Giles Jacob

Every Man his own Lawyer

Giles Jacob

Every Man his own Lawyer

ISBN/EAN: 9783741140006

Manufactured in Europe, USA, Canada, Australia, Japa

Cover: Foto ©Andreas Hilbeck / pixelio.de

Manufactured and distributed by brebook publishing software (www.brebook.com)

Giles Jacob

Every Man his own Lawyer

EVERY MAN
His own Lawyer:

OR,

A Summary of the LAWS of *England* in a New and Instructive Method, under the following Heads,

VIZ.

I. Of Actions and Remedies, Writs, Process, Arrest, and Bail.
II. Of Courts, Attornies and Solicitors therein, Juries, Witnesses, Trials, Executions, &c.
III. Of Estates and Property in Lands and Goods, and how acquired; Ancestors, Heirs, Executors and Administrators.
IV. Of the Laws relating to Marriage, Bastardy, Infants, Idiots, Lunaticks.

V. Of the Liberty of the Subject, *Magna Charta*, and *Habeas Corpus* Act, and other Statutes.
VI. Of the King and his Prerogative, the Queen and Prince, Peers, Judges, Sheriffs, Coroners, Justices of Peace, Constables, &c.
VII. Of publick Offences, Treason, Murder, Felony, Burglary, Robbery, Rape, Sodomy, Forgery, Perjury, &c. And their Punishment.

All of them so plainly treated of that all Manner of Persons may be particularly acquainted with our LAWS and STATUTES, concerning Civil and Criminal Affairs, and know how to defend Themselves and their Estates and ...

IN ALL CASES WHATSOEVER.

The **Eighth Edition**, corrected and improved with many Additions from Lord *Raymond*, *Comyn*, *Strange*, *Foster*, &c. and with the Statute Law down to 18 *Geo*. 3. inclusive.

LONDON:

Printed by W. STRAHAN, and M. WOODFALL, Law-Printers to the King's Most Excellent Majesty;

For W. STRAHAN, J. RIVINGTON and SONS, T. CASLON, R. BALDWIN, T. LONGMAN, J. JOHNSON, F. NEWBERY, G. ROBINSON, and W. GOLDSMITH.

M,DCC.LXXIX.

TO THE

Right Honourable

THOMAS

Lord Viscount GAGE.

My Lord,

IT may at first view seem a little presuming in me, to dedicate a plain law-treatise to a polite nobleman, such as your lordship; but this will be easily reconciled, when 'tis considered, the subject of our law, cannot be made too familiar to the greatest personages, as they live under it's protection, and are by it defended in their rights and properties.

In this address to your lordship, where virtues are so very conspicuous, extraordinary encomiums may be well expected; and I fear I shall require your lordship's pardon for
my

The *DEDICATION*.

my defects; I shall however presume to observe to you, if generosity and greatness of mind, superior sense, learning and judgment, the noblest œconomy, and finest behaviour, with the most extensive publick spirit, are excellencies which deservedly raise a person to titles and honours, they ever belong to your lordship as their possessor.

These great qualities and accomplishments, my lord, shine forth in you, who are universally known and admired; and that you may live long an ornament to your country, attended with prosperity and every satisfaction, is the real wish of,

My Lord,

Your Lordship's

Most obedient, and

Most devoted

Humble Servant,

G. J.

PREFACE

TO THE

SEVENTH EDITION.

IN an age of inquiry into things, it is not to be admired that our great legiſlators ſhould make many new laws well intended for redreſſing publick evils, however ſhort they may fall of it, in the general execution of them: for there is hardly any fence ſo ſtrong, but the fertile genius of the preſent times, by its inventions and ſtratagems, will eaſily break through it.

But I do not here pretend to be a particular advocate, either for or againſt the alteration of our laws, any further than as it makes new books neceſſary; what I ſhall now attempt, is to introduce an inſtructive treatiſe, written in the eaſieſt method, and adapted to every capacity, whereby the unſkilful, and thoſe who are ignorant in practice of the law, may in ſome meaſure be their own adviſers, and readily avoid the common errors too often happening in the proſecution of ſuits.

And in this treatiſe is contained the moſt uſeful and requiſite learning in the law, for

PREFACE.

all degrees of persons to acquire and understand, there being likewise many curious things therein not to be found in any other one law book; so that I may venture to say, the publick will here reap benefit and security to themselves, at the same time attornies and solicitors confess it affords a very just instruction.

Nor will these gentlemen, I hope, make any objection to the popularity of my title, since this work is not designed to defame or abate the profession of the law, tho' it gives some light into it to the ordinary reader.

This edition has been revised and corrected, and many valuable additions inserted from the reports of the late lord chief baron *Comyn*; lord chief justice *Raymond*; *Strange* master of the Rolls; Mr. justice *Foster*, &c. &c. And also from the statute law to the fourth year of the reign of his present Majesty inclusive.

Mich. Vac: 1764.

ADVERTISEMENT concerning the EIGHTH EDITION.

THIS Edition has been revised and corrected, and the *Statute Law* inserted in the second Appendix, to the 18th Year of the reign of his present Majesty inclusive.

Dec. 1778.

EVERY

EVERY MAN
His Own Lawyer:

OR,

A Summary of the Laws of *England*, in a new and instructive Method.

Of Actions and Remedies, Writs, Process, Arrests, and Bail.

THE actions and remedies brought and prosecuted in our courts for recovery of rights and damages for injuries sustained, and for the doing of justice between one subject and another, so that all persons who complain may be relieved, according to the nature and merits of their case, are the following.

1. Of

Of Actions and Remedies.

Action {
1. Of Debt.
2. On the Case.
3. Of Account.
4. Of Covenant.
5. Of Detinue.
6. Of Trover.
7. Of Slander.
8. Of Assault and Battery.
9. Of Trespass.
10. Of Ejectment.
11. Of Assise.
12. Of Waste, &c.
}

Action of *Debt* is a suit given by law where a man oweth another a certain sum of money, by obligation, or bargain for a thing sold, or by contract, &c. and the debtor will not pay the debt at the day agreed; then the creditor shall have this action against him for the same.

If money be due upon any specialty, action of debt only lieth; for no other action may be brought for it: and where a man contracts to pay money for things which he hath bought, and the seller takes bond for the money, the contract is discharged; so that he shall not have action of debt upon the contract, but on the bond. *Nat. Br.* 268.

The usual action of debt, which consists of divers particular branches, lies in all these cases:

1. For money due on bond, or bill.
2. For rent due from tenants.
3. For goods or money delivered.
4. For an attorney's expences.
5. For permitting a prisoner to escape.
6. Upon a judgment, or arbitrament.
7. On an act of parliament.

1. In a bond where several are bound severally, the obligee may have action of debt against all the obligors together, or all of them apart, and have several judgments and executions; though

Of Actions and Remedies.

though he shall have satisfaction but once: but when the bond is joint, and not several, all the obligors must be sued that are bound; and one is not obliged to answer without the rest. Also if a bond is made to three to pay money to one of them, they must all join in the action, for they are but as one obligee. *Dy.* 19, 310. *Yelv.* 177.

If there be several days mentioned for payment of money on a bond, the obligation is not forfeited, nor can be sued, until all the days are past: yet in some cases, the obligee may bring action of debt for the money due by the bond presently, though it be not forfeited; and by special wording the condition, an obligee may be able to sue the penalty on the first default. A man is bound to pay 20*l.* in manner following, that is to say, 10*l.* at one day, and 10*l.* at another; debt will not lie till after the last day, because it is an intire duty: but if one binds himself to pay 10*l.* on one day, and 10*l.* on another, after the first day action of debt lies for 10*l.* it being a several duty. *Co. Lit.* 292. 2 *Danv. Abr.* 501.

In action of debt brought upon a bond against an heir for the debt of his ancestor, it is not good for the heir to say, that the executors have assets in their hands; for the obligee may sue either heir or executor: if an heir hath assets, and the executor also, it is at the obligee's election to have action of debt against the one or the other; but he shall not charge them doubly. Debt lies against the heir of an obligor, who has lands by descent, if the executor have not sufficient: and if an heir has made over lands fallen to him by descent, execution shall be had against him to the value of the land, *&c.* if it be not sold *bona fide* before the action brought. *Dy.*

204. *Plowd.* 433. *Ander.* 7. *Stat.* 3 & 4 *W.*
& *M. c.* 14. perpetuated by 6 & 7 *W.* 3. *c.* 14.

Action of debt lieth on a recognizance; so upon a statute merchant being in the nature of a bond or obligation: but it is otherwise in case of a statute staple. A man owes another a sum of money, and hath his note under hand, without seal, an action of debt on a *mutuatus* lies; but the defendant may wage his law: in action of the case brought upon promise of payment the defendant cannot wage law. 4 *Rep.* 93. 2 *Danv. Abr.* 497.

If debt is brought on a single bill, the defendant may plead payment, before the action brought, in bar: and pending an action on bond, &c. the defendant may bring in principal, interest and costs; and the court shall give judgment to discharge the defendant, by stat. 4 *Ann. c.* 16. *s.* 13.

Upon application to stay an action of debt upon bond, upon payment of principal, interest and costs: cause shewn and opposed, unless costs of a suit in the *Exchequer* relating to the same matter be paid. Lord Ch. Just. *Hardwicke* said he believed it had been ruled upon the above clause that it should be done; and that costs in equity relating to suits on bonds have been referred to, and taxed by the master. Rule absolute to stay the proceedings on payment of principal, interest and costs, and of the costs in the *Exchequer.* M.S.S. Cas. *East.* 8 Geo. 2. *Lock* and *Shermer.* See *Gilb.* Cas. 291.

An executor brought error on a judgment against the testator upon bond; and after affirmance moved on stat. 4 *Ann. c.* 16. *sect.* 13. to pay principal, interest and costs, it was insisted, that as he came for a favour to save the penalty, it was
but

Of Actions and Remedies.

but equitable he should pay the costs in error which he had put the plaintiff to; for if plaintiff had taken execution, equity would never punish him for taking those expences out of the penalty.

On the other side were cited *Banham* v. *Matthews*, 2 *Str.* 871. where an executor discontinued without costs. 2 *Kel.* 70. *pl.* 28. S. P. 2 *Barnard. K. B.* 154. S. C. S. P. and *Sidney* v. *Newinson*. Upon the authority of which case, the Court determined, that as by law the executor was not to pay costs upon a writ of error, a court of law could not direct them to be taxed, though there was a penalty. 2 *Str.* 1072.

The case of *Sidney* v. *Newinson* was, That plaintiff had brought an action of debt upon bond against defendant as administrator, and filed a bill in equity to discover assets; and had instituted a suit in the spiritual court, to oblige her to give in an inventory. After judgment for the plaintiff in the action, a writ of error was brought in *K. B.* and the judgment reversed. That plaintiff brought a new action in *K. B.* and defendant moved to stay proceedings upon stat. 4 *Ann. c.* 16. *sect.* 13. on paying principal, interest, and costs: and now upon motion for the court's direction to the master in taxing the costs, it was insisted for plaintiff, that defendant ought to pay the whole costs of the first suit, proceedings in *Chancery*, and spiritual court.

The court said, that they had nothing to do to order costs for proceedings in another court, which has power to award costs, if the party is intitled to them; and as to the judgment, that is reversed, there is no reason for defendant to pay for plaintiff's error and mistake. The court was of opinion, the proceedings in this court must be stayed on payment of the costs of this suit. *Str.* 699.

2. An action of debt lies for rent in arrear, upon a lease for life or years; at common law it lay not on leases for life, but now by statute it may be had. 8 *Ann. c.* 14. If tenant in fee-simple, or fee-tail die, his executor may have action of debt by the stat. 32 *H.* 8. *c.* 37. for arrears of rent incurred in the life-time of such tenants, or he may distrain for the same; but before this act the executor had no remedy. *Cro. Car.* 471.

The remedy by the common law for rent on a lease for life was assise, if the plaintiff had seisin, or by distress; and if tenant for life died, his executors might bring action of debt for the rent in arrear; but a new remedy is given by the above statute, and that is to distrain. 3 *Rep.* 65. 3 *Salk.* 304.

If a rent or lease for years of land is reserved and made payable at four quarter-days, the lessor may have action of debt after the first day of failure; for every quarter's rent is a several debt, and distinct actions may be brought for each quarter. 5 *Rep.* 81. 2 *Vent.* 129. An assignee of rent upon a lease for years, shall have debt for it: and action of debt will lie against a lessee, for rent due after the assignment of the lease; for the personal privity of contract continues, though the privity of estate is gone: but it is otherwise, if a landlord once accepts the rent of the assignee, knowing of the assignment. *Lev.* 22. 3 *Rep.* 22, 23.

When the lease is ended, the duty in respect of the rent remains, and debt lieth by reason of
privity

privity of contract between leſſor and leſſee. *Cro. Jac.* 227.

3. Action of debt lieth upon a parol contract by word only, and ſo doth action on the caſe: and in ſome caſes, debt will lie, although there be no contract betwixt the party that brings the action, and him againſt whom brought; for there may be a duty created by law. But action of debt lieth not againſt executors, upon a ſimple contract made by the teſtator: though it lies for the arrearages of an account againſt executors, of receipts by the teſtator 2 *Saund.* 343. 9 *Rep.* 87. *Lil Abr.* 403. 2 *Danv. Abr.* 497.

If goods or money are delivered to a third perſon for my uſe, I may have action of debt, or account for them. And where money is delivered to a perſon, to be re-delivered again, the property is altered, and debt lies: but where a horſe, or any goods are thus delivered, there action of detinue lieth. Action of debt lies againſt the huſband, for goods which were delivered or ſold to the wife, if they come to the huſband's uſe: and if one delivers meat, drink or clothes to an infant, and he promiſes to pay for them, action of debt or on the caſe will lie againſt the infant; but what is delivered, muſt be averred to be for the neceſſary uſe of the infant. 2 *Danv. Abr.* 404. *Nelſ. Abr.* 603. 1 *Lil. Abr.* 400, 401.

A man agrees with a taylor to make him a ſuit of clothes, for a certain price; the taylor may bring a general action of debt againſt him for the money; but if the price is not agreed on, action of the caſe only lies, or ſpecial action of debt on the ſpecial contract. *Wood's Inſt.* 9th edit. 563.

Of Actions and Remedies.

4. An attorney shall have action of debt against his client, for money which he has paid to any person for such client, for costs of suit, or to his counsel, &c. And an action of debt, or case, lies for an attorney for his fees against him that retained him in his cause: but attornies are not to demand more than their just fees; nor to be allowed any extraordinary fees to counsel, without tickets signed by them, &c. And it is said to be a good plea to an action brought by an attorney for his fees, that the plaintiff did not give the defendant any bill of charges, according to the statute. *Lil. Abr.* 142. *Stat.* 3 *Jac.* c. 7. *T. Raym.* 245. 2 *Geo.* 2. c. 23. perpetuated by 30 *Geo.* 2. c. 19. *f.* 75. See *Moseley's Rep.* 68. *Str.* 633. *Pract. Reg.* C. P. 36. *Rep. & Caf. Pract.* C. P. 27. *Bac. Abr.* 130.

If a client, when his business in court is dispatched, refuseth to pay the officer his court fees; the court on motion will grant an attachment against him, on which he shall be committed until the fees are paid. *Lil. Abr.* 598.

But officers guilty of extortion shall render treble value: and an action may be brought against attornies for extortion, and the party grieved shall have treble damages and costs. 3 *Ed.* c. 26, 27, 30.

5. Action of debt lies against a gaoler permitting a prisoner committed in execution to escape, for thereupon the law makes the gaoler debtor; and where the party is not in execution, there action on the case lieth for damages suffered by the escape. *Saund.* 218.

If a prisoner escapes who was in execution, his creditor may take him by *capias ad satisfaciendum*; or bring action of debt on the judgment, or or a *scire facias* against him, &c. for he hath still an interest in the body, as a pledge for the debt. If the prisoner makes a tortious escape, the person at whose suit he was taken in execution, may have an *alias cap.* to take him again; or action of the case against the sheriff: but if the sheriff voluntarily permit the escape, debt may be brought against the sheriff. *Ventr.* 269. *Lil. Abr.* 536. 3 *Salk.* 160.

Debt lieth against a sheriff, for money levied in execution: and if a defendant in execution is rescued, the sheriff is liable for the whole debt, and is to have his remedy against the rescuer. *Dy.* 241.

6. A person may have action of debt upon an arbitrament; but not for debt referred to arbitration, which must be action on the case: and debt will lie for breach of a by-law, or for amercement in a court-leet, &c. Action of debt shall be brought for money adjudged to be paid by arbitrators, declaring on the award; and also upon the bond for not performing it. *New Nat. Br.* 267. *Brownl.* 55. *Lill. Abr.* 400.

Debt lies for money recovered upon a judgment, &c. And if a man recovers debt or damages in *London*, on action brought there by the custom of the city, which lies not at common law; when it is become a debt by the judgment, action of debt lies upon this judgment in the courts at *Westminster*. *Nat. Br.* 265. 2 *Danv. Abr.* 499. In actions of debt on bonds, a rule may be made to stay proceedings on payment of principal, interest and costs; but not in actions of debt upon judgments; yet the defendant may plead a tender and *uncore prist*. 6 *Mod.* 60.

7. Action of debt is sometimes grounded on an act of parliament; as for a parson against a parishioner

Of Actions and Remedies.

parishioner for not setting out tithes, wherein the plaintiff shall recover the treble value, by the statute 2 *Ed.* 6. *c.* 13. Against a hundred for a robbery committed on the highway in the day-time of any day, except *Sunday*, when the hundred shall answer it, if the robbers are not taken in forty days, &c. 27 *Eliz. c.* 13. See *Com. Rep.* 345. *Stra.* 406. Against a man for arresting, or causing one to be arrested in another man's name, without his consent, upon the statute 8 *Eliz. c.* 2. And if an * attorney suffer another to follow any suit in his name, he shall forfeit † 20 *l.* and the party grieved shall have debt; by 3 *Jac. c.* 7. And so in many other cases debt lieth.

The manner of Proceeding in actions of Debt.

THE Proceedings upon actions of debt in order to trial in the courts of *Westminster*, are,

1. By writs, process, and arrests.
2. By bail and appearance.
3. By declarations, pleadings, &c.

1. A writ is the king's precept, commanding something to be done touching a suit or action. And of writs there are divers kinds, in many respects; some are real, concerning the posses-

---

* An attorney who gives another leave to practice in his name, is answerable for what he does in his name. 12 Mod. 665.

† By stat. 2 *Geo.* 2. *c.* 23. *sect.* 17. [perpetuated by 30 *Geo.* 2. *c.* 19. *f:8.* 75.] he shall forfeit 50 *l.* and be incapable of acting.

Of Actions and Remedies.

sion of lands, called writs of entry, or of right touching the property, &c. Some are personal, relating to goods, chattels, and personal injuries; and some are mixed, for the recovery of the thing and damages. 2 *Inst.* 39.

The writs in civil actions are either original, or judicial; original writs are issued out of the court of chancery, for the summoning a defendant to appear, and judicial writs issue out of the court where the original is returned, after the suit is begun, to carry on the cause: the originals bear teste in the name of the king; but judicial writs bear date in the name of the chief justice; and a writ without a teste is not good, for the time may be material when it was taken out; and if it be out of the common law courts, it must bear date some day in term (not being *Sunday*) but in chancery writs may be issued in the vacation as well as term-time, as that court is always open: also there are to be fifteen days between the teste and return of writs, where the suit is by original, but by statute, delays in actions by reason of fifteen days between the teste and return in personal actions and ejectments are remedied. *F. N. B.* 51, 147. 2 *Inst.* 40. 13 *Car.* 2. *c.* 2.

An original writ defective in form, is abateable; but it is allowed to be good by pleadings, &c. and though an original may not be amended, yet a new writ may be taken out, where it is not amendable: writs judicial, if erroneous, may be amended; and writs may be renewed every term, until a defendant is arrested, but not after four terms in *B. R.* when a new writ must be issued, and the plaintiff may not renew the old one. And all writs are to be returned and filed in due time, in the court where
returnable;

returnable; for the filing them is the warranty for the proceeding. 2 *Lil. Abr.* 716, 717.

The king's writs cannot be denied to the subject; and after the action is fixed on, for a wrong done, or a right detained, as in debt, on the case, &c. such a writ must be taken out as is suitable to the action, being grounded upon it: and if in the writ several persons are included, (for four defendants may be put in one writ) there must be several warrants from the sheriff to execute the same. *Wood's Inst.* 581.

Attachment lies against sheriffs, &c. for not executing writs; or for doing it oppressively by force, or not doing it effectually, through any corrupt practice. The sheriff's bailiffs cannot execute a writ directed to the sheriff, without his warrant: and sheriffs are not to grant warrants for arrests, before the receipt of the writ; if they do, they shall forfeit 10*l.* and damages. 43 *Eliz. c.* 6.

No high sheriff, under-sheriff, their deputies or agents, shall make out any warrant before they have in their custody the writs upon which such warrants ought to issue, on forfeiture of 10*l. Stat.* 6 *Geo. c.* 21. *f.* 53.

Every warrant to be made out upon any writ of *K. B. C. B.* or *Exchequer*, before judgment, to arrest any person, shall have the same day and year set down thereon as shall be set down on the writ itself, under forfeiture of 10*l.* to be paid by the person who shall fill up or deliver out such warrant. *Id. f.* 54. See *Stat.* 9. *W.* 3. *c.* 15. how penalties to be recovered and divided.

Every warrant upon process for arresting shall, before execution, be subscribed or endorsed with the name of the attorney, clerk in court, or solicitor,

licitor, by whom such process shall be sued forth; and where such attorney shall not be the person immediately employed, then also with the name of the attorney so immediately employed. *Stat.* 2 *Geo.* 2. *c.* 23. *s.* 22. perpetuated by 30 *Geo.* 2. *c.* 19. *s.* 75.

Not subscribing or indorsing the name of the attorney, &c. on any warrant made upon any writ or process, shall not vitiate the same, but such writ, and all proceedings thereon, shall be valid and effectual, provided the writ whereon such warrant be made out be regularly subscribed or endorsed; and every sheriff, or other officer, who shall make out any warrant upon any writ, &c. and shall not subscribe or indorse the name of the attorney, &c. who sued out the same, shall forfeit 5*l.* to be assessed by the court out of which such writ, &c. shall issue; one moiety to be paid to his majesty, and the other moiety to the person grieved. *Stat.* 12 *Geo.* 2. *c.* 13. *s.* 4. See 2 *Barnard. K. B.* 198, 407. *Ld. Raym.* 586. Sir *W. Jones* 346. *pl.* 5. *Cro. Car.* 372. *pl.* 6. *Hawk. Pl. C. chap.* 31. *sect.* 37. *p.* 86. *Str.* 156. *H. H. P. C.* 457. *Barnes's Notes C. P.* 303. *Pract. Reg. C. P.* 441, 442. 2 *Barnes* 327.

If a bailiff be kept off from making an arrest, he shall have an action of assault: and where any bailiff touches a man, which is an arrest, and he makes his escape, it is a rescous, and attachment may be had against him. If a bailiff lays hold of one by the hand, whom he had a warrant to arrest, as he holds it out at the window; this is such a taking of him, that the bailiff may justify the breaking open the house to carry him away: but doors may not be broke open to make an arrest in civil cases, unless it be be in purfuit of one arrefted. *Ventr.* 306. 5 *Rep.* 91. *Salk.* 79. *Foft. Cr. Law* 319, 320.

And arreft in the night, as well as the day, is lawful. 9 *Rep.* 66. *Cro. Jac.* 280. *pl.* 10. 486. 3 *Salk.* 46. *Jenk. Cent.* 291. *pl.* 30. *H. P. C.* 45. 5 *Co.* 92. *b. Ow.* 63. But no writ, procefs, &c. (except in criminal cafes) fhall be ferved on a *Sunday*; on pain that the party ferving them fhall be liable to the fuit of the party grieved, and anfwer damages as if the fame had been done without writ; and action of falfe imprifonment lies for arreft on a *Sunday*, and the arreft is void. *Stat.* 29 *Car.* 2. *c.* 7. 12 *Mod.* 348. *T. Raym.* 250. *Watf. Clerg. law, chap.* 34. *p.* 344, 345. *Gibf. Cod. lit.* 10. *p.* 238. 12 *Mod.* 607. 6 *Mod.* 96. *Hawk. P.C.* 86. *chap.* 31. *fect.* 58. *H. H. P. C.* 457. note (*f.*) *Cro. Jac.* 62. *pl.* 6. *Salk.* 78. *pl.* 1. 5 *Mod.* 95. *Barnes's Notes C. P.* 228. *Stat.* 5 *An.* r. 9. *f.* 3. 1 *An. ft.* 2. *c.* 6. 2 *Salk.* 626. *pl.* 7. 3 *Salk.* 149. *pl.* 1. 2 Ld. *Raym.* 1028. A perfon may be retaken on a *Sunday*, where arrefted the day before, or upon an efcape warrant, when one goes at large out of the rules of the king's bench or fleet prifon, &c. 6 *Mod.* 231. 5 *An. c.* 9. *Fortefc. Rep.* 374.

If, where there are feveral perfons of the fame name, a bailiff arrefts a wrong perfon, he is liable to action of falfe imprifonment: and if he arrefts a man without warrant, though he afterwards receives one from the fheriff; or if he arrefts one after the return of the writ be paft; and where a bailiff demands more than his juft fees when offered, and detains a perfon thereupon; or if a man be any ways unlawfully detained; in all thefe cafes it will be falfe imprifonment;

Of Actions and Remedies.

sonment; and large damages are recoverable in these actions. *Dy.* 244. *Co. Lit.* 124. *Dalt. chap.* 2. *pl.* 111.

No bailiff shall carry any person arrested to a tavern, alehouse, &c. without his consent, so as to charge him with any beer, ale, wine, &c. but what he shall freely call for; nor shall carry him to prison within 24 hours; nor demand any greater sum than the law allows, for the arrest or waiting till bail is given, &c. or receive a greater sum for lodging or a day's diet than is allowed by justices of peace, &c. 32 *Geo.* 2. *c.* 28.

If a debt be under 10 *l.* on writs out of a superior court, or under 40 *s.* in an inferior court, the defendant shall not be arrested, but be personally served with a copy of the process, and not appearing at the return, the plaintiff may enter an appearance for him, and proceed, &c. No person shall be held to special bail on such writs; and affidavit to be made of the cause of action, when it is 10 *l.* &c. or upwards, and the sum indorsed on the writ, for which only bail shall be taken, where a man is arrested. *Stat.* 12 *Geo. c.* 29. perpetuated by 21 *Geo.* 2. *c.* 3. [10 Mod. 14.]

When the cause of action is under 10 *l.* in any superior court, or 40 *s.* in inferior, the process shall be in *English*, and the defendant served with a copy of it, and also notice thereon to appear at the return, &c. And the fee for making and serving the copy of the process and notice, shall be no more than 5 *s.* out of superior courts, and 1 *s.* the inferior courts. 5 *Geo.* 2. *c.* 27. perpetuated by 21 *Geo.* 2. *c.* 3.

The

The form of a bill of *Middlesex* in *K. B.*

This precept must be engrossed on a four sixpenny stampt piece of parchment.

Middlesex. THE *sheriff is commanded to take A. B. if he is to be found in his bailiwick, and that he safely keep him, so that he have his body before our sovereign lord the king at* Westminster, *on* Tuesday *next after the morrow of* All souls *(or other day of return) to answer to* C. D. *in a plea of trespass. And that he then have there this precept.*

By Bill.　Lee.

If the action requires *Bail*, then this clause is added: *And also to a bill of the said* C. *against the said* A. *for twenty pounds of debt, according to the custom of the court of the said lord the king, before the king himself to be exhibited; and that he have there this precept.*

Bail by plaintiff's affidavit for 20 *l.* (The attorney's name indorsed.)

The form of a *latitat* in *K. B.*

This writ must be on a four sixpenny piece of parchment.

GEORGE *the third, by the grace of God, king of* Great Britain, France, *and* Ireland, *defender of the faith,* &c. *To the sheriff of* Norfolk, *greeting. Whereas we lately commanded our sheriff of* Middlesex, *that he should take* C. D. *and* E. F. *if they should be found in his bailiwick, and keep them safely, so that he might have their bodies before us at* Westminster, *at a certain day now past, to answer to* A. B. *in a plea of trespass; and also to a bill of him the said* A. *against the aforesaid* C. *for ten pounds of debt, according to the custom of our court, before us to be exhibited: and our said sheriff of* Middlesex, *at that day made a return*

Of Actions and Remedies. 17

return to us, that the said C. *and* E. *were not found in his bailiwick; whereupon on the behalf of the said* A. *it is sufficiently testified in our court before us, that the aforesaid* C. *and* E. *lurk and wander up and down in your county; Therefore we command you, that you take them, if they are to be found in your bailiwick, and safely keep them, so as you have their bodies before us at* Westminster *on Wednesday next after three weeks of the* Holy Trinity, *to answer to the aforesaid* A. *in the plea and bill aforesaid; and that you have them there this writ. Witness* William *earl* Mansfield *at* Westminster, *the day,*[*] *&c. in the eighteenth year of our reign.*

Lee.

The form of an *alias* and *pluries*.

GEORGE *the Third,* &c. *To the sheriff of* N. *greeting. We command you, as before we commanded you, that you take* C. D. *and* E. F. *if they shall be found in your bailiwick, and safely keep them, so that you have their bodies before us at* Westminster, *on,* &c. *(such a return) to answer to* A. B. *of a plea of trespass, and also to the bill of the said* A. *against the said* C. *and* E. *for ten pounds of debt, according to the custom of our court, before us to be exhibited: and have you then this writ. Witness* William *earl* Mansfield, *&c.*

This also must be on a four sixpenny stamp.

A *pluries capias* varies from the *Alias* only by inserting the word *oftentimes* we commanded, instead of *as before*.

---

[*] If the writ be sued out in term time, it must be tested the first day of the term; if in any of the vacations, then the last day of the preceding term.

C

The form of a *capias* in debt, in C. P.

This also must be on a four six penny stamp.

GEORGE *the Third*, &c. *To the sheriff of* Norfolk, *greeting. We command you that you take* C. D. *late of*, &c. *in your county, gent. and* E. F. *late of the same place in your county, yeoman, if they may be found in your bailiwick, and safely keep them, so that you have their bodies before our justices at* Westminster, *on the morrow of* All Souls, *to answer to* A. B. *of a plea that he render to him thirty pounds, which he owes to, and unjustly detains from him; and have you there this writ. Witness Sir* Charles Pratt, *Knight, at* Westminster,* &c. *in the eighteenth year of our reign.*

If your *capias* be in action of the *case* then say: *To answer to the said* A. B. *according to the custom of our court of Common Bench, in a certain plea of trespass on the case, upon promises, to the damage of the said* A. *twenty pounds,* &c.

2. Bail is security for the appearance of the defendant, at a day and place certain, to answer the plaintiff's suit. And in all cases where process issues forth of *K. B.* to take the defendant's body, if an appearance only, and not special bail is required, there the defendant may appear in court in his proper person, and file common bail. *Lil. Abr.*

There is both common and special bail: Common bail is in actions of small concernment, being called common, because their sureties, as *John Doe* and *Richard Roe*, in that case are taken; whereas in cases of greater weight, as ac-

* See the note in the preceding page.

tions upon bond or specialty, &c. where the debt amounts to 10 *l.* or above, (of which an affidavit of the debt is now to be made) special bail or surety must be taken, such as subsidy-men at least, and they according to the value. 4 *Inst.* 179.

As there are different kinds of bail; so there are divers sorts of bail-pieces, *viz.* 1. A common bail-piece, where the defendant is served with a copy of the process; this is merely to bring the defendant into court, and is in nature of an appearance in the court of Common Pleas. 2. A special bail-piece on a *cepi corpus*, or arrest returned, when the defendant is actually arrested, and the sheriff hath taken a bail-bond. 3. A bail-piece on an *habeas corpus*, in case a defendant lives at a great distance from *Westminster*, and a cause is removed out of an inferior court. 4. Bail-pieces taken before commissioners in the country, by virtue of the stat. 4 *W. & M. c.* 4.

These bail-pieces, if common, are to be filed in the office within six days after the end of the term the attorney appears: and special bail, which is taken before a judge, or by commissioners, when accepted, is to be filed; after 20 days notice given of putting in special bail before a judge on a *cepi corpus*, if there is no exception, the bail shall be filed in four days. Upon a *habeas corpus*, 28 days are allowed to except against the bail, and after that, if it be not excepted against, it shall be filed in four days. *Lil. Abr.* 174. *Salk.* 98.

Bail is not properly such till it is filed; but it shall be accounted good, till the same is questioned and disallowed. And when cognisors of bail are questioned, they must justify themselves in open court by oath of their abilities; or be-

Of Actions and Remedies.

fore one of the judges of the court; or by affidavit before the commissioners who took the bail: and the court may adjudge bail sufficient; when the plaintiff will not accept it. Also a defendant, with leave of the court, may deposit money in court instead of bail: and the court, on motion, or a judge at his chamber will order a common appearance to be taken, when special bail is not required. *Lil. Abr.*

If the defendant doth not find common or special bail, the attorney for the plaintiff is to call upon the sheriff for the return of the writ; on default whereof, a rule being made for it, the sheriff shall be amerced, or summoned before a judge to shew cause, &c. and if on a *cepi corpus* no bail is returned, a rule will be made out to bring in the defendant's body. When a sheriff hath taken good bail of the defendant, he will on a rule return a *cepi*, and assign the bail-bond to the plaintiff; which may be done by indorsement, without stamp, so as it be stamped before action brought thereupon; and then if the bail-bond, &c. be forfeited, the plaintiff may bring his action on the bond in his own name. *Stat.* 4 & 5 *An.* But upon such assignment of a bail-bond and action brought thereon, neither defendant nor bail can be arrested on the bond, but served only with a copy of the process; for otherwise bail might be taken *ad infinitum.*

Sheriffs are to let to bail persons arrested, upon reasonable sureties, having sufficient within the county, to keep their days in such place, &c. as the writs require. 23 *H.* 6. *c.* 10. And the statute 1 *W. & M. sess.* 2. *c.* 2. provides against excessive bail. By late *Orders* of court, bail shall be liable for so much as is sworn to and

indorsed

indorsed on the process, or for a lesser sum; and not be discharged though the plaintiff declares for more. On exception entered against bail, the defendant must procure them to justify in four days, if in term, or on the first day of the next term, if in vacation. *Ord. K. B. East.* 5 *Geo.* 2. Altho' the bail taken by the sheriff on bail-bonds is put in above, yet the plaintiff may except against such bail: Special bail shall be perfected by the defendant within four days after exception, or in default the plaintiff may proceed on the bail-bond; and the like is to be observed on bail put in upon writs of error, or they may be *non-prossed*. No attorney shall be bail; nor shall any bailiff be permitted to become bail in any action or suit. *Ord. C. P. Mich.* 5 *Geo.* 2.

If a plaintiff does not declare against the defendant in two terms after bail is put in, the defendant may *non-pross* the plaintiff, and then the bail are discharged; for in such case the defendant is to go only upon common bail, by the rules of the court. If the defendant render himself to custody in discharge of his bail, upon the day of the return of the second writ of *scire facias* against the bail, the court sitting, the bail shall be discharged: and the bail may bring in the body of the defendant, at any time before the return of the *alias scire facias*, and render him up, which will discharge the bail; but care must be taken that the bail-piece be vacated in the office. *Rol. Abr.* 250. 6 *Mod.* 238. *Salk.* 98.

Of Actions and Remedies.

Form of a *common* bail-piece.

This must be engrossed on a treble sixpenny stampt piece of parchment in this form.

Of Trinity *Term in the fourth Year of the Reign of King* GEORGE *the Third.*

London, (to wit) A. B. *is delivered to bail upon a* Cepi Corpus, *unto*
John Doe *of* London, *Yeoman*, And
Richard Roe *of the same Place, Yeoman.*

H. C.
(*according to the Statute*)
Attorney. } *At the Suit of* C. D.

Of Actions and Remedies.

Form of a *special* bail-piece.

Of the Term of St. Michael *in the fourth Year of King* GEORGE *the Third.*

Middlesex, (to wit) A. B. *is delivered to bail on a* Cepi Corpus, *unto* C. D. *of,* &c. *in the said County, Gent. And* E. F. *of,* &c. *in the said County, Mercer.*

T. W. *Attorney for the Defendant.* } *At the Suit of* C. D.

To be engrossed on a double twelve penny stamps piece of parchment in this form.

There is no difference between the bail-piece upon an *habeas corpus* and a *cepi,* only you say, is delivered to bail on an *hab. corp.* to *C. D. &c.* If it is a *country bail-piece,* the *caption* thereon at the bottom is to be inserted thus: *Taken and acknowledged the 7th day of* May *in the year of our Lord* 1778, *at* Blandford *in the county aforesaid, before* G. P. *a commissioner.* And if it be a bail-piece

piece on a *certiorari*, you say, is delivered to bail on a writ *to cause proceedings to be certified*, or writ of *certiorari*.

It may not be improper here to insert a bail-bond, and an assignment of it by the sheriff to the plaintiff, pursuant to the statute 4 *Ann. c.* 16.

The form of a *bail-bond* to the sheriff.

This must be engrossed on an half crown sheet of paper. For actions on this bond, see Fortesc. Rep. 363. &c. Stra. 399. 2 Stra. 727. 2 Ld. Raym. 1455.

KNOW *all men by these presents, that we* C. D. *of, &c.* E. F. *of, &c. and* J. Doe, *are held and firmly bound to* G. H. *esquire, sheriff of the county aforesaid, in forty pounds of good and lawful money of Great Britain, to be paid to the said sheriff or to his certain attorney, his executors, administrators, or assigns; for which payment to be well and truly made, we bind ourselves, and every of us by himself for and in the whole, our heirs, executors, and administrators, and of every of us, firmly by these presents, sealed with our seals. Dated the Day of, &c. in the year of the reign of the Lord* George *the Third, by the grace of God, of Great Britain, France, and Ireland, king, defender of the faith, &c. the eighteenth, and the year of our Lord* 1778.

THE *condition of this obligation is such, that if the above bound* C. D. *do appear before the justices of our lord the king at* Westminster, *on the day, &c. to answer unto* A. B. *gentleman, of a plea of trespass, and also in a plea of debt for twenty pounds upon demand; then this present obligation to be void and of none effect, or else to stand and remain in full force and virtue.*

Form

Form of the sheriff's *assignment* thereon.

KNOW *all men by these presents, that I G. H. esquire, the sheriff within named, do hereby for myself, my executors and administrators, assign and set over unto A. B. (the plaintiff named in the condition of the within written bond) his executors and administrators, the within mentioned bond, pursuant to an act of parliament for the amendment of the law and the better advancement of justice. In witness whereof I have hereunto set my hand and seal, this — day of —* &c. *in the year of our Lord one thousand seven hundred and seventy-eight.*

To be indorsed on a treble sixpenny stamp; and sufficient if stamped before action brought.

3. The declaration is a shewing in writing of the cause of complaint of the plaintiff against the defendant, wherein the party is supposed to have received some wrong: It is an exposition of the writ, with the addition of time, circumstances, &c. and must be true, clear and certain; for the court is not to take things in it by implication.

A declaration is grounded upon the writ in the *Common Pleas*, and bill of *Middlesex* or *latitat* in the *King's Bench*; and one may not regularly declare in *K. B.* against a person that is not *in custody of the marshal*, or hath not filed bail; unless he is a privileged person. In action of debt upon a bond, the plaintiff in his declaration must alledge a place where the bond was made, because the jury should come from that place: and if one declare upon an obligation, with a *bic in curia prolat*', he must on *oyer* prayed of it, shew the obligation, or the declaration will not be good. Also a plaintiff, declaring

ing as executor or administrator, ought to set forth the probate of the will, and letters of administration granted, with a *profert in curia*. *Dy.* 15. 39. 2 *Lil. Abr.* 412.

If one be in the custody of the marshal of the court, for debt or other cause of action, any plaintiff may file a declaration against him, and he is obliged to plead thereto; and it is the same where he is out upon bail, any other may declare against him, for he is bound to answer every one's suit. *Lil. Abr.* 413. When a declaration is bad, if the defendant demurs, the plaintiff may set it right in a second action; but if the defendant do not take advantage of it, but pleads in bar, and the plaintiff proceeds to issue thereon; if the right is found for the defendant, the plaintiff is estopped by the verdict from bringing a new action: and so it is if he had demurred to the plea in bar. *Mod. Rep.* 20, 207.

In real actions, the declaration is called a *count*; and in all actions it is good to lay sufficient damages therein. A plaintiff's attorney may amend his declaration in *K. B.* in matter of form, after the general issue pleaded, before entry thereof, without paying costs, or giving imparlance; but if he amends in substance, he must pay costs, or give an imparlance: and if he amend in substance, after a special plea pleaded, although he would give imparlance, he is to pay costs. Where a declaration is defective, it is sometimes aided by the statutes of *Jeofails*, &c. but they help only matters of form, not matters of substance; for uncertainty in a declaration, which is matter of substance, is not aided by statute after verdict. 5 *Rep.* 35. *Lil. Abr.* 409.

All declarations are to be filed, before which they are not of record to warrant a judgment: on filing declarations, copies thereof are served on the defendants, or their attornies, &c. and by an *order* of all the judges, 12 *W.* 3. upon delivery or tender of a copy of any declaration, the defendant's attorney shall pay for it after the rate of 4 *d. per* sheet, &c. and if any person refuse to pay for the copy tender'd, the said copy is to be left in the office with the clerk that keeps the files of declarations, and thereupon the plaintiff's attorney giving rules to plead, may for want of a plea sign judgment; and before any plea shall be received, the defendant's attorney is to pay for the copy of the declaration.

If the attorney for the plaintiff does not draw up and deliver a copy of the declaration to the defendant or his attorney, or file the same with the clerk of the declarations, before the end of the next term after the writ is returnable, the plaintiff may be *non-pross'd*, and the defendant shall have costs. So it is where one comes upon an *habeas corpus,* and bail is given thereon; if the plaintiff doth not declare against him within two terms, including the term the defendant was brought in, the action and the bail are to be discharged, and the plaintiff *non-pross'd* with costs. But if a defendant appears in court in person, at the return of the writ, and it be so mentioned in the bail-piece, the plaintiff must declare within three days, or a *non-pross* may be entered against him with costs, by the stat. 8 *Eliz. cap.* 2.

It is *ordered,* that where special or common bail is filed, and notice thereof given, a copy of the declaration shall be delivered to the attorney

torney for the defendant, who is to pay for the same, or on refusal, or not knowing where he lives, it may be left in the office, and notice of it must be forthwith given to the defendant; and such declaration shall be held well delivered from the time of such notice only: and where the cause of action is specially expressed in any writ, by virtue of which the defendant is arrested, and the plaintiff having declared; the defendant shall plead within the usual time, without imparlance, as by original. And if the defendant lives within 20 miles of *London*, the declaration shall be delivered with notice to plead in four days after the delivery thereof; and if he lives above 20 miles off, the declaration is to be delivered with notice to plead in eight days after delivery; and on default of pleading in those times, the plaintiff may sign his judgment. *Ord. K. B. Trin. & Hil.* 2 *Geo.* 2. And *Trin.* 5 & 6 *Geo.* 2.

Where the copy of the process is served upon any defendant, and the plaintiff's attorney enters an appearance for him, pursuant to the late act of parliament, a copy of the declaration shall be left in the office, and an *English* notice delivered the defendant, signifying the nature of the action, and in whose office the declaration is left, &c. and that unless the defendant plead within four days, &c. judgment will be entered against such defendant by default: and if the defendant does not plead by the time the rules for pleading are out, the plaintiff shall sign judgment, without any further calling for a plea; and thereon notice may be given of executing a writ of inquiry, by delivering it to the defendant, or leaving the same at his last or usual place of abode. *Ord. C. P. Mich.* 1 *Geo.* 2. See *Ord. East.* 3 *Geo.* 2.

The

Of Actions and Remedies.

The form of a *declaration* in debt in K. B.

Michaelmas term in the seventeenth year of
King *George* the Third.

Middlesex to wit. A B. complains of C. D. otherwise called C. D. of the parish of St. Clement's Danes in the county of Middlesex aforesaid, gentleman, being in the custody of the marshal of the Marshalsea of our lord the king, before the king himself, of a plea, that he render to him twenty pounds of good and lawful money of Great Britain; which he owes to him, and unjustly detains, for that, to wit, That whereas the said C. the day, &c. in the ——— year of the reign, &c. of the lord George the Third, now king of Great Britain, at the said parish of St. Clement's Danes in the county aforesaid, by his certain writing obligatory, sealed with the seal of the said C. and here shewn to the court of the said lord the king, the date whereof is the same day and year above-mentioned, acknowledged himself to be held and firmly bound to the said A. in the aforesaid twenty pounds, to be paid to the said A. whenever after he should be thereunto required: nevertheless the said C. although thereunto often required, hath not paid to the said A. the said twenty pounds, or any part thereof, but hitherto hath refused, and still doth refuse, to pay the same; whereupon the said A. saith, that he is injured, and hath damage to the value of ten pounds; and therefore he brings his suit, &c.

This and all proceedings at law are to be wrote on treble penny stampt paper.

H. C. for the plaintiff;
T. W. for the defendant. } Pledges of prosecuting { J. Doe.
R. Roe.

Another

Of Actions and Remedies.

Another form of a *declaration* in debt.

London. A B. *complains of* C. D. *being in custody of the marshal,* &c. *of a plea that he render to him thirty pounds of good and lawful money of* Great Britain, *which he owes to, and unjustly detains from him; for that, whereas the said* C. *on the —— day,* &c. *in the year,* &c. *at* L. *aforesaid, to wit, in the parish of* St. Mary Le Bow, *in the ward of* Cheap, *had borrowed of the said* A. *the aforesaid thirty pounds, to be paid to the said* A. *when afterwards he should be thereto required: yet the said* C. *although thereto often requested, hath not paid the said thirty pounds to the said* A. *or any part thereof, but hath hitherto altogether denied, and still doth deny to pay the same to him; to the damage of the said* A. &c. *and thereupon he brings his suit,* &c.

In the *Common Pleas*, the declaration begins: C. D. late of, &c. was summoned to answer *A. B.* of a plea, that he render, &c. And whereupon the same *A.* by, &c. his attorney, complains, that whereas the said *C.* &c. ——And *note*, in *C. P.* in debt, account, covenant, detinue, and replevin, the word *summoned* to answer is used: and in case, trespass, trover, and ejectment, *attached* to answer.

The form of a *plea* in debt.

AND *now at this day, to wit, the —— day of,* &c. *in this same term, came before our lord the king at* Westminster, *as well the aforesaid* A. B. *by his attorney aforesaid, as the aforesaid* C. D. *by,* &c. *his attorney; and the said* C. *defends*

defends the force and injury when, &c. and saith, that he doth not owe to the said A. the said sum of twenty pounds, or any part thereof, in manner and form as the said A. above complains against him; and of this he puts himself upon his country, &c.

All *pleadings* are either general or special; a general plea is drawn on a little piece of 3 d. stamp'd paper, having only the defendant's attorney's name to it, thus: In debt, *He owes nothing*; or if by bond, *'Tis not his deed, &c.* In case, *He hath not promised:* In trespass, *Not guilty,* &c. And special pleas are drawn up in form, setting forth the matter pleaded at large, with a proper conclusion to the declaration or action; and must be signed by counsel; they are of two sorts, pleas in abatement, and in bar. A plea in abatement begins, *That the defendant ought not to answer the bill,* &c. And it concludes in this form; *Whereupon he prays judgment of the bill, or declaration aforesaid,* &c. The plea in bar begins; *That the plaintiff ought not to have or maintain his action:* and concludes to the action, viz. *He prays judgment if he ought to have or maintain his action against him,* &c.

When a defendant hath pleaded, the plaintiff answers the defendant's plea, which is called a *replication:* This must contain certainty, and not vary from the declaration, but must pursue and maintain the cause of the plaintiff's action; otherwise it will be a departure in pleading. The defendant answers the plaintiff's replication by *rejoinder*; and it ought to be a sufficient answer thereto, and enforce the matter of the bar pleaded; if he departs from the plea, the rejoinder is not good. The plaintiff may answer the rejoinder by a *surrejoinder*; also sometimes, though seldom, pleadings come to *rebutter* in answer to the surrejoinder, &c. A faulty plea in bar, in some cases is made good by a replication; and the replication may be allowed good by a rejoinder; but not where they want substance. *Co. Lit.* 304.

After all the above pleadings, there may be a *demurrer* in law: and where the defendant has pleaded in abatement, before he pleads directly in bar, he may demur to the plaintiff's declaration; and refer the points of law that arise thereupon to the judgment of the court, which determines all questions arising on such demurrers. A demurrer is to be signed, and argued on both sides by counsel; and when it is joined the plaintiff enters it, &c. and paper books are delivered to the judges: and on a general demurrer, the party confesseth all matters of fact, that are well pleaded. These demurrers alledge insufficiency in law in the other party's declaration, plea, &c. and if special, say, *That it ought not to be answered, because*, &c. *and therefore prays judgment*: and if the matter be found insufficient, judgment is against him that joined in the demurrer, but if it appear sufficient, judgment is given against the demurrant. Where the points on a demurrer are apparent and easy to determine, the court will proceed to give judgment upon it presently; but if it be doubtful or difficult, they will take time to consider thereof, and give a day to the parties: and sometimes all the judges of *England* are consulted.

By statute, no dilatory plea shall be received in any court of record, unless the truth of it be proved by affidavit, or probable matter is shewn:
And

Of Actions and Remedies.

And the causes of demurrer are to be specially set down, or the judges shall give judgment without regarding imperfections in any writ, pleading, &c. so as sufficient matter appears. *Stat.* 4 *Ann. c.* 16.

A defendant is to demur where he may do it, for if in such case he pleads, he shall not afterwards take advantage in arrest of judgment, &c.

The form of a general *demurrer* to a declaration.

AND *the said C. D. by T. W. his attorney, comes and defends the force and injury, when,* &c. *and the said C. prays judgment of the said declaration, because he saith, that the said declaration and the matter therein contained are insufficient in law for him the said A. to maintain his said action against the said C. to which declaration the said C. is under no necessity, or in any wise bound by the law of the land to answer; and this he is ready to aver: whereupon for want of a sufficient declaration in this case, the said C. prays judgment of the said declaration, and that the same may be quashed.*

Form of a *joinder* in *demurrer*.

AND *the said A. B. saith, that notwithstanding any thing above alledged by the said C. D. the said declaration ought not to be quashed; because he saith, that the said declaration, and the matter therein contained, are good and sufficient in law for him the said A. to maintain his action against the said C. which said matter contained in the said declaration the said A. is*

D ready

ready to aver and prove in such manner as this court shall think fit; and because the said C. hath made no answer thereto, nor hitherto in any manner denied the same, the said A. *prays judgment, and that his damages occasioned by the premisses may be awarded to him*, &c.

Action upon the case is a general action given for redress of wrongs and injuries, done without force, and by the law not provided against: and by an ancient statute, in action on the case, the like process is to be had as in actions of debt, or trespass. 19 *H.* 7. *c.* 9. It is so called, because the whole case as laid in the declaration (except time and place) is set down in the writ; and it is said to lie in few cases where there is another remedy.

As to the kinds of this action, they are as various as the torts and injuries upon which they are founded; but on a general division may be reduced to the heads of,

1. Nonfeazance on promises.
2. Malefeazance, or doing what ought not to be done.
3. Misfeazance, or misdoing any thing.
4. Deceits on contracts, &c.
5. Particular nusances.

1. As to *nonfeazance*, which is the omission of that which a man ought to do; if there be a charge upon any person, by reason of his tenure of house or land, to repair any bank, bridge, or private way, &c. and he doth it not, and thereby another receives special damage, he may have action on the case against him: so where a man is bound by tenure to repair sea-banks, and he neglects it, so that the land of his

his neighbour is drowned; or when one bound by prescription to make his hedge next my lands, doth it not, whereby other men's cattle come into my ground to my damage, &c. And for not paying of toll of a mill or market, &c. this action lies. *Co. Ent.* 11. 10 *Rep.* 139. 2 *Saund.* 112.

Where a man doth not make a good estate of land sold, according to promise; or do not pay money upon a bargain and sale, according to agreement; or not deliver goods upon promise, or demand, action of the case lies on an express *assumpsit*, which may relate to one's real or personal estate, or to a man's person: and implied *assumpsit* is where goods are sold, or work is done, &c. without any price agreed upon; here the law implies a promise and satisfaction to the value. But for breach of promise made by deed, writ of covenant is to be brought; and upon promise of payment of money on a bond, unless there be a collateral promise, action of debt lieth; and on a bill of exchange accepted, an action lies on the custom only. *Danv. Abr.* 28. *Rol. Abr.* 517. *Vent.* 152.

If one desires me to be bound for him, and he afterwards doth not save me harmless, this is *nonfeazance* implied by law; and action of the case lieth. And this action lies against an inn-keeper that refuses to entertain a guest or traveller, on pretence of his house being full, if this be false: also against a smith refusing to shoe a horse, having necessaries for doing it; and against a sheriff for not arresting a person, being present, &c. *Brownl.* 32, 213. *Dy.* 158.

2. *Malefeazance* is where any man does a voluntary tort or injury to another: if a man in riding a horse hurts another person, &c. Or, if

if any one keeps a dog used to bite men and cattle, and knowing thereof continues him unmuzzled; and I, my child, servant, or cattle are bitten, whereby I suffer damage, this action lies against the owner. *Dy.* 25. 4 *Rep.* 188.

If a man is disturbed or hindered in the use of a way to his house or ground, &c. or in putting cattle into a common, he may have an action on the case. And if one commoner surcharge the common, the rest of the commoners, if they cannot have their common as usual, may bring action of the case against him: So where one digs pits or trenches, &c. in the common, by which cattle go in danger of their lives. And for inclosing a man's common, where the damage occasioned by it is special. 2 *Bulst.* 121. *Stile* 164.

Where the parson or any stranger disturbs a person in the using a seat or isle in a church, which he hath as appendant to his house: Or where one is disturbed in his office, or the profits thereof, this action lieth. And when franchises or liberties, are under disturbance from any: If any one shall hinder a person that has the franchise of the execution and return of writs, or process, in a hundred, liberty, &c. or shall disturb an officer in making an arrest, or in attaching or distraining of goods, action of the case lies: But if a man himself do any act to prevent execution upon his own goods, &c. this action doth not lie. *Co. Entr.* 9. *F. N. B.* 102. 5 *Rep.* 91.

For erecting a new market, to the damage of another, &c. And if any person shall entice away a servant, apprentice, or an apprentice maid, &c. whereby the master or mistress loses their service, and have damage, action on the case lies

lies for the same. *Lev.* 296. 2 *Inst.* 198. 2 *Saund.* 169.

3. *Misfeazance* may concern a man's house or lands, or his cattle, goods, &c. If my servant puts a candle or other fire in any place in my house, and this burns all mine and my neighbour's house, action of the case lieth against me: And if a man in burning of heath keep his fire so negligently, that the close of another is burnt down, this action lies; for every man is to take care, that his fire does his neighbour no damage. But action is taken away in case of accidental fires, by statute. *Danv. Abr.* 10. 2 *Inst.* 303. *Reo.* 13 6 *Ann. c.* 31. *s.* 6. perpetuated by 10 *Ann. c* 14

If a carrier takes goods to carry, and wilfully spoils them, or negligently loses or suffers them to be lost or spoiled, action on the case lies: And if such carrier is robbed of goods, he is answerable for the same, because he hath his hire, and therefore took upon him the safe delivery of the goods; and though the carrier be not acquainted with all the particulars in a box, &c. where there is money, he shall answer in an action, if robbed; unless there be a special agreement or acceptance to excuse him. If a waterman or lighterman lose goods, this action lies against such water-carrier; but goods may be thrown over-board in a tempest, to preserve the lives of the passengers, &c. The over-loading an horse, or surcharging a boat, is actionable, if there be a damage by it. *Fitz. Abr.* 14. *Rast. Entr.* 484. 2 *Bulst.* 28. *Danv. Abr.* 13.

Action of the case will lie against an innkeeper for goods stolen in his house; and here the inn-keeper is chargeable, although the guest doth not acquaint him what goods or money he hath;

hath; and tho' he deliver the key of the chamber to the guest, and knows not the persons doing it, &c. But the person robbed must be a traveller, and guest in the inn, or an action will not lie. A man coming to an inn, leaves goods there, and goes away for two or three days; in this case he is no guest; and therefore, if they are stole, no action lieth; though the leaving a horse, &c. by which the inn-keeper hath gain, makes the owner a guest; and the inn-keeper answerable. 8 *Co. Rep.* 33. *Moor* 877.

This action lieth, where an inn-keeper lets a man's horse to hire without his leave: And when a horse that is hired, is abused by the rider, by riding an excessive pace, or further than agreed, neglecting to take care of him, &c. action of the case may be brought; not if the horse die suddenly, without the rider's default. And if a farrier undertake the cure of my horse; or a smith shoeing thereof, and doth it not well, as if he prick the horse so that I lose the use of him, &c. for these action on the case lies. *Brownl.* 8, 9. *Fitz.* 94. 2 *Bulst.* 334.

If a chirurgeon neglects his patient, or gives him unwholesome medicines, whereby the patient receives injury, &c. this action lieth: Also where a taylor undertakes to make a suit of clothes, and he spoils them; and when one undertaking to build a house, does it ill; or if a carpenter promises to mend my house before a certain day, and neglects to do it, by reason whereof my house falls, it is actionable. *Danv. Abr.* 32.

Where a counsellor doth not come to plead his client's cause, being retained to appear, by which the cause miscarries: If an attorney engages in a suit without warrant, or out of negligence

gence or ignorance mifmanage a caufe, or if he plead otherwife than he hath authority to do, or make default, &c. or in cafe any attorney or other officer do any thing contrary to his truſt; for malicious profecution; and where any ſuit is without ground; and for falfe impriſonment, &c. In all theſe caſes, action of the caſe lieth. Alſo if a ſheriff, &c. refuſe to do, or do any thing amiſs relating to his office, to the damage of another; or ſhall make a falſe return of proceſs, &c. this action may be had. 6 *Rep.* 9. *Dy.* 361. 5 *Rep.* 89.

4. For deceits of attornies, &c. in diſcovering evidences, or others ſecrets, to the prejudice of their clients; or if an attorney do a thing in his own name, or for his own uſe, which he ought to do for me in my name, &c. A man perſonating another in any court or other place, to his injury; counterfeiting letters, to receive money; cheating others at play, with falſe dice, &c. and for all deceits in contracts, action on the caſe lies. *Dy.* 25, 75.

If a vintner ſells wine for good, knowing it to be bad, this action lieth: ſo if a man ſells certain packs of wool, as good and merchantable, if they are damaged; or if one promiſe for money to deliver me that which is good, and doth not; and where a perſon ſells to another cattle or goods, that are not his own; for ſelling by falſe weights and meaſures, or warranting clothes to be of ſuch a length, that are deficient of it; ſelling a horſe, &c. affirming it to be ſound, when it hath ſome ſecret diſeaſe; or unwholeſome bread, beer, meat, &c. *Danv. Abr.* 173, 187. *Cro. Jac.* 196, 471.

And in ſome caſes this action ariſes upon the warranty of the ſeller, and in others it will lie without warranty; but if the buyer taste the wares before-hand, and like and accept them, &c. without a warranty, no action lieth: And 'tis said action of the case lieth not, altho' they are warranted, when the fault is so apparent that the buyer may discern it; for the law gives no remedy for a man's own voluntary negligence. It is the same when the warranty is after the thing is sold, so that 'tis no part of the contract; and where any warranty doth extend to a thing to come, as that a horse shall carry a man so many miles a day, or the like. *Cro. Jac.* 631. 3 *Bulst.* 94. 13 *H.* 4. *Finch* 187.

The bare affirmation of a particular sort of diamond, if the seller doth not warrant it, will not maintain an action: But where a man hath the possession of a personal thing, the affirming it to be his own, is a warranty that it is so: 'tis otherwise in case of lands, where the buyer must see that he hath title. For all deceits used by tradesmen in their trades; and if goods in pawn are refused to be delivered, on offering the money, &c. action on the case may be had. *Cro. Jac.* 4. 196. *Salk.* 210. 4 *Rep.* 18. Lord *Raym.* 593.

5. For a particular nusance to a man's house, water, way, light or air, by building, diverting, stopping, digging, &c. whereby he is damnified, action of the case lieth. If one builds his house, so that the eaves thereof hang over and drop upon mine, and cause it to perish, or otherwise trouble my dwelling therein: Or if a man erect a house, upon a new foundation so near to my house, that he stops up my window, and takes away my light; I may have action of the case against him; but not if the building be on an old foundation, where there was a house before. *Co. Lit.* 56. *Bulst.* 116.

The

The erecting of a glass house, a brew-house, or an house of office, &c. may be a nusance for which he, that hath any damage thereby, may bring his action: where a man hath a water running to his house or land for his necessary use, and another stops or turns it; or in case a tanner erects a lime-pit near the water-course, so that the corruption of the pit spoils the water; if dye-houses are erected, the filth of which destroys fish in a river; or if any tallow-chandler sets up a furnace near an inn, and the stink annoys the guests; hogs are kept in a hog-stye near a man's parlour, whereby he loses the benefit of it, &c. These are nusances, for which action lieth: and an action upon the case lies, for hindring of the wholesome air, as well as for corrupting of it. 2 *Rol. Abr.* 140. *Yelv.* 48, 159. 9 *Rep.* 58.

Building a smith's forge near another's house, and making a noise with hammers, was held a nusance; although the smith worked at seasonable times, and had been a blacksmith above twenty years in that place, &c. For though a smith is a necessary trade, and so a lime-burner, and hog-merchant; yet they must be used not to be injurious to the neighbours; or action of the case lieth: also any persons may abate or remove nusances, that are prejudiced by them. *Lutw.* 69.

For the breaking down a wall, or sluice: or if one break down the bank of a river, &c. Also for damming up rivers, or throwing stones or rubbish therein; and stopping, or not scouring of a ditch, &c. action on the case lies. And the continuation of a nusance, is as it were a new nusance: but for a common nusance to a highway, and annoyances of rivers, bridges, &c.

common to every body, the remedy is not by action, but by prefentment or indictment. *Dy.* 248. *Co. Lit.* 401.

The form of a declaration in cafe, for goods fold and delivered, againft a widow, adminiftratrix.

Trinity term in the feventeenth year of the reign of king George *the* Third.

Indebitatus affumpfit for goods fold and delivered.

London, (to wit.) I. C. *complains of* A. H. *(adminiftratrix of all and fingular the goods and chattles, rights and credits, which were of* W. H. *her late hufband, deceafed, at the time of his death, who died inteftate) in the cuftody of the marfhal of the marfhalfea of our lord the king before the king himfelf, for that, Whereas the faid* W. *in his life-time, that is to fay, on the* 30th *day of* March *in the firft year of the reign of our now lord the king in the parifh of* Saint Mary le Bow, *in the ward of* Cheap, *was indebted to the aforefaid* I. *in* 800 l. *of lawful money of* Great Britain, *for divers goods, wares and merchandizes of the faid* I. *to him the faid* W. *before that time fold and delivered; and fo thereof being indebted, he the faid* W. *in confideration thereof afterwards, to wit, the fame day and year at* London *aforefaid, in the parifh and ward aforefaid, affumed upon himfelf, and to the faid* I. *then and there faithfully promifed that he the faid* W. *the aforefaid* 800 l. *to him the faid* I. *when thereof he fhould be required, would well and faithfully pay and content. And whereas the faid* W. *in his life-time, the fame day and year at* London *aforefaid, in the parifh and ward aforefaid, in confideration that the faid* I. *at the like fpecial inftance and requeft of the faid* W.

Quantum valerunt thereon.

Of Actions and Remedies.

W. had sold and delivered to the said W. diverse other goods, wares and merchandizes of him the said I. assumed upon himself, and to the said I. then and there faithfully promised, that he the said W. so much money as the said last mentioned goods, wares and merchandizes, at the time of the sale, and delivery thereof, were reasonably worth, to the said I. when thereof afterwards he should be requested, would well and faithfully pay and content, and the said I. avers, that the goods, wares and merchandizes last mentioned, at the time of the sale and delivery thereof, were reasonably worth other 800 l. of lawful money of Great Britain, whereof the said W. then and there had notice. And whereas the said W. in his life-time afterwards, to wit, the same day and year aforesaid, at London aforesaid, in the parish and ward aforesaid, was indebted to the said I. in other 800 l. of like lawful money, for so much money by him the said I. at the like special instance and request, and for the proper use of him the said W. before that time laid out and expended, and being so indebted, he the said W. in consideration thereof, afterwards, to wit, the same day and year at London aforesaid, in the parish and ward aforesaid, assumed upon himself, and to the said I. then and there faithfully promised, that he the said W. the aforesaid 800 l. last mentioned, to the said I. when therefore afterwards he should be required, would likewise well and faithfully pay and content: And whereas also the said W. in his life-time, to wit, the day and year aforesaid, at London aforesaid, in the parish and ward aforesaid, accompted with the said I. of diverse sums of money, to him the said I. by the said W. before that time owing, and then being behind and unpaid; and upon that account the said W. was found in arrears towards the said I. in other 800 l. of like lawful money of

Indebitatus assumpsit for money laid out for defendant's use.

Insimul computasset.

Great

Of Actions and Remedies.

Great Britain, and so in arrear being found, be the said W. in his life-time in consideration thereof, afterwards, to wit, the same day and year aforesaid, at London aforesaid, in the parish and ward aforesaid, assumed upon himself, and then and there faithfully promised, that he the said W. the said 800 l. last mentioned, to the said I. when thereof afterwards she should be required, would likewise well and faithfully pay and content. Nevertheless the said W. in his life-time, and the said A. (to whom administration of all and singular the goods and chattles, rights and credits which were of the said W. at the time of his death, to wit, at London aforesaid, in the parish and ward aforesaid) after his death, the several promises and assumptions aforesaid, so as aforesaid made, little regarding, but contriving and fraudulently intending him the said I. in this behalf craftily and subtilly to deceive and defraud, the aforesaid sums of money, or any part thereof to the said I. he the said W. in his life-time, and the said A. after the death of the said W. at any time hitherto have not nor hath either of them paid, although so to do the said W. in his life-time, that is to say, the day and year aforesaid, at London aforesaid, in the parish and ward aforesaid, and also she the said A. after his death, and after committing administration to the said A. to wit, the 9th day of June in the first year of the reign of our now lord the king, at London aforesaid, in the parish and ward aforesaid, and often afterwards by the said I. were requested, but the same to the said I. have altogether refused to pay, and the said A. the same to the said I. still refuses to pay. To the damage of the said I. of 1000 l. and therefore he brings suit, &c.

Pledges to prosecute } J. Doe. & Rich. Roe.

Form

Form of a *declaration* in a cafe for deceit upon a warranty of goods.

Berks, to wit. **A**. B. *complains of* C. D. *being in cuſtody of, &c. For that whereas the ſaid* C. *the —— day of —— in the —— year, &c. at* N. *in the county aforeſaid, in conſideration of ſeventeen pounds of lawful money of Great Britain, by the aforeſaid* A. *to him the ſaid* C. *then and there in hand paid, did bargain and ſell unto the ſaid* A. *one hogſhead of white* Liſbon *wine, and upon making the ſaid bargain and ſale, he the ſaid* C. *did then and there warrant the ſame wine to be neat and perfect wine, and in good condition: but he the ſaid* A. *in fact ſaith, that the wine aforeſaid, at the time of the bargain and ſale aforeſaid, was corrupted and adulterated wine, and if drank, would be hurtful to man's body; whereby the ſaid* A. *upon the ſaid bargain and ſale and warranty aforeſaid, was very much deceived and defrauded, to the damage of the ſaid* A. *&c. And therefore he brings his ſuit, &c.*

The form of a *declaration* in caſe for a nuſance to a man's water.

Wilts, to wit. **A**. B. *complains of* C. D. *being in the cuſtody of the marſhal, &c. For that whereas the ſaid* A. *on the —— day of —— in the —— year of the reign, &c. and always from thence hitherto, was and hath been, and ſtill is poſſeſſed of a meſſuage or tenement, ſituate, lying and being in the pariſh of, &c. in the county aforeſaid, for a certain term of years,*

then

then and yet to come: and whereas the said A. and all those whose estate he now hath, of and in the messuage with the appurtenances aforesaid, have, and, from the time whereof the memory of man is not to the contrary, were accustomed to have, and of right ought to have, for themselves and their tenants, as to the said messuage belonging and appertaining, in the garden of the said A. in and out of the river running down and descending between the meadow of the said C. called, &c. and the said garden of the aforesaid A. at all times of the year at their pleasure, clean, pure, and wholesome water, to dress all manner of victuals, for the necessary sustenance of men inhabiting and residing in the tenement aforesaid, with the appurtenances, or any part thereof: nevertheless the said C. not ignorant of the premisses, but contriving and maliciously intending the said A. in this behalf unjustly to grieve, the ——— day of ——— &c. in the ——— year, &c. at, &c. aforesaid, certain tan-pits in the aforesaid meadow, called, &c. then and there made and digged, and continued; and the mud, filth, and other unclean things into the said meadow of the said C. near to the river, and near the said garden of the said A. then and there out of the tan-pits aforesaid did cast and evacuate; and from thence the said mud, filth and uncleanness, into the said river out of the aforesaid meadow of him the said C. near to the garden of the aforesaid A. out of the same tan-pits then and there being evacuated and cast into the water of the said A. then and there did run down and descend; whereby the said water of him the said A. out of the river near the garden of the said A. for the necessary use of him the said A. and his whole family taken and had, became putrid, corrupt, and to human bodies altogether

Of Actions and Remedies.

together unwholesome; whereupon the said A. saith that he is injured, and hath damage, &c. and therefore he brings his suit.

Form of a *plea* in case of payment in satisfaction of a promise, and *replication*.

AND *the aforesaid C. D. by T. W. his attorney, comes and defends the force and injury, when, &c. and saith, That the said A. B. ought not to have or maintain his action aforesaid against him; because he says, that after the several promises and assumptions so made as aforesaid, to wit, on the —— day, &c. in the —— year of the reign, &c. at, &c. aforesaid in the county aforesaid, he the said C. paid to the said A. twenty pounds, in full satisfaction of all the money due by the several promises and assumptions in the declaration of the said A. above mentioned: and this he is ready to aver and prove; whereupon he prays judgment, if the said A. ought to have or maintain his said action thereof against him.*

And the said A. B. saith, that for any thing by the said C. before in pleading alledged, he ought not to be barred or precluded from having his action aforesaid against the said C. because he says, that the said C. did not pay to the said A. the aforesaid twenty pounds, in manner and form as the aforesaid C. hath above alledged: and he prays that this may be inquired of by the country.

Plea that the defendant made no such promise, &c. in case.

AND the said C. by, &c. his attorney, comes and defends the force and injury, when, &c. and saith, that the said A. ought not to have or maintain his action aforesaid against him; because he says, that he the said C. did not make any such promise, in manner and form as the said A. above complains against him; and this he is ready to verify; wherefore he prays judgment, if the said A. ought to have or maintain his action thereupon against him.

A *plea* of Not guilty, in case.

AND the said C. by, &c. his attorney comes and defends the force and injury, when, &c. and saith, that the said A. ought not to have or maintain his action against him, because he saith, that he is not guilty of the premisses above laid to his charge, in such manner and form as the said A. above complains against him; and this he is ready to aver; whereupon he prays judgment, &c.

Action of *account* lies against a bailiff or receiver, &c. to a lord or others, who by reason of their offices and businesses, are to render accounts, but refuse to do it: and this writ or action may be brought against,

1. A bailiff or receiver of rents and debts.
2. Where one was not bailiff or receiver.
3. Before auditors assigned, &c.

Of Actions and Remedies.

1. If a man makes one his bailiff of a manor, &c. he shall have a writ of account against him as bailiff: also where a person makes another his receiver, to receive his rents or debts, &c. he shall have action of account against him as receiver; and if he appoint him his bailiff and receiver, he then may bring account against him in both ways: but a bailiff cannot be generally charged as a receiver, nor a receiver as bailiff. *Danv. Abr.* 220.

A bailiff or receiver makes a deputy; action of account lies against them, and not against the deputy: if account is brought against one as bailiff, he shall have his costs and expences; 'tis said to be otherwise where such action is brought against him as receiver. An action of account may be brought against a factor, who sells goods and merchandizes; and if a man have a servant, whom he orders to receive money, the master shall have account against him, if he were his receiver: but an apprentice is not chargeable in action of account. *Co. Lit.* 172. *Lon.* 32. 2 *Mod.* 100.

If money be received by a wife, account lies against the husband; but action of account lieth not properly of a thing certain, only of uncertain things; if a man delivers 10*l*. to merchandize with, he shall not have account of the 10*l*. but of the profits, which are uncertain. It is no plea in an accountant, that he was robbed; but he may plead that it was without his default and negligence, and it will be good. *Danv. Abr.* 215. *Co. Lit.* 89.

2. By the statute 4 *Ann. c.* 16. actions of account may be brought against the executors and administrators of guardians, bailiffs and receivers; and by one jointenant, &c. against

the other, his executors and administrators, as bailiff for receiving more than his share. If one receive money for my use, I shall have account against him as receiver, &c. So if a man enter into land to my use, and receive the profits of it, I shall have action of account against him as bailiff. *Fitz. Abr. Account,* 6.

Where a person receives money due to me upon a bond or obligation; or for rents owing to me, I may have account against him as my receiver; or action of debt, or on the case, as owing me so much money that he hath received. A man delivers money to one to pay me; if it be not paid, I shall have an action of account against him; and if I pay money to another person, I may bring action against him for so much received for my use; but he may discharge himself, by saying it was for some debt, or to be paid over by my order to some other, which he hath done, &c. *Lil. Abr.* 30, 33.

Money is delivered to another, to be delivered over, account lies if it be not delivered: and if I deliver money to one to deliver over to another for my use, and he gives it him, account lieth. *Danv. Abr.* 215.

3. In actions of account, auditors are to be assigned, who are judges of record; but what may be pleaded in bar to the action, shall not be allowed to be pleaded before them: the plaintiff or defendant, may join issue, &c. before the auditors, which shall be certified to the court, and there tried; and they may grant a further day to the defendant to account; but if he is remiss, they must certify the court that he will not account. *Cro. Car.* 161. *Danv. Abr.* 231.

If the accountant be found in arrear, the auditors have power to commit him to prison, to remain till he makes agreement with the party; though if he be charged with more receipts than he ought, or be not allowed reasonable expences, he may have a writ *ex parte talis* out of the chancery directed to the sheriff, to take four mainpernors for bringing his body before the barons of the exchequer at a certain day, and to warn the lord to appear at the same time, &c. by statute 13 *Ed.* 1. *cap.* 11. *Co. Lit.* 380.

And the auditors appointed by the court, where an action of account shall be depending, may administer an oath, and examine the parties touching the matters in question; and for their pains shall have a reasonable allowance, to be paid by the party on whose side the balance shall appear, by 4 *Ann. c.* 16.

The judgment in this action being only to account, and no damages given therein, it is seldom used at this day.

Form of a *declaration* in an action of account.

South'ton to wit.

A. B. *complains of* C. D. *being in custody of the marshal,* &c. *of a plea that he render to him a reasonable account for the time that he was bailiff of him the said* A. *and the receiver of the monies of the same* A. *at,* &c. *in the county aforesaid; for that whereas the said* C. *was the bailiff of the said* A. *of one messuage or farm, and sixty acres of land,* &c. *with the appurtenances in* H. *aforesaid in the county of* S. *aforesaid, from the day,* &c. *in the year,* &c. *until the day and year,* &c. *and for all that time having the care thereof, and power to let and improve the messuage or farm aforesaid with the appurtenances, and the rent for the same*

E 2 *messuage*

messuage and lands, to the use of him the said A. during the said time to collect and receive, as receiver of the monies of the said A. for the same time, had received of the money of the said A. at H. aforesaid, by the hands of, &c. twenty pounds, and by the hands of, &c. ten pounds, and there also by the hands of, &c. of lawful money of Great Britain, *to render a reasonable account thereof to the said A. when he should be thereunto required: nevertheless the said C. tho' often thereto required, his reasonable account of the same to the said A. hath not as yet rendered, but the same to him to render hitherto hath denied, and still doth deny; whereupon the said A. saith, that he is the worse, and hath damage, &c. And therefore he brings his suit, &c.*

Action of covenant is brought where a man is bound by covenant in a deed, entered into by two or more persons, to do or not to do some act or thing agreed betwixt them, when he hath broke the same: and is divided into,

1. Covenant personal for doing any thing.
2. Covenant real concerning lands.

1. A covenant between persons must be to do what is lawful and possible, or it will not be binding: and in such case, where there is any agreement under hand and seal, action of covenant may be brought on it; and if one is party to a deed, his agreement to pay amounts to a covenant. 2 *Mod.* 91.

Upon a bond action of covenant lies, it proving an agreement; and if a person covenants to pay another a certain sum of money at a day, tho' he may bring action of debt for it, yet may
writ

writ of covenant be had at his election: but when only a hand is to a writing, and not a seal, covenant lieth not, but action of the case upon breach of the agreement. And by release of all covenants from the covenantee, a covenant is discharged, with the action thereon, &c. 2 *Danv. Abr.* 228. *Lil.* 346. *Allen* 39.

If a man covenant with one to pay him money on a time to come, and do not say to his executors, &c. If the covenantee die before the day, his executors or administrators shall have action of covenant for the money, and recover the same: also in every case where a testator is bound by a covenant, the executor shall be liable, if it be not determined by the testator's death. Not only parties to deeds, but their executors and administrators, may take advantage of covenants: but there may be an agreement and covenant, only to be performed by the parties themselves. *Dy.* 12. 5 *Rep.* 16. *Cro. Eliz.* 552. 2 *Danv. Abr.* 235.

In deeds and articles of covenant, sometimes a clause for performance, with a penalty, is inserted; and other times, and more frequently, bonds are given for the performance, with a sufficient penalty, separate from the deed; which last being sued, the jury must find the penalty, but on covenant the damages only. And commonly the party damnified in this action shall recover nothing but damages for the breach; except in real actions. *F. N. B.* 145.

2. Where it is agreed, that one man shall pay 100 *l.* to another for lands in such a place, this is a mutual real covenant; and action of covenant lies, if the other party refuses to convey, &c. And when covenants are distinct and mutual, several actions may be brought against the

parties;

parties; but if there be mutual covenants, and the one not to be performed before a covenant precedent, there the covenant is not suable till the other is performed. *Sid.* 423. 2 *Mod.* 74.

A person covenants expressly to repair a house and it is burnt down by lightning, or any other accident, yet he ought to repair it, or action of covenant lies against him; for it was in his power to have guarded against it by his contract, by exception, &c. tho' a tenant is not so bound, by covenant in law. But where the use of a thing is demised, and it runs to decay, so that the lessee or tenant cannot have the benefit of it; for this no action of covenant lieth for the lessee and if the lease, &c. is not good, there can be no covenant, or any breach. *Lil. Abr.* 349. *Yelv.* 19. 2 *Danv. Abr.* 233.

If a man makes a lease of lands for years, and then turns out the lessee, he shall have covenant against the lessor, tho' there be no express covenant in the deed: but in case a stranger enters before such lessee, the lessee shall not have an action of covenant upon this ouster, because he was never a lessee in privity to have the action; yet a stranger to the deed may not take advantage of a covenant. *Yelv.* 18.

A covenant for the lessee to enjoy against all men, extends not to tortious acts and entries, &c. for which the lessee hath his proper remedy against the aggressors. If a person covenants in a deed, that he hath good right to grant, &c. and he hath no right, it is a breach of covenant, for which action of covenant lieth: and where a man by his own act disables himself to perform a covenant, it is a breach thereof; and no duty or cause of action arises upon any covenant, till it be broken. *Vaugh.* 123. 5 *Rep.* 21. 2 *Bulst.* 12.

Of Actions and Remedies.

On covenants in general, if the plaintiff have judgment in an action for one breach, and afterwards the covenator breaks his covenant again, a new action may be brought, and so for every breach: or in covenants perpetual, upon a new breach, a *scire facias* may be had on the former judgment, and the plaintiff need not bring any new writ of covenant. Co. Rep. 154. Cro. El. 5.

Form of a *declaration* in covenant.

London, to wit.

A. B. *complains of* C. D. *in the custody of,* &c. *of a plea of covenants broken,* (*or breach of covenants,*) *for that, whereas by certain articles of agreement, indented and made at* L. *aforesaid, that is to say, in the parish of St.* Mary le Bow, *in the ward of,* &c. *on the* —— *day,* &c. *in the* —— *year of the reign,* &c. *by and between the aforesaid* A. *by the name of* A. B. *of,* &c. *gentleman, of the one part, and the said* C. *by the name of* C. D. *of,* &c. *of the other part,* (*which other part of the said articles, sealed with the seal of the said* C. *bearing date the same day and year above, the said* A. *brings here into court*) *it was concluded and agreed between the said* A. *and* C. *their executors, administrators, and assigns, that,* &c. (*reciting the articles, or the particular clause for payment of money,* &c. *wherein the breach is to be assigned, with the penalty annexed*) *as by the said articles of agreement indented doth most fully appear: and the said* A. *in fact saith, that the aforesaid articles of agreement indented were sealed and executed at* L. *within the parish and ward aforesaid, on the day,* &c. *in the year abovesaid, and that the said* C. *neither on the said* —— *day of,* &c. *in the* —— *year,* &c. *aforesaid, or at any time afterwards hitherto, although thereunto often required by the said* A. *hath paid to him the said* A. *the said sum of,* &c. *in the said articles of agreement indented specified,* &c. *And also the said* A. *in fact further saith, that the said* C. *tho' often required thereto by the said* A. *hath not performed all or any of the articles of agreement or covenants in the aforesaid indenture contained, which on the part and behalf of the said* C. *ought to be done and performed, according to the form and effect of the said indenture; but to do or perform the same hath hitherto refused, and still doth refuse; whereupon the said* A. *saith, that he is injured, and hath sustained damage,* &c. *And therefore he brings his suit.*

A *plea* that all covenants are performed.

AND *the said* C. *comes and defends,* &c. *and saith, that all and singular the covenants, grants, articles and agreements in the indenture above contained, on the part and behalf of the said* C. *to be observed, performed, fulfilled and kept, are and from the time of the making of the indenture aforesaid, until the day of exhibiting of the bill of the said* A. *were well and truly observed, performed fulfilled and kept, according to the true intent and meaning of the said indenture; and this he is ready to verify: whereupon he prays judgment if the said,* &c.

Action of detinue lies for recovery of goods or chattels, lent and delivered to a man to keep, or to deliver over to a third person, who refuses to redeliver them, and detains them in his hands. It is used in these two cases:

1. For recovering goods detained.
2. For recovery of deeds and charters.

1. The

1. The action lies for any thing certain and valuable, wherein one may have a right or property; as for cattle, cloth, houshold goods, plate, jewels, bags of money sealed, or chests of money locked, sacks of corn, loads of wood, &c. but for money out of a bag, or corn out of a sack, &c. detinue lies not, because they cannot be distinguished from another man's corn or money; and therefore the party must have an action on the case, &c. *F. N. B.* 138. *Co. Lit.* 286.

The thing detained must be once in the possession of the defendant; which is not to be altered by act of law, as seizure in execution, &c. and the nature of the thing must continue without alteration, to intitle to this action; so that if leather be made into shoes, or timber be used in building, &c. the writ of detinue will not lie. In case of delivery of goods, if a person to whom a thing is delivered dieth, detinue may be brought against his executors, or against any person to whom the same comes; as if things be delivered to be kept, whether by the party, or his father, ancestor, &c. he may bring this action, if detained. 11 *Rep.* 89. 4 *Rep.* 83.

If one lends me a horse, or such like thing, he must have the very thing restored, &c. or detinue lieth against me: tho' where goods, &c. are delivered by way of loan, as if one lend another money, corn, or the like, he cannot expect the same thing again; but the same in specie and quantity. Grantees of goods, and persons to whom they are to be delivered over, &c. shall have action of detinue: and if a man bargain and sell goods, upon condition to be void, on payment of money at a day; if he pays it, he may have detinue for the goods. *Co. Lit.* 89. *Cro. Eliz.* 267. *Bulst.* 69.

A general action of detinue lies against one that finds a man's goods; though if I deliver any thing to a person, to re-deliver to me, and he loses it, if another finds the thing, and delivers it to one who has right to the same, he is not chargeable to me in detinue: but where any goods are delivered to a man, and he delivers them to another, action of detinue may be had against the second person; and if he deliver the goods to a party having right thereto, yet 'tis said he is answerable. 9 *H.* 6. 58. 2 *Danv. Abr.* 511.

If a person receives goods of me for my use, I may take my goods again without request; or if they are left or delivered to deliver to another man, before they are delivered I may countermand the authority, and require the goods again; and may bring an action, or take the goods where I find them. *Co Lit.* 498.

2. Action of detinue may be had for charters, which make the title of lands; and the heir shall have a detinue of charters or writings, altho' he hath not the lands: and in this action, judgment is given to deliver the deed found by verdict to be detained, or the value, &c. But if the issue be upon the detinue, and it is found that the defendant hath burnt or destroyed the charters, the judgment shall be for the plaintiff to recover the land in damages; and not the deeds, which it appears cannot be had. *F. N. B.* 308. 2 *Rol. Abr.* 101.

Where the charters relate to the freehold, detinue must be brought in the *Common Pleas,* and in no other court: and the defendant cannot wage law upon a detinue of writings concerning the inheritance of lands nor of any indenture of lease for years; but a defendant may wage

Of Actions and Remedies.

wage his law in detinue in almost all cases touching goods or chattels; to prevent which trover may be brought, when the conversion changes the detinue to action of the case, and he cannot wage his law. *Co. Lit.* 286.

Form of a *declaration* in action of detinue.

A. B. *complains of* C. D. *being in custody of the marshal,* &c. *of a plea, that he render him chattels to the value of twenty pounds, which he unjustly detains from him,* &c. *For that whereas the said* A. *on the* —— *day,* &c. *in the* —— *year of,* &c. *at* M. *in the county aforesaid, delivered to the said* C. *divers chattels, that is to say, one yellow mohair bed, with the feather-bed, bolster and two pillows,* &c. *belonging, and one walnut-tree table, a pier locking-glass,* &c. *of the value of,* &c. *to be safe kept by the said* C. *and to him the said* A. *to be re-delivered, when he should be thereunto required; yet the said* C. *though often required, the chattels aforesaid hath not re-delivered to the said* A. *but the same to him hitherto to re-deliver hath denied, and still doth deny, and unjustly detain; whereupon the said* A. *faith, that he is injured, and hath damage to the value,* &c. *And thereof he brings his suit,* &c.

Action of trover and conversion is a special action of the case, lying where a man having found goods refuseth to deliver them to the owner upon demand. Or if one hath in his possession my goods, by delivery to him, and he sells or uses them without my consent, this is a conversion for which trover lies; and so if he doth not actually convert them, but doth not deliver them to me on demand.

An

Of Actions and Remedies.

An action of trover, or detinue, may be brought for goods detained; for the party shall have his goods detained, if they may be had, or damages to the value for the detaining and conversion of them: after the goods are demanded, if the person having them denies the delivery thereof, detinue or this action lies; and a denial to deliver is a conversion in law: also trespass or trover lies for the same thing; and the alledging the conversion of the goods in trespass, is to aggravate damages. If where a bond, &c. is detained, the money be received thereon, action of account lies against the receiver, &c. *Cro. Jac.* 50. 2 *Lutw.* 1526.

For any live goods, or things inanimate, trover will lie; and a plaintiff may chuse to have his action of trover against the first finder of the goods, or any other who gets them afterwards; and an executor may bring trover for the goods of the testator: and either by finding or delivery of goods, as the defendant hath a lawful possession, there must be a demand and refusal to make the conversion; but if the possession was tortious, as if the defendant take away my hat, &c. the very taking is a sufficient proof of a conversion, without any thing farther. *Sid.* 264. 3, *Salk.* 365.

The action of trover and conversion lieth for goods, although they come into the possession of the plaintiff before the action brought, which doth not satisfy for the detainer, or purge the wrong: in case a person takes the horse of another, and rides him, and then delivers the same to the party, he may notwithstanding have trover, it being a conversion, and re-delivery is no bar: but where a defendant generally tenders the goods, if the plaintiff refuse to receive them, that

Of Actions and Remedies.   61

that will go in mitigation of damages; though the plaintiff may bring trover still. *Danv. Abr.* 21. 3 *Nelf. Abr.* 424.

One puts out cattle to pasture, and then sells them, the buyer may have trover against the farmer, &c. if he refuses to let them go till paid for; and his remedy must be by action for what is due to him for depasturing the cattle: for he may not detain them for the debt; as in case of an inn-keeper, or taylor, &c. for things in their custody. *Cro. Car.* 27. 2 *Lil. Abr.* 622.

If a man finds goods, he ought not to abuse or use them, for therein lies the offence, to found this action, the point of which is the conversion; in this case, the party finding is to deliver them on demand, &c. though he may answer, that he knows not whether the plaintiff is the true owner. And where goods lost are found in the hands of another, if he bought them in open fair or market, this alters the property, and the plaintiff cannot recover them from him. *Dan. Abr.* 22. *Co. Lit.* 498.

In action of trover, if a conversion cannot be proved, then proof is to be had of a demand made of the thing, before the action brought, and that it was not delivered; and the property of the plaintiff must be proved, before the goods came to the defendant's hands, &c.

The form of a *declaration* in trover.

London, } A B. *complains of* C. D. *being in the*
to wit. } *custody of,* &c. *For that whereas the said* A. *the* — *day of,* &c. *in the* —— *year of the reign,* &c. *at* L. *aforesaid, in the parish of St.* Mary le Bow, *in the ward,* &c. *was possessed of one large silver tankard, marked with the letters,*

Of Actions and Remedies.

letters, &c. of the price of six pounds, as of his own proper goods; and being so thereof possessed, the said A. afterwards, that is to say, the —— day of, &c. in the —————— year aforesaid, at L. aforesaid, in the parish and ward aforesaid, the said tankard out of his hands and possession did casually lose, and was deprived of the same; which said tankard afterwards, that is to say, the said day, &c. in the, &c. year abovesaid, at L. aforesaid, in the parish and ward aforesaid, by finding came to the hands and possession of the said C. Nevertheless the said C. knowing the said tankard to be the proper tankard of the said A. and to him the said A. of right to belong and appertain, contriving and intending craftily and subtilly to deceive and defraud the said A. in this particular, the tankard aforesaid to the same A. altho' thereunto often required, hath not delivered; but the said tankard afterwards, that is to say, the —— day of, &c. in the year aforesaid, at L. aforesaid, in the parish and ward aforesaid, the said C. to his own proper use did then and there dispose of and convert; to the damage of the said A. &c. And therefore he brings his suit.

Form of a *plea* in trover, with a traverse of the conversion.

AND *the said C. by, &c. his attorney, comes, and defends the force and injury, when, &c. and saith, that the said A. ought not to have or maintain his action aforesaid against him; because he says, that the city of L. is an ancient city, and in the said city there is had, and, from the time whereof the memory of man is not to the contrary, there always was had and kept a common market every day in the week, in the day-time,*
from

from the rising until the setting of the sun of the same day, in all open places of the said city (Sundays and festival days only excepted) for all persons freely to buy or sell, in which one party of the contractors is a citizen and freeman of the same city: and the said C. further saith, That on the ―― day of, &c. in the ―― year, &c. abovesaid, being Tuesday, and no festival day, one E. F. at L. aforesaid, in the parish and ward aforesaid, was possessed of the silver tankard aforesaid, and so being possessed thereof, then and there in the day time of the said day, &c. after sun rising and before the sun setting of that day, that is to say, at e'even o'clock in the forenoon of the said day, for four pounds of lawful money of Great-Britain, unto the said E by him the said C. in hand paid, then and there in the open market of the said city, the said tankard in the said open market then being, did bargain and sell unto the said C. the tankard aforesaid, and the said C. then being a freeman and citizen of the said city, that is to say, free of the art or mystery of, &c. of the city of L. whereby he the said C. was possessed of and intitled to the said tankard, as of his proper goods; and being so intitled thereto, the aforesaid tankard, afterwards, that is to say, the said ― day, &c. in the ― year, &c. abovesaid, at L. in the parish and ward aforesaid, to the proper use of him the said C. did dispose and convert, as it was lawful for him to do: Without that, that he is guilty of any other conversion of the said tankard, to his use in manner and form as the said A. by his declaration aforesaid hath alledged; and this he is ready to verify: whereupon he prays judgment if the said A. ought to have or maintain his said action against him, &c.

Action

Action of slander lieth for defaming a person in his reputation; being no more than an action on the case for words, &c. And when words spoken affect a man's life, or liberty, office, trade, or tend to loss of preferment in marriage, service, &c. or to his disinheritance, or which occasion any particular damage, this action may be brought. There are several divisions of actions of slander as follow:

1. For charging a man with particular crimes.
2. Slander of persons in their offices and professions.
3. Slandering a man's title to an estate, &c.
4. Of defamation by libels.

1. Where any words are maliciously spoken of another, for which, if true, they would touch his life, or he might be punished, action of slander lies; as to call a man traitor, robber, felon, &c. or charge him with the committing any of these crimes; or to say of one, if he might have his will, he would do such a thing, which thing is actionable. 10 *Rep.* 130. *Dy.* 19.

To reproach a person with a heinous crime, as that he lay in wait to rob or murder any one; to charge a man with a rape, that he did ravish or was guilty of ravishing a certain woman; or say he should have been hanged for a rape, &c. and charging one with sodomy or buggery, &c. being very penal by the law, for these action lieth. The charging a person with stealing things, or as a receiver of stolen goods, are actionable; tho' the words must import a certain charge of felony, and not be of cutting and taking away standing corn, apples from trees, &c. This action

Of Actions and Remedies.

action of slander may be had for calling a person thief; unless something of qualification be coupled to prove the thing no felony: and for conspiring to indict a man falsly and maliciously of felony, or other offence, on his acquittal, &c. but not if it appears on the trial there was probable cause for the indictment. *Rep.* 589. *Bulst.* 112.

For saying of another, that he hath killed, or concealed the murder of such a man, action lies; but the defendant may shew that the party is or was alive at the speaking of the words, and then no action will lie thereon. To say of one formerly that he was a witch, and did bewitch a certain person, &c. was actionable; tho' not for calling a woman witch, without more words importing that she had bewitched some body, or his goods, &c. For saying one is a pirate, or maintainer of pirates, action of slander lieth; and so it is to say of a man, that he did burn a dwelling-house, or a barn with corn, &c. *Dy.* 236. *Brownl.* 15. 2 *Bulst.* 234. *2 elv.* 154.

Such words as charge a person with forgery of false deeds, or with perjury, bribery, extortion, maintenance, &c. all which are punishable by the common and statute laws, and affect a man's liberty and estate; for these words an action of slander may be brought. If one say of a person, that he could prove him perjured in a court of record; or call him perjured knave, action lies; so where a man says he gave another money for forswearing himself; and when the words charge the party with subornation of perjury. *Brownl.* 18. 3 *Inst.* 163. *Dawv. Abr.* 87.

2. To say of a member of parliament, or a bishop, &c. that he is a papist, is actionable: and for saying a parson preaches lies in the pulpit, action of slander lieth; not if words are, he is a preacher of false doctrine. If one call a justice of peace false justice, &c. A doctor of physick fool, ass, empirick and mountebank; or say that a counsellor is no lawyer; call an attorney rogue and knave in his profession; or to say to him that he is not fit to be an attorney; and calling a clerk in a court a corrupt man, &c. in these cases action lies. 2 *Brownl.* 166. *Danv. Abr.* 119, 113. 4 *Rep.* 15.

An action of slander will lie for words spoke against a sheriff, receiver, steward of a court, mayor, constable, &c. but the words spoken must relate to the office, and the person be an officer at that time. For saying of a merchant or tradesman, that he is a beggarly fellow, and not able to pay his debts; or to call him bankrupt, or say he will be a bankrupt shortly; and saying of any other, that he is a runaway, and dares not shew his face: that a man is a cheating knave in his trade; or that he keeps a false book in his shop, &c. whereby he is injured, action lies. But words of heat, as where a person in a passion calls another rogue, knave, or villain, unless he apply the words, by saying villain to such man, or knave in such an affair, &c. will bear no action. 10 *Rep.* 61. *Danv. Abr.* 114. *Hob.* 93. *T. Raym.* 184.

If one say, that an alehouse-keeper keeps a bawdy-house, action lieth; but to say an innkeeper harbours rogues, &c. is not actionable, for his house is common to all guests. For calling a man whore-master, or a woman whore, except in *London* by the custom of the city, no
action

action lieth: tho' to say of a man that he is a common whore-master, and lay with a certain woman, and is a drunken fellow, &c. Or that a woman hath a bastard, or is with child, and lay with such a man, &c. whereby either of them lose their marriage, are actionable; but not without special damage on action at common law. *Cro. Eliz.* 582. 2 *Rol. Rep.* 136. 4 *Rep.* 16. 2 *Salk.* 696. 2 Ld. *Raym.* 959.

Where a man is courting a woman, if another say of him, that he hath the *French* disease, &c. or for saying of a person, he hath the pox, leprosy, &c. by reason of which he ought by law to be separated from society, action of slander lies: but 'tis otherwise if the words are that he has the pox, after cured. The saying of one who stands for a place, that he is an ignorant man, and not qualified; or of a parson, that he is an excommunicate, &c. if thereby he loseth his preferment, and the servant his service, 'tis actionable. *Cro. Jac.* 430. *Danv. Abr.* 87, 103. *Lev.* 248.

3. Slandering the title of another person is actionable; as to say he has no right to such a house or lands, or that he hath no good estate therein, &c. when he is about to sell or let the same, and by this slander the chapman falls off. And for calling a man bastard, that is heir to an estate, action lieth; tho' he be not about to sell it, and he have no particular loss by speaking the words, for thereby the title of the land may be drawn in question: but 'tis said, if he be an heir apparent, the action lies not till he is disinherited or prejudiced by it; and if he who spoke the words claim the estate as next heir, the action will not lie, which may be set forth

Of Actions and Remedies.

by way of bar. *Rep.* 77. 4 *Rep.* 18. *Danv. Abr.* 83.

As to slander of persons, tho' scandalous words are spoken before a man's face, or behind his back, by way of affirmation or report, in jest or earnest, when sober or drunk, &c. they are actionable; and so it is if the words are spoke directly or indirectly, or obliquely; and tho' they are pronounced in any language, if understood: but where they can have a double interpretation, they shall be taken in the mildest sense, that no action shall lie. 4 *Rep.* 14. *Hob.* 236. *Cro. Jac* 438.

If one say that another said a third person did a certain scandalous thing, such third person may have his action of slander against the first man, with an averment that the second never said so, whereby the first is the author of the scandal. In case the slander proceeds from a man's wife, the husband and wife must be sued for it, and not she alone: and for any scandal against the wife, he and she are to bring the action; but for words against both a man and his wife, the husband may prosecute one action for his slander, and he and the wife may afterwards sue another action for hers. *Cro. Jac.* 406. *Styles* 113, 161.

When the words are utterly incertain, no *innuendo* or averment can make them good; and to these actions the defendant may plead the general issue, Not guilty; or if the plaintiff declares on some of the words only, when altogether they are not actionable, he may set them forth at large as he spoke them, and traverse or justify the whole, &c. Also if the defendant can make proof of the words, he may plead special justification; but if the plea be not made good,

Of Actions and Remedies.

good, damages will be aggravated. *Styles* 70. *T. Raym.* 61. *Co. Ent.* 26.

4. Defamation by libel, as by scandalous writing, &c. is likewise actionable; and printing or writing may be libellous, if the scandal is not charged in direct terms, but ironically, or tho' there be only the first and last letter of the name, if the jury will find it to point at a particular person: and the person who is the author or contriver, and the procurer, and publisher of a libel, knowing it to be such, are all punishable; as are booksellers, &c. who sell libels, altho' they know not the contents thereof. 5 *Rep.* 125. *Moor* 862. 5 *Mod.* 167.

And a libeller shall be punished, though the party of whom the words be spoken is dead; and notwithstanding the matter of the libel is true, for it is not material whether it be true or false, if the prosecution be by way of indictment or information; but in an action of the case, one may justify that it is true. *Hob.* 253. *Hardr.* 470.

But scandalous matter in legal proceedings, alledged in a court of justice, amounts not to any libel, &c.

The form of a *declaration* in an action of slander.

A. B. *complains of* C. D. *being in the custody of the marshal,* &c. *For that whereas the said* A. *is a good, true and faithful subject of our Lord the now King, and hath hitherto, from the time of his birth, behaved himself as a good, true and faithful subject of our said Lord the King, and his predecessors, Kings and Queens of this realm; and for the whole time aforesaid was reckoned, esteemed and reputed of good name, fame, behavi-*

our, condition and conversation, as well among his neighbours as all other faithful subjects of our said Lord the now King, to whom the said A. was known; and whereas the said A. now is, and for the space of fifteen years last past has been a linen-draper, and hath skilfully exercised and used the said trade and mystery during all that time, that is to say, at, &c. in the county aforesaid; and in all the said time hath sufficiently got and gained his living, and a support for him and his family by exercising the art or mystery aforesaid; and the said A. hath justly and honestly for the whole time aforesaid bought divers wares and merchandizes, and other things appertaining to the trade of him the said A. for the better support of himself and family, and to the great increase of his riches, of several persons creditors of the said A. residing and dwelling at, &c. aforesaid, as well upon credit, as for ready money in hand paid; and hath always, upon request, paid and satisfied all and singular sums of money, for the things or wares whatsoever by him upon credit bought and received of any persons for all the time aforesaid, or in any manner had, and all other his debts, without fraud or delay; and by that means obtained to himself great credit, reputation and esteem of divers faithful subjects of our said Lord the King, with whom the said A. did trade and deal in the art or mystery aforesaid, or in any other manner. Yet the said C. not ignorant of the premisses, but contriving and maliciously intending not only to hurt, impair and injure the good name, fame, credit, and reputation of the said A. but to draw him the said A. into great mistrust and discredit, among the subjects of our said Lord the now King, with whom the said A. had any commerce or dealings in his art and mystery aforesaid, and so that for the future no person should give any credit to the said A.

and

and likewise to lessen the knowledge of the said A. in his art aforesaid, on the — day of, &c. at, &c. aforesaid, discoursing with certain subjects of our said Lord the King, of the said A. and of his art or mystery aforesaid and his knowledge therein, in the presence and hearing of very many persons, then and there being present, did falsly, maliciously, and publickly speak, affirm, report, utter and publish of the said A. these false, scandalous and malicious words following, that is to say, He (meaning the said A.) doth not understand his business, *(meaning the art or mystery of him the said* A) and he *(meaning again the said* A.) is broke, and hath no linen to shew; *by the speaking, uttering and publishing of which said false and scandalous words, the said A. is not only injured in his good name, fame, credit and esteem aforesaid, and greatly scandalized in his art and mystery aforesaid, but also upon that account, his neighbours and divers other subjects of our said Lord the now King, with whom the said A. then before used to deal in his art or mystery, and who before that time had sold divers goods and merchandizes upon credit to the same A. have kept themselves from the acquaintance of him the said A. and daily more and more do withdraw themselves; and have intirely refused to have any commerce with the said A. in buying, selling and bargaining in his art or mystery aforesaid, and to give any credit to the said A. and still do refuse and desist: whereupon the said A. saith, that he is injured, and hath damage to the value,* &c. *And therefore he brings his suit.*

Of Actions and Remedies.

Form of a *declaration* for slandering a man's title.

Wilts, to wit. A B. *complains of* C. D. *being in the custody of*, &c. *For that whereas the said* A. *was, and yet is lawfully seised in his demesne as of fee of and in one messuage and ten acres of land, with the appurtenances, situate, lying and being in* M. *in the county aforesaid; and being so seised, the said* A. *afterwards, that is to say, the —— day, of,* &c. *in the —— year,* &c. *had a conference with one* E. F. *gentleman, concerning the bargaining, selling and assuring of the said messuage and land, with the appurtenances and the whole estate, right, title, and interest of the said* A. *in the same, for the sum of five hundred pounds, of lawful money of* Great Britain, *to the said* A. *by the said* E. *to be paid, to the said* E. *his heirs and assigns; to which bargain and sale of the messuage and lands aforesaid, for the consideration aforesaid, the said* E. *with the aforesaid* A. *had actually agreed, or intended to agree: nevertheless the aforesaid* C. *not being ignorant of the premisses, but maliciously intending the said* A. *in that particular to oppress and injure, and altogether to hinder the said* A. *from the sale and alienation of the said messuage and ten acres of land, with the appurtenances, and of his whole right, title and interest in the same, and also the right, estate and title of the said* A. *of, in and to the said messuage and land, with the appurtenances, greatly to scandalize, afterwards, that is to say, on the —— day of,* &c. *in the —— year,* &c. *abovesaid, at* M. *aforesaid, in the presence and hearing of one* G. H. *and of divers other faithful subjects of our Lord the now King, did scandalously, maliciously and openly say, affirm, repeat and publish*

of

of the said A. *these* English *words following, that is to say,* Mr. A. B. *(meaning the aforesaid* A.*)* hath no right or title to the messuage and land in, &c. *(meaning the aforesaid messuage and ten acres)* And if you *(the aforesaid* G. H. *meaning)* will give me *(meaning the said* C.*)* five shillings, I will give you ten pounds, if the lands *(meaning the said ten acres)* be not recovered against the said A. B. by reason of which scandalous words aforesaid, so spoken, affirmed and published, the aforesaid E. doubting and fearing the estate, right and title of the said A. of and in the said messuage and ten acres of land, with the appurtenances, not to be good and valid in law, his bargain aforesaid with the said A. for the said messuage and land, and the right, title, and interest of the said A. in the same, to hold and perform altogether refused; and also divers other subjects of our said lord the king, who before the sayings and publishing of the scandalous words aforesaid, with the said A. for the aforesaid messuage and ten acres of land, and for his right and interest in the same, would have bargained and contracted, by occasion of the saying of the said words, with him the said A. concerning the said messuage and land, in any way to meddle intirely did refuse; to the damage of the said A. &c. *And therefore he brings his suit,* &c.

Action of assault and battery is an action for a trespass against a man's person, where any injury is done to another in a violent manner; as by striking or beating of a man, pushing, jolting, filliping upon the nose, &c. and as in indictment for this offence for a breach of the peace, the party shall be fined; so on an action he shall render damages. *Dalt.* 282.

Of Actions and Remedies.

If a man in anger lift up or stretch forth his arm, and offer to strike or menace another; or hold up any weapon to strike at him, being within his reach; or shall thrust or push a person; cast a stone at him, tho' he be not struck therewith; throw wine in another's face, or upon his clothes, &c. These are trespasses and assaults in law, for which action lies: and if one threaten to beat or do me some bodily mischief, or lieth in wait to do it; if I dare not follow my business as at other times, and I have any loss thereby, I may have this action. *Bro. Tresp.* 236. *Finch* 29. 18 *Ed.* 4. 28.

To hold a person by the arm is an assault, if not battery; and to strike one, altho' he is not hurt with the blow; and striking at him, if he be neither hit nor hurt, have been held an assault: for it does not always imply a hitting or blow, because in trespass for assault and battery, a defendant may be found guilty of the assault, and excused of the battery. But if any one strike at another, at a great distance; or if it be near, or he threw stones at him, &c. merrily or accidentally, and not purposely, no action will lie. 22 *Ass.* 60. *Finch* 40.

It is said the least touching of another in anger is a battery; and tho' battery may not be committed by attempting to beat, but generally a stroke must be actually given; yet if one comes to the assistance of another who is beating a third person, tho' he do not touch him, he is guilty of battery; and he who commands or procures a battery to be done, may be charged as a principal in this action. And spitting in a man's face, &c. is battery; if not done by accident. *Hob.* 176. *Co. Lit.* 57. 6 *Mod.* 149, 172.

If

If two or more persons meet in a narrow passage, and without any violence or design of harm, the one touches the other gently, it will be no battery: though if any of them use violence to force his way in a rude manner, or any struggle is made about the passage to that degree as to do hurt; it will be a battery, for which action of assault and battery lieth. 6 *Mod.* 149.

To lay hands gently on another, not in anger, is no battery to found an action; the law will not presume any damage: and in this case the defendant may justify *molliter manus imposuit.* Also a man may justify an assault, in defence of his person or goods; or of his wife, father, mother, master, &c. and for the maintenance of justice: and when a person is beaten by another, he may return it, and plead that the other's battery was occasioned by his own assault. *Cro. Eliz.* 770. *Kel.* 64. 2 *Inst.* 316.

A man and his wife may have this action together, for any the least beating of the wife; in case it be such a battery, as thereby he loses her company or service, he alone may bring it: and actions for loss and injury done to the husband, in depriving him of the conversation and service of his wife, are generally laid for assaulting and detaining the wife, &c. whereupon large damages are given. 3 *Rep.* 113. 10 *Rep.* 130. *Cro. Jac.* 538.

For the assault and battery of a man's wife, child or servant, the husband, father and master shall have action of trespass: but a husband himself may by law moderately correct his wife; a master his servant or apprentice, a school-master his scholar, &c. and it will not be battery. 2 *Rol. Abr.* 546.

Where

Of Actions and Remedies.

Where any man is assaulted or beaten, and he hath no witnesses to prove the same, the party instead of this action may bring an information in the crown-office.

Form of a *declaration* in assault and battery.

South'ton, to wit.

A. B. *complains of* C. D. *being in custody of the marshal,* &c. *of that, that he the said* C. *on the* —— *day of,* &c. *in the* —— *year of the reign,* &c. *with force and arms, to wit, with swords, staves, fists and knives, in and upon the said* A. *at,* &c. *in the county aforesaid, made an assault, and him then and there did beat, wound and evilly treat, so that his life was greatly despaired of; and other injuries then and there did to him the said* A. *against the peace of our lord the now king; to the damage of the said* A. *&c. And therefore he brings his suit.*

Action of trespass lies generally for any wrong or damage, which is done with force and arms by one private man to another; sometimes against the person of a man, and sometimes against his goods and lands, &c. And I shall here divide this action into,

1. Trespass to a man's lands or goods.
2. Where divers actions are brought and trespasses continued.
3. Action of trespass by statute.

1. In all trespasses, there ought to be a voluntary act, and a damage: and action of trespass lieth where a man makes an entry on the lands of another, and does damage; and trespass

pass *vi & armis* may be brought by him that hath the possession of goods, or of a house, if he be disturbed in his possession. 2 *Rol. Abr.* 572.

Trespasses actionable are done with pretence of title, by which the property is altered, or without pretence of title; and they are local, that is, annexed to a place, as breaking the close of another, &c. or transitory, as the carrying away a person's goods, &c. A person that hath but a bare possession of a house or land, may maintain trespass against him who has no right; and he who has but the herbage, may have it for a wrong done him in the grass or ground. *Finch* 198, 303. *Plowd.* 144.

Entring into a house against the will of the owner, is trespass for which action lies; but a man may lawfully come into the house of another, to demand or pay money, &c. for breaking of a man's close and ground; or driving a cart of horses over the land of another person, where there is no lawful way for it; for chasing of cattle by which means they die or are damaged; the taking away piles, and breaking the doors, windows, &c. of a house, or fences of land; for eating corn of another with cattle; fishing in another man's pond, and breaking the pond; for digging in a person's coal-mines, and carrying away coals; plucking up garden herbs and roots; tearing of a bond or other writing, &c. in all these cases, all persons, that do any such wrongs, may be sued in action of trespass. *Co. Lit.* 57. *Cro. Jac.* 463. *Saund.* 202.

Executors may have this action for the testator's goods, taken out of their possession; also administrators for goods of intestates: and churchwardens may bring trespass for the parish
goods

goods, belonging to the church, &c. But in common actions of trespass for taking of goods, the plaintiff must alledge a property in himself; for there may be two intendments; one that they were the defendant's own goods, and then the taking is lawful; and the other, that they were the goods of the plaintiff, when the taking will be wrongful; tho' where-ever it is indifferent in construction, it shall be taken most strongly against the plaintiff in the action. *F. N. B.* 92. 117. *Bro. Tref.* 389. 2 *Lev.* 20.

In trespass against three persons, one of them commits battery, another imprisonment, and the third takes the goods, &c. all at one time; all are guilty of the whole, and action lies against them; so where many come to do a trespass, and they are all present when done, altho' some of them only look on; if they do not declare their dissassent thereto. *Co. Lit.* 57. 10 *Rep.* 60. 3 *Lev.* 324.

2. If several actions of trespass be brought for the same cause, and they are brought to vex the defendant, he may get them joined into one; but then the trespasses must not be of several natures, which may not be tried in one action: and a man may have action of trespass for divers trespasses; or for a trespass done in several places, if they are in the same county; for otherwise they cannot receive one trial, they being local causes of action triable in the county where done. 2 *Lil. Abr.* 596.

Action of trespass *vi & armis* lies not but in a court of record; and in this action, perfect notice must be taken of the day when the trespass was committed, whether there were not several trespasses at several times, and the place where done, with the damages sustained: trespasses

continued

continued may be laid with a *continuando* divers days, &c. but things muſt lie in continuance: and it is beſt to ſet forth that the defendant, between ſuch a day and ſuch a day, cut ſeveral trees, &c. (and not from ſuch a time to ſuch a time) when evidence may be given of cutting on any day within thoſe days. 2 *Salk.* 638. 2 Ld. *Raym.* 974.

3. As to treſpaſſes by ſtatute, perſons maliciouſly maiming, wounding, or hurting any cattle, deſtroying any plantation of trees, or throwing down incloſures, ſhall forfeit treble damages, in action of treſpaſs: tho' if the jury give not 40 s. damage in treſpaſs, the plaintiff ſhall have no more coſts than damages; unleſs the title come in queſtion, or ſomething of the plaintiff's be carried away, or the battery be well proved, &c. 23 *Car.* 2. *c.* 7. 9. If in treſpaſs defendants are acquitted, they ſhall have coſts; except the judge certify cauſe for the making them defendants, by 8 & 9 *W.* 3. *c.* 11.

If the defendant in treſpaſs diſclaims any title to the land, and the treſpaſs is involuntary or by negligence, he may plead a diſclaimer, and tender of amends before the action brought, &c. 21 *Jac.* 1. *c.* 16. And where a perſon juſtifies for a treſpaſs, he muſt confeſs it; and ſhall not be excuſed, but upon an inevitable neceſſity. 2 *Salk.* 644.

The form of a *declaration* in treſpaſs.

A B. *complains of* C. D. *being in cuſtody,* &c. *of that, that be the ſaid* C. *on the* ―― *day of,* &c. *in the* ―― *year,* &c. *with force and arms, the houſe of the ſaid* A. *in the pariſh of,* &c. *in the county of* S. *aforeſaid, broke and entered,*

tered, and the door of him the said A. to the value of forty shillings, then and there found, be broke, cut, tore down and spoiled, and also of that, that the said C. on the same day and year abovesaid, in the parish aforesaid, in the said county, the wainscot, glass windows, and walls of the house aforesaid of the said A. to the value of three pounds in like manner then and there found, be broke, tore, and spoiled; and other wrongs to the said A. then and there did, against the peace of our sovereign lord the king, and to the damage of the said A. &c. And therefore he brings his suit, &c.

Form of a *declaration* in action of trespass, for several trespasses.

Dorset, to wit.

A. B. complains of C. D. &c. of that, that he the said C. the ———— day of, &c. in the ———— year, &c. with force and arms, that is to say, with clubs, staves, &c. the close of the said A. called, &c. at M. in the county aforesaid, broke and entered, and the grass of him the said A. to the value of one hundred shillings, then and there growing, with his feet in walking, he trod down and consumed; and also other grass or corn of the said A. to the value of fifty shillings, in like manner there growing, with certain beasts, that is to say, with horses, oxen, cows and sheep, eat up, trod down and consumed: and also in the ground of the said A. called, &c. did dig, and his earth, to wit, fifty cart loads of earth, to the value, &c. there cast up, took and carried away; whereby he the said A. lost the whole profit of his ground aforesaid, for a long 'ime, that is to say, for the space of, &c. And the trespass above-mentioned, as to the treading down and consuming the grass aforesaid, with the

afore-

aforesaid beasts, from the aforesaid day, &c. in the year abovesaid, until the day, &c. then next following, at divers days and times continued; and other wrongs then and there did to the said A. against the peace, &c. and to the damage of the said A. &c. And therefore he brings his suit.

Form of a *plea* in action of trespass.

AND *the said C. by, &c. his attorney, comes and defends the force and injury, when, &c. and as to the coming with force and arms, or whatsoever else is against the peace of the said lord the king, he saith, that he is not guilty thereof; and of this he puts himself upon his country; and the said A. doth likewise: and as to the residue of the said trespass above supposed to be done, the said C. saith, that the said A. ought not to have or maintain his action aforesaid against him; because he says, that the close aforesaid, called, &c. in which the trespass in the declaration above is supposed to be done, is and at the same time of that supposed trespass was the soil and freehold of the said C. by which the said C. at the said time, the close aforesaid as the proper soil and freehold of him the said C. then entered; and the grass aforesaid, as the proper grass of the said C. in the same close, in which, &c. as in the proper close, soil and freehold of the said C. then growing with the cattle aforesaid eat up, trod down and consumed, &c. as to him it was lawful to do: and this he is ready to verify; wherefore he prays judgment, whether the said A. ought to have or maintain his action aforesaid against him.*

Action of ejectment is brought to recover possession of lands, &c. illegally kept from the right owner: and partakes of the nature both of a

G real

real and personal action; for the land and damages are recovered thereon.

And this action lieth, where one makes a lease to another for a term of years, and a third ousts the lessee, then such lessee shall bring ejectment against the person that ousted him, and recover his term and damages: also ejectment may be brought by a lessor against the lessee holding over his term; or on non-payment of rent, &c. But this is now become the common action for trial of titles to lands; yet when entry is taken away by descent, fine, disseisin, &c. ejectment must not lie, so that all titles cannot be tried by it. *Reg. Orig.* 227. *F. N. B.* 220.

Ejectment must be brought for a thing that is certain: as of the manor of *A.* and so many messuages, cottages, acres of arable land, meadow, &c. with the appurtenances, in the parish of, &c. for the nature of the land must be set forth, and be distinguished how much of one sort, and how much of another. If a person brings ejectment of an acre of land, in two parishes, and the whole is in one, she shall recover; so where ejectment is of an acre of land in *A.* and part of it lieth in *B.* he may recover for such part as lies in *A.* And if a man hath title to a fourth part only, and he bring this action for the whole, he shall recover his fourth part of the lands. *Cro. Eliz.* 339. *Plowd.* 429.

In this action no arrest is to be made, as commonly prosecuted; only a declaration in ejectment, &c. And if it appears that the plaintiff was ejected after the lease made, it is sufficient, tho' no certain day be alledged in which it was done; the day is not material, being before the action brought: but the time of entry of the

plaintiff

plaintiff must be shewn, that it may appear he was not a disseisor, by entring on the lands before the commencement of his term, &c. Also where lands in the lease or other deed differ from those in the declaration, and are not exactly the same; or the term is different, altho' one hath a verdict in ejectment, he cannot have judgment. *Cro. Jac.* 311. 2 *Lutw.* 963.

The action of ejectment is now made short and easy; for there is no occasion for a lease to be made and delivered upon the premisses to the lessee, and ouster and ejectment of him as formerly, unless there be no tenants in possession, &c. but instead of the old way of sealing a lease on the premisses, the course is to draw a declaration, feigning a lease for years to him that would try the title, and a casual ejector or defendant, who is generally some friend of the plaintiff's; the declaration is delivered to the ejector named, and he serves a copy of it on the tenant in possession, or his wife, and gives notice at the bottom for him to appear and defend his title, or that he the feigned defendant will suffer judgment by default; whereby the true tenant will be turned out of possession: to this declaration, the tenant appears by attorney, and consents to a rule to be made defendant, in the place of the casual ejector, and to confess lease, entry and ouster, and at the trial stand upon the title only; and then the new defendant is put into the declaration, and his attorney pleads not guilty; whereupon the cause proceeds to issue, &c. But if the tenant doth not appear in due time, and enter into such rule, on affidavit of service of the declaration, the court will order judgment to be entered against the casual ejector, and the tenant is thereby ousted of his possession. 1 *Lil. Abr.* 498, 499. 1 *Danv.* 665.

A plaintiff in this action recovers according to the right which he hath at the time of bringing the action; and one that hath title to the land in question, may on motion be made a defendant with the tenant in possession, to defend his title: and the landlord may be made defendant by the tenant, with consent of such landlord. For as the possession of the land is primarily in question, and to be recovered, that concerns the tenant; and the title of the land, which is tried collaterally, is concerning some other, who may be admitted a defendant with such tenant: tho' none other shall be admitted, but he that hath been in possession, or receives the rent of the lands. *Neif. Abr.* 694. *Lil. Abr.* 497.

Where there is a recovery by verdict in ejectment, action may be brought for the mesne profits of the land from the time of the defendant's entry, laid in the declaration: and if there be a judgment against the plaintiff, he may bring another action of trespass and ejectment for the lands, it being only to recover the possession, &c. wherein judgment is not final; and 'tis not like a writ of right, where the title alone is tried. *Trin.* 23 *Car. B. R.*

In ejectment for non-payment of rent, proceedings have been ordered to be stayed, on payment of the rent and costs; and a new lease to be made at the defendant's charge. *Lil. Abr.* 501. in cases between landlord and tenant, when half a year's rent is due from any tenant, the landlord may, without formal demand or re-entry, serve a declaration in ejectment against the

the tenant, or affix it on the door of the demised messuage, &c. and proving the rent due, and no sufficient distress, shall have judgment to recover the lands: but upon the tenant's paying his rent in arrears, with the costs, the proceedings in ejectment to cease; and the tenant may file a bill in equity to be relieved in six months, &c. and thereon shall hold the premisses according to the lease, without a new one. 4 *Geo.* 2. *c.* 28.

Tenants to whom declarations in ejectment are delivered by strangers, for any lands, &c. are to give their landlords notice thereof on pain of forfeiting three years rent, to be recovered by action of debt; and the court shall suffer the landlord to make himself defendant with the tenant, if he appears; but if not, judgment shall be signed against the casual ejector, for want of such appearance. Though in case the landlord desires to appear by himself, and consents to enter into the like rule, that the tenant, if he had appeared, ought to have done; the court may permit it, and stay execution 'till further order, &c. Stat. 11 *Geo.* 2. *c.* 19.

The form of a *declaration* in ejectment.

Wilts, to wit. A. B. *complains of* C. D. *being in custody of the marshal,* &c. *whereas* T. B. *gentleman, on the* —— *day of,* &c. *in the* —— *year of the reign,* &c. *at* D. *in the county of* Wilts *aforesaid, had demised, granted, and to farm let to the said* A. *two messuages, two gardens, and twenty acres of arable land,* &c. *with the appurtenances, situate and lying in the said parish of* D. *in the county abovesaid: to have and to hold the said tenements with the appurte-*

nances, to the said A. B. and his assigns, from the ―――― day of, &c. then last past, to the full end and term of five years from thence next ensuing, and fully to be complete and ended: by virtue of which said demise, he the said A. entered into the said tenements, with the appurtenances, and was thereof possessed, until the aforesaid C. D. afterwards, that is to say, on the same day of, &c. in the year, &c. aforesaid entered with force and arms into the said tenements, with the appurtenances, in and upon the possession of the said A. and ejected, expelled, and removed the said A. from his said farm, during his term aforesaid therein not yet expired; and the said A being so ejected, expelled and removed, the said C. hitherto hath withheld from him, and still doth with hold, the possession thereof; and then and there other injuries did to him against the peace of our said sovereign lord the king, and to the damage of the said A. thirty pounds; and thereupon he brings his suit, &c.

Form of a *notice* for the tenant to appear, &c.

Mr. E, E.

I AM informed, that you are in possession, or claim title to the premisses mentioned in this declaration of ejectment, or some part thereof; and I being sued in this action as a casual ejector, and having no title to the same, do advise you to appear next Trinity *term in his majesty's court of* King's Bench *at* Westminster, *by some attorney of that court, and then and there by a rule of the same court, to cause yourself to be made defendant in my stead; otherwise I shall suffer judgment to be entered against me, and you will be turned out of possession.*

Your loving friend,

C. D.

Of Actions and Remedies.

Action or writ of assise lieth where a man is put out of his lands or tenements, and thereby disseised of his freehold therein: and tenants in fee-simple, fee-tail, or for term of life, may have *assise of novel disseisin* of these things following:

1. Assise of lands and tenements.
2. Assise of rents, commons and tolls.
3. Of an office held for life, *&c.*

1. An assise may sometimes be brought for entries, and disturbance in the possession of lands, where trespass *vi & armis* may not be had: and assise will lie in some particular cases that ejectment doth not, because the things may be put in view to the jury. *F. N. B.* 7. 8 *Rep.* 47.

As the grand assise serves for the right of property; so the petit assise serveth for the possession: but assise must be of an actual freehold, not a freehold in law; and if lessee for years, or tenant at will be ousted, the lessor or he in remainder may have assise, for the freehold was in him at the time of the disseisin: also if a person, who hath title to enter, set his foot upon the land, and is ousted, that is a sufficient seisin to bring an assise. *Horn's Mirr. Kel.* 109.

In assise, when the party purchaseth the writ, he ought to find sureties in the Chancery; and the court of Common Pleas, or King's Bench, may hold plea of assises of land in the county of *Middlesex*, by writ out of Chancery; in other counties, such pleas must be tried at the court of assises: and in actions of assise the land, damages and costs are recovered. *Lil. Abr.* 105.

The complaint need not be so certain in assise as in other writs; but the plaintiff must prove his title, then his seisin and disseisin: and the demandant in assise may abridge his plaint after the jury are charged, before verdict given. In this action the judgment is to recover the land, &c. by view of the recognitors; and if they may put the demandant in possession, it is well enough; and the party recovering shall have writ of seisin, &c. *Dy.* 84. *Danv. Abr.* 580, 583.

2. If a man have a rent issuing out of land for life, in tail, or in fee, if he be disseised of the rent, he shall have an assise: and if certain rent be granted out of the house, &c. and *sixpence* is given in the name of seisin, it is good; so that the rent being demanded at the house whence it issues, on non-payment it is a disseisin, for which assise lieth. *New Nat. Brev.* 440. *Cro. Car.* 500.

A man is seised of a parcel of a rent payable at a day, and afterwards the tenant will not pay the residue thereof due at the same day; he who hath right to the rent, may bring an assise of novel disseisin for the whole rent, as well of that which he is seised, as of the residue: and that seisin of part of the rent shall be a seisin of the whole. But if a person distrains for his rent pending an assise, he shall abate it; and assise lies not for an annuity, &c. *Bro. Assis.* 302. *Fitzb.* 289.

Assise may be had of several rents, or of land and rent, and offices and profits, all in one writ. An assise lies for common of pasture for a man's cattle, &c. which is so necessary, as without it his freehold cannot be manured: and if a man have any profit whatsoever granted to him out of lands for life, or in fee, he shall have assise,

if

if he be disseised of it; so of toll, tronage, pontage, or pannage. *Br. Assis.* 127, 145. 2 *Inst.* 411.

3. An assise lay at common law for an office; and therefore, tho' the statute of *Westm.* 2. mentions only offices in fee, yet assise lies for an office for life: and assise may be brought by officers where their proceedings are according to the civil law, for the right of such offices is determinable at common law. But if the office be only of charge, not of profit, assise doth not lie thereof. 8 *Co. Rep.* 47. *Danv. Abr.* 579.

The taking 3 *d.* of *A.* for a *capias* against *B.* is a sufficient seisin of the office of filazer of the Common Pleas; and seisin of an office may be alledged by taking money for the business done, and the place where the officer sat be put in view: if the office extends into divers towns, or counties, assise lies for the profits in any town or place, &c. And if one be ousted of parcel of the profits of his office, this, may be alledged to be an ouster of the whole: tho' by *Coke's Reports*, he shall have assise only of the part of the profits whereof he is disseised; and not of the whole office, unless he be disseised of the whole. *Dy.* 114, 63. 8 *Rep.* 49.

In assise for an ancient office, the demandant in his plaint need not shew what fee or profit is belonging to it; but in a newly erected office he must: and if the assise concerns the king and his prerogative, the judges may be prohibited to proceed therein, by writ *de non ulterius prosequendo rege inconsulto.* 8 Rep. 49. Nell. Abr. 277.

There is an *assise of mortdancestor, that lies* where a man's father, mother, brother, sister, uncle, aunt, &c. died seised of lands in feesimple,

Of Actions and Remedies.

simple, and after their deaths a stranger abateth or enters into the same: which is good as well against the abator, as any other in possession; but it lieth not against brothers or sisters, *&c.* only against strangers. *Reg. Orig.* 223. *Co. Lit.* 242.

And *assise of darrein presentment*, where a man and his ancestors have presented a clerk to a church, and after the church becoming void, a stranger presents his clerk to the same church, whereby the person having right is disturbed, *&c. Reg. Orig.* 30.

The form of a *declaration* in assise, for a rent.

Soth'ton. **T**HE *assise come to recognize, whether C. D. unjustly and without judgment did disseise A. B. of his freehold in R. within thirty years last past,* &c. *And whereupon the said A. by T. P. his attorney, complains, that he the said C. did disseise him of fifteen pounds rent, with the appurtenances issuing out of the messuage or tenement with the appurtenances in R. aforesaid,* &c. *And for such title to the tenement and assise of the rent aforesaid, the same A. saith, that F. B. father of him the said A. long before the obtaining of the original writ of assise aforesaid was seised of the messuage aforesaid with the appurtenances, in his demesne as of fee; and being so thereof seised the day and year,* &c. *at R. aforesaid, by his certain indendure, made between him the said F. B. of the one part, and the aforesaid C. D. of the other part, which other part thereof, with the seal of the said F. affixed thereto, and by him signed, the said A. here in court shews forth, the date whereof is*

the

Of Actions and Remedies.

the same day and year above, he did grant, release and convey to the said C. his heirs and assigns, the above-mentioned messuage or tenement with the appurtenances, subject to the payment of the rent of fifteen pounds aforesaid, to the said A. during his life, &c. And the said A. further saith, that after the making and executing of the release or conveyance aforesaid, and before the day of the purchasing of the original writ of assise aforesaid, that is to say, the day of, &c. in the year, &c. he came to the messuage aforesaid, and then and there claimed of the said C. tenant of the freehold of the said messuage with the appurtenances, the aforesaid rent of fifteen pounds, which said rent the said C. to the said A. afterwards, and before the obtaining of the original writ of assise aforesaid, at R. aforesaid did once pay, whereby the said A. was seised of that rent with the appurtenances, during his life, &c. And because forty-five pounds of the rent aforesaid, for three years ending at the feast of, &c. in the year of the reign, &c. to the said A. after the conveyance aforesaid in form aforesaid made, were in arrear and not paid, the said A. afterwards, and before the day of the original writ aforesaid, that is to say, the day, &c. in the year, &c. came to the messuage aforesaid with the appurtenances, between the hours of ten and eleven before noon of the same day, and then and there did demand the aforesaid forty-five pounds of the rent aforesaid, in form aforesaid being in arrear, to be paid unto him; but for that no man would then and there pay the said forty-five pounds to the said A. he the said A. would have entered into the messuage aforesaid to distrain for the same, but the door of the said messuage was then shut with a lock against him the said A. so that the same A. could not enter into the said messuage to distrain for the rent aforesaid, by reason *of the shutting of the door aforesaid; and so the said C. the said A. thereof unjustly and without judgment did disseise; and this he is ready to verify; whereupon he prays assise, &c.*

Action of waste is that which is brought on any destruction being made in houses, lands, *&c.* by tenant for life, or years, to the damage of him in reversion or remainder: It lieth,

1. For any waste done or suffered to houses.
2. For cutting down timber trees, or other trees on an estate.
3. For ploughing up meadow ground, diging mines, destroying deer, *&c.*
4. And who shall bring his action, for the land, *&c.* and damages.

1. To pull down a house by any tenant, except the same be ruinous, and in order to rebuild it of the same dimensions only, is waste in such tenant; so if he suffer his house to be uncovered, or in decay, though there be no wood upon the premisses: and it is the same to permit a house to be burnt by negligence, if the tenant do not repair the same; and in these cases action of waste lies. But if the house be consumed or destroyed by thunder, lightning, tempest, floods, enemies, *&c.* it is no waste in the lessee. *Co. Lit.* 52, 53. *Kelw.* 87.

The converting of a brewhouse into tenements, altho' of a greater value; or if a cornmill be converted into a fulling-mill, *&c.* it is waste; for things must be used in their natural and proper manner, and not be altered. Taking away or breaking down wainscot, doors, windows, benches or coppers fixed to a house, will

be

be waste actionable: though if any of these are set up by the lessee, he may take them down before the end of his term, so as he do not thereby weaken the freehold. *Lev.* 309. *Cro. Jac.* 182. *Salk.* 368.

If a lessee covenants to leave a house at the end of the term in as good condition as he found it; and during the term he doth waste therein, action doth not here lie presently, because the house may be repaired before the time expires; but 'tis otherwise in such covenant for leaving wood or timber, if it is cut down by the lessee; for then it is not possible for him to perform his agreement, to leave the same as he found it. 4 *Rep.* 62. 5 *Rep.* 11, 21.

2. Timber on an estate is parcel of the inheritance, and reserved by law to the lessor, or landlord; and therefore if it be cut down by the lessee, or tenant, the lessor may take it away. and the lessee having an interest only in trees while standing, as in the fruit, shrowd, shadow, *&c.* if he fells timber-trees, or doth any other act whereby they may decay, 'tis waste in the lessee. 4 *Rep.* 61, 62.

The felling or cutting down of timber-trees, such as oak, ash, elm, or lopping them to sell, or any intent, but for repairs: and if they are so felled for building a new house, or young trees be cut for reparations, when there is other timber, these are waste, for which this action lieth: and so it is, to cut down beech-trees, where used as timber in building; or willows, maple-trees, *&c.* standing in defence of a house, or planted for fencing a manor. *Co. Lit.* 53, 88.

Cutting down fruit-trees, if they grow in an orchard, or garden, tho' used for repairs of the house, *&c.* is waste; but 'tis not so if they
grow

Of Actions and Remedies.

grow in a field: the suffering young germins to be destroyed by cattle; or stubbing up a quickset hedge, &c. are waste; as are also cutting down green wood, if there is dry, or more firebote than is necessary. *Co. Lit.* 53. 3 *Nels. Abr.* 540.

But tenants may cut underwood, and take wood sufficient to repair the pales, hedges, and fences, and what is called by law plough-bote, fire-bate, and other house-bote.

3. If ancient meadow-ground is ploughed up, it is waste; but where meadow hath been at any time arable, or sometimes meadow and sometimes pasture, it will be no waste to plough it up. The ploughing of lands, that have not been ploughed up time out of mind, or to plough up wood-lands; and it is said, if a tenant converts arable land into wood, meadow into arable land, arable into meadow, or pasture into arable; they will be waste. 2 *Rol. Abr.* 814. *Co. Lit.* 53.

A lessee for years converts a meadow into hop-ground; it is no waste, because it may be easily made meadow again: but the converting it into an orchard is waste, tho' it may be more profitable. It is waste to suffer a wall of the sea to be in decay, by reason whereof the meadow-ground is surrounded with salt-water, and rendered unprofitable; also the not scouring of a mote or ditch, whereby the groundsils of the house, &c. are rotten, is waste actionable. 2 *Leon.* 174. *Owen* 43.

The digging mines of metal, coals, &c. hidden in the earth, and that were not open when the tenant came in; or for lime, brick, stone, &c. without power by covenant, will be waste: tho' the tenant may dig in an open mine, and

for

for gravel, clay, earth, &c. for reparations of the house. Destroying deer in a park, doves in a dove-house, or fish in a pond, &c. or if such stores be not left by the lessee, as he found when he entered on the land, it is waste; and so is any thing which abridges the lessor's annual profits of the lands. *Co. Litt.* 53, 54. 5 *Rep.* 12. 3 *Leon.* 76.

If a lease be made without impeachment of waste, it takes off all restraint from the tenant of doing it; and in such case he may pull up, or cut down wood or timber, or dig mines, &c. at his pleasure, and not be liable to any action of waste. *Plowd.* 135.

4. This action must be brought by one who hath an estate in fee-simple, or fee-tail; and it ought to be he that hath the immediate estate and inheritance in fee-simple, &c. For if there be any estate for life between the first estate and that of the remainder-man in fee, the waste will not be *ad exhæreditationem* of him in remainder. 5 *Rep.* 76.

Action of waste is maintainable against tenant by the curtesy, in dower, for life, &c. and if tenant in dower, or by the curtesy, assign their estates, the heir or he in remainder may have this action against them for waste done after the assignment: but it lieth not against tenants in fee-simple, or in fee-tail, or tail after possibility of issue extinct; nor against tenants by statute-merchant, staple, or elegit, tenant in mortgage, or at will; or against any executor or administrator, for waste committed by the testator, &c. *Co. Lit.* 54, 310. 6 *Rep.* 37. 9 *Rep.* 138.

If a man makes a feoffment to the use of himself for life, and after his death, to the use
of

Of Actions and Remedies.

of another person and his heirs; in this case, if the feoffor commit waste, it has been adjudged that the feoffee shall have a special writ against him. And before any waste is done, a *prohibition* may be had, directed to the sheriff, not to permit it; or he in remainder, &c. may have an *injunction* out of the chancery, to stay the waste, and enter a house or lands to see if waste is committed. *Hell.* 79. *F. N. B.* 55. *Co. Lit.* 53. 2 *Inst.* 306.

On any waste being done in any houses, or in woods, so much will be recovered wherein the waste is done; but if the waste be here and there through the whole, then all shall be recovered in this action; and the judgment in action of waste is, that the plaintiff shall recover the place or places wasted, and treble damages. 2 *Inst.* 303.

The form of a declaration *in action of waste.*

Dorset, to *wit.*
'A B. complains of C. D. of a plea wherefore, whereas by
' the common council of the realm of the
' King of *England* it is provided, that it shall not
' be lawful for any one to commit waste, spoil
' or destruction in any lands, woods, or gar-
' dens to them demised for term of life, or years;
' the said C. in a house, lands and woods at S.
' which he holdeth for term of years, of the de-
' mise of the aforesaid *A.* &c. did waste, spoil
' and destruction, to the disinheriting of him the
' said *A.* and against the form of the provision
' aforesaid, &c. And whereupon the said *A.* saith,
' that whereas the same *A.* was seised of a mes-
' suage called, &c. and twenty acres of land,
' ten acres of pasture, and five acres of wood,
' with

'with the appurtenances, in S. aforesaid, in his
'demesne as of fee, and being so thereof seised,
'the—day of, &c. in the—year of the reign, &c.
'by indenture made between him the said *A*. by
'the name of *A. B.* of, &c. in the county of *D.*
'aforesaid, of the one part, and the aforesaid *C.*
'by the name of, *C. D.* of, &c. in the said coun-
'ty, of the other part, one part of which said
'indenture, sealed with the seal of the said *C.*
'the said *A.* brings here into court, whose date
'is the same day and year above, he the said *A.*
'demised, granted and to farm let unto the
'said *C.* all that the messuage or tenement,
'aforesaid, with the appurtenances, &c. To
'have and to hold the said messuage or tene-
'ment, and all and singular other the premisses
'aforesaid, by the said indenture so demised,
'with their appurtenances, to the said *C.* his ex-
'ecutors, administrators, and assigns, from the
'feast of, &c. unto the full end and term of one
'and twenty years, from thence next ensuing,
'and fully to be complete and ended: by vir-
'tue of which said demise, the said *C.* into the
'messuage and premisses aforesaid, with the ap-
'purtenances, in form aforesaid demised, enter-
'ed and was thereof possessed; and the said *A.*
'being seised of the reversion of the said pre-
'misses as of fee, and the said *C.* so thereof pos-
'sessed, the same *C.* made waste, spoil and de-
'struction in the messuage or tenement afore-
'said, with the appurtenances, *to wit*, in throw-
'ing down and flatting to the ground of one
'barn and stable, parcel of and adjoining to the
'said messuage, and taking away the timber and
'other materials of the same, of the value of,
'&c. and in cutting down and selling of ten
'timber-trees, in, &c. wood, parcel of the te-

H   'nement

'nement aforesaid, with the appurtenances, the
'price of every tree twelve shillings, through
'the said whole wood here and there growing;
'and in digging in six acres of land in *S.* afore-
'said, parcel of the tenement aforesaid, to the
'said *C.* demised, twenty loads of clay, taking
'for the price of every load thereof, &c. to the
'disinheriting of the said *A.* and against the
'form of the provision aforesaid; whereupon
'he saith he is injured, and hath damage to the
'value of seventy-five pounds; and thereof he
'brings his suit, &c.

Form of a *plea*, &c. in action of waste.

AND *the said C. by,* &c. *his attorney, comes and defends the force and injury, when* &c. *and saith that he made no waste, spoil or destruction in the tenement aforesaid, with the appurtenances, as the said A. by his writ and declaration aforesaid above hath supposed; and of this he puts himself upon his country, and the said A. doth likewise: Therefore,* &c.

Here follow some particular cases, and instructions relating to,

1. *Distresses* for rent, and proceedings therein.
2. *Replevins* on taking distresses.

1. Distress is a thing which is taken and distrained upon land, for rent behind, or other duty: and a man may distrain for rents reserved upon a gift in tail, lease for life, or years, &c. altho' there be no clause of distress in the deed or lease, so as the reversion be in himself;
but

but it is otherwise on a feoffment in fee. *Co. Lit.* 57, 205.

A distress taken for rent must be of goods or things valuable, whereof some body hath property, not the distrainer; and ought to be made of such things whereof the sheriff may make replevin: a horse with a rider on it, or any thing one carries about him; utensils of trade, cattle of the plough, beasts of husbandry, horses joined to a cart, or sheep, may not be distrained; nor may a horse in an inn, goods in a market, another man's garment in the house of a taylor, &c. neither shall any thing fixed to the freehold, as a furnace, &c. *Rol. Abr.* 664, 665. *Co. Lit.* 47. *Ventr.* 36. *Sid.* 440.

But corn thrashed, and in the straw; carts with corn, not victuals; and hay in a barn, &c. may be destrained: so may money in a bag sealed; tho' not money out of a bag, &c. And a distress may be taken of cattle driving to market, if put into pasture by the way; also beasts of a stranger, in the landlord's ground, being levant and couchant, and having well rested themselves there; and another's goods in the tenant's house &c. And distresses are to be taken on the premisses; in the taking whereof, one may not break open *gates, or enter houses, if the doors are open. *Co. Lit.* 47. 161. *Lut.* 214. 4 *Mod.* 385.

If a landlord comes into a house, and seises on some goods in the name of all of them, it is a good seisure and distress of all; 6 *Mod.* 215.

---

* Upon a question about taking a distress it was held, that a padlock put on a barn-door could not be opened by force to take the corn by way of distress; by lord Ch. Just. *Hardwicke.* 8 *Vis. Abr.* 128. *pl.* 6, at top.

9 *Vin. Abr.* 127. Ld. *Raym.* 54. 2 *Bac. Abr.* 114, 115. 2 Ld. *Raym.* 1424. *Barnard. K. B.* 34. 2 *Stra.* 717, 851, 1272. 10 *Mod.* 265, 266. but the goods are generally to be removed immediately, unless it be corn or hay, by statute: and when a distress is taken of the household goods, or other dead things, they are to be locked up and impounded in a house; and if the distress is damaged, the distrainer must answer it. A distress of cattle must be brought to the common pound, or kept in an open place; when notice is to be given the owner to feed them; and cattle distrained may not be used, except by milking, &c. for the owner's benefit. *Cro. Jac.* 141. 5 *Rep.* 90. *Co. Lit.* 96.

In case a tenant or any other, to prevent the landlord's distress, drives the cattle off the ground, the landlord may make fresh pursuit, and distrain them: and debt will lie for rent, where a distress may not be taken for one rent there cannot be two distresses, if there were sufficient goods, when the first was made; but if there be not then enough for a distress, it may be taken afterwards; or distress may be for part of the rent, and, action of debt for the rest thereof. But if the owner of goods tenders his rent, and a distress is afterwards taken, it is wrongful: and if any person shall distrain another on purpose to injure him, he shall pay treble damages. If where no rent is due, distress and sale be made, the owner of the goods distrained may recover double value and costs. *Co. Lit.* 160. 2 *Lev.* 8 *Rep.* 147. 2 *Inst.* 107. 13 *Ed.* 1. *Stat.* 2 *W. & M. seff.* 1. c. 5.

All distresses are to be reasonable, by our ancient statutes; and none shall take an unreasonable distress, on pain to be amerced: they shall not

not be taken in the highway, nor in the ancient fees of the church; and no distress of cattle shall be driven out of the county, or out of the hundred where it is taken, except to a pound overt within the same shire, not above three miles distant from the place where taken; neither shall a distress be impounded in several places, whereby the owner may be constrained to sue several replevins for the delivery thereof, under the penalty of 5 *l.* and treble damages: and not above 4 *d.* to be taken for the poundage of one distress, (or less where usually given, on the same penalty, &c.) *Stat.* 51 *H.* 3. 52 *H.* 3. *c.* 4. 3 *Ed.* 1. *c.* 16. 9 *E.* 2. *c.* 9. 1 & 2 *P.* & *M. c.* 12.

And by statute, where any goods or chattels shall be taken as a distress, (in the day-time, it must not be in the night) for rent reserved and due upon any lease or contract, and the tenant or owner of the goods shall not within five days after such distress taken, and notice thereof, with the cause of taking, left at the mansion-house, or other most notorious place on the premisses charged with the rent distrained for, replevy the same, with sufficient security to be given to the sheriff according to law; then the landlord or person distraining, with the sheriff or under-sheriff of the county, or with the constable of the hundred, parish, or place where the distress shall be taken (who are required to be aiding and assisting therein) may cause the goods and chattles to be appraised by two sworn appraisers, whom such sheriff or constable are impowered to swear to appraise the same truly; and after such appraisement made, may lawfully sell the goods for the best price that can be gotten, towards the satisfaction of the rent, and the charges of the distress, appraisement and sale;

leaving the overplus, if any be, in the hands of the sheriff or constable, for the owner's use. *Stat.* 2 *W. & M. Sess.* 1. *c.* 5.

It shall be lawful to distrain, for rent arrear, any sheaves or cocks of corn, or loose corn or hay in any barn or granary, or upon any hovel, stack, or rick, or otherwise; and to lock up and detain the same in the place where found, 'till it be replevied as aforesaid; and in default thereof, within the time aforesaid, to sell the same after the appraisement made, *&c.* so that nevertheless it be not removed by the persons distraining, to the damage of the owner, but kept where it shall be found and seised, as impounded, 'till the same is replevied or sold. *Stat. ibid.*

And if any pound-breach or rescous shall be made of goods or chattels distrained for rent, the person grieved shall have a special action upon the case for the wrong thereby sustained, and recover treble damages and costs of suit against the offenders, or against the owner of the goods distrained, if they afterwards come to his use or possession.

Where rent is reserved on lease, if the tenant shall fraudulently or clandestinely convey away or carry off his goods, the landlord or any person impowered by him, may, in five days after, take and seize such goods and chattels wheresoever they shall be found, as a distress for the rent in arrear, and sell the same, as if they had been actually distrained on the premisses; except goods sold for a valuable consideration, before the seizure made: and where leases are expired, distress may be taken for arrears of rent, after the determination of the said leases, as if they had not been ended; provided such distress be made within six kalendar months after the end of

the

the lease, and during the continuance of the landlord's interest or title, and the possession of the tenant from whom the rent is due. And these distresses shall be liable to such sales, and in such manner, and the money be distributed, as by the act 2 *W. & M.* is directed. *Stat.* 8 *Ann. c.* 14.

If there is an execution against goods or chattels of a tenant for life, or years, &c. the plaintiff, before removal of the goods by the execution, shall pay the rent of the land, &c. so as there be not above a year due; otherwise they shall not be taken or extended; and if more rent is in arrear, paying a year's rent, the plaintiff may proceed in his execution, and the sheriff or other officer is to levy as well the money so paid for rent, as the execution money. *Ibid.*

For cases on this clause of the statute. See Fortesc. Rep. 359, 360. Stra. 214. 11 Vin. Abr. 133, 134, in Marg. Stra. 97.

An ejectment may be brought for rent due, where there is no sufficient distress, &c. And all persons shall have the like remedy by distress and sale, for rents seck, rents of assise and chief rents, as in case of rent reserved upon lease. *Stat.* 4 *Geo.* 2. *c.* 28.

Gilb. Eq. Rep. 223. 2. 4. Stra. 112. 11 Vin. Abr. 110. pl. 30. Stra. 543. 2 Stra. 787. 1024.

Andr. 218, 219. Bunb. 41, 43. Barn's Just. 410, 313.

And it is ordained, that tenants of lands, &c. fraudulently carrying away their goods, to prevent distress for rent; the landlords in thirty days after may distrain them wherever they are, as if upon the premisses; and such tenants, and other persons assisting in the fraud, shall forfeit double the value of the goods, recoverable by action of debt, &c. And where the goods are under 50 *l.* value, two justices of peace may examine into it, and order such offenders to pay the forfeiture, leviable on their goods and chattles, or for default, to be committed to the house

house of correction for six months. 11 *Geo.* 2. *c.* 19.

Order made by two justices, reciting that a complaint had been made to them in writing, by *A. Clavey* against *J. Bissex*, that he the said *Clavey* demised his estate in the parish of *Skelly*, in the county of *Somerset*, to *William Thatcher*, at the yearly rent of 44*l.* and that there was due and in arrear from *Thatcher* to him for rent of the said estate, on the 5th day of *April* last, 24*l.* 15*s.* 8*d.* ¾; and that he the said *Clavey* would have distrained the goods and chattels of the said *W. Thatcher* upon the said estate, in order to obtain satisfaction of the said rent; but to prevent him from so doing, the said *Bissex*, on or about the 27th, 28th, and 29th days of *August* last, did knowingly and wilfully aid and assist the said *Thatcher* in fraudulently conveying and carrying off from the said estate his the said *Thatcher*'s goods and chattels, and also in concealing the same, being under the value of 50*l.* that is to say, two cows, one heifer, ten hundred weight of cheese, of the value of 20*l.* whereby the said *Clavey* was prevented from distraining the same, in order to obtain satisfaction for the said rent, and contrary to the statute 11 *Geo.* 2. and therefore praying us to grant him our warrant of summons, requiring you the said *J. Bissex* to appear before us, and that we would examine the facts, and thereupon make such order therein for his relief, as the said statute directs and requires, and as should be agreeable to justice: whereupon we the said justices, residing near the said estate from whence the said goods and cattle were removed, and neither of us any way interested in the said estate, did issue our warrant of summons,

mons, requiring you the said *J. Bissex* to attend us thereon to answer the said complaint; and you having attended accordingly, and we in your presence having examined the witnesses produced by the said *A. Clavely* upon oath, and heard what was alledged by you in your defence, do adjudge that the said complaint is true; and that the said goods and cattle of the said *W. Thatcher*, in which you so aided and assisted in conveying and carrying off from the said estate, and also in concealing the same, were of the value of 20*l.* and that you have thereby forfeited double of the value of the said goods and cattle, being the sum of 40*l.* to the said complainant *A. Clavely*, by virtue of the statute: we therefore, in pursuance of the said statute, do adjudge, order, and require you the said *J. Bissex* within the space of three days from the date hereof, to pay to the said *A. Clavely* the sum of 40*l.* which if you shall neglect to do, such further proceedings will be then had against you to inforce the payment thereof, as the said statute directs and requires. Given under our hands and seals this 5th day of *January* 1756. This order was affirmed by the sessions upon appeal. Both the orders were removed by *certiorari* into the King's Bench. It was moved to quash the same. Objections taken: 1. The complaint is said to be taken in writing, but not upon oath. 2. It is only said, that he demised to *W. Thatcher*; but not said for what estate or term. 3. It is stated, so much due for rent, but not said for what term: it might be due twenty years ago. It is not stated to be due when *Thatcher* moved the goods. 4. The words of the order are, goods and *cattle*; of the statute, goods and *chattels*. 5. No certain time is alledged

ledged when the defendant aided and assisted; only said on or about the 26th, 27th, or 28th of *August*. 6. Not stated that *Thatcher* did carry off his goods: only that *Biſſex* did aid and assist him in carrying them off. 7. They adjudge the complaint true, but do not state the evidence, and this is a conviction, not an order: and for any thing that appears, it might be upon *Clavey*'s evidence alone. 8. It is not stated that the goods were under the value of 50 *l.* which is the ground of the justices jurisdiction. 9. The words of the statute are, 'if any person shall be a tenant of any lands, tenements, or hereditaments: the word used in the order is estate, which may be a thing incorporeal, or may mean the interest in the land, and so not within the statute. 10. It shall appear, whether the landlord had a right to distrain: by 8 *An. c.* 14. the landlord may distrain at any time within six months after the expiration of the term: it doth not appear these six months were not expired, and if they were, this is no offence. After consideration, Mr. Justice *Dennison* delivered the resolution of the court: I think the most material objection is, whether this is an order or a conviction. If a conviction, the evidence ought to have been set out. And there has been no doubt (notwithstanding the case of *K.* and *Pulleine, Salk.* 369.) that in a conviction the evidence must be set out, that the court may judge upon it. So it was held by Lord *Hardwicke* in the case of *K.* and *Lloyd.* 2 *Stra.* 996. 2 *Bernard. K. B.* 302, 310, 338, 466. *Seſſ. Caſ.* 233. *pl.* 190. and in that case it was objected, that as it subjected the party to a penalty, though in the statute it was called an order, yet it should be construed as a conviction: but the court said, every act of the justices,

tices, which subjects the party to a penalty, shall not be construed as a conviction. *K.* and *Venables. Stra.* 630. 2 Ld. *Raym.* 1406. *Fortesc. Rep.* 325. *Sess. Caf.* 267. *pl.* 210. *Caf. of Set. and Rem.* 163. upon the stat. for licensing alehouses, considered as an order. *K.* and *Blackwell. M.* 4 *Geo.* which the court said was a strong case, and must be considered as an order. I understood from my Lord *Hardwicke,* in the case of *K.* and *Lloyd,* that his ground of the difference was founded upon the expressions of the statute, and not upon the penalty; as where the words of the statute are, " of which he shall be convicted," it is to be construed as a conviction. Here it is extremely strong; the statute calls it an order: and in the nature of it, it is an examination upon a complaint. If the party was never summoned, this court upon affidavit will grant an information against the justices: but the summons need not be set out: and the court will intend the justices have done right, in case the contrary does not appear upon the face of the order. As to the first objection: this is is not an information, but a complaint: when the party is summoned, the witnesses are to be examined upon oath, but the complaint need not be upon oath. In answer to the second objection: as the order has followed the words of the statute, we will not intend it a case wherein the justices had not a jurisdiction. The court will not, in case of an order, intend that the justices have done wrong. As to the third objection: it is sufficiently alledged in an order; his assisting the tenant to carry away the goods, as it is here alledged, is sufficient, the rent continued then to be in arrear; and the rather as the defendant might have availed himself of the rent paid, by
prov-

proving it before the justices. I much doubt, whether in a declaration it would not be sufficient to say, the rent was in arrear at such a day; and I think it would lie upon the defendant to prove that the rent does not remain in arrear. As to its not being said, for what time the rent was due; this is mere matter of form. As to the fifth objection: *about*, in common parlance, means in this case three days or near it. They might be three days in carrying the goods away. The days are not material, even in legal proceedings. 1.d. *Raym.* 581. and in the case of *K.* and *Simpson*, H 3 *Geo. Stra.* 46. the day and hour in a conviction are not material. By this statute no time is limited, when the complaint shall be made: it may be made at any time. Suppose the defendant had paid the penalty on a different complaint made, he might easily have shewn it. As to the sixth, the answer is obvious; if *Thatcher* had not carried his goods away, the defendant could not have aided in carrying them. The statute makes two offences, one carrying the goods away; the other, aiding in carrying them away. It is only necessary here to state the offence which the defendant had been guilty of, which this order does in the words of the statute. In the case of *K.* and *Monk*, M. 13 *Geo.* 2. there was a conviction for aiding and assisting in killing a buck. It was objected, that it was not charged the buck was killed. But the court held, that as the conviction was in the words of the statute, it was sufficient; and the court held they were all principals, as well those that killed the buck, as those that assisted. And this was the case of a conviction. All the other objections may have this general answer; that in the case of orders, where the

justices

Of Actions and Remedies.

justices have jurisdiction, we will intend they have acted right; and if they have done wrong, they may be punished by an information. Let the orders be confirmed. *Burn. Juft.* 4*to.* 304.

Landlords may take and seize goods concealed in any house or out-house, &c. and in case of a dwelling-house, on oath made before a justice, of reason to suspect that the goods are therein, may with the assistance of a constable break open such house to distrain. Stat. 11 *Geo.* 2. *c.* 19.

But except it be in this case where the goods are clandestinely conveyed, it may seem from what has been said, that the landlord hath no mean to come at the goods in order to make distress, if the tenant shall think fit to lock up his gates, and shut the doors: which matter may seem to require consideration. *Burn's Justice,* 4*to. pag.* 307.

And any cattle feeding on commons, or corn, grass, or other things growing on the land, shall and may be distrained for rent; and when ripe, cut and cured, a week's notice being given to the tenant where lodged, may be appraised and disposed of towards satisfaction of the landlord, if the tenant do not before pay the rent and charges. 11 *Geo.* 2. *c.* 19. See *action of ejectment.*

The form of a landlord's *warrant* to distrain for rent.

KNOW *all men by these presents, that I* T. B. *of,* &c. *do hereby authorise and appoint* A. B. *of,* &c. *to take any person or persons to his assistance, and enter into the house*
of

of C. D. in, &c. and there make a distress of all such goods and chattels, as are in and upon the premisses, for ten pounds, for half a year's rent due to me the said T. B. at, &c. last: and after the said goods are so distrained, if the said C. D. doth not, within the time limited, by the act of parliament for that purpose made, replevy the same, or pay the said rent; then, and in such case, I do hereby authorise you the said A. B. to cause the said goods so distrained, to be appraised, and according to such appraisement to make sale thereof to any person or persons, as will buy the same; and to dispose of the money arising by the sale, in such manner as by the said act is directed: and for your so doing, this shall be your sufficient warrant. Witness my hand and seal this 3d of May 1777.

T. B.

Note; this warrant or authority is requisite, where the landlord lives at a distance in another place, or would be free from the trouble of distraining himself; and therefore he empowers some other person to do it.

Form of an *appraiser's oath*, to appraise goods distrained.

YOU shall swear that you will faithfully appraise and value the goods now taken in distress, and mentioned in the inventory to you shewn, as between buyer and seller, according to the best of your skill and understanding: you shall not through partiality, interest or otherwise, over or under estimate the said goods, but impartially do your duties herein. *So help you God.*

The appraisers valuing the goods too high shall be obliged to take them at the price appraised. *Stat.* 13 *Ed.* 1. 2 *Show. Rep.* 87. *pl.* 78.

The form of an *inventory* and *appraisement* of the goods taken in distress.

AN *inventory of the goods seized and distrained by A. B. &c. in the house of C. D. of, &c. for ten pounds, one half year's rent due to the said A. B. at Michaelmass last: taken the day, &c. in the year, &c. for the rent aforesaid.*
Imprimis *in the fore parlour a round mahogany table, a pier looking-glass, and six beech matted chairs.* } value, &c.
In the chamber one pair of stairs, a red china bed, &c. }
In the kitchen, &c.

Valued in all at

By us, witness our hands this day, &c.

   E. F. }
   G. H. } *sworn appraisers.*
   J. K. *constable.*

Form of *notice* of the distress to the tenant.

Mr. C. D.

THIS *is to inform you, that I have this ———— day of, &c. seized upon your goods in your house in, &c. for ten pounds, half a year's rent due to me at, &c. last, and have taken an inventory thereof, and locked the same up in your chamber one pair of stairs, &c. and if you do not pay the rent due, or replevy the goods mentioned in the inventory, I shall in five days make*

sale

sale thereof, according to the direction of the act of parliament; of which take notice from,

Yours,   A. B.

Witness, that a copy hereof was this day delivered to Mrs. M. D. *the wife of* C. D. *by*
       G. H.

There is a distress for *damage-feasant*, where the beasts of a stranger are found in another man's ground, without leave of the owner thereof, and there feed, or do other damage to the grass, corn, &c. And here distress may be taken in the night, as well as day, lest the beasts escape before taken: also beasts belonging to the plough, sheep, and horses joined to a cart, or a horse with the rider on it, &c. are liable to this distress, though not for rent; but it must be while the cattle are damage-feasant, and the party may tender amends, until they are impounded, and then detainer is unlawful. Co. Lit. 142. 2 *Inst.* 107. 5 *Rep.* 76. 2 *Danv. Abr.* 633.

2. *Replevin* is grounded upon a distress, and is a re-deliverance of it, that the thing distrained may remain with the first possessor, on surety given by him to try the right with the distrainer, and answer the same at law; and if he do not pursue his action, or it be judged against him, then he that took the distress shall have it again, by the writ *returno habendo.* Co. Lit. 145, 161.

If notice be not given in writing, on taking a distress, of the things distrained, and for what you distrain them, they may not be sold by the statute 2 *W. & M.* but the distress is to be detained

tained till replevin, or satisfaction: and replevins are by writ at common law; or on plaint by statute, for the party's more speedy having again of his cattle and goods distrained. Here the sheriff ought to take two sorts of pledges, one by the common law, to prosecute; and another by the statute, to return the distress, if the taking be judged lawful; and if the sheriff deliver a distress without these pledges, he must answer the price thereof. *Co. Lit.* 145. *F. N. B.* 69.

Replevin by writ lies in the courts at *Westminster*, and action of replevin may be removed out of other courts, into those courts, and tried there: replevin by plaint may be brought in the county-court, hundred-court, and court-baron. The most usual method to obtain a replevin is by plaint; and the sheriff may take a plaint by statute, and make a replevin presently, and enter it in the county-court afterwards: also sheriffs of counties shall depute four deputies to make replevins, not dwelling above twelve miles distant from one another, under a certain penalty. *Dy.* 246. *Co. Lit.* 139. *Stat.* 1 *P. & M. c.* 12.

If the defendant in replevin claims the property of the goods, the sheriff cannot proceed till it is decided before him by writ *de proprietate probanda*; and if found for the plaintiff, the sheriff is to make replevin or deliverance; but if for the defendant he is to do nothing further: though the plaintiff may replevy by writ afterwards; and if the sheriff returns the property claimed, it shall be put in issue and tried in the Common Pleas. *Finch* 316, 317.

Where cattle or goods are not delivered upon a first replevin, the party distrained may have an *alias*, and a *pluries* replevin, in the general prosecution of it; and if the cattle are put into any strong place, the sheriff may take the *posse comitatus*, and break into it, to make the replevin: when they are driven out of the county, &c. so that the sheriff cannot make replevin, a writ of *Witkernam* shall go to take so many of the distrainer's cattle, till the party make deliverance of the first distress, &c. and in this case, the cattle taken shall be to the value of those that were first taken and detained. 52 *H*. 3. *c*. 21. 1 *P. & M.* 2 *Inst.* 140. 13 *Ed.* 1.

On bringing a replevin, it must be certain in setting forth the number and kinds of cattle distrained; that the sheriff may know how to make deliverance of the cattle, if a writ be directed to him to do it; and the time and place are to be named in the declaration: if the plaintiff in replevin makes default, or is nonsuit, or judgment be given against him, the defendant may have his writ *retorno habenda* of the goods taken in distress. And when the plaint is removed into *C. B.* &c. and the plaintiff nonsuited, before or after avowry made, the defendant may distrain again for the same cause; but the plaintiff may sue a writ of *second deliverance* upon the same record, to revive the first suit; upon which writ, the sheriff is to take security for the suit, and so make a return of the cattle or price of them, if the return shall be adjudged. *Heb.* 16. *T. Raym.* 33. *F. N. B.* 72.

And after this second deliverance and trial thereon; or if the plaintiff be again nonsuit upon a declaration, there must be awarded a *returnum irreplegiabile* to the defendant; and then he may make his avowry, or plea in justification of his distress, to ground a writ of inquiry of damages; or hold the beasts till he is satisfied:

in case the defendant make default, the plaintiff shall have judgment to recover all in damages; as well the value of the cattle, as damages for the taking of them, and his costs. And in a replevin, damages and costs are given the defendant, if found for him, such as the plaintiff would have had, if he had recovered in the action, &c. *F. N. B.* 69. *Wood's Inst.* 553. *Stat.* 21 *H.* 8. *c.* 9. 17 *Car.* 2. *c.* 7.

In replevin, if the plaintiff be nonsuit, the defendant may make suggestion as in an *avowry* for rent, and on prayer a writ shall be awarded to the sheriff, to inquire of the sum in arrear, and value of the distress, and upon the return thereof, the defendant shall recover the arrears, or the value of the distress, with costs, &c. And if the jury do not inquire of the value of the cattle distrained for the rent, that they may be sold according to the statute, and also of the rent due, there shall be no writ of inquiry to supply it. 17 *Car.* 2. *c.* 7. *Lev.* 255.

The defendant in replevin may avow, or justify; but if he justifies, he cannot have a return, as he shall have if he avows: and an avowry is where the taker of the distress avows the taking, if in his own right; and if for another, makes cognizance thereof, as bailiff, or servant, &c. It is in the nature of a declaration, and must contain sufficient matter for judgment to have return: but the avowant need not alledge seisin within the time of the statute of limitations; though the lord must have seisin by the hands of his tenant in certain. 3 *Lev.* 206. 7 *Rep.* 25. *Co. Lit.* 268.

The defendant in a replevin is allowed to avow generally, that the plaintiff or other tenant of the land, &c. whereupon distress was made,

made, held it at such certain rent, during the time the rent distrained for incurred, &c. without setting forth the landlord's grant or title; and if the plaintiff became nonsuit, the defendant shall have double costs. Sheriffs and other officers granting replevins, and taking bonds to prosecute with effect, &c. shall at request assign them to the avowant or defendant by indorsement, which if forfeited, the avowant may bring an action, and recover thereupon in his own name; and the court may give reasonable relief to the parties, by rule of the same, &c. by the *Stat.* 11 *Geo.* 2. *c.* 19.

An avowry may be made either on a distress for rent, or for damage-feasant, &c.

The form of a *count* or *declaration* in replevin.

Wilts, to wit. A. B. *and* T. B. *were summoned to answer* C. D. *gent. of a plea, wherefore they took the cattle of the said* C. *and them unjustly detained against sureties and pledges,* &c. *And whereupon the said* C. *by,* &c. *his attorney, complains, that the said* A. *and* T. *the day of,* &c. *in the year of the reign,* &c. *at* D. *in a certain place there called,* &c. *close, took the cattle, to wit, two heifers, and one bay horse, of the said* C. *and the same unjustly detained, against sureties and pledges, until,* &c. *whereupon he saith, that he is the worse, and hath damage, to the value of twenty pounds; and therefore he brings his suit,* &c.

An *avowry* in replevin for arrears of rent.

AND the said A. B. and T. B. by, &c. their attorney, come and defend the force and wrong, &c. and the said A. well avoweth, and the same T. as bailiff of the said A. well acknowledgeth the taking of the cattle aforesaid, in the same place in which, &c. and justly, &c. because he saith, that the same place, in which the taking of the cattle aforesaid is supposed to be done, doth contain, and at the time of the taking of the said cattle did contain, ten acres of pasture with the appurtenances in D. aforesaid; and that long before the same time, in which, &c. one E. D. was seised in fee of one messuage and twenty acres of pasture with the appurtenances in D. aforesaid, whereof the same place in which, &c. is, and from the time that the memory of man is not to the contrary, was parcel, and those tenements with the appurtenances, whereof, &c. held of the said A. B. as of his manor of, &c. with the appurtenances in the county aforesaid, by homage, fealty, and by the rent of twenty shillings, yearly and every year, to be paid at the feast of St. Michael the archangel, &c. of which said services the said A. was seised by the hands of the said E. D. as by the hands of his true tenant, to wit, of homage, fealty, and of the rent aforesaid, &c. in his demesne as of fee, and of which manor, with the appurtenances, the said A. was and is seised in his demesne as of fee, and being so thereof seised, and the said E. D. of the tenements aforesaid, whereof, &c. in form aforesaid being seised, the said E. before

the

the same time in which, &c. at D. *aforesaid died of such his estate therein seised, held in bomage of the said* A. *after whose death the tenements aforesaid, with the appurtenances thereof, &c. descended to the aforesaid* C. D. *son and heir of the said* E. D. *by which the same* C. *before the time in which, &c. into the tenements aforesaid, whereof, &c. entered, and was therefore seised in fee, &c. And because ten pounds for the rent aforesaid, for ten whole years ending at the feast of St.* Michael *in the year, &c. to the said* A. B. *after the death of the said* E. D. *at the same time in which, &c. were in arrear and unpaid, the said* A. *well avoweth, and the said* T. B. *as bailiff of the same* A. *well acknowledgeth the taking of the cattle aforesaid in the same place in which, &c. as in parcel of the tenements aforesaid, with the appurtenances of the said* A. *in form aforesaid held, for the same ten pounds of the rent aforesaid, so as aforesaid being in arrear, and justly, &c. according to the form of the statute in this case made and provided.*

The statutes of limitation *of actions are* 32 H. 8. c. 2. *and* 21 Jac. 1. c. 16.

BY the stat. 32 *H. 8. c.* 2. no person shall have any writ of right for recovery of lands, of the possession of his ancestors, but of a seisin within sixty years next before the *teste* of writ, *&c.* In assise of *Moridanceslor,* writ of entry *sur disseisin,* or other possessory action upon the possession of an ancestor, it must be brought within fifty years; and in

assise,

assise, &c. upon the party's own possession, within thirty years, and the plaintiff is barred, not proving such possession, &c. And writs of *formedon* for title to lands *in esse* shall be prosecuted within twenty years after the title accrued, by stat. 21 *Jac.* 1. *c.* 16.

But there is a proviso in the statutes to relieve infants, feme-coverts, persons beyond sea, or in prison, and the heirs of such persons, so as they commence their suits within the times limited after their impediments are removed. And it has been adjudged, that the act 32 *H.* 8. doth not extend to rent, or services, &c. out of land: also that one who hath been out of possession for sixty years, if his entry be not taken away, may enter and bring an action for his own possession. *Wood's Inst.* 557.

By statute 21 *Jac.* 1. *c.* 16. actions of debt, actions upon the case, (except for words) actions of account (except concerning merchandize) of detinue, * trover and trespass, are to be commenced within six years after the cause of action, and not after; actions of assault and battery, within four years; and for slander, within two years after the cause of action, &c. And if these personal actions are not brought in the time limited by this statute, they are barred: though where money is to be paid on request, or the consideration of a promise is executory, &c. it is not material when the promise was made, but when the cause of action did arise; and the defendant ought to plead, that *causa actionis non accrevit infra sex annos*, &c. 2 *Salk.* 422.

7 Mod. 143.
1 Ld. Raym. 838.

The exception in the statute of limitations in actions of account, relates to accounts current

* See 15 Vin. Abr. 115.

only

only between merchants; for when an account is stated and balanced, debt lies, and the action must be brought within six years. In actions of slander, when words are actionable in themselves, there damages shall be recovered accordingly as they were first spoken, if the action be brought within two years, as required by the statute of limitations; and otherwise the party will be barred thereby: but where the words are actionable in respect of the special damage which happens after the speaking; in such case, if the damage is seven years afterwards, it is no bar. *Mod.* 70, 268. *Sid.* 95.

An action barrable by the statute 21 *Jac.* I. a fresh promise will revive it; so it is of an acknowledgment of a debt, because that is evidence of a promise: and taking out a writ, and entring and filing it, is an avoidance of the statute; for 'tis a demand, and a good bringing of an action within the time mentioned by the statute of limitations. 3 *Salk.* 228, 229. *Lil. Abr.* 19.

Personal actions die with the person; as of battery, &c. A man attainted of treason or felony, convict of recusancy, an outlaw, excommunicate person, &c. cannot bring an action 'till pardon, reversal, absolution, &c. A feme covert must sue with her husband, and infants by guardians, &c. *Lit.* 196. *Co. Lit.* 128.

How controversies are determined, without action at law, by award, &c.

AWARD is the judgment and arbitration of one or more persons, at the request of two parties at variance, for ending the matter in dispute, without publick authority: and this is
done

done by arbitrators chosen by the parties, on a bond to submit themselves to their judgment.

And arbitrators are generally where parties think it more safe to refer the matters in controversy to the determination of friends, than to venture a trial at law; they proceed at their own discretion, without solemnity of process, &c. to hear and determine the controversy referred to them: and they have as great power as other judges, though they are not tied to the formalities of law; and if they observe the submission, their award is definitive. *Dy.* 356.

The submission to arbitrators may be general, of all demands, &c. or special, of some matters in dispute: and the award must be made of the thing submitted, according to the submission; it must be equal between the parties, and not on one side only; and the performance of it is to be lawful and possible; also the award must be certain and final: if an award is of things not submitted, or to pay money to a stranger, &c. it will be void. *Co. Lit.* 206. *Rol. Abr.* 242. 2 *Saund.* 122.

Where arbitrators award a thing against law, it is void; so if more is awarded than should be: but on a general submission, the award may be of part, without the residue, and be good. An award may be void for some part, and good in another part, if it makes an end of all the differences submitted; and if the award is good in part, and void in part thereof, the good shall be performed. And the Chancery will not give relief against the award of arbitrators, unless for corruption, exceeding authority, &c. *Cro. Eliz.* 161. *Danv. Abr.* 536. *Rol. Abr.* 244.

If

Of Actions and Remedies.

If all debts and demands are submitted to arbitration, the arbitrators may award a release of bonds, specialties, &c. by which the debts and demands are due: and where the award is according to the submission by bond, though it be void in law, if it is not performed, the obligation will be forfeited. Things relating to freeholds, leases, debts due on certain contract, matters concerning matrimony, and criminal offences, are not arbitrable by awards. *Danv. Abr.* 513, 515.

<small>10 Mod. 332. Stra. 1. 2 Stra. 1024. 9 Mod. 232.</small> Sometimes matters are referred by the judges at the assises to the three foremen of the jury, in nature of arbitrators; and after their award is made, the plaintiff may have an attachment, &c. to oblige performance: and attachment lies for not performing an award made a rule of court; after personal demand of performance. *Salk.* 83, 84. Submissions to awards, by agreement of the parties, may be made a rule of any of his majesty's courts of record; and on a rule of court thereupon, the parties shall be finally concluded by such arbitrament: and in case of disobedience thereto, the party refusing to perform the same shall be subject to the penalties of contemning a rule of court, &c. except it appears on oath, that such award was unduly procured, when it shall be set aside: but this extends only to personal matters for which there is no other remedy but by personal action, or by suit in equity. *Stat.* 9 & 10 *W.* 3. *c.* 15.

When there is but one arbitrator, which happens where the matter is referred to two, and if they cannot agree in the award, it is left to a third person, this is called an *umpirage*; and the umpire has the same power as the arbitrators, if they do not agree in their award. Tho'
the

the arbitrators are to refuse, and declare they will make no award, before the umpire shall proceed. 8 *Rep.* 98. 2 *Saund.* 130.

The umpire's award shall be good, where the arbitrators make a void award, which is no award. *Lil. Abr.* 170.

The form of an award of differences.

TO all people, *to whom this present writing indented of award shall come, greeting.* Whereas *there are several accounts depending, and divers controversies and disputes have lately risen between* A. B. *of,* &c. *and* C. D. *of,* &c. *all which controversies and disputes are chiefly touching and concerning,* &c. And whereas, *for the putting an end to the said differences and disputes, they the said* A. B. *and* C. D. *by their several bonds or obligations bearing date,* &c. *are become bound each to other of them in the penal sum of one hundred pounds, to stand to and abide the award and final determination of us* E. F. G. H. &c. *so as the said award be made in writing, and ready to be delivered to the parties in difference on or before,* &c. *next, as by the said obligations and conditions thereof may appear:* Now know ye, *that we the said arbitrators, whose names are hereunto subscribed, and seals affixed, taking upon us the burden of the said award, and having fully examined and duly considered the proofs and allegations of both the said parties, do, for the settling amity and friendship between them, make and publish this our award, by and between the said parties in manner following, that is to say:* First, *we do award and order, that all actions, suits, quarrels, and controversies whatsoever, had, moved, arisen, or depending*

This instrument must be engrossed on a crown stamped sheet of paper.

pending between the said parties in law or equity, for any manner of cause whatsoever touching the said &c. to the day of the date hereof. shall cease and be no further prosecuted; and that each of the said parties shall pay and bear his own costs and charges. in any wise relating to or concerning the same premisses. And we do also award and order that the said A. B. *shall pay, or cause to be paid, to the said* C. D. *the sum of,* &c. *within the space of three months, and at his own charges do,* &c. And further we do award and order that the said C. D. *shall pay, or cause to be paid, to the said* A. B. *the sum,* &c. *on or before,* &c. *or give sufficient security for the same to the said* A. B. And we do award and order that, &c. And lastly, we award and order that the said A. B. and C. D. *on receipt of the several sums,* &c. *above-mentioned, shall in due form of law execute each to the other general releases, sufficient for the releasing, by each to the other of them, his executors and administrators, of all actions, suits, arrests, quarrels, controversies and demands whatsoever touching or concerning the premisses aforesaid, or any matter or thing thereunto relating, from the beginning of the world until the ——— day of,* &c. *last.* In Witness *whereof we have hereunto set our hands and seals the* ——— *day,* &c. *in the year,* &c.

Sealed, &c.

Of Courts, Attorneys and Solicitors, Juries, Witnesses, Trials, Executions, &c.

A Court is the place where justice is judicially administered: and there are many courts, some of record, and some not; courts superior, as those at *Westminster*, and courts inferior, in the country, &c. A court of record is that which hath power to hold plea according to the course of the common law, of real, personal and mixed actions, where the debt or damage is 40 s. or above: and a court not of record is when it cannot hold plea of debt, &c. amounting to 40 s. but of pleas under that sum; or where the proceedings are not according to the course of the common law, nor inrolled. *Cromp. Jurisd. Co. Lit.* 260, 117.

In courts where writs lie not, the suit is begun by plaint, *viz.* by entring the action, and cause of complaint, &c. and in inferior courts having particular jurisdictions, it must be set forth at large; for there nothing shall be extended to be within the jurisdiction, but what is expresly alledged to be so: but at the courts at *Westminster*, the plaintiff doth not shew at large in his declaration, that the cause of action arises within their jurisdiction, which is general; and pleading to issue, &c. allows the jurisdiction of courts. *Sid.* 331. 2 *Inst.* 219. 1 *Lil. Abr.* 371.

The courts of law and equity I shall here treat of, are the following.

1. The

Of Courts, Juries,

1. The high court of Chancery.
2. The King's Bench.
3. The court of Common Pleas.
4. The Exchequer.
5. The court of Assises, &c.

1. The *court of Chancery* is the highest court of judicature in this kingdom next to the parliament, and of very ancient institution. Its jurisdiction is of two kinds; ordinary or legal; and extraordinary, or absolute: The ordinary court is that wherein the lord chancellor, in his proceedings and judgments, observes the order and method of the common law; and in such cases, the proceedings are filed or inrolled in the *Petty-Bag* office.

This court holds plea of recognizances acknowledged in Chancery; writs of *Scire facias* for repeal of letters patent, writs of partition, &c. and also of all personal actions, by or against any officer of the court; and by acts of parliament, of several offences and causes: all original writs, commissions of bankrupts, charitable uses of idiots and lunacy, &c. issue out of this court for which it is always open; one from hence may have an *habeas corpus*, prohibition, &c. In the vacation, which are to be had out of the other courts only in term-time; and here a *subpœna* may be issued to force witnesses to appear in other courts, when they have no power to call them. But in prosecuting causes, if the parties descend to issue, this court cannot try it by jury; but the record is to be sent into the King's Bench, and try'd there, and afterwards remanded into the Chancery: though if there be
a de-

a demurrer in law, it shall be argued and adjudged here. Upon a judgment given in this court, a writ of error lies returnable in *B. R.* 4 *Inst.* 78, 80, &c. *Danv. Abr.* 776.

The extraordinary or unlimited court exercises jurisdiction in cases of equity, by way of *English* bill and answer in abating the rigour of the common law, and where the courts of law are defective to give remedy: it gives relief for and against infants, notwithstanding their minority; and for or against married women, called feme coverts, notwithstanding their coverture; all frauds and deceits are here relievable; as also all accidents to mortgagors, obligors, &c. against penalties, and forfeitures, where the intention was to pay the debt; all breaches of trust, unreasonable engagements, &c. This court may force unreasonable creditors to compound debts; make executors, &c. give security, and pay interest for money long in their hands; and here executors may sue one another, or one executor alone be sued without the rest: order may be made for performance of a will, decree made who shall have the tuition of a child; and this court may relieve copyholders against the ill usage of their lords; confirm title to lands, where the deeds are lost; make conveyances, defective thro' fraud or mistake, good and perfect; oblige men to come to account with each other; avoid the bar of actions by the statute of limitations, &c. 4 *Inst.* 84. *Rol. Abr.* 373. 1 *Danv.* 749, 750, 752, &c.

But in all cases, where the plaintiff can have his remedy at law, he ought not to be relieved in Chancery; and long leases, as for 1000 years naked promises; verbal agreements not executed: estates derived under concealed titles, &c.

have been refused relief in this court: and mortgages are not relievable in equity after twenty years, where no demand has been made, or interest paid, &c. Also this court will not retain a suit for any thing under 10 *l.* value, except it be in cases of charity; nor for lands, &c. under 40 *s. per annum*; and it refuses to relieve persons in suits where the substance of them tends to the overthrow of any fundamental point of the common law, or an act of parliament. *Danv. Abr.* 763, 754. 2 *Vent.* 340.

And altho' the power of the court of Chancery, in its equitable proceedings, is so great in the foregoing particulars, yet it is no court of record; and therefore 'tis said can bind the person only, and not the estate of the defendant; and if the party will not obey the decree of this court, he must be committed until he does: in this case, if there be an order that one shall stand committed to the *Fleet*, for breach of a decree, in pursuance of the order, there must be a writ awarded for taken and imprisoning him. 4 *Inst.* 84. *Danv.* 749, 776.

It is ordained by the *stat.* 36 *Ed.* 3. That whosoever shall find himself grieved with any statute, he shall have his remedy in the Chancery. No *subpoena* or process is to issue out of this court 'till a bill is filed; except in injunctions to stay waste, and suits at law, &c. and on a plaintiff's dismissing his bill, or the defendant for want of prosecution, the plaintiff to pay full costs, &c. 5 *Ann. c.* 16. A defendant not appearing on *subpœna* issued, and absconding to avoid being served therewith, the court may make an order for his appearance at a certain day, which shall be published in the *gazette*; and if he do not then appear, the plaintiff's bill

shall

shall be taken *pro confesso*, and the defendant's estate sequestered to satisfy the plaintiff, &c. 5 *Geo.* 2. *cap.* 25.

2. The *Court of King's Bench at Westminster*, is a court that hath supreme authority, the king himself being supposed to be there, and was sometimes wont to sit in his own person. The court and the Chancery are to follow the king; and the King's Bench was originally the only court in *Westminster-hall*; out of which the courts of Common Pleas and Exchequer seem to have been derived. 4 *Inst.* 73. 2 *Hawk. P. C.* 6.

It is divided into a crown-side, and a plea-side; the one determining criminal, and the other civil causes: the crown-side takes notice of all treasons, felonies, breaches of the peace, and of all causes prosecuted by way of indictment, or information; and into this office, indictments from all inferior courts, orders of sessions, &c. may be removed by *certiorari*: also here inquisitions of murder are certified: and hence issue attachments, &c. On the plea-side, it hath cognizance of all pleas by bill for debt, account, covenant, in action upon the case, and other personal actions, ejectment, &c. against any person in custody of the marshal, as every one sued here is supposed to be; and in all personal actions, for or against any officer, minister, or clerk of the court, who in respect to their attendance have privilege of court. *Cromp. Jurisd.* 67, 68. 4 *Rep.* 57. 9 *Rep.* 118.

In ancient times this court was ordinarily exercised only in criminal matters, and pleas of the crown: and it awards execution against persons attainted or condemned by parliament, or any other court, when the record is removed, and their persons brought thither by *habeas corpus*, and there pardons of offenders are allowed, on removing the records and prisoners, &c. This court may bail any person whatsoever; grants *habeas corpus*'s to relieve persons wrongfully imprisoned; restores freemen unjustly disfranchised; and grants prohibitions to keep other courts within their proper jurisdictions, &c. 4 *Inst.* 70. 2 *Danv. Abr.* 279.

The court of *B. R.* regulates all the courts of law in the kingdom, so that they do not exceed their jurisdictions, nor alter their forms, &c. and may grant an attachment against any inferior court, usurping a jurisdiction not belonging to it; but generally a writ of prohibition is first issued to such court. The judges of this court are the sovereign justices and coroners of the land: and their jurisdiction is general over all *England*, which, when the king hath appointed them, they have from the law. 4 *Inst.* 74.

3. The *court of Common Pleas* is one of the king's courts held in *Westminster-hall*, or other certain place: it is not to follow the king and his court, but to be held at some place certain; nor shall be removed without warning by adjournment. *Stat.* 9 *H.* 3. *c.* 12. & 2 *Ed.* 3. *c.* 11.

All actions belonging to this court come here either by original, as on arrests and outlawries; or by privilege or attachment, for or against privileged persons; or out of inferior courts not of record: and all civil causes, real, personal, or mixed, are here brought and determined; tho' regularly this court cannot hold plea in any action real or personal, &c. but by writ out of Chancery, returnable here; unless it be by bill for or against an officer, or other privileged person of the court. 4 *Inst.* 99, 100.

The

Witnesses, Trials.

The Common Pleas is said to have been the only court for real causes concerning lands; and, in personal and mixed actions, it hath a concurrent jurisdiction with the King's Bench: but it hath no cognizance of pleas of the crown; and common pleas are all pleas that are not such. It's jurisdiction, like that of the other courts at *Westminster*, is general, and extends throughout *England*: and hither suits are removed out of other courts by divers writs; as by *pone*, *recordare*, writ of false judgment, &c. 4 *Inst.* 118. *Fortescue* 50, 51.

And this court, besides having jurisdiction for punishment of it's officers and ministers, may grant prohibitions to keep temporal and ecclesiastical courts within due bounds. *Ibid.*

4. The *court of Exchequer* is a very ancient court of record, set up to order and determine the rights and revenues, debts and duties due to the crown, &c. And in the Exchequer there are divers courts, consisting of many branches; but, according to the usual division, it is divided into two parts only, for dispatch of business. 4 *Inst.* 112, 115.

This is the last of the four courts at *Westminster*; and the lord chief baron and barons are the sovereign auditors of *England*, and hear and determine all causes in law or equity: for the judicial part of the Exchequer is a court both of law and equity; the court of law being in the office of Pleas, after the course of the Common law, *coram baronibus*; and the court of equity held in the Exchequer-chamber, before the lord treasurer, chancellor or under treasurer, and barons: but generally before the barons only, the lord chief baron being the chief judge. 4 *Inst.* 118.

Here the proceedings are according to the practice of the Chancery, by bill and answer; but the plaintiff must set forth in his bill, that he is debtor or accountant to the king, though whether it so or not, is not material: in this court the clergy usually exhibit their bills for recovery of tithes; and here the attorney general brings bills against persons for any matters concerning the king; also any person grieved with any prosecution on behalf of the king, &c. may bring his bill against the attorney general, and be relieved therein. *Ibid.*

In the court of law, all the officers, and clerks, the king's tenants and farmers, all debtors, and accountants of the Exchequer, are privileged to sue and implead one another, or any stranger, in like manner as in the King's Bench and Common Pleas; and the writs of *subpœna* and *quo minos* go into *Wales*, where no process of the courts of *B. R.* or *C. B.* ought to run, except the *Capias Utlagatum*.

There is a court of *Exchequer-chamber*, being the assembly of all the judges of *England*, for difficult matters in law; into which causes are adjourned when there are two judges against two, that they cannot be determined in other courts, &c.

5. The *court of Assizes* is the court, place or time, when and where the writs and processes of assise are handled or taken, before an assembly of knights, and other gentlemen, with the justice appointed, &c. And assize is general, as when the justices go their several circuits with commission to take all assizes; or special where a special commission is granted to certain persons, (formerly oftentimes done) for taking an assise upon one or two disseisins only: and concerning

cerning the general assise, all the counties of *England* are divided into six circuits, and two judges assigned by the king's commission to every circuit, who hold their assises twice a year in every county, (except *Middlesex*, where the king's courts of record do sit, and where his courts for his counties palatine are held,) and have five several commissions:

1. A commission of *Oyer* and *Terminer*, directed to them and many other gentlemen of the county, by which they are impowered to try treasons, felonies, &c. 2. Of *Gaol-delivery*, directed to the judges and clerk of assise associate, which gives them power to try every prisoner in the gaol committed for any offence whatsoever; but none but prisoners in the gaol. 3. Of *Assise*, directed to themselves only and the clerk of assise, to take assises, and do right upon writs of assise brought before them by such as are wrongfully thrust out of their lands and possessions, &c. 4. Of *nisi prius*, directed to the judges and clerk of assise, by which civil causes grown to issue in the courts above are tried in the vacation by a jury of twelve men of the county where the case of action arises; and on return of the verdict of the jury to the court above, the judges there give judgment. 5. A commission *of the peace*, in every county of the circuits; and all justices of peace of the county are bound to be present at the assises; and sheriffs, &c. shall also give their attendance on the judges, or they shall be fined. 4 *Inst.* 158. *Bacon's Elem.* 15, 16, &c.

Justices of assise, &c. are to hold their sessions in the chief towns of each county; and their records shall be sent into the Exchequer: and if causes are too difficult for them, they shall be referred

ferred to the justices of the Bench, there to be ended. *Stat.* 9 *H.* 3. *c.* 12. 6 *R* 2. *& 9 Ed.* 3.

The inferior courts in the county may be reduced to the heads of,

1. The County-Court.
2. The Court-Leet.
3. The Court-Baron.

1. The *County-Court* is a court kept by the sheriff of every county, and divided into two sorts; one retaining the general name, as the county-court held every month, before the sheriff or his deputy: the other called the turn, held twice in every year, *viz.* within a month after *Easter* and *Michaelmas*. Cromp. Jurif. 241.

By the Common law, every sheriff ought to make his turn or circuit, throughout all the hundreds in his county, in order to hold a court in every hundred for the redressing of common grievances, and preservation of the peace, &c. and the turn is the king's leet thro' all the county; it being a court of record, of which the sheriff is judge: also, before the courts at *Westminster* were erected, the county-courts were the chief courts of the kingdom. *Glanvil, lib.* 1. *cap.* 2, 3. *Fleta, lib.* 2. *c.* 62.

But the power of the county-court was much reduced by the statute of *Magna Charta, c.* 17. and 1 *Ed.* 4. *c.* 1. It hath now the determination of certain trespasses and debts under 40 *s.* and this court holdeth no plea of any debt or damage to the value of 40 *s.* or more; nor of trespass *vi & armis*, &c. But of debt and other actions personal above that sum, the sheriff may hold plea by force of a writ of *justicies*, which is in nature of a commission to him to do it. *Brit. c.* 27 *&* 28. 4 *Inst.* 266.

Witnesses, Trials.

No sheriff is to enter in the county court any plaint in the absence of the plaintiff; nor above one plaint for one cause, on pain of 40 *s.* and the defendant in this court shall have lawful summons, &c. And out of the county-court causes are removed by *recordare, pone* &c. into K. B. and C. P.

2. The *Court-leet* is a court of record incident to a hundred, ordained for punishing offences against the crown; it is derived out of the sheriff's turn, and inquires of all offences under treason; but those, which are to be punished with loss of life or member, are only inquirable and presentable there; and must be certified over to the justices of assise. 4 *Inst.* 261. *Stat.* 1 *Ed.* 3.

And this court is called the *view of frank-pledge*, for that the king is to be there certified by the view of the steward, how many people are within every leet, and have an account of their good manners and government; and all persons above twelve years of age, which have remained there for a year and a day, may be sworn to be faithful to the king, and the people are to be kept in peace, &c. Also every one, from the age of twelve to sixty years, that dwells within the leet, is obliged to do suit in this court; except peers, clergymen, &c. 4 *Inst.* 261, 263.

In the court-leet, or view of frank-pledge, formerly all persons were bound with sureties or pledges for their truth to the king: the steward is here the judge, as the sheriff is in the turn; and this court is to be kept twice a year, one time in a month after *Easter*, and the other within a month after *Michaelmas*, at a certain place within the precinct: and the steward hath power, to elect officers, as constables, tithingmen, &c. as well as punish offenders. The usual method of punishment in the leet is by fine and amercement, and a presentment here subjects the party to them; the former is assessed by the steward, and the latter by the jury; for both of which, the lord may have an action of debt, or take a distress. *Kitch.* 70. *Co. Lit.* 115. 6 *Rep.* 12. 2 *Inst.* 199.

This court inquires of and punishes misdemeanors, incroachments, nusances, &c. purprestures in lands or woods; or houses set up, or beat down, and other annoyances; bounds taken away; ways or waters turned, or stopped; of thieves, and hues and cries not pursued; of bloodshed, escapes, persons outlawed, money coiners, treasure found: assise of bread and ale, persons keeping alehouses without licence; false weights and measures, unlawful games, offences relating to the game; of tanners selling insufficient leather; forestallers and ingrossers of markets, &c. of victuallers and labourers, unlawful fishing, idle persons, &c. All which particular articles are to be inquired into by statute. 18 *Ed.* 2. 14 & 15 *H.* 8. 2 & 3 *Ed.* 6. 31 *Eliz.*

And the lord of the leet ought to have a pillory and tumbrel, &c. to punish offenders; or for want thereof he may be fined, or the liberty seised; and all towns within the leet are to have stocks in repair; and the town that hath none, shall forfeit 5*l.* 2 *Danv. Abr.* 289.

3. The *Court-Baron* is that court which every lord of a manor (who in ancient times were called barons) hath within his own precinct: and a court-baron is an inseparable incident to a manor; it must be held by prescription, for it

cannot

cannot be created at this day, and is to be kept on some part of the manor. *Co. Lit.* 58. 4 *Inst.* 268.

This court is of two natures, 1. By the common law, which is the barons or freeholders court, of which the freeholders being suitors are the judges. 2. By custom, which is called the customary court, and concerns the customary tenants and copyholders, whereof the lord or his steward is judge: the court-baron may be of this double nature, or one may be without the other. The freeholders court hath jurisdiction for trying actions of debt, trespass, &c. under 40 s. and may be held every three weeks; being something like the county-court: but on recovery in debt, they have not power to make execution, only to distrain the defendant's goods, and retain them till satisfaction is made. The other court-baron is for taking and passing of estates, surrenders, admittances, &c. and is kept but once or twice in the year, (usually with the court-leet) unless it be on purpose to grant an estate, and then it may be holden as often as required. 4 *Rep.* 26. 6 *Rep.* 12. 2 *Inst.* 119.

In this court the homage jury are to inquire that the lords do not lose their services, duties, or customs; but that the tenants make their suits of court; pay their rents, heriots, &c. and keep lands and tenements in repair, &c. and every public trespass may be punished here by amercement or presenting the same. *Stat.* 4 *Ed.* 1.

No steward of a leet, or court-baron, shall receive profits to his own use, that belong to the lord, on pain of 40 l. and disability. 1 *Jac.* 1. c. 5.

Next

Of Courts, Juries,

Next I shall mention *attornies* and *solicitors* in the courts of law, who are allowed, admitted and regulated,

 1. By the orders of court and common law.
 2. By ancient and late statutes.

1. Attornies at law are those persons as take upon them the business of other men, by whom they are retained: and in respect of the several courts, there are attornies at large; and attornies special, belonging to this or that court only. *Rol. Abr.* 17.

By order of all the judges, attornies are to be admitted into some of the inns of court or chancery, and take chambers there or near, (except house-keepers in *London* and *Westminster*, &c.) and none shall be sworn an attorney until he is thus admitted: no attorney shall put himself out of the society that he is of, till he is admitted of some other society, and deliver a certificate thereof; all attornies are to be in commons the times ordered by the society to which they belong, and offending therein shall be put out of the roll of attornies. Attachments have been granted against those that have disobeyed this order, in not being admitted of some inn of court, &c. and attornies may be committed for any ill practices. *Ord. Mich.* 3 *Ann. Lil. Abr.* 129, 130.

Action lies for a client against his attorney, if he appear for him without warrant; and if he pleads a plea, for which he hath not his warrant: but in case the attorney appears without warrant, and judgment is had against his client, the judgment shall stand if the attorney be responsible;

sponsible; otherwise if the attorney be not responsible. Action lies against an attorney for suffering judgment against his client by *nil dicit*, when he had given him a warrant to plead the general issue; though this is understood where it is done by covin. Action lies not for what any attorney does generally, although he knows the plaintiff has no cause of action; he only acting as a servant in the way of his profession. *Danv. Abr.* 185. 4 *Inst.* 117. *Mod.* 209. *Salk.* 88.

He that is attorney at one time is attorney at all times pending the plea: and the plaintiff or defendant may not change his attorney, while the suit is depending, without leave of the court, which would reflect on the credit of attornies; nor until the attornies fees are paid; and attornies and solicitors may detain writings which come to their hands by way of business, till their just fees are satisfied: if there be no fees due, the court will compel the delivery of them on motion, without forcing the party to an action. A cause shall proceed notwithstanding the death of an attorney therein, and not be delayed on that account. *Lil. Abr.* 148. 2 *Keb.* 273.

Attornies have the privilege to sue and be sued only in the court at *Westminster*, where they practise: they are not obliged to put in special bail, when defendants; but when they are plaintiffs, they may insist upon bail in * all cases: and they shall not be chosen into offices against their will, &c. *Ventr.* 299. Ld. *Raym.* 342, 533. 2 *Stra.* 1141.

* Not unless plaintiff makes an affidavit of a debt of 10 *l.* or upwards, by stat. 12 *Geo.* c. 29. perpetuated by 21 *Geo.* 2. c. 23.

2. By

2. By the statutes, the justices shall examine attornies, and by their discretion they shall be put into the roll; and they shall swear to execute their offices truly, &c. The number of attornies may be restrained, by an ancient statute; and where they are unskilful or insufficient, they shall be removed by the justices, and their clients have notice thereof: when any die, or cease to practise, the justices shall appoint others; and if an attorney be found notoriously in the fault, he shall forswear the court. *Stat.* 4 *H.* 4. *c.* 18. 33 *H.* 6. *c.* 7.

None shall be admitted attornies of any court of record, but those that have been brought up in the said courts, or were well practised and skilled in the law, and of an honest disposition; and no attorney shall suffer any other to follow a suit in his name, on pain that each of them shall forfeit 20 *l.* And attornies, solicitors, &c. are to take the oaths to the government, under penalties and disabilities to practise. An attorney shall not be allowed any fees laid out for counsel, or otherwise, unless he have tickets thereof signed by them who receive such fees; and attornies shall give in true bills to their clients of all the charges of suits, under their hands, before the client shall be charged with the payment thereof; if they delay their clients suits for gain; or demand by their bills more than their due fees and disbursements, the clients shall recover costs and treble damages, against them; and they shall be for ever after disabled to be attornies, &c. 3 *Jac.* *c.* 7. 13 *W.* 3. *c.* 6.

Attornies are to enter and file warrants of attornies, in every suit, on pain of 10 *l.* and imprisonment: and the plaintiff's attorney is to file his warrant the term he declares, and the defendant his the term he appears. If any who hath been convicted of forgery, perjury, or common barretry, shall practise as an attorney or solicitor in any suit or action brought in any court; on complaint, the judge, where such action shall be depending, hath power to transport the offender for seven years, by such ways, and under such penalties as felons. 4 *Ann. c.* 16. 12 *Geo. c.* 29. perpetuated by 21 *Geo.* 2. *c.* 3. *Stra.* 633. *Moseley* 68. *Barnes's Notes, C. P.* 91. *Comb.* 348. *Salk.* 89. 2 *Stra.* 1056. *Andr.* 276.

All attornies and solicitors shall be sworn, admitted and inrolled by the judges, before allowed to sue out writs in the courts at *Westminster*, &c. and every writ served on a defendant, shall be indorsed with the name of the attorney by whom sued forth; and sworn attornies permitting others to sue forth writs in their names, to be disabled: for the future, no persons shall practise but such as have served a clerkship and five years to an attorney, &c. duly sworn and admitted; and shall be examined, sworn and admitted in open court; and attornies shall not have more than two clerks at one time, &c. persons sworn as attornies, may be admitted solicitors in courts of equity: and attornies or solicitors shall not bring any action for fees till a month after delivery of their bills subscribed with their hands; also the parties chargeable may get them taxed in the mean time, and upon the taxation the sum remaining due is to be paid in full of the said bills; or in default, the party shall be liable to attachment, &c. but if any bill is reduced a sixth part, the attorney must pay the costs of taxation. 2 *Geo.* 2. *c.* 23. perpetuated by 30 *Geo.* 2. *c.* 19. *sect.* 75.

The

Of Courts, Juries,

The judges of any court of record may not admit any greater number of attorneys, than by the usages of such court hath been accustomed: and if any person shall sue out any writ, or defend an action in any courts of law or equity, as an attorney or solicitor, for any gain or fee, without being admitted and inrolled, he shall forfeit 50 *l.* and be incapable to maintain an action for fee or reward; the penalty to be recovered by action of debt, bill, plaint, *&c.* *Stat. ibid.*

In order to trials in courts, after attornies and other practisers therein, I am to consider of,

1. Juries, to try causes.
2. Witnesses, and other evidence necessary.

1. *Jury* signifies a certain number of men, sworn to enquire of matter of fact, and declare the truth upon such evidence as shall be delivered them in a cause. And there are two sorts of juries in criminal cases; a *grand jury*, which usually consists of twenty-four men of greater quality than the other; and a *petty jury*, consisting of twelve men, called the jury of life and death: the grand jury finds the bills of indictment against criminals: and the petty jury convicts them by verdict, in the giving whereof all the twelve must agree; and according to the verdict the judgment passeth. Also besides the common jury in civil cases; there is a *special jury*, in causes of consequence, tried at the bar, when the court makes a rule for the secondary to name forty-eight freeholders, and each party is to strike out twelve, one at a time, and the remainder to be the jury for the trial. A jury

jury of *merchants* may be returned to an issue between two merchants touching merchants affairs: and where an alien is plaintiff or defendant, the jury shall be half foreigners and half *English, per medietatem linguæ*; but 'tis not necessary that the foreigners be all of the same country. *Co. Lit.* 154. 3 *Inst.* 30, 221. *Lil. Abr.* 125.

By the common law jurymen are to be returned, in all cases, for trial of general issues, from the county where the fact was done: and they are to be freemen, indifferent, and not outlawed, or infamous; men attainted of any crime ought not to serve on juries, nor aliens generally; and infants, persons seventy years old, clergymen, apothecaries, &c. are exempted by law from serving upon juries. By statute, jurors impanelled shall be the next neighbours, most sufficient and least suspicious; or the officer shall forfeit double damages: and their qualification, which was formerly but 40 s. *per annum* estate, is 10 l. *per annum* freehold or copyhold, within the same county; and talesmen 5 l. a year. *S. P. C.* 154. 3 *Inst.* 221. 2 *Inst.* 447. *Stat.* 13 *Ed.* 1. 4 & 5 *W.* & *M. c.* 24.

The constables of parishes at *Michaelmas* quarter-sessions yearly, are to return to the justices of peace there, lists of the names and places of abode of persons qualified to serve on juries, between the age of twenty-one and seventy, attested upon oath, on pain of forfeiting 5 l. and the justices of peace shall order the clerk of the peace to deliver a duplicate of those lists to the sheriff, &c. from which they are to make their panels of jurors: but no sheriff, or bailiff, &c. shall return any person to serve on a jury, unless he he hath been summoned six days before the day of appearance, &c. And if a trial is for any thing which concerns the sheriff or under-sheriff, the coroner is to return the jury: the process to bring in a jury in *B. R.* is a *distringas*, and in *C. B. venire fac.* and then *habeas corpora jurator'*, to bring in the jury. Stat. 4 & 5 *W.* & *M. c.* 24. 7 & 8 *W.* 3. *c.* 32. 3 *Ann. c.* 18: 2 *Lil. Abr.* 126.

Lists of jurors, qualified according to the acts of 4 & 5 *W.* & *M.* and 7 & 8 *W.* 3. shall be made and given in from the rates of each parish, and fixed on the doors of churches, &c. twenty days before the feast of St. *Michael*, that notice may be given of persons qualified omitted, or of persons inserted who are not so, &c. and the lists being set right by the justices of peace in quarter sessions, duplicates are to be delivered to the sheriffs of counties, by the clerks of the peace; the names contained in which, with the additions of the persons, shall be entered alphabetically by the sheriffs in a book, and none others to serve on juries, &c. If any sheriff, or other officer, shall return other persons; or the clerk of assise record any appearance when the party did not appear, they shall be fined by the judges not exceeding 10 *l.* nor less than 40 *s.* The like penalty for sheriffs taking money to excuse persons from serving; and the judges may fine the sheriffs, &c. not above 5 *l.* for returning jurors who have served two years before in any county, except of *York*, &c. In the county of *Middlesex*, no person shall be returned as a juror, that hath served two terms before. *Stat.* 3 *Geo.* 2. *c.* 25. 4 *Geo.* 2. *c.* 7.

On

On the return of writs of *venire facias*, she- | It has been
riffs are to annex thereto a panel, or little piece | held since this
of parchment, of the names of a competent | statute, that a
number of jurors named in the lists, not less | *tales circum-*
than 48, nor more than 72; (without direction | *stantibus* was
of the judges) who shall be summoned to serve | allowable up-
at the assise, &c. and the names of the persons | on special ju-
impanelled shall be written in distinct pieces of | ries, by Ray-
paper, and delivered by the under sheriff to the | mond, Ch.
judge's marshal, and he is to cause them to be | Just.
rolled up and put together in a box; and when | 2 Kel. 77.
any cause shall be brought on, some indifferent | pl. 39.
person shall in open court draw out twelve of | 2 Sess. Caf.
the said papers of names, one after another, | 333. pl. 183.
who, not being challenged, are to be the jury to | 3 Bac. Abr.
try the cause; but if any are challenged, or | 248.
do not appear, then a further number is to be
drawn till there be a full jury, &c. and their
names after sworn shall be kept apart in some
other box or glass, till they have given in their
verdict; and then these names shall be rolled
up again, and returned to the former box, to
be kept with the other names, as long as any
cause remains for trials: and if a cause comes
on before the jury in any other shall have given
their verdict, the court shall order twelve of the
residue of the papers to be drawn, &c. Jurors
whose names shall be drawn, if they do not appear after three times called, upon oath made
that they were lawfully summoned, shall forfeit
not above 5 *l*. nor under 40 *s*. *Stat.* 3 *Geo.* 2.
c. 25.

In trials of issues on indictments, &c. and all | There can be
actions whatsoever, the courts at *Westminster* | no special ju-
may order a special jury to be struck, as on | ries granted
trials at bar, upon motion in behalf of the king, | in cases of
or of any plaintiff or defendant; and when or- | treason or fe-
dered | lony, 21 Vin.
 | Abr. 301. pl. 5.

L

dered by rule of court in causes arising within any city, &c. the jury shall be taken out of lists, or books of persons qualified, which are to be brought by the sheriffs, &c. before the proper officer, as the freeholders book is for causes arising in counties. Persons who have estates, held for 500 years, or 99 years, or other term determinable on lives, &c. of the yearly value of 20 l. are declared qualified to serve on juries, and to be inserted in the freeholders book, &c. And leaseholders on leases where the rent amounts to 50 l. a year, are liable to serve as jurors in the county of *Middlesex:* and sheriffs of any county or city shall not impanel persons on any jury for the trial of capital offences, who would not be qualified to serve in civil causes. In *London*, jurors are to be housekeepers that have lands or goods of 100 l. value, who may be examined on oath, &c. *Ibid.*

By stat. 6 *Geo.* 2. *c.* 37. the acts of 3 *Geo.* 2. *c.* 25. 4 *Geo.* 2. *c.* 7. for the regulation of juries, are made perpetual: and the justices of the session or assizes, for the counties palatine of *Chester*, *Lancaster* and *Durham*, on motion in behalf of his majesty, or any prosecutor or defendant in any indictment or information, &c. may, if they think fit, order a jury to be struck before the officers of each court, in such manner as special juries in the courts at *Westminster*.

' The party who shall by virtue of 3 *Geo.*
' 2. *chap.* 25. or 6 *Geo.* 2. *chap.* 37. apply for
' a special jury, shall not only pay the fees for
' striking such jury, but shall pay all the ex-
' pences, occasioned by the trial of the cause by
' such special jury, and shall not have any other
' allowance for the same upon taxation of costs,
' than

' than such party would be intitled unto, in
' case the cause had been tried by a common
' jury; unless the judge before whom the cause
' is tried, immediately after the trial certify in
' open court under his hand upon the back of
' the record, that the same was a cause proper
' to be tried by a special jury.' *Stat.* 24 *Geo.* 2.
c. 18. *sect.* 1.

' No person who serves upon any jury ap-
' pointed by authority of the said acts, shall
' take for serving on such jury more than the
' sum which the judge who tries the issue thinks
' reasonable, not exceeding one pound one shil-
' ling, except in causes wherein a view is directed.'
Ibid. sect. 2.

' To prevent delays, where a peer is party by
' challenges to the array for want of a knight
' being returned on the panel, no challenge
' shall be taken to any panel of jurors, for want
' of a knight being returned in such panel, nor
' any array quashed by reason of any such chal-
' lenge.' *Ibid. sect.* 4.

' Every person duly impanelled and summon-
' ed to serve upon any jury for the trial of any
' cause to be tried in any court of record within
' the city of *London*, or in any other city or
' town corporate, liberties or franchises within
' *England*, who shall not appear and serve on
' such jury (after being called three times, and
' on proof on oath of the person so making de-
' fault, having been duly summoned) shall for-
' feit for every such default, such fine not ex-
' ceeding 40 *s*. nor less than 20 *s*. as the judge
' of the respective courts wherein such default
' is made shall impose, unless some just cause
' for such defaulter's absence be made appear

'by oath or affidavit to the satisfaction of the judge.' 29 *Geo.* 2. *chap.* 19. *sect.* 1.

The plaintiff or defendant in a cause may use their endeavours for a juryman to appear, but not one who is party to the suit. If a juror appears, and refuseth to be sworn, or to give any verdict; and if he endeavours to impose upon the court, or is guilty of any misbehaviour after departure from the bar, he may be fined, and attachment issue against him: and if a juryman withdraw from his fellows, or keep them from giving their verdict, without alledging any reasons for it, he shall be fined; not if he differ from them in judgment. *Moor* 882. *Dy* 53.

Jurors are not to meddle with any matters which are not in issue; they are fineable if unlawfully dealt with to give their verdict; though they are not fineable for giving a verdict contrary to the evidence, or against the direction of the court; for the law supposes the jury may have some other evidence, than what was given in court; and they may not only find things of their own knowledge, but they go according to their consciences: but in a civil cause, an attaint will lie against them, if they give a false or corrupt verdict. 3 *Leon.* 147. *Vaugh.* 144, 149, 153.

If the jury take upon them the knowledge of the law, and give a general verdict, it is good; but in cases of difficulty they may find the special matter, and leave it to the judges to determine what law is upon the fact. And after the evidence is given, the jury are to be kept together till they bring in their verdict, without meat, drink, fire or candle, otherwise than with leave of the court; and the court may

not

not give them leave to eat or drink, out of court: if jurors after sworn eat or drink, tho' the verdict be good, they are fineable; and if it be at the charge of either party, the verdict is void. When a juror is sworn, he may not go from the bar until the evidence is given, for any cause whatsoever, without leave of the court, and having a keeper with him: and when the jury are gone from the bar, a witness may not be called by them to repeat the same evidence he gave in court. *Co. Lit.* 227. *Dalif.* 10. *Cro. Jac.* 21. 2 *Lil. Abr.* 123, 127.

In capital cases a verdict must be actually given by jurors; and if the jury do not agree upon it, they may be carried round the circuits, and shall not be discharged till they do: in civil cases it is otherwise, as where there are non-suits, &c. and oftentimes in a civil case, when the evidence hath been heard, the parties doubting of the verdict do consent that the jury shall be drawn or discharged. Jurors by the common law are liable to no prosecution for giving their verdict except by way of attaint; in which case being found guilty they are punishable by loss of lands and goods, their houses to be rased, and their bodies cast into prison; and the party is to be restored to all that he lost by their false verdict; but this is altered by the statute 23 *H.* 8. *c.* 3. *Co. Lit.* 227, 154. 2 *Hawk. P. C.* 147.

If a juror takes any thing of either party, to give his verdict, he shall pay ten times as much as taken; or suffer a year's imprisonment: and a juryman guilty of bribery is disabled to be of any assises or juries, and to be imprisoned and ransomed at the king's will; also, being accused of this, may be tried presently by a jury then taken.

taken. But jurymen, where there is a full jury, and they try the cause, are to have their charges allowed them. *Stat.* 38 *Ed.* 3. *c.* 12. 5 *Ed.* 3. and 34 *Ed.* 3. 2 *Lil. Abr.* 125.

The *challenge* of jurors is in respect of partiality, or default of the sheriff, by reason of kindred, &c. to the plaintiff or defendant; or where one of the parties is of affinity to any juror; a juror hath given a verdict before in the same cause, or if he hath been an arbitrator therein, &c. And jurors may be challenged for defect of age, or want of estate; and being convicted of felony, perjury, &c. *Plowd.* 425. *Hob.* 294. 2 *Rol. Abr.* 636, &c. *Co. Lit.* 172.

2. A witness is one that proves and makes out any thing to a jury on a trial, by lawful testimony; and ought to be an indifferent person to each party, and not concerned in the cause: and evidence is used for some proof by men on oath, or by writings or records; it is called evidence, as thereby the point in issue is made evidence to the jury. *Co. Lit.* 283.

As to persons who may or may not be witnesses: an alien, * infidel, (not a *Jew* who may be sworn on the Old Testament) a person of *non-sane memory*, one interested in the suit, a † wife for or against her husband, (except in cases of treason) person convicted of felony, or perjury, &c. may not be witnesses in a cause: but kinsmen, though never so near, tenants, servants, masters, attornies for their clients, and all others that are not infamous, which want not understanding, or are not parties in interest, may be

* 2 Eq. Caf. Abr. 397. pl 15.   2 Stra. 1104. *feem* contrary.
† Wife's declaration where evidence against her husband. Stra. 527.

witnesses;

witnesses; though the credit of servants is left to the jury. A judge who is to try the person, may give testimony going off from the bench: and a juror may be a witness, as to his particular knowledge; but then it must be on examination in open court, not before his brother jurors. Members of corporations will not be generally admitted to be witnesses in a cause that concerns the corporation; though inhabitants that are not freemen will be allowed: a counsellor, attorney, or solicitor, is not to be examined as a witness against their clients, being obliged to keep their secrets; but of their own knowledge before retained, not as counsel, attorney, &c. that they may be examined. *Co. Lit.* 6. 4 *Inst.* 279. 2 *Rol. Abr.* 685. 2 *Hawk.* 432. 2 *Lev.* 231. *Ventr.* 197. 2 *Bac. Abr.* 266. &c.

In case divers persons are made parties to a suit, and some found not guilty, &c. they may be witnesses in the cause. A man that hath a legacy given by will, is not a good witness to the will; but he may release his legacy, and then he shall be a witness: a person who claims any benefit by a deed, may not prove that deed, in regard of his interest; and one any ways concerned in the same title of land in question, will not be permitted to be a witness in the suit depending. But in criminal cases, as of robbery on the highway, in action against the hundred; in rapes of women, or where a woman is married by force, &c. a man or woman may be a witness in their own cause: so in private notorious cheats, where no persons else can be witnesses, but those who suffer. 2 *Lil. Abr.* 704, 705. 2 *Rol.* 625. *Ventr.* 243. *Salk.* 286. 2 *Ld. Raym.* 1179.

If one by judgment hath stood in the pillory, or been whipt; for this infamy he shall not be allowed to give evidence, whilst the judgment is in force: but the record of conviction must be produced; and you may not ask the witness any question to accuse himself, though his credit and character in general, may be impeached by other witnesses so as not to make proof of particular crimes whereof he hath not been convicted. Although judgment of the pillory infers infamy at common law; by the civil and canon law it is no infamy, unless the cause for which the person was convicted was infamous: and it hath been adjudged, that 'tis not standing in the pillory, disables a person to give evidence; but the standing there upon a judgment for some infamous crime, as forgery, &c. If for a libel, a man may be a witness; and so in other cases, when he is pardoned. 3 *Inst.* 219. 3 *Lev.* 426, 427. 5 *Mod.* 16, 74. 3 *Nels. Abr.* 557.

The testimony of one single witness to a jury is sufficient; and one witness is enough for the king in all causes, except for treason, where there must be two witnesses: for the common law required not a certain number of witnesses; but they are required by statute in some cases. And if a witness, served with process, refused to appear and give evidence in a criminal cause, the court may put off the trial, and grant * attachment against him: in a civil cause, if any witness refuse to appear, being tendered reasonable charges, and having no lawful excuse, action of the case may be brought, whereupon 10 *l.* damages, and other recompence to the

* *Stra.* 510. 2 *Stra.* 810. 2 Ld. Raym. 1378. Barnard. K. B 45. 2 *Stra.* 1054.

party, shall be recovered. And a feme covert not appearing, action lies against the husband and her. *3 Inst.* 26. *Leon.* 112. *Stat.* 5 *Eliz. c.* 9. perpetuated by 29 *Eliz. c.* 5. & 21 *Jac. c.* 28. *f.* 8.

Evidence by writings and records is where acts of parliament, statutes, judgments, fines and recoveries, proceedings of courts and deeds, &c. are admitted as evidence in a cause.

General acts of parliament may be given in evidence, upon the statute book, and need not be pleaded; but where there is a private act, a copy of it must be examined by the records of parliament, and it ought to be pleaded: records and inrolments prove themselves; and a copy of a record sworn to may be allowed as evidence: the part indented of a fine is the usual evidence that there is such a fine; tho' it is said, the fine must be shewed, with the proclamations under seal. A record of an inferior court hath been rejected in evidence; and the party put to prove what was done: an ancient deed proves itself, possession having gone accordingly; but later deeds are to be proved by witnesses; and if they are dead, their hand-writing must be proved. Although a seal is broken off, a deed may be evidence; but it cannot be proved by a counterpart or copy, when the original is in being, and may be had; if it be burnt, &c. the judges may allow proof by witnesses, that there was such a deed, and this be given in evidence. *Co. Lit.* 117, 262. 10 *Rep.* 92. 2 *Rol. Abr.* 574. 2 *Inst.* 118. *Lev.* 25.

A writing allowed to be read, to prove one part of an evidence, may be read to prove any other part of the evidence given to a jury, and if a copy is permitted, it must be the intire copy of the whole, that the court may judge of it.

The probate of a will is admitted as evidence for personal estate; but if title of land is made under the will, it must be shewn, not a copy of it, or the probate. If the will is proved in Chancery, copies of the proceedings there will be evidence. Of things done in a foreign country, the testimony of a publick notary is good evidence. *Lil. Abr.* 548. 2 *Rol.* 678. 6 *Rep.* 57.

Depositions of witnesses in Chancery, between the same parties, may be evidence at law, 2 *Bac. Abr.* 314. but in a court of Common law, a decree in Chancery is no evidence: the depositions before a coronor have been admitted as an evidence, the witnesses being dead; depositions in the ecclesiastical court cannot be given in evidence, tho' a sentence may in a cause of tithes, &c. church-books are not allowed as evidence; yet some say they may: a shop book is evidence, but not after a year for goods sold, &c. unless it be in buying and selling, between one tradesman and another. An almanack, wherein the father had writ the nativity of his son, was held evidence to prove his son's non-age; and an inscription on a grave-stone, had been judged good to make a pedigree for the heir. *Trials per pais* 167, 207, 235. *Lev.* 180. 7 *Jac.* c. 12. *T. Raym.* 84. 5 *Mod.* 10.

Matter of fact shall be given in evidence at a trial; in debt, a release may be given in evidence, on *nil debet*; and entry and expulsion, in debt for rent, &c. On the general issue, fraud may be given in evidence: but many things are to be pleaded; and cannot be given in evidence, upon Not guilty. By statute, justices of peace, constables, &c. may plead the general issue, and yet give the special matter in evidence in their justification. *Vaugh.* 443, 147. 4 *Mod.* 18.

Witnesses, Trials.

Trials *per pais* 404. Stat. *Jac. c.* 5. (perpetuated by 21 *Jac. c.* 12.) 21 *Jac. c.* 12.

Form of a writ of *subpœna* for witnesses to testify.

GEORGE *the Third, by the grace of God, king of* Great Britain, *&c. To* T. F. M. H. *and* N. J. *We command you, and every of you, firmly enjoining you, that, laying aside all and all manner of businesses and excuses whatsoever, you and every of you be before our faithful and well beloved* William *Earl* Mansfield, *our chief justice appointed to hold pleas in our court before us, on the ——— day of,* &c. *next following, at* Guildhall, London, *&c. to testify all and singular those things, which you or either of you shall know, in a certain cause now depending and undetermined in our court before us, between* A. B. *plaintiff and* C. D. *defendant, in a plea of debt,* &c. *and on that day to be tried by a jury of the county; and this you and every of you are by no means to omit, under the penalty of one hundred pounds.* Witness, *&c.*

If it be at the *assizes*, then it must be; *that you and every of you be in your proper persons before our justices of the* assizes *appointed to be held in the county of* W. *on the —— day of,* &c. *next following, at,* &c. *in the county aforesaid, to testify,* &c.

A *subpœna* ticket for a witness to appear.

Mr. M. H.

BY *virtue of a writ of* subpœna *to you and others directed, and herewith shewn unto you, you are personally to be and appear before* William *Earl* Mansfield, *chief justice,* &c. *Or before his majesty's justices of assize, on the —— day of,* &c. *next, being* &c. *at ten of the clock in the forenoon*

*of the same day, at the court then to be holden at,
&c. in the county of* W. *to testify the truth, according to your knowledge, in a certain cause now depending, and then and there to be tried between* A. B. *plaintiff, and* C. D. *defendant, in a plea of,* &c. *on the part of the plaintiff; and hereof you are not to fail, on pain of one hundred pounds. Dated the—day of,* &c. *in the—year of the reign of the lord* George, *&c. and in the year of our Lord* 17—.

The head *trial*, in pursuance of my present method, I shall divide into,

1. Things to be known preparatory thereto.
2. The form of trial in the courts of *Westminster*.
3. How trials are managed at the assizes.
4. New trials and executions, *&c.*

1. Trial, in its common definition, is the examination of a cause civil or criminal, before a judge, who has jurisdiction to try it according to the laws of the land. And the most general rule has been, that every trial shall be out of that town, precinct, *&c.* within which the matter of fact triable is alledged, or the nearest thereunto, for the better cognizance of the fact committed. *Co. Lit.* 125

All trials for murder must be had in the county where the fact was done: but if the stroke is in one county, and the death in another, the indictment may be found by the jury of the county where the party died; and there the matter be tried, as well as if the stroke had been in the same county: and when an indictment is found against a person in the proper county, it may be heard

Witnesses, Trials.

heard and determined in any other county by special commission, &c. In a civil case, if a foreign issue which is local should happen, it may be tried where the action is laid; and for that purpose the plaintiff may enter a suggestion on the roll, that such a place in such a county is next adjacent; and it shall be tried in the court of *B. R.* by a jury from that place, according to the laws of that county, which may be given in evidence. 5 *Inst.* 27. *Cro. Car.* 247. 5 & 6 *Ed.* 6. 2 *Salk.* 651.

Where civil causes are grown to issue, if they are to be tried in *London* or *Middlesex*, and the defendant lives not forty miles from *London*, in that case eight days notice of trial must be given the defendant; and if he live that distance from *London*, or further off, he must have fourteen days notice from the plaintiff, before he try his cause. But at the *assizes* eight days notice of trial is good, let the defendant live where he will; and if the defendant go to trial without sufficient notice given him, the trial is not binding. A defendant, on due notice given, must go to trial, or judgment will pass against him by default: and where the plaintiff will not try his cause in such time as he ought to do, by the rules of the court; the defendant may give a rule and notice for trying the cause by *proviso*, and so discharge himself of the action. 2 *Lil. Abr.* 613. *Stat.* 23 *Hen.* 8. *c.* 15.

In case the court sees that one of the parties is surprised, through some casualty, without any fault of his own, they may at their discretion put off the trial to another time, until such party is better prepared: also if a defendant is not ready to try his cause, on petition; and affidavit of the reasons, the judge will order it to be stayed till

Of Courts, Juries,

till another day the same assizes; and in *London* until the next term, on payment of costs. A cause is to be entered in the judge's book two days before the time of trial, or it shall not be set down to be try'd that term; and if the issue is not joined between the plaintiff and defendant, which consists of an affirmative on the one part and a denial of the charge on the other part, &c. it will not be a good trial. 2 *Lil. Abr.* 609.

2. To proceed to trial in the courts at *Westminster*, after the bill or writ issued and executed against the defendant, and appearance thereupon made by him, the declaration is to be drawn and delivered with an imparlance to the defendant's attorney; and it must be entered that term on the prothonotary's roll, and docquetted: the term following the plaintiff's attorney gives a rule with the secondary for the defendant to plead by such a day, or the plaintiff to have judgment; and the defendant having pleaded to the plaintiff's action and declaration, according to the case, so that the parties are at issue, the attorney for the plaintiff makes a copy of the issue, and gives it to the defendant's attorney, with notice of trial; in order to which the *venire facias* must be made out and returned by the sheriff, and after is sued forth the *habeas corpora* to bring in the jury, and the record is made up; whereupon a trial is had, and a verdict being brought in by the jury, judgment is given accordingly, &c.

But if the defendant do not plead, but lets it go by default, then, upon entering judgment, a writ of inquiry of damages is to be awarded, returnable the next term, of the execution, whereof notice is to be given the defendant's attorney; which being executed, with the damages inserted in a schedule annexed to the writ, and returned by the sheriff to the prothonotary's office, &c. and on a rule being given upon it, he taxes costs: then it is carried to the clerk of the judgments, and on giving him the number roll and term that the judgment was entered, he will make out a writ of execution, either a *capias ad satisfaciendum*, or *fieri facias*, for the damages and costs.

3. In the proceedings to trial at the *assises*, when any cause comes on, a *distringas* of the jury is to be first returned by the sheriff, and then the record must be delivered to the judge's marshal; upon which, the counsel being instructed with their briefs, &c. and all parties ready, the marshal gives the record to the judge, and the cryer calls over the names of the jury, and when they are sworn, being first elected by ballot, they are bid to stand together, and hear their charge; which done, the counsel on both sides open the case, first of the side of the plaintiff, as the proof lies on him, and looking over their *Breviates*, argue the matter in contest, producing the witnesses to prove what they alledge; and then the judge sums up the evidence, and gives it in charge to the jury, to do impartially therein; at which time the clerk of assise, or his associate, files the writ, panel and record together, and makes a copy of the jury's names, and of the issue they are to try, which he delivers to the jury; and a bailiff being sworn to keep them without meat, drink, &c. they are then kept together till they all agree on the verdict.

The jury, when they are agreed, return to give in their verdict, and the plaintiff is then called; and if he do not appear, a nonsuit shall be be recorded, &c. but if he appears, the clerk asks the jury who they find for, and what costs and damages, and so enters it on the back of the panel, and repeats it to the jury, which finishes the trial: and after that is over, the associate delivers to the plaintiff's attorney the record with the *distringas*, and the names of the jury annexed, on the back of which he writes the substance of the verdict; then upon the back of the record is ingrossed the *postea* (that afterwards the plaintiff and defendant came before such a judge, and the jury was elected and sworn, &c. and found such verdict and costs, &c.) and after it is to be carried to the clerk of the *postea's* to be marked, and then 'tis delivered to the clerk of the rules, and he makes a four days rule for judgment; which rule being out, if judgment be not arrested, the record is to be stamped with a 2 s. 6 d. stamp on the back, and carried to the master of the office, who will tax further costs, when the judgment is fit to be entered, &c.

And in trials at the assises, the record and *distringas* are generally kept by the associate till the next term, and he indorses the *postea*, receiving his fee for it at the trial; and then he is to be called upon for the same, and you proceed to have it marked, take out a rule, and sign judgment, as before is directed, and the judgment must be entered on a roll: also if a trial is had the last day of term, or at the sittings after, or the assises, judgment cannot be given thereupon until the first day of the next term; and judgment being entered, execution is awarded, and writs of *capias ad satisfaciendum*, &c.

4. There

4. There may be new trials granted, in several cases; as where sufficient notice was not given the defendant of the former trial; if excessive damages are assessed by the jury; or a verdict is given against evidence; and when there was any fraud, &c. But generally a new trial shall not be had for too small damages, except action of covenant is brought for a sum certain, and the jury give damages under that, &c. and it should not be granted for want of any evidence at a former trial, that the party might then have produced, &c. 2 *Salk.* 647.

Trials at bar are ordained by statute, where causes require great examination, and the title in question is difficult or intricate, for the better satisfaction of the parties concerned; and officers of the court, and barristers at law may insist upon a trial at bar, after which no new trial will be permitted. After a motion in arrest of judgment, the party shall not move for a new trial; but after motion for new trial, he may move in arrest of judgment. *Stat. Westm.* 2. 13 *Ed.* 1. 2 *Lil. Abr.* 609. 2 *Salk.* 648.

The causes of arrest of judgment are, Want of notice of trial; where the record differs from the deed pleaded; for any material defect in pleading; where persons are misnamed; the declaration doth not lay the thing with certainty, &c. and here all matters of fact are proved by proper affidavits. *Comp. Attorn.* 329, &c.

M   Form

Form of the record of an issue and trial of a cause in K. B.

PLEAS before the lord the king at *Westminster*, of *Hilary* term in the 17th year of the reign of our sovereign lord *George* the Third, king of *Great Britain, &c. Roll*

Berks, to wit.
BE it remembered, that heretofore, that is to say, in, &c. *Term last past, before the lord the king at* Westminster, *came* A. B. *by, &c. his attorney, and brought here into the court of the said lord the now king, then there held, his certain bill against* C. D. *in the custody of the marshal, &c. of a plea of debt, and there are pledges of prosecuting, to wit,* John Doe, *and* Richard Roe; *which said bill follows in these words; that is to say:* Berks, to wit, A. B. *complains of* C. D. *otherwise called* C. D. *of the parish of* W. *in the county aforesaid, gentleman, being in the custody of the marshal of the marshalsea of our sovereign lord the king, being before the king himself, of a plea that he render to the said* A. *thirty pounds, of lawful money of* Great Britain, *which he owes to him, and unjustly detains; for that whereas the said* C. *the—day of, &c. in the first year of the reign of the lord* George *the Third, now king of* Great Britain, *&c. at* W. *aforesaid, in the county aforesaid, by his writing obligatory, sealed with the seal of the the said* C. *and now here shewn to the court of the said lord the king, the date whereof is the same day and year above, acknowledged himself to be held and firmly bound to the said* A. *in the aforesaid thirty pounds, to be paid to the said* A. *when he should afterwards be thereunto required: yet the said*

said C. *altho' he hath been often required to pay the same, hath not paid to the said* A. *the said thirty pounds, or any part thereof, but hitherto hath refused, and still doth refuse, to pay it to him; to the damage of the said* A. &c. *and therefore he brings his suit,* &c. *(and hath good proof of the premisses, when the court will consider thereof.)*

And now at this day, to wit, on the—*day,* &c. *next after,* &c. *in this same term, to which day the said* C. *hath licence to imparl, and then to answer, came before the lord the king at* Westminster, *as well the said* A. *by his attorney aforesaid, as the said* C. *by,* &c. *his attorney; and the said* C. *defends the force, and injury, when,* &c. *and saith, that he paid to the said* A. *upon the* — *day of,* &c. *in the year,* &c. *the aforesaid thirty pounds, which he on the same day ought to pay, according to the form and effect of the aforesaid bond or writing obligatory, to wit, at* W. *aforesaid; and this he is ready to verify,* &c. *and the said* A. *saith, that he ought not to be barred, because he saith, that the said* C. *hath not paid to him the aforesaid thirty pounds, as the said* C. *hath above alledged in his plea; and this he prays may be inquired of by the country; and the said* C. *doth likewise,* &c. *Therefore let there come a jury before the lord our king at* Westminster, *on Monday next after,* &c. *to try this issue between the said parties, and who are in no wise a-kin either to the said* A. *the plaintiff, or to the said* C. *to recognize and make a jury of the country between the said parties; because as well the said* A. *as the said* C. *(between whom the matter is in variance) have thereof submitted themselves to the jury: the same day is given to the said parties here,* &c.

And afterwards the process between the parties aforesaid was continued of the plea aforesaid; and the jurors aforesaid impanelled thereupon are respited before our said lord the king at Westminster until Wednesday next after, &c. then next following, unless the justices of the lord the king, assigned to hold the assises in the county aforesaid, shall on Tuesday the — day of, &c. at R. in the county aforesaid, according to the form of the statute in that case made and provided, first come for default of the jurors; therefore let the sheriff have their bodies, &c. The same day is given to the parties aforesaid there, &c. and be it known, that the writ of the said lord the king thereof, on the — day of, &c. (the return of the venire) in the same term, before the lord the king at Westminster, was delivered of record to the deputy sheriff of the county aforesaid, in due form of law to be executed, &c.

Afterwards, to wit, on the day and at the place within contained, before W. lord M. chief justice of the lord the king of his court of King's Bench, and, &c. to him associated, and Sir J. Y. knight, one of the justices of the said lord the king of his said court of K. B. appointed to hold the assises in the county of B. by virtue of the writ of the lord the king, &c. according to the form of the statute, came as well the within named A. B. as the within written C. D. by their said attornies within mentioned; and the jurors of the jury, being summoned and ballotted, according to the form of the statute in such case lately made and provided, and tried and sworn to declare the truth of what is within contained, say upon their oath, that the within written C. D. on the — day of, &c. after the, &c. did not pay to the said A. B. the within mentioned sum of thirty pounds, which on the same day he ought to have paid pursuant to the bond or writing obligatory within specified, as the said C. hath within for that purpose alledged in his plea; and

they

they assess the damages of the said A. *by reason thereof, besides his costs and charges by him laid out in prosecuting this cause, to twelve pence, and for his expences and costs twenty shillings,* &c. *Therefore it is considered, that the said* A. *do recover against the said* C. *his said debt, and the damages assessed by the jury aforesaid, by reason of detaining the same, and also thirteen pounds for his expences and costs awarded by this court to the said* A. *with his consent, by way of increase; which said damages, expences and costs, amount in the whole to fourteen pounds and one shilling; and the said* C. *is in mercy,* &c.

After trials, *execution* follows, for obtaining possession of the thing recovered by judgment of law. And execution is either in personal, real or mixed action: in personal actions it may be three ways, viz. by *capias ad satisfaciendum* against the body; *fieri facias* against the goods, or *elegit* against the lands, &c. And in real and mixed actions, the writs of execution are *habere fac. seisinam*, to put the party in possession of freehold land recovered; and *habere fac. possessionem* to put him in possession of his term, &c. Co. Lit. 289. 5 Rep. 86.

When a judgment is signed, execution may be taken out immediately upon it; but if it be not issued within a year and a day after, where there is no fault in the defendant, there must be a *scire facias* to revive the judgment: and if the plaintiff proceed not on the *Sci. fa.* he may upon the judgment bring an action of debt, &c. In action where special bail hath been given, the plaintiff may have execution against the defendant, or prosecute his bail: tho' if you first take out a *cap. ad satisfaciend.* you are debarred

barred from taking out any other writ of execution. *Co. Lit.* 290. 2 *Inst.* 471. 395.

If a person in execution dies, a new execution may issue against his lands, *&c.* as if he had never been taken in execution, by statute: and writs of execution bind the property of goods from the time of delivery of the writ to the sheriff, *&c.* But land is bound from the day of the judgment. Sheriffs may deliver in execution all lands, whereof others shall be seised in trust for him against whom the execution is had on a statute, judgment, *&c.* though, if there are chattels sufficient, a sheriff ought not to take the land. *Stat.* 21 *Jac. c.* 24. perpetuated by 1 *Jac.* 2. *c.* 17. *s.* 5. 29 *Car.* 2. *c.* 3. *Lil. Abr.* 565.

One may not generally be delivered out of prison when there in execution, but by writ of *supersedeas*: and if a man committed to prison, for any misdemeanor, is there taken in execution, he shall not be set at large. The *capias ad satisfaciendum* lies not against a peer of the realm; nor against executors or administrators except on a *devastavit, &c. T. Raym.* 58. *Cro. Jac.* 143.

Form of a writ of *capias ad satisfaciendum.*

GEORGE *the Third,* &c. *To the sheriff of* B. *greeting. We command you, that you take* C. D. *if he shall be found in your bailiwick, and safely keep him, so that you have his body before us at* Westminster *on* Monday *next after,* &c. (*the day of the return*) *to make satisfaction to* A. B. *of a debt of thirty pounds, which the said* A. *lately recovered in our court before us, and also,* &c. *which in the same court were awarded to the said* A. *for his damages that he sustained, as well by occasion of the detaining the said debt, as for his costs and charges*

charges laid out by him about his suit in that behalf; whereof the said C. *is convicted, as appears to us of record: and have you then there this writ. Witness,* &c.

The writ *fieri facias* lieth for debt or damages, as well against executors or administrators, as any others, to be levied of the testator's goods, &c. But goods of a stranger in the possession of the defendant shall not be subject to the execution; for the sheriff at his peril must take notice whose they are: and on this writ, a sheriff cannot break open doors, to take goods. The sheriff is to sell the goods and chattels of the defendant, and after the debt is levied, is debtor to the plaintiff: and the sale of the sheriff shall take effect, tho' the judgment is afterwards reversed; but the defendant shall be restored to the value. *Dalt. Sher.* 60. *Rol Abr.* 892. 8 *Rep.* 96.

There may be a *testatum fieri fac.* into another county, if the defendant hath not goods enough in the county where the action is laid to satisfy the execution; and if all the money be not levied on this writ, there may be a second writ of execution, on return of the first, reciting the same. 2 *Salk.* 589. *Salk.* 318.

A sheriff having taken goods, and levied the money by virtue of a *fieri facias*, ought to bring it into court, and not to pay it to the plaintiff. *Godb.* 147. *pl.* 188. in 2 *Show.* 87. *pl.* 78. the contrary is held.

Form of a writ of *fieri facias*.

GEORGE *the Third,* &c. *To the sheriff of* S. *greeting. We command you, that you cause to be made of the goods and chattels of* C. D. *in your bailiwick, fifty pounds, which* A. B. *lately in our court before us at* Westminster, *recovered against him for a debt, and also, &c. which were adjudged to the said* A. *in the same court before us, for his damages which he sustained, occasioned as well by the detaining of his said debt, as for his expences and costs laid out by him in and about his suit in that behalf, whereof the said* C. *is convicted, as appears to us of record; and have you the said money before us at* Westminster *on* Monday *next, &c, to render to the said* A. *his debt and damages aforesaid; and have you there at the same time this writ.* Witness W. *lord* M. *at* Westminster *the —— day, &c.*

The writ *elegit* commands the sheriff to deliver to the person recovering, all the goods and chattels of the defendant, (beasts of the plough excepted,) and half of his lands, &c. to be held until the whole debt and damages are satisfied: and it is done by a jury, summoned by the sheriff to require what land the defendant had, at the time of the judgment. This writ may be sued after a *fieri facias* returned *nulla bona, &c.* And if tenant by *elegit* be put out of possession before satisfaction received, he may have action of trespass, or re-enter, and hold over till satisfied; after which, the defendant may enter, and if more be levied than the debt, *&c.* shall have damages. *F. N. B.* 267. *Hib.* 57. *Cro. Eliz.* 656. 4 *Rep.* 67.

If lands are once taken in execution, on an *elegit,* and the writ is returned and filed, the plaintiff shall have no other execution: where the defendant hath lands in more counties than one, and the plaintiff awards *elegit* to one county, and extends the lands thereupon; if he then files it, he cannot sue out an *elegit* into the other counties: but immediately after entry of the judgment, he may award as many *elegits* into as many counties as he thinks fit, and execute all, to any of them. *Lev.* 92. *Cro. Jac.* 246.

The plaintiff, at the return of an *elegit*, prays a new *elegit*; he shall have it, if he hath not accepted of the first: so if all the lands extended are evicted by better title, &c. *Cro. Eliz.* 310. 4 *Rep.* 66. *Stat. Westm.* 2. c. 18.

Form of the writ of *elegit*.

GEORGE the Third, &c. To the sheriff of W. greeting. *Whereas* A. B. *lately in our court before us at* Westminster, *by bill, without our writ, and by a judgment of the same court hath recovered against* C. D. *of, &c. seventy-five pounds for a debt, and also forty shillings for his damages, which he hath sustained, as well by occasion of the detaining the said debt, as for his expences and costs laid out by him about his suit in that behalf, whereof the said* C. *is convicted, as appears to us of record; and afterwards the said* A. *came into our court before us, and hath elected to be delivered to him all the goods and chattels of the said* C. *except the oxen and beasts of the plough; and likewise a moiety of all and singular the lands and tenements of the said* C. *in your bailiwick, according to the form of the statute in that case made and provided, until the debt and damages aforesaid should be thereof fully levied: Therefore we command you, that to the aforesaid* A. *all the goods and chattels of the said* C. *in your bailiwick, besides the oxen and beasts of the plough, and likewise the moiety of all the lands and tenements of the said* C. *in your bailiwick, whereof the said* C. *the day of, &c. in the eighth year of our reign on which day the judgment aforesaid was obtained, or at any time afterwards he was seis'd, to*

the

the said A. you cause to be delivered without delay, by a reasonable price and extent; To hold the said goods and chattels to him as his own proper goods and chattels, and also to hold the said moiety of the lands and tenements aforesaid, as his freehold, to him and his assigns, according to the form of the statute aforesaid, until the debt and damages aforesaid shall be thereof levied; and how and in what manner this writ you shall have executed, make certainly known to us at Westminster, *on* Wednesday *next after,* &c. *under your seal, and the seals of those by whose oaths you shall make that extent and appraisement; and have you then there this writ. Witness,* &c.

To writs of execution the defendant cannot plead; but he may have *audita querela* for any matter since the judgment, to discharge him of the execution; upon which the justices shall hear the complaint, and do right. And the writ *audita querela* is usually where judgment is given against a man, &c. and his body in execution, upon suggestion of just cause why execution should not be granted; as a release, &c. This writ lies not after judgment upon a matter which the party might have pleaded before; and 'tis granted where no other remedy can be had, when persons are unreasonably charged, &c. *Co. Lit.* 290. 2 *Inst.* 396.

If a debt is released after verdict, or after judgment or execution, and it is so that the defendant hath not a day in court to plead it; there he must be relieved by *audita querela*: and on allowance of the *audita querela*, bail shall be given; by which the party is in custody of the law; and if he make not out his complaint, he must render his body in execution again, or pay the debt for which he is in execution,

Witnesses, Trials.

cution, or else his bail must pay it. 36 *H*. 6. 24. *Cro. Jac.* 645.

Where after judgment against bail to an action, the judgment against the principal is reversed, or the money paid by the principal, the bail may have *audita querela*. 8 Rep. 143.

Form of a writ of *audita querela*.

GEORGE *the Third*, &c. *To our justices assigned to hold pleas before us, greeting. We having received information, by the grievous complaint of* C. D. *that whereas* A. B. *in* Trinity *term last obtained a judgment against the said* C. &c. *and since that hath released,* &c. *but nevertheless the said* A. *doth threaten to levy by execution,* &c. *to the damage of the said* C. &c. *whereof the said* C. *hath besought us to provide him relief; and being unwilling that the said* C. *should be any ways injured, and desirous that what is right and just should be done in this case, we command you, that in order to hear the complaint of the said* C. *you call before you the aforesaid parties, and such others as it shall seem meet to you to convene; and having heard the aforesaid parties, and their several reasons, you cause to be done full and speedy justice to the said parties, which of right, and according to the laws and customs of our kingdom, you shall see ought to be done. Witness,* &c.

By *statute*, persons charged in execution for any sum not exceeding 100*l*. in any gaol or prison, being minded to deliver up all their effects to their creditors towards satisfaction of their debts, may exhibit a petition to the court from whence the process issued, certifying the cause of their imprisonment, and an account of their estate, &c. and thereupon the court is by order

order or rule to cause the prisoner to be brought up, and the creditors to be summoned to appear at a day appointed, when the court shall in a summary way examine the matter, and hear what shall be alledged on both sides, for or against the discharge of such prisoner, tendering to the prisoner on oath, that the account delivered in is a full and true account of all his estate, (except wearing apparel and bedding, &c. not exceeding 10 *l*. value;) and if thereupon the creditors are satisfied, the court may order the lands, goods and effects contained in the said account to be assigned to the creditors, by indorsement on the back of the petition signed by the prisoner; and upon such assignment executed, the prisoner shall be discharged out of prison, without paying any fee, by order of court: but in case the creditors shall not be satisfied with the oath, the court shall remand the prisoner, and order him and his creditors to appear at another day; and then if the creditors cannot discover any estate or effects of the prisoner omitted, &c. the court shall immediately cause the prisoner to be discharged, unless any creditor insists upon his being detained, and agree to give him 2 *s*. 4 *d*. per week, and on failure of any payment, he shall be discharged. 32 *Geo*. 2. c. 28.

The person so discharged out of prison shall never after be arrested for the same debt; but the judgment against him is to stand in force, and execution may be taken out thereon against his lands or goods, &c. afterwards: and if any prisoner shall be convicted of perjury in his oath, he shall suffer the pains inflicted for such offences, and may be retaken, and charged again in execution. *Stat. ibid.*

And prisoners in execution as aforesaid, in any prison (except in *London* and *Westminster*)

before

before they petition the court to be discharged, &c. are to give notice to their creditors at whose suit they were charged, that they design to petition, with a true copy of the account of their whole estates intended to be delivered in to the court, &c. and then on such petition, the prisoner shall have a rule of court to be brought to the next assises for the county; and the creditors shall be summoned to appear there thirty days before, and at the assises the judges on examination shall determine the matter, and give judgment and relief, &c. The charge of carrying the prisoners to the assises not to be above 12 *d.* a mile, to be paid out of their effects, or, if they have none, out of the county stock. 32 *Geo.* 2. *c.* 28.

Writs of error *to reverse and set aside judgments and executions.*

A Writ of error issues out of Chancery, and lies where any one is grieved by the proceedings and judgment in any court of record; it is returnable in *B. R.* and if upon the transcript of the record sent into that court, it appears there is error in the process, or in the giving of judgment, then 'tis reversed: but if there appear to be none, then is the judgment affirmed with double costs.

On judgments given in the *King's Bench*, where the suit is by bill, writ of error lies out of the Chancery returnable in the *Exchequer-chamber*, before the judges of *C. B.* and barons of the Exchequer, &c. But if the suit is by original writ, or where the king is party, or if it be after judgment affirmed in the *Exchequer-chamber*, writ of error lies only in *parliament:* to reverse a judgment

ment in the *Common Pleas*, the writ is to be returned in *B. R.* and error is not to be brought in parliament; except a judgment of that court is affirmed, *&c.* in the King's Bench: and erroneous judgment given in the *Exchequer* is to be examined and corrected by the lord chancellor, *&c.* and some of the justices. *Stat.* 27 *Eliz. c.* 8. 31 *Eliz.* 1. 31 *Ed.* 3. *c.* 12.

When a writ of error is brought the party is in the time appointed by the rule to certify the record; and he must cause the roll where the judgment is entered to be marked with the word *error* in the margin, whereby the other party may take notice of it; and the plaintiff's attorney may take out execution upon the judgment, if a *supersedeas* be not taken forth, allowed with the sheriff of the county: and in all cases after verdict, in actions of debt on bond, for the payment of money, or upon any contract, *&c.* the person that brings writ of error must put in good bail, to prosecute his writ with effect; and to pay the debt and damages, and also all costs and damages for delaying of execution, if judgment be affirmed. For if bail be not put in, the writ of error is no *supersedeas* to the execution; but the writ is in being, until a *nolle prosequi* entered, or judgment affirmed, *&c.* 3 *Jac. c.* 8. made perpetual by 3 *Car. c.* 4. 6 *Rep.* 26.

Any person damnified by error in a record may bring a writ of error to reverse it; and the chief justice only, or the eldest judge, ought to allow a writ of error: the errors of a judgment are to be assigned upon the record, to appear to the court; and if they are not assigned in the term, the writ of error shall abate. A judgment cannot be reversed in part, and stand

good

good for other part; but if there be error in awarding execution, the execution only, and not the judgment, shall be reversed: and if a judgment is reversed by writ of error, the plaintiff may bring a new action for the same cause. *Cro. Jac.* 534. *Yelv.* 112. *Hob.* 90.

All writs of error, wherein there shall be any variance from the original record, or other defect, may be amended by the court; and where any verdict hath been given, in any action in the courts at *Westminster*, or other court of record, the judgment thereon shall not be stayed or reversed for any defect or fault in form, or substance, in any bill, writ, &c. or for variance in such writs from the declaration or other proceedings. 5 *Geo. c.* 13.

2 Ld. Raym. 1587.
2 Stra. 902.
Barnard. K.B. 462.

Form of a *writ of error* in *K. B.*

GEORGE *the Third,* &c. *To our beloved and faithful,* &c. *greeting. Because in the record and process, and also in giving judgment of the plea, which was in our court before you and your companions, our justices of the bench, by our writ between* A. B. *and* C. D. *of a certain trespass on the case, done to the damage of the said* A. 100 l. *as 'tis said, error manifest hath intervened to the great damage of him the said* C. D. *as by his complaint we are informed; we, willing that the error, if there be any, should be corrected in due manner, and that full and speedy justice be done to the parties aforesaid in this behalf, command you, that if judgment be thereupon given, then that record and process of the plea aforesaid, with all things concerning it, to us under your seal, distinctly and openly you send, and this writ; so that those we may have the day,* &c. *to the end*

end that looking into the record and process aforesaid further, we may cause to be done thereupon for correcting that error, what of right, and according to the laws of our kingdom, ought to be done therein. Witness, &c.

Of Estates in Lands and Goods, and how acquired; Ancestors, Heirs, Executors and Administrators.

ESTATE is that title or interest which a man hath in lands, tenements, or other things. And estates are real, of lands and tenements; or personal, of goods and chattels; otherwise distinguished into freeholds, that descend to the heir, and chattels which go to the executors: also some estates are made by words, and others implied by law; and the word *estate* in deeds and grants generally comprehends the whole in which the party hath an interest or property, and will pass the same.

The estates and lands we have in this kingdom, are obtained and held in divers manners:

1. By discent and right of blood.
2. Conveyance, or grant from one man to another.
3. Ancient tenures and holdings of lands.

Discent is where a man hath land or other estate of inheritance in fee-simple, and dieth without making any disposition thereof, but leaveth it to go (as the law calleth it) to the heir: it is a means whereby lands or tenements are

are derived to a man, as heir and by right of blood, from an ancestor; and this is the worthiest means whereby lands can be acquired. *Co. Lit.* 13, 257.

In difcents, the next and moft worthy of blood shall inherit; as the male and all defcendants from him, before the females; and the elder brother and his pofterity, before any younger brother, &c. A fifter of the whole blood shall be preferred before the younger brother of the half blood: but fuch younger brother may be heir to his father or uncle; though not to a brother, for want of the whole blood. And a perfon to have land in fee-fimple, by difcent, muft be heir of the whole blood: by which rule, where lands defcend to the fon from the father, and he enters and dies feifed, without iffue, this land shall go to the heirs of the part of the father; and if there be none fuch, it shall efcheat. *Co. Lit.* 14. 3 *Rep.* 4.

And difcent is lineal, or collateral; lineal is downwards in a right line, from grandfather to father, father to fon, &c. and the lineal heirs shall firft inherit: collateral is a difcent which springeth out of the fide of the whole blood; as the grandfather's brother, father's brother, and fo downwards: fo that if a man purchafe lands in fee-fimple, and dies without iffue, for default of the right line, he who is next of kin in the collateral line of the whole blood, shall have the land, by difcent as heir to him. In cafe of difcents, when land defcends on the part of the father, the heirs of the mother shall not inherit; and where lands defcend on the part of the mother, the heirs of the father shall not inherit: 'tis otherwife in cafe of purchafe, where a fon purchafes lands, and dies without leaving iffue; if there be no heirs on the part of the father, those on the mother's side shall inherit the lands. 1 *Inst.* 10, 11, 13. 1 *Vent.* 415.

Inheritances may lineally descend, but not ascend; and in the right line, children shall inherit their ancestors without limitation; but the ancestors may not take from the children, for the father can never come to the lands which his son hath purchased by lineal ascent; though he may by collateral ascent, where the land of the son comes to his uncle, and then to his father: in the collateral line, the uncle inherits the nephew, and the nephew the uncle. The elder brother of the whole blood shall have land by discent, that is purchased by a middle or younger brother, if they die without issue: and when there is no brother or sister, the uncle shall have it as heir; but it may afterwards descend to the father, as heir to the uncle; and if after the discent to the uncle, the father hath issue another son or daughter, that issue shall enter upon the uncle, and hold the estate. *Co. Lit.* 11. 3 *Rep.* 40. *Vaugh.* 244.

There is a difference between discents from father and mother to their children, and between brothers and sisters; a son or daughter need be only of the blood either of father or mother, which hath the inheritance: but the brothers and sisters must be of the same father and mother, to inherit one another. From this it is, that if a man hath issue two sons by divers venters, the younger brother of the half blood shall not have the land purchased by the elder brother, on his dying without issue; but the elder brother's uncle or next cousin. If a man hath two wives, and by one wife he has a son and a daughter, and a son by the other, and then dies seised of land in fee-simple; here, if the elder son die without any issue, before actual seisin, the land shall descend to the younger brother; but if the elder brother had entered, then the sister shall have the land as heir to him. *Co. Lit.* 14, 15. 3 *Rep.* 41. *Noy* 68.

As in discents one must be heir to him that was last actually seised; so none can inherit lands as heir, but the blood of the first purchaser. Though the law takes no notice of the disability of the father in case of discent, relating to brothers and sisters, as to their estates: a man, who had issue a son and a daughter, was attainted of treason, the son having purchased lands, and died without issue; and it was held, that notwithstanding the attainder of the father, the daughter shall take by descent from her brother, because the estate between them was immediate, and therefore the father's inability shall not hinder it. *Co. Lit.* 12. *Lit.* 8. 4 *Leon.* 5.

By discent, lands in fee-simple shall go, 1. To the eldest son as heir, and to his issue; the sons first, in order of birth, and for want of sons to all the daughters equally, who are called parceners, and all of them inherit as one heir. 2. If the eldest son hath no issue, then to his next eldest brother of the whole blood, and his issue; and for want of a brother, to a sister or sisters of the whole blood, and her and their issue. 3. If there be no brother or sister, then to the uncle, and his issue; and for want of an uncle, to an aunt or aunts, and their issue. 4. And if there be no uncles or aunts, then to cousins, in the nearest degree of consanguinity. And where lands are purchased by *brethren*; after uncles and aunts, the land shall go to the father, and the half blood, and their issue; and for want of uncle, aunt, father and half blood, to the next of kin in the collateral line: here the half blood come in after the father, as being of the whole blood to him; tho' not to their brethren. *Co. Lit.* 163, 12, &c. *Wood's Inst.* 221. In difcent of *eftates-tail* half blood is no hindrance; for the iffue are in *per formam doni*, and always of the whole blood to the donee. 3 *Rep.* 41.

Sometimes difcent is by cuftom of fee-fimple lands to all the fons, or to all the brothers, where one dies without iffue, as in *Gavelkind* in the county of *Kent*: all the fons fhall inherit, like unto fifters at common law; and the heir at the age of fifteen years may give and fell his lands, and though his father be attainted of treafon or felony he fhall inherit. *Co. Lit.* 140.

And there is a cuftomary difcent of lands in fome ancient boroughs and manors to the youngeft fon, and fometimes to the eldeft daughter, &c. as in *Borough Englifh*; and by other cuftoms: but where the youngeft fon dies, having no iffue, the eldeft fon is heir to him. *Kitcb.* 102.

As to difcents of *Borough Englifh* lands, the cuftom goes with the land, and guides the difcent to the youngeft fon; altho' there be devifes, &c. to the contrary. 2 *Lev.* 138.

In the learning of difcents in general, there are fome things further to be taken notice of:

1. Where parties are in by difcent, or purchafe.
2. Where difcents to an entry.

1. Difcent being created by law, and the moft ancient title, an heir is in by that, before a grant, or devife. If a man gives fee-fimple lands by will to one who is heir at law, the devife

Of Estates, Ancestors, Heirs, &c.

vise is void, and he shall take by discent: and where a father devises his land to his wife for life, and after her decease to his eldest son; tho' the son doth not take the estate presently on the death of the father, he shall be in by discent, and not by purchase, and the devise shall be void as to him. *Dr.* 126. *Style* 148.

When the heir takes that which his ancestor would have taken if living, he shall take it by discent; and not by purchase: but generally where an estate is devised to the heir at law, attended with a charge, as to pay money, debts, &c. in such case he takes by purchase, and not by discent. And a man can have lands no other way than by discent or purchase. 2 *Danv. Abr.* 557. *Latw.* 593.

2. A discent which takes away an entry is where one dies seised of lands, in which another hath right to enter, and it descends to his heir; such discent shall take away the other's right of entry, and put him to his action for recovery thereof: but a discent shall not take away the entry of lessee for years, &c. who hath no freehold; and if it be of such things as lie in grant; as advowsons, rents, commons in gross, &c. it puts not him that hath right to his action. And though where a disseisor dieth seised, and the law casteth the lands upon his heir, this is a discent which tolls an entry at common law; by statute, it is only where the disseisor had peaceable possession five years. *Co. Lit.* 237, 238. *Stat.* 32 *H.* 8. *c.* 33.

The heir is to enter into lands descended to him, to intitle him to the profits, &c.

A *conveyance* is a deed which passeth lands and tenements from one man to another: and of these

these deeds and conveyances there are several sorts.

LANDS CONVEY'D,

1. By feoffment.
2. By lease and release, and confirmation.
3. By bargain and sale.
4. By fine and recovery.
5. By surrender.
6. By gift and grant.
7. By lease.
8. By mortgage.
9. By assignment.
10. By will.

1. Feoffment is a grant or conveyance of any manors, messuages, land or tenements to another in fee to him and his heirs for ever, by the delivery of seisin and possession of the thing granted: and in every feoffment the grantor is called the feoffor, and he that receives by virtue thereof is the feoffee. And the livery and seisin is made in the presence of witnesses, all persons being removed from the lands, &c. when the feoffee or his attorney makes an entry on the premisses. *Lit. lib.* 1.

The deed of feoffment is our most ancient conveyance of lands; and it is said to excel the conveyance by fine and recovery; for it clears all disseisins, abatements, intrusions, and other wrongful estates, which no other conveyance doth; and for that it is so solemnly and publickly made, it has been of all others the most observed. It bars the feoffor of all present and future right, and collateral benefit, as conditions, power of revocation, &c. and destroys contingent uses: but feoffment may not be of such things whereof livery of seisin cannot be made; the livery being a ceremony used by which the common people may see the passing or alteration of the estate;

estate; and if either of the parties die before livery and seisin, the feoffment will be void. *West. Sym.* 235. *Plowd.* 214, 554. *Co. Lit.* 5.

As a feoffment is a common law conveyance, and executed by livery, it makes a transmutation of estate; but a conveyance on the statute of uses, such as a covenant to stand seised, &c. makes only a transmutation of possession, and not of estate. If a feoffment in fee be inrolled, but no livery made: it is no good feoffment, but the inrollment shall conclude the person to say that it was not his deed: but where a bargain and sale of lands is not inrolled, and the bargainor delivers livery and seisin of the land, according to the form of the deed, it has been held a good feoffment. 2 *Lev.* 77. *Poph.* 6. 2 *Ander.* 68.

Where a man makes a feoffment, without any consideration; by that the estate passes, but not the use, which shall descend to the heir. A feoffment in fee, made by tenant in tail, doth not give the inheritance of the tail to the feoffee, nor is he thereby tenant in tail; for none shall be such but he who is comprehended in the gift made by the donor: but it gives away all the immediate estate the feoffor had: though if lessee for life, and the reversioner in fee, make a feoffment by deed, each grants his estate; the lessee his by livery, and the fee from him in remainder. *Leon.* 182. *Plowd.* 562. *Hob.* 335. 6 *Rep.* 15.

A deed of feoffment is always applied to a corporeal and immoveable thing; as a house or land, &c. And a feoffment of lands, to hold to the feoffee and his heirs, after the death of the feoffor, though livery be made upon it, yet it is a void feoffment; for an estate of freehold in lands cannot begin at a day to come: but a lease for life in reversion, after the death of another, is a good estate in reversion. *Hob.* 171. 2 *Nels. Abr.* 846.

At Common law, before lease and release, feoffment was the general conveyance; but if livery and seisin could not be made, by reason there was a tenant in possession, the reversion was granted, and the particular tenant attorned. *Co. Lit.* 49. Now the deed of lease and release has taken place of this deed; the statute 27 *H.* 8. *c.* 10. uniting the use to the possession, without actual entry, &c.

The form of a deed of *feoffment*.

THIS *indenture, made the day of,* &c. *in the fourth year of the reign of our sovereign lord* George *the Third, by the grace of God king of* Great Britain, France, *and* Ireland, *defender of the faith,* &c. *and in the year of our Lord* 1764. *Between* A. B. *of the parish of,* &c. *in the county of* S. *gent. of the one part, and* C. D. *of,* &c. *in the county aforesaid, esq; of the other part,* Witnesseth, *That the said* A. B. *for and in consideration of the sum of three hundred pounds of lawful money of* Great Britain, *to him in hand paid by the said* C. D. *the receipt whereof the said* A. B. *doth hereby confess and acknowledge, and for other good causes and considerations him hereunto moving, he the said* A. B. *hath granted, bargained and sold, aliened, enfeoffed, released and confirmed, and by these presents doth grant, bargain and sell, alien enfeoff and confirm unto the said* C. D. *his heirs and assigns for ever,* All *that messuage or tenement situate,* &c.

now

now in the possession of, &c. *and also the reversion and reversions, remainder and remainders, rents and services thereof; and all the estate, right, title, interest, claim and demand whatsoever of him the said* A. B. *of, in and to the same premisses, and of, in and to every part and parcel thereof:* To have and to hold *the said messuage or tenement, and all and singular the premisses above-mentioned, with the appurtenances, unto the said* C. D. *his heirs and assigns, to the only proper use and behoof of him the said* C. D. *his heirs and assigns, for ever.* And *the said* A. B. *for himself, his heirs and assigns, doth covenant and grant, to and with the said* C. D. *his heirs and assigns, that he the said* A. B. *now is lawfully and rightfully seised in his own right of a good, sure, perfect, absolute and indefeasible estate of inheritance in fee-simple, of and in all and singular the said messuage and premisses, above-mentioned, and of every part and parcel thereof, with the appurtenances, without any manner of condition, mortgage, limitation of use or uses, or other matter, cause or thing, to alter, change, charge or determine the same:* And also *that he the said* A. B. *now hath good right, full power and lawful authority in his own right to grant, bargain, sell and convey the said messuage and premisses above-mentioned, with the appurtenances, unto the said* C. D. *his heirs and assigns, To the only proper and use and behoof of the said* C. D. *his heirs and assigns for ever, according to the true intent and meaning of these presents:* And also *that he the said* C. D. *his heirs and assigns, shall and may from time to time, and at all times for ever hereafter, peaceably and quietly have, hold, occupy, possess and enjoy all*

and

and singular the said premisses above-mentioned to be hereby granted, with the appurtenances, without the let, trouble, hinderance, molestation, interruption and denial of him the said A. B. his heirs or assigns, and of all and every other person and persons whatsoever claiming or to claim, by, from or under him, them or any of them. And further, that he the said A. B. and his heirs, and all and every other person and persons, and his and their heirs, any thing having or claiming in the said messuage and premisses above-mentioned, or any part thereof, by, from or under him, shall and will at all times hereafter, at the request and costs of the said C. D. his heirs or assigns, make, do and execute, or cause or procure to be made, done and executed, all and every further, and other lawful and reasonable grants, acts and assurances in the law whatsoever, for the further, better, and more perfect granting, conveying, and assuring of the said premisses hereby granted, with the appurtenances, unto the said C. D. his heirs and assigns, to the only proper use and behoof of the said C. D. his heirs and assigns for ever, according to the true intent and meaning of these presents, and to and for none other use, intent or purpose whatsoever. And lastly, the said A. B. hath made, ordained, constituted, and appointed, and by these presents doth make, ordain, constitute and appoint E. F. and G. H. of, &c. his true and lawful attornies jointly, and either of them severally, for him and in his name, into the said messuage and premisses, with the appurtenances hereby granted and conveyed, or mentioned to be granted and conveyed, or into some part thereof, in the name of the whole to enter, and full and peace-

peaceable poffeffion and feifin thereof for him, and in his name to take and have;' and after fuch poffeffion and feifin fo thereof taken and had, the like full and peaceable poffeffion and feifin thereof, or of fome part thereof, in the name of the whole, unto the faid C. D. *or to his certain attorney or attornies in that behalf, to give and deliver*; To hold *to him the faid* C. D. *his heirs and affigns for ever, according to the purport, true intent and meaning of thefe prefents, ratifying, confirming and allowing all and whatfoever his faid attornies, or either of them, fhall do in the premiffes.* In witnefs *whereof the parties firft abovenamed have to thefe prefent indentures interchangeably fet their hands and feals, the day and year above written.*

2. Leafe and releafe is the moft common deed of conveyance now in ufe; to convey any right or intereft in lands or tenements, to another who hath the poffeffion thereof. And this conveyance by leafe and releafe amounts to feoffment, the ufe drawing after it the poffeffion, and fupplying the place of livery and feifin, required in that deed.

In the making of it, a leafe or bargain and fale for a year, or fuch like term, is firft prepared and executed; to the intent that by virtue thereof the leffee may be in poffeffion of the lands intended to be conveyed by the releafe, and thereby, and by force of the ftatute 27 *H.* 8. *c.* 10. for transferring of ufes into poffeffion, be enabled to take a grant of the reverfion and inheritance of the faid lands, *&c.* to the ufe of himfelf and his heirs for ever: upon which, the releafe is made, reciting the releafe for a
year,

year, and declaring the uses. And in these cases, a pepper-corn rent in the lease for a year is a good reservation, and sufficient to raise an use, to make the lessee capable of a release. 2 *Vent.* 35.

The lease for a year must have the words *bargain and sell* for money; and 5 *s.* or any other sum, although never paid, will be a good consideration; whereupon the bargainee for a year is immediately in possession, on the executing of the deed, without actual entry: but if only the words *demise, grant, and to farm let* are used, in that case the lessee cannot accept of a release of the inheritance until he hath actually entered, and is in possession. 2 *Lil. Abr.* 435.

A lease and release make but one conveyance, being in the nature of one deed: and to the perfection of this deed, it is required that he who makes the release have an estate in himself, out of which the estate may be derived to the relessee; the relessee is to have an estate in possession, in deed or in law, in the land whereof the release is made, as a foundation for the release; and there must be sufficient words in law, not only to make the release, but to create and raise a new estate, or the release will not be good. It is necessary in all cases where a release of lands is made, that the estate be turned to a right, and there are two rights to the estate and also to the possession: or else there must be privity of estate between the tenant in possession and the relessor, without which a release will not operate. *Co. Lit.* 22. *Mod.* 252. 2 *Lil. Abr.* 435.

In case a release be made by one, that at the time of the making thereof had no right; or to a man that at the time had nothing in the lands,

lands, such release is void, because he ought to have a freehold, or a possession, or privity. But if a man make a lease for life, remainder for life, and the first lessee dies; and then the lessor releases to him in remainder, before entry, this is a good release to enlarge his estate; he having an estate in law capable of enlargement by release before entry had. *Ney Max.* 74. *Co. Lit.* 270.

A release to a man and his heirs, will pass a fee-simple; and if made to a person and the heirs of his body, by this the relessee hath an estate-tail. And where a man releases to another all his right which he hath in the land, without using any more words, as to hold to him and his heirs, &c. the relessee hath only an estate for life. *Dy.* 263.

These releases, that enure by way of passing away an estate, may be made upon condition, or with a defeazance; so as the condition, &c. be contained in the release, or delivered at the same time with it: and there may be in this deed a recital, covenant, warranty, &c.

A confirmation is in nature of a release, where one having right unto lands makes a deed to him who has possession of them, to enlarge his estate, or make his possession perfect. And it is likewise a means whereby a voidable estate is made sure and unavoidable. *Co. Lit.* 295.

And this confirmation, which is often joined to lease and release, may be for perfecting an estate, by making a conditional estate absolute, or for encreasing it; as where an estate for years is made lease for life, &c. or it may be for diminishing, by confirming the estate of a tenant at a less rent: but the prior estate must not be void; for a confirmation will have no effect upon

Of Estates, Ancestors, Heirs, &c.

upon an estate that is void in law, or determined. *Co. Lit.* 301.

If tenant for life grant a rent-charge, &c. to one and his heirs, he in reversion is to confirm it; otherwise it is good only for the life of tenant for life. *Lit.* 529.

Form of a *lease for a year*, whereon to ground a release.

THIS *indenture, made,* &c. Between A. B. *of,* &c. *of the one part, and* C. D. *of,* &c. *of the other part,* Witnesseth, *that the said* A. B. *for and in consideration of the sum of five shillings of lawful* British *money to him in hand paid by the said* C. D. *the receipt whereof is hereby acknowledged, he the said* A. B. *hath granted, bargained and sold, and by these presents doth grant, bargain and sell unto the said* C. D. All *that messuage or tenement,* &c. *with the rights, members and appurtenances thereof, situate, lying and being in,* &c. *in the county of* S. *and all houses, edifices, buildings, gardens, orchards, lands, meadows, commons, pastures, feedings, trees, woods, underwoods, ways, paths, waters, water-courses, easements, profits, commodities, advantages, emoluments and hereditaments whatsoever to the said messuage or tenements belonging, or in any wise appertaining, or which now are or formerly have been accepted, reputed, taken, known, used, occupied or enjoyed, to or with the same, or as part, parcel or member thereof, or of any part thereof; and the reversion and reversions, remainder and remainders, rents and services of*

the

Of Estates, Ancestors, Heirs, &c.

the said premisses above-mentioned, and of every part and parcel thereof, with the appurtenances: To have and to hold the said messuage or tenement, lands, hereditaments and premisses above-mentioned, and every part or parcel thereof, with the appurtenances, unto the said C. D. his executors, administrators and assigns, from the first day of this instant, &c. for and during and unto the full end and term of one whole year, from thence next and immediately ensuing and following, and fully to be complete and ended: yielding and paying therefore one pepper-corn in and upon the feast of St. Michael the archangel, if demanded: To the intent that by virtue of these presents, and by force of the statute for transferring of uses in possession, he the said C. D. may be in the actual possession of all and singular the said premisses above-mentioned, with the appurtenances, and thereby be enabled to accept and take a grant and release of the reversion and inheritance thereof, to him and his heirs, to the only proper use and behoof of him the said C. D. his heirs and assigns for ever. In witness, &c.

The form of the *release* and conveyance of the lands.

THIS *indenture, made the day and year,* &c. *Between* A. B. *of,* &c. *of the one part, and* C. D. *of,* &c. *of the other part,* witnesseth, *that the said* A. B. *for and in consideration of the sum of six hundred pounds of lawful money of* Great Britain, *to him in hand paid by the said* C. D. *the receipt whereof*

Of Estates, Ancestors, Heirs, &c.

of the said A. B. *doth hereby confess and acknowledge, and for divers other good causes and considerations him thereunto moving, he the said* A. B. *hath granted, bargained and sold, aliened, released and confirmed, and by these presents doth fully, freely and absolutely grant, bargain and sell, alien, release and confirm unto the said* C. D. *(in his actual possession now being, by virtue of a bargain and sale to him thereof made for one year, by indenture bearing date the day next before the day of the date of these presents, and by force of the statutes for transferring of uses into possession) and to his heirs and assigns for ever, All that messuage or tenement, &c. with the rights, members and appurtenances thereof, situate, lying and being in, &c. in the county of, &c. aforesaid, and all houses, edifices, buildings, gardens, orchards, lands, meadows, commons, pastures, feedings, trees, woods, underwoods, ways, paths, waters, water-courses, easements, profits, commodities, advantages, emoluments and hereditaments whatsoever to the said messuage or tenement belonging, or in any wise appertaining, or which now are, or formerly have been accepted, reputed, taken, known, used, occupied or enjoyed, to or with the same, or as part, parcel or member thereof, or of any part thereof; and also the reversion and reversions, remainder and remainders, rents and services of all and singular the said premisses above-mentioned, and of every part and parcel thereof, with the appurtenances; and also all the estate, right, title, interest, claim and demand whatsoever, as well in equity as in law, of him the said* A. B. *of, in, and to all and singular*

gular the said premisses, and of, in and to every part and parcel thereof, with the appurtenances: and also all deeds, evidences and writings, touching or concerning the said premisses only, or only any part thereof, together with true copies of all other deeds, evidences and writings, which do concern the said premisses, or any part thereof, jointly with any other lands or tenements, now in the custody or possession of him the said A. B. or which he can or may get or come by without suit in law, the said copies to be made and written at the request, costs and charges of the said C. D. his heirs and assigns: To have and to hold the said messuage or tenement, lands, hereditaments, and all and singular the premisses above-mentioned, and every part and parcel thereof, with the appurtenances, unto the said C. D. his heirs and assigns, to the only proper use and behoof of the said C. D. his heirs and assigns for ever. And the said A. B. for himself, his heirs and assigns, doth covenant and grant to and with the said C. D. his heirs and assigns, that he the said A. B. now is the true, lawful and rightful owner of the said messuage, lands, tenements, hereditaments and premisses above-mentioned, and of every part or parcel thereof, with the appurtenances. And also that he the said A. B. now is lawfully and rightfully seised in his own right, of a good, sure, perfect, absolute and indefeasible estate of inheritance in fee-simple, of and in all and singular the premisses above-mentioned, with the appurtenances, without any manner of condition, mortgage, limitation of use and uses, or other matter, cause or thing to alter, change, charge or determine the same.

And *that he the said A. B. now hath good right, full power, and lawful authority, in his own right, to grant, bargain, sell and convey the said messuage, lands, tenements, hereditaments, and all and singular the premisses above-mentioned, with the appurtenances, unto the said C. D. his heirs and assigns, to the only proper use and behoof of the said C. D. his heirs and assigns for ever, according to the true intent and meaning of these presents. And also that he the said C. D. his heirs and assigns, shall and may, at all times for ever hereafter, peaceably and quietly have, hold, occupy, possess and enjoy all and singular the said messuage, lands, tenements, hereditaments and premisses above-mentioned, with the appurtenances, without the let, trouble, hindrance, molestation, interruption and denial of him the said A. B. his heirs or assigns, and of all and every other person or persons whatsoever: And that freed and discharged, or otherwise well and sufficiently saved and kept harmless and indemnified of and from all former and other bargains, sales, gifts, grants, leases, mortgages, jointures, dowers, uses, wills, intails, fines, post fines, issues, amerciaments, seizures, bonds, annuities, writings obligatory, statutes merchant and of the staple, recognizances, extents, judgments, executions, rents and arrearages of rent, and of and from all other charges, estates, rights, titles, troubles and incumbrances whatsoever, had, made, committed, done or suffered, by the said A. B. or any other person or persons whatsoever, claiming or to claim, by, from or under him, them, or any of them. And further, that he the said A. B. and his heirs, and all and every*

every other person and persons, and his and their heirs, any thing having or claiming in the said premisses above-mentioned, or any part thereof, by, from or under him, shall and will from time to time, and at all times hereafter, upon the reasonable request, and at the costs and charges of the said C. D. his heirs or assigns, make, do and execute, or cause or procure to be made, done and executed, all and every such further and other lawful and reasonable act and acts, thing and things, device and devices, conveyance and conveyances in the law whatsoever, for the further, better, and more perfect granting, conveying and assuring of all and singular the said premisses above-mentioned, with the appurtenances, unto the said C. D. his heirs and assigns, to the only proper use and behoof of the said C. D. his heirs and assigns for ever, as by the said C. D. his heirs or assigns, or his or their counsel learned in the law, shall be reasonably devised or advised and required. And lastly, it is covenanted, granted, concluded and agreed upon by and between the said parties to these presents, and the true meaning thereof also is, and it is hereby so declared, that all and every fine and fines, recovery and recoveries, assurance and assurances, conveyance and conveyances in the law whatsoever already had, made, levied, suffered, executed and acknowledged, or at any time hereafter to be had, made, levied, suffered, executed and acknowledged, by or between the said parties to these presents, or either of them, or by or between them or either of them, and any other person or persons whatsoever, of the said premisses above-mentioned, with the appurtenances, or

Of Estates, Ancestors, Heirs, &c.

any part thereof, either alone by itself, or jointly with any other lands, tenements or hereditament, shall be and enure, and shall be adjudged, esteemed and taken to be and enure, as for and concerning all and singular the premisses above-mentioned, with the appurtenances, to and for the only proper use and behoof of the said C. D. *his heirs and assigns for ever, according to the true intent and meaning of these presents, and to and for none other use, intent or purpose whatsoever.* In witness, &c.

3. Bargain and sale is a deed or instrument, whereby the property of lands and tenements is for valuable consideration granted and transferred from one person to another: it is called a real contract, upon a valuable consideration, for passing of lands, tenements and hereditaments, by deed indented and inrolled. Also 'tis where a recompence is given by both the parties to the bargain; as of land for money, and money for the land, &c. 2 *Inst.* 612. *Lil. Abr.* 206.

Where lands are bargained and sold for money only, the deed is to be inrolled; if in consideration of money and natural affection, &c. the estate will pass without it. And a bargain and sale passes the freehold of the lands, also reversions, remainders, &c. without livery and seisin; and a rent may be reserved out of it by deed inrolled: but if the bargain and sale be for money, it cannot be to one man to the use of another, but to the bargainee only. If one bargain lands of which another person is in possession, and claims title to, the deed is not good; unless the bargainor enter, and deliver

the

the deed on the ground, &c. and hath good title: and a bargain and sale by a man who is not in possession, nor receives the rents, tho' in consideration of money, will not be good, without livery. *Lev.* 56. 8 *Rep.* 93. *Dy.* 155. *Lil. Abr.* 209.

There must be a good consideration given, or at least said to be given for lands in these deeds; and for a competent sum of money, is a good consideration, but not the general words for divers considerations, &c. If money is mentioned to be paid in a bargain and sale, and, in truth, no money is paid; some of our books tell us this may be a good bargain and sale, because no averment will lie against that which is expressly affirmed by the deed; except it comes to be questioned whether fraudulent or no. Although a deed express a consideration upon a purchase, by *Style* this will be no proof upon a trial, that the money was actually paid; but it is to be made out by witnesses. *Co. Rep.* 176. 11 *Rep.* 25. *Dy.* 169. *Style* 370.

The deed of bargain and sale being made on good consideration, neither the death of the bargainor or bargainee before inrollment hinders the passing of an estate: but until the deed is inrolled, the estate of freehold is in the bargainor; and the bargainee cannot bring an action of trespass before entry had, though he may surrender, alien, &c. and a bargainee before inrollment, 'tis said, may suffer a recovery: also he shall have rent which grows due after the date of the bargain and sale, and before the inrollment. *Hob.* 136. *Jac.* 52. *Vent.* 361. *Sid.* 310.

This inrollment is to be in one of the courts at *Westminster*, or in the county where the lands lie, before the *Custos Rotulorum*, justices of peace, &c.

&c. and the deeds are to be thus inrolled within six months by statute, to be accounted at twenty-eight days by the months: though this extends only to bargains and sales of inheritance and freehold; and not to a bargain and sale of leases for years, *&c.* which are good though not inrolled, nor by deed indented, *&c.* If several seal a deed of bargain and sale, and but one acknowledge it, and thereupon the deed is inrolled; this is a good inrollment within the statute 27 *H.* 8. *c.* 16. *Style* 462.

In case two bargains and sales are made of the same lands to two several persons, and the last deed is first inrolled; if afterwards the first deed is also inrolled within six months, the first buyer shall have the land; for when the deed is inrolled, the bargainee is seised of the land from the delivery of the deed, and the inrollments shall relate to it. The statute of inrollment says, that the estate shall not vest, except the deed be inrolled; and then it vests presently, by the statute of uses, and settles *ab initio.* Wood's Inst. 260. Danv. Abr. 696.

Not only lands, but rents, advowsons, tithes, *&c.* may be granted by bargain and sale, in fee-simple, fee-tail for life or years; but commonly it is of land in fee-simple. If a tenant in tail grants all his estate to a man and his heirs; the grantee hath but an estate for the life of tenant in tail: and where tenant for life, bargains and sells his land, by deed inrolled, 'tis a forfeiture of his estate. *Rep.* 176. *Lit.* 613. 4 *Leon.* 251.

Form

Form of a common *bargain* and *sale* of lands.

THIS *indenture, made,* &c. Between A. B. *of,* &c. *of the one part, and* C. D. *of,* &c. *of the other part,* witnesseth, *that the said* A. B. *for and in consideration of the sum of,* &c. *to him in hand paid by the said* C. D. *the receipt whereof the said* A. B. *doth hereby acknowledge,* He *the said* A. B. Hath granted, bargained and sold, aliened and confirmed, and by these presents doth grant, bargain and sell, alien and confirm unto the said* C. D. *his heirs and assigns for ever,* All *that messuage or tenement, situate and lying,* &c. *and also all lands, trees, woods, underwoods, tithes, commons, common of pasture, profits, commodities, advantages, hereditaments, ways, waters and appurtenances whatsoever to the said messuage or tenement and premisses above-mentioned belonging or any wise appertaining: and also the reversion and reversions, remainder and remainders, rents and services of the said premisses, and of every part thereof; and all the estate, right, title, interest, claim and demand whatsoever of him the said* A. B. *of, in and to the said messuage, tenement and premisses, and every part thereof:* To have and to hold *the said messuage or tenement, and all and singular the said premisses above-mentioned, and every part and parcel thereof, with the appurtenances, unto the said* C. D. *his heirs and assigns, to the only proper use and behoof of the said* C. D. *his heirs and assigns for ever.* And *the said* A. B. *for him and his heirs, the said messuage or tenements, and premisses, and every part thereof, against him and his heirs, and against all and every other person and persons whatsoever to the said* C. D. *his heirs and assigns,*

Of Estates, Ancestors, Heirs, &c.

assigns, shall and will warrant and for ever defend by these presents. In witness, &c.

The deed of *bargain* and *sale* is *inrolled* as follows:

IT is to be remembred, *That the day, &c. thither in the same term, before the lord the king at* Westminster, *came* A. B. *of*, &c. *in the county of* S. *gentleman, in his proper person, and brought here in the court of the said lord the now king before the king himself at* Westminster, *a certain indenture, which he acknowledged to be his deed: and he desired that that indenture in the court of the lord the new king, before the said lord the king at* Westminster, *might be inrolled of record; and it is inrolled in form following, that is to say,* This indenture, made, &c. *(and so inrolled the deed verbatim.)*

4. Fine and recovery. A fine is a final agreement or conveyance upon record, for the settling and assuring of lands and tenements, acknowledged in the king's court by the cognisor to be the right of the cognisee. Or it is a covenant made before justices, and entered of record, for conveying lands, tenements, or any thing inheritable, to cut off all controversies.

Anciently a fine was a determination of a real controversy; but now it is generally a feigned action upon a writ of covenant, &c. and supposes a controversy where in reality there is none, to secure the title that a man hath in his estate against all men; or to cut off intails, and with more certainty convey the title of lands, &c. and pass the inheritance thereof, though it be not controverted, to whom we think fit,

Of Estates, Ancestors, Heirs, &c.

fit. And a fine may be levied on a writ of right, &c. in any real action: and being levied in the King's court, therefore it binds women covert, being parties, and others whom ordinarily the law disables to act. *West. Symb. par.* 2.

There are four sorts of fines: a *fine sur cognizance de droit come ceo*, &c. single, which is the principal, and surest kind of fine, it giving present possession to the cognisee, without writ of execution: a *fine sur done, grant and render*, called a double fine, whereby the cognisee after a release and warranty to him by the cognisor, grants and renders back the lands, &c. and this render is sometimes of the whole estate, and sometimes of a particular estate with remainders over; also sometimes with reservation of rent, and clause of distress, &c. A *fine sur cognizance de droit tantum*, which is a fine executory, generally used to pass a reversion; and sometimes made use of by tenant for life, to release to him in reversion: when a reversion is passed by it, then it is expressed in the fine that the particular estate is in another, and the cognisor willeth that the cognisee shall have the reversion, or that the land shall remain to him after the other estate is spent. A *fine sur concessit* is where the cognisor is seised of the lands, and the cognisee hath no freehold therein, but it passeth by the fine; it is used to grant away estates for life, or years, and is also executory, so that the cognisee must enter, or have a writ of *habere facias seisinam* to obtain possession, if the party to whom the estate is limited, be not in possession at the time of levying the fine. 2 *Inst.* 513. 2 *Rep.* 56. 5 *Rep.* 38. *Plowd.* 268.

Fines are likewise with proclamations or without; a fine without proclamation is a fine at the

Of Estates, Ancestors, Heirs, &c.

Common law; and the fine with proclamations is termed a fine according to the statutes, and this is the best sort, and most used: and if there be error in the proclamations, it shall be a good fine at Common law. And fines are now levied in the court of *Common Pleas*, at *Westminster*, on account of the solemnity thereof, ordained by the statute of 18 *Edw.* 1. They may be acknowledged before the lord chief justice of C. P. as well in as out of court; and two of the justices of the same court have power to take them in open court: also justices of assise may do it; but they do not usually certify them without a special writ of *dedimus potestatem:* and by commissioners in the country fines may be taken, impowered by *dedimus potestatem*, one whereof named 'tis said must be a knight; these commissions, general and special, issue out of the Chancery. *Stat.* 18 *Ed. c.* 7. 1 *R.* 3. *st.* 4. 4 *H.* 7. *c.* 24. 32 *H.* 8. *c.* 36. 3 Rep. 86. 2 Inst. 512. Dy. 224.

A person seised of an estate in fee-simple, fee-tail general or special, tenant in remainder, or reversion, may levy a fine: so may tenant for life, to hold to the cognisee for the life of tenant for life; but tenant for years cannot levy a fine of his term. These fines may be levied of all things *in esse* at the time of the fine, which are inheritable; though not of things uncertain, or of lands held in tail by the king's letters patent, &c. And lands bought of divers persons, by several purchasers, may pass in one fine, to save charges; but the writ of covenant must be brought against all vendors, and every vendor warrant against him and his heirs: and on a fine uses may be raised and created, &c. declared by indentures before or after levying the fine.

Also.

Also by fine, almost any kind of contract may be made and expressed. 3 *Rep.* 77. 5 Rep. 124. Co Rep. 76.

And there are in every fine several parts. 1. An original writ, usually a writ of covenant. 2. The *licentia concordandi*, or king's licence, for which the king hath a fine, called the king's silver. 3. The concord itself, containing the agreement between the parties how the land, &c. shall pass, being the foundation and substance of the fine: and 'tis said, the concord being the complete fine, it shall be adjudged a fine of that term in which the concord was made, and the writ of covenant returnable. 4. The note of the fine, or abstract of the original contract, left with the chirographer. 5. The foot of the fine, which includes all, setting forth the day, year and place, and before what justices the concord was made, &c. of this there are indentures made forth in the office, which is called the ingrossing of the fine. In the levying of fines, if either of the parties cognisors die, after the king's silver is entered, the fine shall be finished, and be good: tis otherwise if they die before, it shall avoid the fine. *Rep.* 76. 2 *Inst.* 511, 517. *Co. Lit.* 9. *Salk.* 341.

If there be want of an * original, or not writs of covenants for lands in every county; or if there is any notorious error in the suing out a fine, or any fraud or deceit, &c. Writ of error may be brought to make void the fine, but a fine shall not be reversed for small variance, which will not hurt it: nor is there occasion for a precise form in a render upon a fine, because it is only an amicable assurance upon record. No single fine may be with a remainder to any other

---

* See *Cake's* Law Tracts, 253. in notes.

person

person not contained in it: though if *A.* levy such a fine to *B.* who, by the same concord, grants and renders back the land again to *A.* for life, remainder to his wife for life, remainder to *A.* and his heirs; this will be a good fine. *Co. Lit.* 9. 5 *Rep.* 58. *Plowd.* 248.

A feme covert levying a fine with her husband, is to be examined in private whether she does it voluntarily, and not by compulsion, for without her voluntary consent the fine cannot pass: and women coverts, and infants ought to be cautious in levying fines; if a married woman levy a fine with her husband of her own lands, she cannot reverse it during the husband's life, or after his death; and if it be of her jointure, she will lose her thirds: fines levied by infants must be reversed during their minority, or they are good against them. *Assis. pl.* 53. 50 *Edw.* 3. *Dy.* 359.

After a fine is passed, the privies in blood, as the heirs of the cognisor, are barred presently; but strangers to the fine have five years to enter and claim their rights, &c. And the like time have infants after their full age; feme coverts after the death of their husbands; prisoners after their enlargement; persons out of the realm after their return, &c. But if a feme covert dies while she is covert, being no party to the fine; or a person in prison dieth whilst there; or one beyond sea at the time of the fine levied never returns; in these cases the heir is not limited to any time. A future interest, as in remainder or reversion, cannot be barred by a fine, until five years after it comes in being: and where there is no present nor future right to the lands, only a possibility at the time of levying the fine, &c. a person may enter and claim when he will. *Plowd.* 367. 1 *Rich.* 3. *c.* 7. 2 *Inst.* 519. 2 *Rep.* 93. *T. Raym.* 151. 10 *Rep.* 49.

If a fine according to the Common law, be now levied, he that hath right may make his claim or entry, &c. at any time to prevent the bar: by statute, claim or entry to avoid the bar of a fine, is to be made in five years; and no entry or claim, shall make an avoidance of any fine with proclamations, unless an action be commenced within one year after such entry, and prosecuted with effect. *Co Lit.* 254, 262. *Stat.* 1 *R.* 3. *c.* 7. 4 *Ann. c.* 16.

An estate must be devested and put to a right, before a fine bars; when it is turned to a right, and then there comes a fine, and non-claim, 'tis a perpetual bar. One that at the time of the fine levied, had not any title to enter, shall not be barred thereby: this in case of a future interest, not turned to a right, wherein a man is not bound to claim; and extends not to tenant in tail, barring his issue. If a person doth levy a fine of my land, while I am in possession, this fine will not hurt me; nor when a stranger levies a fine of my lands let to a tenant, if the tenant pays me his rent: and if there be tenant in tail, remainders in tail, &c. and the first tenant in tail bargains and sells the land by deed inrolled, and levies a fine to the bargainee; here the remainders in tail are not bound, tho' five years pass without claim; for the law adjudges them always in possession. 9 *Rep.* 106. 32 *H.* 8. *c.* 36. *Carter* 82, 163.

If tenant in tail be disseised, and the disseisor levy a fine, and five years pass, without claim, that shall bind his issue. And a fine will bar the heirs in tail; but not the remainders or reversions:

sions: but recoveries bar them all. *Cro. Eliz.* 896.

A *recovery* is *fictio juris*, or a formal act by consent, used where a man is desirous to cut off an estate-tail, &c. and for the better assurance of lands and tenements, upon which uses may be limited and raised. It is much of the same nature of a fine, though better in regard it bars remainders and reversions: and recoveries are much favoured by the law, many of the inheritances of the kingdom depending upon these assurances. 5 *Rep.* 40.

This common recovery supposes a recompence in value, to all persons that lost the estate: and it is either with single, double or treble voucher. The recovery with single voucher is used to bar the tenant in tail, and his heirs, of such estate-tail which is in his possession, with the remainders depending upon it, and the reversion expectant thereon which others have; and of all leases and incumbrances derived out of such remainder or reversion. The recovery with double voucher is to bar the first voucher, and his heirs, of every estate at any time in him, or any of his ancestors, whose heir he is of such estate; and all others of right to remainders and reversions dependant and expectant upon the same, and all leases and incumbrances derived out of them; also it will be a bar of the estate whereof the tenant was then seised in reversion or remainder, &c. The recovery with treble voucher is to make a perpetual bar of the estate of the tenant, and of every such estate of inheritance that at any time had been in the first or second vouchee, or their ancestors, whose heirs they are; and as well of every reversion thereupon depending, as of all leases, estates, charges and incumbrances,

derived

derived out of any reversion or remainder. *Co. Lit.* 102. 10 *Rep.* 37. 2 *Roll Abr.* 204. *Noy* 81.

In prosecuting recoveries there is a colourable suit; wherein there is a demandant, and a tenant, and one called to warrant upon a supposed warranty, who is the common vouchee; the demandant is supposed to come into court, and the common vouchee to make default; and withdraw in contempt of the court; whereupon judgment is had, that the demandant, against whom there is no defence shall recover the land. And in a recovery with single voucher, the writ of entry must be brought against tenant in tail in possession, and he is to vouch the common vouchee: but if the recovery be with double or treble voucher, then by fine, feoffment or lease and release, &c. you are to discontinue the estate, and make a tenant of the freehold of the land; and thereupon bring the writ against that tenant, and he is to vouch the tenant in tail, and he the common vouchee, and then judgment is given for the demandant against the tenant, and for the tenant to recover in value against the vouchee, and so the first vouchee against the second, &c. as the recovery is brought. 10 *Rep.* 39, 42. *Co. Lit.* 224. *Wood's Inst.* 252.

To every recovery there must be a good tenant to the *præcipe*, or it will be void: a recovery has been held good where a stranger that had nothing in the land was made tenant to the *præcipe* with the tenant in tail; for the supposed recompence in value shall go to him who lost the estate. If tenant for life, and he in remainder in tail suffer a common recovery, and both vouch the common vouchee: it is no good recovery to bar the issue in tail, because he in
remainder

remainder was not tenant to the *præcipe*, being not in poffeffion. But where there is tenant for life, the remainder in tail, with reverfion, or remainder in fee; if the tenant for life is impleaded by agreement, and he vouch the tenant in tail, and he vouch over the common vouchee; this will bar the remainder and reverfion in fee, though he in remainder or reverfion did never affent to the recovery. 2 *Lil. Abr.* 425. *Vent.* 358. *Co. Rep.* 15. 3 *Rep.* 60.

In cafe tenant for life furrenders to him in remainder in tail, he may bind the remainder and reverfion expectant upon his eftate: though if tenant for life alone fuffer a recovery, without the confent of him in remainder the recovery is void. And here if tenants in tail after poffibility of iffue extinct, tenants by the curtefy, or for life, fuffer a common recovery by covin, without the affent, and to the prejudice of him in remainder or reverfion; not only the recovery fhall be void, but it will be a forfeiture of the eftate of fuch tenants. *Co. Lit.* 362. *Stat.* 14 *Eliz. c.* 8.

It was formerly a queftion, if there was a tenant in tail, remainder for years, and tenant in tail fuffers a recovery, whether the leafe for years be barred or not? becaufe it was infifted, that no recompence can go to this, being a chattle: but the court adjudged, that this leafe fhould be barred, and fo the conftant experience had been. 2 *Lev.* 30. *Mod. Rep.* 110. A recovery fuffered by tenant in tail, after he himfelf hath made a leafe of the lands, or entred into a ftatute, will make the leafe or charge, that before was voidable, good againft the iffue in tail, and him in remainder or reverfion; and the recoveror

veror shall hold the lands charged, and subject to the lease made by tenant in tail. *Co. Rep.* 25.

A common recovery is the best assurance a man can have, so as to sell or dispose of his estate as he pleases; except an act of parliament. But a recovery bars only where there is a privity in law; as the issue of tenant in tail, and he in remainder, reversion, &c. Strangers are not barred by a recovery and non-claim, as they are by a fine: nor shall it bar the heir, who claims as a purchaser, and not by descent; or when there is an executory estate, which depends upon a contingency; nor a rent granted by the tenant in tail, &c. And recoveries may be avoided if suffered by fraud, to deceive purchasers, &c. like any other fraudulent conveyance. 3 *Rep.* 5. *Carter* 53. *Lutw.* 1224. *Cro. Eliz.* 792.

These recoveries are suffered in the Common Pleas, by the tenants and vouchers personally in court, or by attornies; and sometimes by attorney in the country on a *dedimus potestatem*, &c. And most errors in a recovery are amendable the first time after the recovery had; but for gross error in the proceedings in matter of substance, a recovery may be made void, either by writ of error, or by pleading; or by motion in court, praying a *vacat* of the judgment. 8 *Rep.* 162. *Co. Lit.* 104.

As a fine and recovery are a bar, and dock the estates before mentioned; so by indentures to lead the uses thereof, new estates and intails are limited and created subject to farther fines and recoveries.

P

The form *of a præcipe and concord* of a
fine *sur cognizance de droit*, &c.

Wilts, *to wit,* Command A. B. *that be justly and without delay, perform to* C. D. *the covenant made between them, of one messuage, one cottage, ten acres of land, twenty acres of pasture,* &c. *with the appurtenances in* W. *And unless* &c.

AND *the agreement is such, to wit, that the said* A. *hath acknowledged the said tenements, with the appurtenances, to be the right of the said* C. *as those which the said* C. *hath of the gift of the said* A. *and those be both remised and quit-claimed, from him and his heirs, to the said* C. *and his heirs, for ever. And moreover the said* A. *hath granted for himself and his heirs, that they will warrant to the said* C. *and his heirs, the said tenements, with the appurtenances, against the said* A. *and his heirs for ever. And for this,* &c.

*Taken and acknowledged the
day and in the year,* &c.
before, &c.

Form of a *præcipe and concord* of a fine by husband and wife, of his land.

Somerset, *to wit, Command* A. B. *and* E. *his wife, that they justly,* &c. *perform to* C. D. *the covenant made between them, of two messuages, two tofts, thirty acres of land,* &c. (naming the rest of the parcels) *with the appurtenances in* M. *And unless,* &c.

AND *the agreement is such, that is to say, that the said* A. *and* E. *have acknowledged the said tenements, with the appurtenances, to be the right of the said* C. *as those which he the said* C. *hath of the gift of the said* A. *and* E. *and those they have remised, and for ever quit-claimed, from them the said* A. *and* E. *and the heirs of the said* A. *to the said* C. *and his heirs for ever. And moreover, they the said* A. *and* E. *have granted for themselves, and the heirs of the said* A. *that they will warrant to the said* C. *and his heirs, the said tenements, with the appurtenances, against the said* A. *and* E. *and the heirs of the said* A. *for ever. And for this,* &c.

Taken and acknowledged, the day and year, &c.

Of Estates, Ancestors, Heirs, &c.

The form of an *indenture* to declare *the uses* of a fine.

THIS *indenture, made,* &c. Between A. B. *of,* &c. *esq; and* E. *his wife, of the one part, and* C. D. *of,* &c. *of the other part, witnesseth, that the said* A. B. *and* E. *his wife, for the settling and assuring of the manor, lands, tenements and hereditaments herein after mentioned, to the several uses herein after declared and limited, and for divers other good causes and considerations,* He *the said* A. B. *hath covenanted and granted, and by these presents doth for himself, his heirs and assigns, covenant and grant, to and with the said* C. D. *his heirs and assigns; and the said* E. *wife of the said* A. B. *doth hereby consent and agree, that they the said* A. B. *and* E. *his wife, shall and will, before the end of* Trinity *term next ensuing, acknowledge and levy in due form of law, before his majesty's justices of the court of Common Pleas at* Westminster, *unto the said* C. D. *his heirs and assigns, one fine* sur cognizance de droit come ceo, &c. *with proclamations to be thereupon had, according to the form of the statute in that case made and provided, of* All *that the manor of,* &c. *and of all that messuage or farm called,* &c. *situate, lying and being,* &c. *and also of the reversion and reversions, remainder and remainders, rents and services of the said manor and premisses above-mentioned, and of every part and parcel thereof, with the appurtenances, by the names of twenty messuages, five cottages, two mills, three hundred acres of land, two hundred*

hundred acres of meadow, four hundred acres of pasture, fifteen acres of wood, and twenty pounds rent, and common of pasture for all manner of cattle, with the appurtenances in, &c. aforesaid. And it is hereby agreed by and between the said parties to these presents, and the true meaning hereof also is, and it is hereby so declared, That the fine so as aforesaid, or in any other manner to be had and levied of the said manor and premisses, or any part thereof; and also all and every other fine and fines already had, levied, or to be had or levied, of the same premisses, or any part thereof, shall be and enure, and shall be adjudged, esteemed and taken to be and enure; and the said C. D. and his heirs, and all and every other person and persons, and his and their heirs, now standing and being seised, or which at the perfecting of the said fine shall stand or be seised of the said manor and premisses, or any part thereof, shall, at all times hereafter, stand and be seised thereof, and of every part thereof, with the appurtenances, to and for the several uses, intents and purposes herein after limited, expressed and declared, (that is to say) As for and concerning the said manor of, &c. with it's rights, members and appurtenances, and all and singular the messuages, cottages, lands, tenements, commons, wastes, waste-grounds, mines, royalties, profits, rents and hereditaments whatsoever, to the same manor belonging or appertaining, or accepted, reputed or taken as part, parcel, or member thereof; to the use and behoof of the said A. B. and E. B. for and during the term of their natural lives, and the life of the longest liver of them, without impeachment of or for any manner of

waste,

Of Estates, Ancestors, Heirs, &c.

waste, &c. and from and after the decease of the said A. B. and E. his wife, and the survivor of them, then to the use and behoof of the right heirs of the said A. B. for ever. And as for and concerning all and singular the said messuage, or farm called, &c. with the appurtenances, whereof the said fine shall be so levied, and whereof no use is herein before declared, to the only proper use and behoof of the said A. B. his heirs and assigns for ever; and to and for none other use, intent or purpose whatsoever. In witness, &c.

The form of a *writ of entry* sur disseisin, &c. in order to suffer a recovery.

GEORGE the second, &c. to the sheriff of W. greeting. Command A. B. that justly, and without delay, be render to C. D. two messuages, two gardens, twenty acres of land, &c. with the appurtenances in D. which he claims to be his right and inheritance, and into which the said A. hath not an entry: but after a disseisin, which Hugh Hunt thereof unjustly and without judgment hath made to the said A. B. within thirty years now last past, as he saith; and whereupon he complains, that the said A. B. deforced him; and unless he shall so do, and the said C. D. shall give you security that his suit shall be prosecuted, then summon by good summoners the said A. B. that he be before our justices at Westminster, in three weeks from the day of St. Michael, to shew, wherefore he will not; and you have there this summons and this writ. Witness ourself at Westminster the day, &c. in the eighth year of our reign.

The

The form of a deed to lead the uses of a *fine* and *recovery*, on a purchase.

THIS *indenture tripartite, made, &c. Between A. B. of, &c. and S. his wife, C. D. of, &c. and J. his wife, of the first part, E. F. and G. G. both of, &c. of the second part, and J. K. of, &c. and T. M. of, &c. of the third part, witnesseth, that for and in consideration of the sum of one thousand pounds of lawful money of Great Britain to the said A. B. and S. his wife, and C. D. and J. his wife, in hand paid by the said J. K. and T. M. the receipt whereof they do hereby acknowledge, and in consideration also of* 5 s. *of, &c. to the said A. B. and S. his wife, and C. D. and J. his wife, in hand paid by the said E. F. and G. H. the receipt whereof they do also hereby acknowledge; and the said A. B. and C. D. for their barring, docking, cutting off and destroying of all estates-tail and remainders over, now in being in and upon the messuage, lands, tenements and hereditaments herein after mentioned; and for the conveying and assuring the same premisses to the only proper use and behoof of the said J. K. and T. M. and their heirs; they the said A. B. and C. D. have, and each of them have covenanted and granted, and by these presents do and each of them doth covenant and grant, to and with the said E. F. and G. H. their heirs and assigns, that they the said A. B. and S. his wife, and C. D. and J. his wife, shall and will on this side, and before the end of* Easter *term next coming, before his majesty's justices of the court of Common Pleas at* Westminster,

minster, *in due form of law, levy and acknowledge unto the said* E. F. *and* G. H. *and their heirs, or to the heirs of one of them, one fine sur conuzance de droit come ceo,* &c. *with proclamations to be thereupon had, according to the form of the statute in that case made and provided, of* All *that messuage or tenement,* &c. *in the tenure of,* &c. *and all those pieces or parcels of land lying and being,* &c. *with all and singular their appurtenances; and also of the reversion and reversions, remainder and remainders, rents and services of the said premisses as above-mentioned, and of every part and parcel thereof, with the appurtenances, by such name and names, quality and number of messuages, acres and things, and in such manner and form, as by the said* E. F. *and* G. H. *or their counsel learned in the law, shall be reasonably devised or advised and required:* Which *said fine so to be had and levied in manner aforesaid, and all and every other fine and fines already had, or at any time hereafter to be had, levied, sued or prosecuted of the said premisses, or any part thereof, by itself, or jointly with any other lands or tenements, by or between the said parties to these presents, or by or between them, or any or either of them, and any other person or persons before the end of the said next* Easter *term, as for and concerning all and singular the said premisses above-mentioned, with the appurtenances, shall be and enure, and shall be adjudged, esteemed and taken to be and enure, to and for the only proper use and behoof of the said* E. F. *and* G. H. *their heirs and assigns, to the intent and purpose, that they may become perfect tenants of the freehold of the said premisses:*

misses: And to this further end, *intent and purpose, that they the said* E. F. *and* G. H. *shall and will on this side, and before the end of,* &c. *term next, permit and suffer the said* J. K. *and* T. M. *to sue and prosecute one or more writ or writs of entry* for disseisin en le post, *returnable before his majesty's justices of the said court of Common pleas, against them the said* E. F. *and* G. H. *of all and singular the said premisses above-mentioned, and of every part and parcel thereof, with the appurtenances, by such name and names, quantity and number of messuages, acres and things, and in such sort, manner and form, as by the said* J. K. *and* T. M. *shall be thought fit and convenient*; *unto and upon which said writ of entry so to be brought, the said* E. F. *and* G. H. *shall appear and vouch to warranty the said* A. B. *and* S. *his wife, and* C. D. *and* J. *his wife, who shall likewise appear, either in their several persons, or by their attornies lawfully authorised, and enter into the said warranty, and after their entry into the said warranty, shall vouch over the common vouchee, who shall also enter into the said warranty and imparl, and afterwards make default, to the end one perfect common recovery shall and may of all and singular the said premisses above-mentioned be had, prosecuted, and executed in all things, according to the usual form of common recoveries for assurance of lands, tenements and hereditaments, in such cases used and accustomed; and the same recovery shall in due form of law be executed by one writ of* habere facias seisinam *accordingly. And it is covenanted, granted, concluded and agreed upon, by and between the said parties to these presents, and the true meaning hereof is, and it is hereby so declared, that the said recovery so, or in any other manner to be had and suffered, and all and every other recovery and recoveries to be had, suffered and executed of the said premisses, or any part thereof, by or between the said parties to these presents, or by or between them or any or either of them and any other person and persons, on this side and before the end of the said, &c. term next coming, and the full force and execution of them, and every of them, and all other conveyances and assurances of the said premisses, or any part thereof, had, or to be had or made between the said parties, or any of them, shall be and enure, and shall be adjudged, esteemed and taken to be and enure, to and for the only proper use and behoof of the said J. K. and T. M. their heirs and assigns for ever: And each of them the said A. B. and C. D. for himself severally and apart, and not jointly, and for his several and respective heirs and assigns, doth severally and apart, and not jointly, covenant and grant to and with the said J. K. and T. M. their heirs and assigns, that they the said A. B. and S. his wife, and C. D. and J. his wife, are or some or one of them now is lawfully and rightfully seised of a good, sure, perfect, absolute and indefeasible estate of inheritance in fee-simple, or fee tail, of and in the said premisses abovementioned, with the appurtenances, in their or some, or one of their own rights or right, without any condition, mortgage, limitation of use or uses, or other matter or thing, to alter, charge, change and determine the same: And also, that they the said J. K. and T. M. their heirs and assigns, shall and may from time to time, and at all times hereafter for ever, peaceably and quietly enter into, have,*

hold,

hold, occupy, possess and enjoy all and singular the said premisses above-mentioned, and every part and parcel thereof, with the appurtenances, without the let, trouble, hindrance, molestation, interruption, and denial of them the said A. B. and S. his wife, and C. D. and J. his wife, their heirs or assigns, or any of them, and of all and every other person or persons whatsoever, claiming or to claim by, from or under them, or any or either of them, or by, from, or under &c. deceased: And further, that they the said A. B. and S. his wife, and C. D. and J. his wife, and their heirs, and all and every other person and persons, and his and their heirs, any thing having or claiming in the said premisses above-mentioned, or any part thereof, by, from or under them, or any or either of them, or under the said, &c. shall and will at any time or times hereafter, upon the reasonable request, and at the costs and charges of the said J. K. and T. M. their heirs or assigns, make, do and execute or cause or procure to be made, done and executed, all and every such further and other lawful and reasonable grants, acts and assurances in the law whatsoever, for the further, better, and more perfect granting, conveying and assuring of all and singular the said premisses above-mentioned, with the appurtenances, unto the said J. K. and T. M. their heirs and assigns, to the only proper use and behoof of the said J. K. and T. M. their heirs and assigns for ever, according to the true intent and meaning of these presents, as by the said J. K. and T. M. their heirs or assigns, or their or either of their counsel learned in the law, shall be reasonably devised or advised and required. In witness, &c.

A sur-

A surrender is a deed or instrument testifying that the particular tenant, for life or years, of lands and tenements, doth yield up his estate to him who hath the immediate reversion or remainder, that he may have the present possession thereof; and where the estate for life or years may merge or drown, by the mutual agreement of the parties. *Co. Lit.* 337.

The usual surrender at common law is of two sorts, a surrender in deed or by express words in writing, when the words of the lessee to the lessor prove a sufficient assent to give him his estate back again; and a surrender in law, being that which is wrought by operation of law, and not actual; as if lessee for life or years take a new lease of the same land during their term, it will be a surrender in law of the first lease: and in some cases this surrender is of greater force than the surrender in deed; for if a man make a lease for years to begin at a day to come, the future interest cannot be surrendered by deed, because there is no reversion wherein it may drown; but if the lessee before the day takes a new lease of the same thing, 'tis a good surrender in law of the former lease. Also this kind of surrender by taking a new lease holds good, though the second lease is for a less term than the first, &c. *Co. Lit.* 338. 5 *Rep.* 11. 10 *Rep.* 67. *Perk.* 601.

To make a good surrender in deed of lands, the following things are required; the surrenderor is to be a person able to make the surrender, and the surrenderee capable to receive and take it; the surrenderor must have an estate in possession of the thing surrendered, and not a future right: and the surrender is to be made to him
that

Of Estates, Ancestors, Heirs, &c.

that hath the next estate in remainder or reversion, without any estate coming between; the surrenderee must have a higher or greater estate in his own right, and not in the right of his wife, &c. than the surrenderor hath in the lands, so that the surrenderor's estate may be drown'd therein; there is to be privity of estate between the surrenderor and surrenderee; and the surrenderee must be sole seised of his estate in remainder, not in jointenancy; and agree to the surrender, &c. *Co. Lit.* 338. 2 *Rol. Abr.* 494. *Noy's Max.* 73.

A surrender may be of any thing grantable, either absolute or conditional; and may be made to an use, being a conveyance tied and charged with the limitation of an use: but it may not be of an estate in fee; nor of rights or titles only to estates for life or years; or for part of any such estate; nor may one termor regularly surrender to another. If lessee for life surrender to him in remainder for years, &c. it is a void surrender: though it has been held, that if a tenant for life, and one in remainder for life, surrender to him in reversion, it shall pass as several surrenders; first of him in remainder to the tenant for life, and then by the tenant for life to the reversioner. *Perk. Sect.* 675. *Cro. Eliz.* 688. *Leon.* 303. *Poph.* 157.

There are surrenders of copyhold or customary estates; and where things will not pass by surrender, the deed may enure to other purposes, and take effect by way of grant, having sufficient words. *Perk.* 624.

Form

Form of a *surrender of lands*.

TO all people to whom these presents shall come, A. B. of, &c. sendeth greeting. Whereas the said A. B. is possessed of and interested in one messuage or tenement called, &c. and lands containing, &c. situate, &c. for the remainder of a certain term of ninety-nine years, &c. the reversion whereof doth belong to C. D. of, &c. Gentleman: Now know ye, that the said A. B. for and in consideration of the sum of sixty pounds of lawful money of Great Britain to him in hand paid by the said C. D. the receipt whereof the said A. B. doth hereby confess and acknowledge; He the said A. B. Hath *surrendered and yielded up,* and by these presents doth surrender and yield up, unto the said C. D. his heirs and assigns for ever, All the said messuage or tenement, lands and premisses above-mentioned, and all the estate, right, title, interest, term of years, claim and demand whatsoever of him the said A. B. of, in and to the said premisses, and every part thereof, with the appurtenances; so that neither he the said A. B. his executors, administrators or assigns, or any of them, shall or may have, claim, challenge or demand the said premisses, or any part thereof, or any estate, right, title or interest, of, in and to the same, but shall at all times hereafter, of and from all right, title and interest, of and in the said premisses, and every part thereof be barred and for ever excluded by these presents. And the said A. B. for himself, his executors, administrators and assigns, doth covenant and grant to and with the said C. D. his heirs and assigns, that be the said C. D. *his heirs and assigns, shall and may, at all times hereafter, peaceably and quietly enter into, have, hold, occupy, possess and enjoy all and singular the said messuage or tenement, lands and premisses above-mentioned, and every part thereof, with the appurtenances; without the let, trouble, hindrance, molestation, interruption or denial of him the said* A. B. *his executors administrators or assigns, or of any other person or persons whatsoever, claiming or to claim, by, from or under him.* In witness, &c.

6. Gift and Grant. A deed of gift is an instrument that passeth lands or goods; and is applied to two kinds of conveyances, for either of those purposes, where there is no bargain and sale. And a gift is of a larger extent than a grant, extending to things moveable and immoveable: though as to things immoveable, when taken strictly, it is applicable only to lands and tenements given in tail; but gifts and grants are often confounded. *Wood's Inst.* 263.

In this deed the person who gives is called the donor, and he to whom the thing is given is called the donee, and in like manner there is grantor and grantee, &c. The deed must have apt words to describe and set forth the persons of the donor and donee, that they be duly named, and also the thing given, &c. and all necessary circumstances, as sealing and delivery, and livery of seisin are to be observed: and if a deed of gift, or any other deed, be procured by duress of imprisonment of the party that makes it, for this it may be made void. *Perk. Sect.* 16. *F. N. B.* 202.

A deed

Of Estates, Interests, Heirs, &c.

A deed of gift is good without any consideration; and a gift may be upon condition: but great care must be taken that there be no fraud in the case; for if a deed of gift and conveyance of lands is made with intent to defraud a purchaser upon good consideration, as against such purchaser it shall be void, and parties justifying the same to be *bona fide* made, shall forfeit a year's value of the lands, &c. And so it is if any deed of gift, or grant, be made to defeat creditors of their just debts, &c. The statute makes the deed void, against such creditors; but not against the party himself, his executors or administrators, against whom it remains good. *Co. Lit.* 351. *Cro. Jac.* 271. *Stat.* 13 *Eliz. c.* 5. perpetuated by *Stat.* 29 *Eliz. c.* 5. 27 *Eliz. c.* 4. perpetuated by *Stat.* 39 *Eliz. c.* 18. *Sect.* 32.

The words give and grant, in deeds of gift, &c. of things which lie in grant, will amount unto a grant, a feoffment, a gift, release, confirmation or surrender, and may be pleaded, as a gift, or grant, release, &c. at the election of the party: and the deeds of gift and grant are said to be alike in nature, and equal in power. 1 *Inst.* 301.

Grant signifies a conveyance in writing of incorporeal things, not lying in livery; as of reversions, advowsons, tithes, services, rent, common in gross, &c. And grants are made by such persons as cannot give but by deed. *West. Symb.* 234.

A grant shall be taken most strongly against the grantor, and for the grantee: And the grantee himself is to take by the grant immediately, and not a stranger, or any one *in futuro*. The use of any thing being granted, all is granted necessary to enjoy such use; and in the grant of things,

things, what is requisite for the obtaining thereof is included: so that if timber trees are granted, the grantee may come upon the grantor's ground to cut and carry them away. Where the principal thing is granted, the incident shall pass with it; but not the principal by the grant of the incident. *Co. Lit.* 56, 151. 2 *Inst.* 309. *Plowd.* 15.

If lands are granted by deed, the houses which stand thereon will pass; for houses and mills pass by the grant of all lands, as land is the most durable thing on which they are built. By grant of all the lands the woods will pass: if a man grants all his trees in a certain place, this passeth the soil; tho' an exception of wood extends to the trees only, and not the soil of the land: and trees in boxes, &c. pass not by the grant of land, because they are separated from the freehold. When a first description of lands in a grant is true, if the second be false, this grant is good; but if the first be false, notwithstanding the second be true, nothing will pass by it. 4 *Rep.* 86. 5 *Rep.* 11. 3 *Rep.* 10. 6 *Mod.* 170.

Grants are to be of things certain; and the law will not allow of a grant of imperfect interests, or of such as are merely future: in all grants there must be a foundation of interest, or they will not be good; the thing granted must be what is grantable; and it is to be granted in that manner the law requires; also there must be an acceptance of the grant, by him to whom made. One attainted of treason or felony may make a grant; and be good against all persons but the king, and the lord of whom the lands are held: grants made by persons *non sunt memoriæ* are voidable by their heirs, &c. but good

against

Of Estates, Ancestors, Heirs, &c.

against themselves; and though infants, and feme coverts, are not capable to be grantors, yet they may be grantees, subject to disagreement of the husband, and the infant at his full age. *Perk. Sect.* 15, 26, 31. *Co. Lit.* 2.

Deeds of grant may be void by incertainty, impossibility, being against law, &c. But where the grant is impossible, according to the letter, the law may make such construction as by possibility it may take place: and constructions of grants shall be agreeable to the intent of the parties. *Co. Lit.* 183, 313. *Co. Rep.* 46.

The form of a deed of *gift* of land.

THIS *indenture, made the day and year,* &c. Between A. B. *of,* &c. *esquire, of the one part, and* E. B. *of,* &c. *son of the said* A. B. *of the other part,* witnesseth, *that the said* A. B. *for and in consideration of the natural love and affection which he hath and beareth unto the said* E. B. *and for the better maintenance of him the said* E. B. Hath given, granted, aliened, enfeoffed and confirmed, *and by these presents doth give, grant, alien, enfeoff and confirm unto the said* E. B. All *that messuage or tenement,* &c. *situate, lying and being,* &c. *with all and singular its appurtenances, and all houses, out-houses, lands,* &c. *And the reversion and reversions, remainder and remainders, rents and services of the said premisses; and also all the estate, right, title, interest, property, claim and demand whatsoever of him the said* A. B. *of, in and to the said messuage or tenement, lands and premisses, and of, in and to every part and parcel thereof, with the appurtenances; and all deeds, evidences*

evidences and writings concerning the said premisses only, now in the hands or custody of the said A. B. or which he may get or come by without suit in law: To have and to hold the said messuage or tenement, lands, hereditaments and premisses hereby given and granted, or mentioned or intended to be given or granted unto the said E. B. his heirs and assigns, to the only proper use and behoof of him the said E. B. his heirs and assigns for ever. And the said A. B. for himself, his heirs, executors and administrators, doth covenant, promise and grant, to and with the said E. B. his heirs and assigns, by these presents, that he the said E. B. his heirs and assigns, shall and lawfully may from henceforth for ever hereafter, peaceably and quietly have, hold, occupy, possess and enjoy the said messuage or tenement, lands, hereditaments and premisses hereby given and granted, or mentioned or intended so to be, with their and every of their appurtenances, free, clear and discharged, or well and sufficiently saved and kept harmless, of and from all former and other gifts, grants, bargains and sales, feoffments, jointures, dowers, estates, entails, rents, rent-charges, arrearages of rent, statutes, **judgments**, recognizances, statute merchant and **of** the staple, extents, and of and from all other titles, troubles, charges and incumbrances whatsoever, had, made, committed, done or suffered, or to be had, made, committed, done or suffered, by him the said A. B. his heirs, executors or administrators, or any other person or persons lawfully claiming, or to claim, by, from, or under him, them, or any or either of them. In witness, &c.

7. A

7. A lease is a demise or letting of lands, tenements or hereditaments to another, for term of life, years, or at will, for a rent reserved. All leases, interests of freehold, and terms for years in lands, &c. are to be in writing, or shall have no greater effect than estates at will; except leases not exceeding three years from the making, &c. And if the substance of a lease be put in writing, and signed by the parties, though it be not sealed, it shall have the effect of a lease for years, &c. Articles with covenants to let and make a lease of lands, for a certain term, at so much rent, have been adjudged a lease: and a licence to occupy, and take the profits, &c. which passeth an interest, amounts to the same. 29 *Car.* 2. *Co. Lit.* 43. *Cro. Eliz.* 486. 3 *Salk.* 223.

Leases may be for life or years, of any thing that lies in livery or grant; but a lease for life, which requires livery of seisin, cannot be made to commence at a day to come; for by the common law an estate of freehold must take effect presently, and livery cannot be made to a future estate: tho' a lease for life in 'reversion is good. Leases for years should be made of such lands, &c. whereunto the lessor or landlord may come to distrain; not of incorporeal inheritances; and a lease for years may commence from a day past, or to come; as *Christmas* next, three or ten years after, or after the death of the lessor, &c. and be good. This lease may have a certain commencement and determination, and have all the usual ceremonies, &c. A demise having no certain commencement, is void. *Co. Lit.* 47. 5 *Rep.* 94. *Plowd.* 273. *Vaugh.* 85.

A man seised of an estate in fee-simple, in his own right, of any lands or tenements, may make

make a lease of it for what lives or years he will; and one, that is seised of an estate tail in lands, may grant a lease of it for his own life, but not longer; except it be by fine or recovery, or lease warranted by the statute 32 *H*. 8. *c*. 36. by which statute, tenants in tail are enabled to make leases, not exceeding three lives, or twenty-one years, of lands commonly let to farm, under the accustomed yearly rent, &c. He that is seised of an estate for life, may make a lease for his life, according as he is seised; and if tenant in tail, or for life, make any lease generally, it shall be construed for his own life. Where a lease for years is made by tenant for life, it will be good as long as the estate for life doth last; and if lessee for years makes a lease for life, it may be enjoyed accordingly, if the term of years lasts so long; but if he gives livery and seisin upon it, this is a forfeiture of the estate for years: a person possessed of lands for years, may make a lease of all the years, except one pay, or any short part of the term; it is to be granted for a less term than the maker hath in the premisses, for if all the estate is granted, it is an assignment. *Co. Lit.* 42. *Wood's Inst*. 266, 267.

Leases may be made for any number of years, months, or weeks; and be from week to week, month, &c. for three or four years. If one makes a lease for a year, and so from year to year, it is a lease for two years; and if from three years to three years, it is a good lease for six years; and in case 'tis made for a year, to hold from year to year, so long as both parties agree 'till six years expire, this is a lease for the six years, but determinable every year, at the will of either party; but if 'tis for a year, and

Of Estates, Ancestors, Heirs, &c.

so from year to year, until six years determine, it will be a certain lease for six years. A man makes a lease for years to one person, and afterwards makes a lease for years to another of the same lands; the second lease shall be good for so many years thereof as shall be to come after the first lease is ended. *Co. Lit.* 6. 6 *Rep.* 35. 6 *Mod.* 215. *Noy's Max.* 67.

A person out of possession cannot make a lease of lands, without entering and sealing the lease upon the land: and when a lease is sealed by the lessor, though the lessee hath not sealed the counterpart, action of covenant may be brought upon the lease against the lessor. The lessee is to enter on the premisses let; and such lessee for years is not in possession, so as to bring trespass, &c. until actual entry; but he may grant over his term before entry. On a lease for life or years, the lessee hath but a special interest in the timber-trees, as things annexed to the land, to have the mast and shade for his cattle, &c. and when they are severed from the land, the lessee's interest is determined, and the lessor may take them as part of his inheritance: but if an house falls down by tempest, &c. the lessee may take the timber to re-edify it, &c. *Dalif.* 81. *Co. Lit.* 46. 4 *Rep.* 62. 11 *Rep.* 81.

The lessor making a lease may not reserve rent to any other but himself, his heirs, &c. and if he reserves a rent to his executors, the rent shall be to the heir, as incident to the reversion of the land: if a lessor dies before the day of payment of rent, the heir shall have it; but if it becomes due in the lessor's life-time, and be not received, it shall go to his executors. The lessor may distrain in the tenements letten

for

for the rent, &c. Also land leased is subject to those lawful remedies which the lessor provides for recovery of his rent, possession, &c. into whose hands soever the land comes. *Co. Lit.* 47. *Raym.* 213. 10 *Rep.* 127, 129. *Cro. Jac.* 300.

If any lessor tenant for life dies on the day rent is made payable to him, by lease determining at his death; the executors, &c. in action of the case may recover from the under-tenants the whole; or if he die before such a day, a due proportion of the rent: and when demises are not by deed, landlords shall have satisfaction, for the use of what the tenants hold. Where tenants or lessees of lands, &c. held at a rack-rent, being in arrear one year's rent, leave the same uncultivated or unoccupied, two justices of peace, at request of the landlord, may go upon and view the premisses; and if, on notice fixed on the most notorious place, and a second view, the rent be not paid, the lease shall become void: but these proceedings are examinable by the next justices of assise, who may order restitution, &c. Tenants holding over lands, after the end of their leases, or on notice of quitting the premisses, after the time appointed, shall pay double rent. *Stat.* 4 *Geo.* 2. *c.* 28. 11 *Geo.* 2. *c.* 19.

Tenant in tail, remainder to the defendant in fee, lease for years, and dies without issue a week before the day of payment of the half year's rent; the lessee at the day pays all the half year's rent to the defendant; the executor of the tenant in tail brings his bill for apportionment of the rent. By the lord chancellor *Hardwicke:* This point has never been determined; but this is so strong a case, that I shall make it a precedent. There are in it two grounds for relief in equity; the first arises on the statute of the 11 *Geo* 2. the second arises on the tenant's having submitted to pay the rent to the defendant; the relief arising upon the statute, is either from the strict legal construction, or equity founded upon the reason of it: and here it is proper to consider what the mischief was before the act, and what remedy is provided at common law; if tenant for life, or any who had a determinable estate, died but a day before the rent reserved on a lease of his became due, the rent was lost, for no one was intitled to recover it; his representatives could not, because they could only bring an action for the use and occupation; and that would not lie where there was a lease, but debt or covenant; nor could the remainder-man, because it did not accrue in his time. Now this act appoints the apportioning the rent, and gives the remedy. But there are two descriptions of the persons, to whose executors the remedy is given; in the preamble, it is one having only an estate for life; in the enacting part, it is tenant for life; now tenant in tail comes expressly within the mischief. I do not know how the judges at common law would construe it; but I should be inclined in this court to extend it to them; I should make no doubt, were this the case of tenant in tail after possibility of issue extinct, for he is considered in many respects as tenant for life only; he cannot suffer a recovery; he may be injoined from committing waste, such as hurts the inheritance, as selling timber; tho' not for committing common waste, being considered as to that as tenant in tail: were it the case of tenant for years determinable on lives, he certainly must be included within the act, tho'

it

it says only tenant for life: it would be playing with the words to say otherwise; the cases shew the necessity of construing this act beyond the words; tenant in tail has certainly a larger estate than a mere tenant for life, for he has the inheritance in him, and may when he pleases turn it into a fee; but if he does not, at the instant of his death he has but an interest for life: such too is the case of a wife tenant in tail *ex provisione mariti*: upon this point I give no absolute opinion. As to the equity arising from this statute, I know no better rule than this, *æquitas sequitur legem*: where equity finds a rule of law agreeable to conscience, it pursues the sense of it to analogous cases; if it does so as to maxims of the common law why not as to the reasons of acts of parliament? nay, it has actually done so, on the statute of forcible entry; upon which, this court grounds bills, not only to remove the force, but to quiet the possession; that act requires a legal estate in possession: this court extends the reason to equitable interest, but I ground my opinion in this case upon the tenants having submitted to pay the rent; he has held himself bound in conscience to pay it, for the use and occupation of the land the last half year; he paid it to the defendant, which he was not bound to do in law; and in such a case, the person he pays it to shall be accountable, and considered as receiving it for those who are in equity intitled to it. The division must be that prescribed by the statute, and then the plaintiff is intitled to such a proportion of the rent as accrued during the testator's life, and accordingly it was decreed. *Burn's Just. quarto* 313.

The

The remedy given by *Stat.* 4 *Geo.* 2. *c.* 28. *f.* 1. seemeth not altogether adequate to the evil; for three reasons: 1. Because such action is certainly tedious and expensive. 2. It is uncertain when the action is over, whether the tenant will be able to pay. 3. What is chiefly wanted, namely, putting the landlord into possession, is not obtained by such action, but for that he shall be still to seek; a more short and easy method of ousting the tenant in his possession, seemeth more eligible in the like cases. *Ibid.* 311.

This clause also proceedeth upon a supposition, which perhaps may not be true, namely, that the tenant is a man of substance; it is more likely, that if he were able to live elsewhere, he would not chuse to hold over under such circumstances, nor perhaps would the landlord want to be rid of him: the putting him out of possession by some expeditious and easy method seemeth the more adequate remedy in this case also in like manner as is provided in the case where the tenant deserteth the premisses. *Ibid* 312.

A man demiseth lands for term of years, &c. the law intends a covenant that the lessee, on paying his rent, shall quietly enjoy the land during the term. And in case a lessee for years loses his lease, if it can be proved there was such a term let to him by lease, and that it is not determined, he shall not lose his term; so it is of any other estate in lands, if the deed that created it be lost: for the estate in the land is derived from the party that made it, and not from the deed otherwise than instrumentally and declarative of the mind and intent of the party, &c. *Co. Lit.* 384. 2 *Lil. Abr.* 152.

No

Of Estates, Ancestors, Heirs, &c.

No tenant shall take leases of above two farms in any town, village, *&c.* nor hold two, unless he dwell in the parish, under penalties and forfeitures by statute 25 *Hen.* 8. *c.* 13.

See more of leases and tenants, under the heads, *Action of waste, Ejectment, Distresses* and *Replevins,* also *Tenures.*

The form of a lease *for years of a* house.

'THIS Indenture made, *&c. Between A. B.*
' of, *&c.* of the one part, and *C. D.* of, *&c.*
' of the other part, *Witnesseth,* that for and in
' consideration of the rent and covenants herein
' after reserved and contained, on the part and
' behalf of the said *C. D.* his executors and ad-
' ministrators, to be paid, kept and performed,
' *He* the said *A. B. Hath* demised granted and
' to farm letten, and by these presents doth de-
' mise, grant, and to farm let unto the said *C.*
' *D. All* that messuage or tenement, known by
' the name or sign, *&c.* situate and lying in,
' *&c.* with all and singular cellars, sollars, cham-
' bers, rooms, lights, ways, waters, water-
' courses, easements, profits, commodities and
' appurtenances, to the said messuage or tene-
' ment belonging or appertaining; together
' with the use of the goods in the schedule
' hereunto annexed mentioned: *To have and to*
' *hold* the said messuage or tenement, and all
' and singular the premisses, with their and
' every of their appurtenances herein before-
' mentioned, or intended to be hereby demised
' unto the said *C. D.* his executors, admini-
' strators and assigns, from the day of, *&c.*
' for and during and unto the full end and
' term of fourteen years, from thence next
                            ' ensuing,

Of Estates, Ancestors, Heirs, &c.

'ensuing, and fully to be complete and ended:
'*Yielding and paying* therefore yearly and every
'year, during the said term, unto the said *A.*
'*B.* his executors, administrators or assigns,
'the rent or sum of twenty-five pounds of law-
'ful money of *Great Britain*, on the four most
'usual feasts or terms in the year, that is to
'say, the Annunciation of the blessed virgin
'*Mary*, the Nativity of Saint *John* the Baptist,
'the Feast of Saint *Michael* the archangel, and
'the Birth of our Lord *Christ*, by even and
'equal portions. *And* if it shall happen, the
'said yearly rent of twenty-five pounds, or any
'part thereof, shall be behind and unpaid by
'the space of eight and twenty days, next after
'any of the said feast days, on which the same
'ought to be paid as aforesaid (being lawfully
'demanded), that then, and at all times then
'after, it shall and may be lawful to and for
'the said *A. B.* his executors, administrators
'and assigns, into the said demised messuage or
'tenement and premisses, or into any part
'thereof, in the name of the whole, to re-
'enter, and the same to have again, re-possess
'and enjoy as in his and their former estate,
'and the said *C. D.* his executors, administra-
'tors and assigns, thereout and from thence
'to expel and put out; any thing herein con-
'tained to the contrary thereof in any wise
'notwithstanding. *And* the said *C. D.* for him-
'self, his executors, administrators and as-
'signs, doth covenant and grant to and with
'the said *A. B.* his executors, administrators and
'assigns by these presents, that he the said *C.*
'*D.* his executors, administrators or assigns,
'shall and will, during the said term hereby
'demised, well and truly pay, or cause to be
' paid,

'paid, unto the said *A. B.* his executors, administrators or assigns, the said yearly rent of twenty-five pounds, on the days and times, and in the manner and form above-mentioned, for payment thereof, according to the reservation thereof as aforesaid, and the true intent and meaning of these presents: *And also*, that he the said *C. D.* his executors, administrators and assigns, or some or one of them, shall and will, at his or their own proper costs and charges, well and sufficiently repair, uphold, support, maintain and keep the said messuage or tenement and premisses, with the glass windows, pavements, privies, sinks, gutters and wydraughts belonging to the same, in, by and with all and all manner of needful and necessary reparations and amendments whatsoever, when and as often as need or occasion shall be or require, during the said term, (the casualty of fire, which may burn down or destroy the said messuage or tenement and premisses, or any part thereof, only excepted); and the said messuage or tenement and premisses being so well and sufficiently repaired, upheld, supported, maintained and kept, at the end of the said term, or other sooner determination of this present demise, unto the said *A. B.* his executors, administrators and assigns, shall and will, peaceably and quietly, leave and yield up, (except as before excepted) and shall and will then also leave unto the said *A. B.* his executors, administrators and assigns, all such goods as are mentioned in the said schedule hereto annexed, in as good condition as they are now in, reasonable usage of them *&c.* excepted. *And further*, that it shall and may

Of Estates, Ancestors, Heirs, &c.

'may be lawful to and for the said *A. B.* his
'executors, administrators or assigns, or any of
'them, with workmen or others, or without,
'twice in every year, during the continuance
'of this demise, at seasonable times in the day-
'time, to enter and come into and upon the
'said demised premisses, or any part thereof,
'and view, search and see the state and condi-
'tion of the reparations of the same; and of
'all defects, defaults, and want of repairs,
'then and there found, to give or leave notice
'or warning in writing, at and upon the said
'demised premisses, to and for the said *C. D.*
'for the repairing and amending thereof, within
'the space of three months then next follow-
'ing: in which said space or time of three
'months, after every or any such notice or
'warning, he the said *C. D.* for himself, his
'executors, administrators and assigns, doth
'hereby covenant and grant to and with the
'said *A. B.* his executors, administrators and
'assigns, well and sufficiently to repair and
'amend the defects and want of reparations so
'to be found as aforesaid, (except as is before
'excepted.) *And also,* that he the said *C. D.*
'his executors, administrators and assigns, shall
'and will at all times hereafter, during the
'term hereby demised, bear, pay and discharge
'all taxes, charges, impositions and parish du-
'ties which shall be taxed, charged, imposed
'or assessed upon the said messuage or tene-
'ment aforesaid, or any part thereof, (except
'the land-tax and window-tax, charged by act
'of parliament, and payable to the king's ma-
'jesty, his heirs and successors.) *And* the said
'*A. B.* for himself, his executors, administra-
'tors and assigns, doth covenant and grant

' to

'to and with the said *C. D.* his executors, ad-
'ministrators and assigns, that he the said *C.
'D.* his executors, administrators and assigns,
'paying the said yearly rent of twenty-five
'pounds above reserved in manner aforesaid,
'and performing all and every the covenants and
'agreements herein before contained, shall and
'may peaceably and quietly have, hold, use,
'occupy, possess and enjoy the said messuage or
'tenement and premisses hereby demised, for
'and during the term hereby granted, without
'any lawful let, suit, trouble or interruption
'of or by the said *A. B.* his executors, admi-
'nistrators or assigns, or any of them, or by any
'other person or persons lawfully claiming, or
'to claim, by, from or under him, them, or
'any of them, or by or through his, their, or
'any of their acts, means or procurement. *In
'witness,* &c.

8. A mortgage is defined to be a pawn of lands or tenements for money borrowed, to be the creditor's for ever, if the money be not repaid at the day agreed: but on the mortgagor's paying the interest of the money, mortgages are continued a long time without disturbing the possession or parties. *Lit.* 332.

These mortgages are usually made by lease for a long term of years, lease and release, assignment, &c. and therein is contained a *proviso,* that if the money be paid on the day, the deed to be void: until failure in payment, the mortgagor generally holds the lands; and if failure be made, and the mortgagee doth enter into the land, yet the mortgagor hath an equity of redemption, and may call the mortgagee to account: but the mortgagee may bar the equity of redemption, and oblige the mortgagor to pay what is due, or be foreclosed; which the court of chancery will order in convenient time. A feoffment in fee or lease for life or years, may be made with proviso, that if the feoffor or grantor, their heirs or executors, pay to the feoffee or grantee, &c. such sums of money at a certain day, then the feoffor or grantor may re-enter; and this hath been a common condition in a mortgage, or of an estate upon condition in a deed: in the former case of mortgages, the mortgagor keeps possession till failure; but here the mortgagee has possession presently, and 'till payment, and is in the mean time called tenant in mortgage, &c. *Co. Lit.* 205.

A mortgagee is esteemed in possession, on executing the mortgage; and if the mortgage-money be not paid, whereby the land is forfeited, he may bring ejectment, without actual entry. The interest in the lands mortgaged is in law, in the mortgagee, before forfeiture; he hath as it were purchased the same upon a valuable consideration, as the law will intend; and although the mortgagor may redeem, it is not certainly known whether he will do it or not: and if he do not redeem the land, the estate is absolute in the mortgagee; but still subject to an equitable right of redemption by the morgagor. 2 *Lil. Abr.* 203, 204.

If persons having once mortgaged lands mortgage the same a second time, without discovering the first mortgage, they shall forfeit their equity of redemption, and the second mortgagee shall have the power of redeeming, &c. And where any action of ejectment shall be brought by a mortgagee for the recovery of the possession of morgaged lands, and no suit is

depending

depending for foreclosing or redeeming such land; if the person that hath right to redeem shall, pending the action, pay the mortgagee, or bring into court all the principal money and interest and costs, it shall be a full satisfaction of the mortgage; and the mortgagee shall reconvey the land, and deliver up all deeds, &c. And on a bill in equity to compel the defendant having right to redeem, to pay the mortgage-money, or on default to be foreclosed, &c. the court upon the defendants application may make orders therein before the cause is brought to hearing, &c. *Stat.* 4 & 5 *W.* & *M. c.* 16. 7 *Geo.* 2. *c.* 20.

The mortgagor's heir, who is interested in the condition, may pay the money and save the forfeiture; and so may executors, &c. unless it be where no time is limited for payment, and the mortgagor, having time during his life, do not pay it: in this case, his heir or executors shall not be received to pay the money after his death. The executors are to have money due on mortgages, if a mortgagee in fee dies before the day of payment; except the heir be particularly named, as the executors do more represent the testator than the heir: and mortgages have been looked upon as part of the personal estate, if it be not otherwise declared by the mortgagee in fee; also personal estate of a mortgagor shall be applied to discharge the mortgage, where there are personal assets to pay all legacies. *Co. Lit.* 206, 210. 2 *Vent.* 348. 2 *Salk.* 450. *Eq. Caf. Abr.* 269. *pl.* 2. *Gilb. Lex. Præt.* 315. 15 *Vin. Abr.* 441. *pl.* 18. 2 *Wil. Rep.* 455.

An old mortgage assigned to another ought to be taken as a new mortgage from the time of

R the

the assignment: and when a mortgage is forfeited the mortgagee shall have interest for his interest; so shall an assignee for all interest, from the time the mortgage was assigned. For where the mortgagee assigns his mortgage, all money paid by the assignee, if due at that time, shall be accounted principal, to the mortgagor, whenever he comes to redeem: but an agreement made at the time of a mortgage will not make future interest principal; the interest must be first due, before any agreement concerning it may make the same principal. *Chanc. Rep.* 218, 258. 2 *Salk.* 449.

Where there are mortgages upon an estate intended to be sold, assignments are to be made in trust, from the mortgagees, &c. to the purchaser; reciting the mortgages, and assigning them in trust to attend the fee, which is conveyed absolutely to the purchaser by lease and release. A purchaser coming in upon a valuable consideration, purchasing a precedent incumbrance, shall protect his estate against any person that hath a mortgage subsequent: and it hath been allowed in equity, that a third mortgagee may buy in the first incumbrance, to protect his own mortgage, &c. 2 *Ventr.* 538.

Form of a common mortgage *of an estate.*

'THIS indenture, made, &c. Between *A. B.*
' of, &c. of the one part, and *C. D.* of,
' &c. of the other part, *witnesseth*, that the said
' *A. B.* for and in consideration of the sum of
' one hundred pounds of lawful money of *Great*
' *Britain*, to him in hand paid by the said *C. D.*
' the receipt whereof the said *A. B.* doth hereby
' confess and acknowledge; *He* the said *A. B.*
' hath

Of Estates, Ancestors, Heirs, &c.

'hath granted, bargained and sold, and by these
'presents doth grant, &c. unto the said C. D.
'*All* that messuage or tenement, &c. and all
'those lands, &c. situate, &c. and also the re-
'version and reversions, remainder and remain-
'ders, rents and services of all and singular the
'said premisses above-mentioned, and of every
'part and parcel thereof, with the appurte-
'nances; *To have and to hold* the said messuage
'or tenement, lands and premisses above-men-
'tioned, and every part and parcel thereof, with
'the appurtenances, unto the said C. D. his
'executors, administrators and assigns, for and
'during the term of five hundred years, next
'and immediately ensuing and following, and
'fully to be complete and ended: *Yielding and*
'*paying* therefore yearly, during the said term,
'one pepper-corn, in and upon the feast of St.
'*Michael* the archangel, if demanded. *Provided*
'always, and upon condition, that if the said
'*A. B.* his heirs or assigns, do and shall well and
'truly pay, or cause to be paid unto the said
'*C. D.* his executors, administrators or assigns,
'the full sum of one hundred and five pounds of
'lawful *British* money, in and upon the day, &c.
'which will be in the year, &c. without any de-
'duction or abatement for taxes, assessments,
'or any other impositions whatsoever, either or-
'dinary or extraordinary; that then and from
'thenceforth these presents, and every thing
'herein contained, shall cease, determine and be
'void; any thing herein contained to the con-
'trary notwithstanding: *And* the said *A. B.* for
'himself, his heirs and assigns, doth covenant
'and grant, to and with the said *C. D.* his execu-
'tors, administrators and assigns, that he the said
'*A. B.* his heirs or assigns, shall and will well

'and

'and truly pay or cause to be paid unto the said
'C. D. his executors, administrators or assigns,
'the said full sum of one hundred and five
'pounds, in and upon the said day, &c. which
'will be in the said year, &c. without any de-
'duction as aforesaid, according to the true in-
'tent and meaning of these presents: *And also*
'that he the said *C. D.* his executors, administra-
'tors and assigns, shall and may, at all times,
'after default shall be made in performance of the
'proviso or condition herein contained, peacea-
'bly and quietly enter into, have, hold, occupy,
'possess and enjoy all and singular the said mes-
'suage or tenement, lands and premisses above-
'mentioned, and every part and parcel thereof,
'with the appurtenances, for and during the re-
'sidue and remainder of the said term of five
'hundred years hereby granted, which shall be
'then to come and unexpired, without the let,
'trouble, hindrance, molestation, interruption,
'and denial of him the said *A. B.* his heirs and
'assigns, and of all and every other person and
'persons whatsoever: *And further*, that he the
'said *A. B.* and his heirs, and all and every other
'person and persons, and his and their heirs, any
'thing having or claiming in the said messuage
'or tenement and premisses above-mentioned,
'or any part thereof, shall and will at any time
'or times, after default shall be made in perform-
'ance of the proviso or condition herein con-
'tained, make, do and execute, or cause or pro-
'cure to be made, done and executed, all and
'every such further and other lawful and reason-
'able grants, acts and assurances in the law what-
'soever, for the further, better and more perfect
'granting and assuring of all and singular the
'said premisses above-mentioned, with the ap-
'purte-

'purtenances, unto the said *C. D. To hold* to him
' the said *C. D.* his executors, administrators and
' assigns, for and during all the rest and residue
' of the said term of five hundred years above
' granted, which shall be then to come and un-
' expired, as by the said *C. D.* his executors, ad-
' ministrators or assigns, or his or their counsel
' learned in the law shall be reasonably devised,
' or advised and required. *And lastly*, it is cove-
' nanted, granted, concluded and agreed upon,
' by and between the said parties to these pre-
' sents, and the true meaning hereof also is, and
' it is hereby so declared, that until default shall
' be made in performance of the proviso or con-
' dition herein contained, he the said *A. B.* his
' heirs and assigns, shall and may hold and enjoy
' all and singular the said premisses above-men-
' tioned, and receive and take the rents, issues
' and profits thereof, to his and their own pro-
' per use and benefit; any thing herein con-
' tained to the contrary thereof notwithstanding.
' *In witness,* &c.

The form of an assignment of a mortgage *to attend the fee.*

' THIS indenture tripartite, made, &c. Be-
' tween *A. B.* of, &c. of the first part,
' *C. D.* of, &c. of the second part, and *E. F.* of,
' &c. and *G. H.* and *J. K.* of, &c. of the third
' part. *Whereas* the said *C. D.* by his indenture
' of mortgage, bearing date, &c. did demise,
' grant, bargain and sell unto the said *A. B. All*
' that messuage, &c. and the reversion and re-
' versions, remainder and remainders, rents,
' issues and profits thereof, and all the estate,
' right,

'right, title, interest, claim and demand whatsoever, of him the said *C. D.* of, in and to the same, or any part or parcel thereof; *To be had and holden* unto the said *A. B.* his executors, administrators and assigns, from the date thereof, for and during the term of 500 years, from thence next ensuing, and fully to be complete and ended; at and under the yearly rent of, &c. which said recited indenture was defeasible on repayment by the said *C. D.* unto the said *A. B.* of the sum of, &c. at a certain day therein mentioned, then to come, and now since past, as in and by the said recited indenture may more fully appear. *And whereas* upon an account this day made up between the said *C. D.* and *A. B.* of and concerning the said debt of, &c. and the interest thereof, there remains justly due and owing from the said *C. D.* to the said *A. B.* for principal and interest on the said mortgage, the full sum of, &c. *And whereas* the said *E. F.* hath lately contracted and agreed with the said *C. D.* for the absolute purchase of all and singular the said messuage, &c. and premisses above-mentioned, for the sum of three hundred and fifty pounds, and in pursuance thereof, in and by certain indentures of lease and release, bearing date, &c. last past, made between the said *C. D.* of the one part, and the said *E. F.* of the other part; he the said *C. D.* hath granted and conveyed the said messuage, lands and premisses, unto the said *E. F.* and his heirs, as by the said indentures of lease and release may more fully appear: *Now* to the end the said term of 500 years may be preserved and kept on foot, to attend and wait on the reversion and inheritance of the said premisses, to protect and defend the same from all

'all incumbrances, subsequent to the creation of the said recited term, *This present indenture witnesseth*, that the said *A. B.* for and in consideration of the sum of, &c. to him in hand paid by the said *E. F.* (by and with the consent of the said *C. D.* testified by his being a party to, and signing and sealing of these presents) the receipt whereof the said *A. B.* doth hereby confess and acknowledge, and in consideration also of five shillings, of, &c. to the said *A. B.* in hand paid by the said *G. H.* and *J. K.* the receipt whereof the said *A. B.* doth hereby also acknowledge; *He* the said *A. B.* by and with the consent and agreement of the said *C. D.* testified as aforesaid, *Hath* bargained, sold, assigned and set over, and by these presents doth bargain, sell, assign and let over unto the said *G. H.* and *J. K.* (by the nomination and appointment of the said *E. F.*) *All* and singular the said messuage and premisses above-mentioned, and every part and parcel thereof, with the appurtenances; and also all the estate, right, title, interest, claim and demand whatsoever of him the said *A. B.* of, in and to the said premisses, and of, in and to every part and parcel thereof, with the appurtenances: *To have and to hold* all and singular the said messuage and premisses, and every part and parcel thereof, with the appurtenances, unto the said *G. H.* and *J. K.* their executors, administrators and assigns, for and during all the rest and residue of the said term of 500 years above mentioned, which is yet to come and unexpired; *In trust* for the said *E. F.* his heirs and assigns, and such other person and persons to whom the freehold and inheritance of the said premisses shall appertain

and

'and belong, to protect and defend the same
'from all subsequent incumbrances. *And* the
'said *A. B.* for himself, his executors and ad-
'ministrators, doth covenant and grant, to and
'with the said *E. F.* his executors, administra-
'tors and assigns, that he the said *A. B.* hath
'not done or committed any act, matter or
'thing whatsoever, whereby or wherewith the
'said premisses above-mentioned, or any part
'thereof, are, is, shall or may be charged or
'incumbred in title, estate or otherwise howso-
'ever. *In witness,* &c.'

9. An assignment is the setting over or tranf-
ferring the interest a man hath in a lease or other
thing to another. And assignments may be
made of lands held in fee, for life or years; of
an annuity, rent-charge, judgment, statute, &c.
but as to lands they are usually of leases and
estates for years.

Where tenant for years assigns his estate, no
consideration is required; for the tenure being
subject to payment of rent, &c. is sufficient to
vest an estate in the assignee: in other cases,
some consideration must be paid. And if lessee
for years assigns all his term in his lease to another, he cannot reserve a rent in the assignment;
for he hath no interest in the thing, by reason
of which the rent reserved should be paid; and
where there is no reversion, there can be no dif-
tress: but debt may lie upon it as on a contract.
Mod. 263. *Rep. Lil. Abr.* 99.

Although a lessee make an assignment over of
his term, yet action of debt lies against him for
the rent, by the lessor or his heir, (not having
accepted rent from the assignee:) but where a
lessee assigns his term, and the lessor his rever-

Of Estates, Ancestors, Heirs, &c.

sion, the privity is determined, and action of debt doth not lie for the reversioner against the first lessee. On an assignment of the lessee, before acceptance of rent from the assignee, the lessor may charge either the lessee or assignee with the rent, at his election; tho' if he once accepts the rent from the assignee, knowing of the assignment, he cannot afterwards bring debt against the lessee for rent. As the rent issues out of the land, the assignee generally who has the land, and is privy in estate, is debtor in respect thereof; yet if an assignment be made by an assignee, to any one whatever, the first assignee is not suable for any rent; here, if he be accepted by the lessor, the admission of one assignee is the admission of twenty. *Moor* 472. *3 Rep.* 23, 32.

An assignee is he who hath the whole estate of the assignor; and there is assignee in deed, being such person to whom a lease or estate is assigned by deed; and assignee in law, whom the law makes so without deed, as an executor appointed by will is in law assignee to the testator: but if there be assign in deed, the assign in law is not allowed. Where a grant is made to a man and his heirs, though the word *assigns* be not expressed, he may assign at his pleasure; for the word *assigns* is included in his heirs: and assignees may take advantage of forfeitures on conditions, when they are incident to the reversion, as for rent, &c. and regularly every assignee of the land may have advantage of inherent covenants; also assigns are bound by such covenants as a covenant to repair, &c. for the benefit of the estate, although not named. *Co. Lit.* 215. *Dy.* 6. *Ander.* 2. *Cro. Eliz.* 552.

But

Of Estates, Ancestors, Heirs, &c.

But when a covenant concerns a thing not in being at the time of the demise, as to make a new edifice, &c. the assignee is not bound, except he be named in express words; nor is he when named, if the thing to be done doth not concern the thing demised; or in contracts merely personal. A lessee covenanted for himself and his assigns, to rebuild a house before such a time, which he did not do, but after the time expired he assigned the term; and it was held that this covenant would not bind the assignee, because it was broken before the assignment. *Rol. Abr.* 915. *Plowd.* 284. *Salk.* 199.

Bonds and debts, &c. are said to be assigned; but must be sued for in the assignor's name: bills of exchange are assignable by indorsment, whereon the assignees may sue and recover in their own names, by Stat. 3 & 4 *Ann. c.* 9. perpetual by 7 *Ann. c.* 25. *s.* 3. If a man makes an assignment, and yet keeps possession of the land, &c. it shall be adjudged fraudulent. *F. N. B.* 98.

The form of an *assignment* of a lease.

THIS *indenture, made,* &c. Between A. B. *of,* &c. *of the one part, and* C. D. *of,* &c. *of the other part.* Whereas N. B. *of,* &c. *in and by this indenture of lease, bearing date,* &c. *for the consideration therein mentioned, did demise, grant, and to farm let unto the said* A. B. *All that messuage or tenement,* &c. *situate,* &c. To hold *unto the said* A. B. *his executors, administrators, and assigns, for and during the term of one and twenty years, thence next and immediately ensuing and following-*

lowing, and fully to be complete and ended; yielding and paying *unto the said* N. B. *his heirs and assigns, during the said term, the yearly rent or sum of,* &c. *at and upon the days,* &c. *and under divers covenants and agreements in the said recited indenture of lease contained, as in and by the said indenture may more fully appear.* Now this indenture witnesseth, *that the said* A. B. *for and in consideration of the sum of,* &c. *to him in hand paid by the said* C. D. *the receipt whereof is hereby acknowledged,* He *the said* A. B. Hath *granted, bargained and sold, assigned and set over, and by these presents doth grant, bargain,* &c. *unto the said* C. D. All *and singular the said messuage or tenement, and premisses above-mentioned, with the appurtenances; and also all the estate, right, title, interest, term of years, claim and demand whatsoever of him the said* A. B. *of, in and to the said premisses above-mentioned, and of, in and to every part and parcel thereof with the appurtenances, together with the said recited indenture of lease;* To have and to hold *the said messuage or tenement, and premisses above-mentioned, and every part and parcel thereof, with the appurtenances, unto the said* C. D. *his executors, administrators and assigns, for and during all the rest and residue of the said term of one and twenty years above recited, which is yet to come and unexpired; under the said yearly rent of,* &c. *payable to the said* N. B. *his heirs and assigns, and by and under all and every the covenants, conditions and agreements in the said recited indenture of lease mentioned and contained, which on the part and behalf of the said* A. B. *his executors and administrators, before the*

making

making of this present assignment, should and ought to have been paid, observed and performed: And the said A. B. *for himself, his executors and administrators, doth covenant and grant, to and with the said* C. D. *his executors, administrators and assigns, that the said lease and term of twenty-one years hereby assigned, are still in being and fulfilling, not surrendered, discharged or otherwise avoided:* And also, *that he the said* C. D. *his executors, administrators and assigns, shall and may, by and under the rent, covenants and conditions in the said recited lease contained, peaceably and quietly enter into, have, hold, occupy, possess and enjoy all and singular the said messuage, tenement and premisses above-mentioned, with the appurtenances, for and during the rest, residue and remainder of the said term of one and twenty years hereby granted and assigned, now to come and unexpired, without the let, trouble, hindrance, molestation, interruption and denial of him the said* A. B. *his executors, administrators or assigns, or of any other person or persons, claiming or to claim, by, from or under him or them, or any of them.* And further, *that he the said* A. B. *his executors and administrators, shall and will, at any time or times hereafter, make, do or execute all and every such further and other lawful and reasonable act and acts, thing and things in the law whatsoever, for the further and more perfect assigning, and transferring of the said recited indenture of lease and premisses above-mentioned, with the appurtenances, unto the said* C. D. *his executors, administrators and assigns, for and during all the rest and residue of the said term of twenty-*

one

one years above recited, now to come and unexpired, as by the said C. D. his executors, administrators or assigns, or his or their counsel learned in the law shall be reasonably devised, or advised and required. In witness, &c.

10. A will is the declaration of a man's mind and intent, as to the disposition of his lands or goods, of what he would have done after his death. The common law calls that a will, when lands and tenements are devised; and where it concerns chattels alone, it is termed a testament. *Co. Lit.* 111.

In a will made of goods there must be an executor named; but not of lands only, without goods, for executors have nothing to do with the freehold. If lands are given by will, 'tis called a devise, and goods and chattels a legacy; and there is this diversity between lands and goods given by a will, that when lands are devised in fee, or for life, the devisee shall enter without any appointment of others: but in case of goods, there must be the assent of the executor, &c. Where lands or tenements only are devised by will, the will ought to be proved in the chancery; if of goods and chattels it must be done in the spiritual court; and a will both of lands and goods may be proved in that court. *Co. Lit.* 111. *Swinb.* 24.

All persons, who have a sole estate in fee-simple of any lands, tenements or hereditaments, may give and devise the same by last will and testament, at their free will and pleasure; so as such persons are not feme coverts, infants, persons *Non sanæ memoriæ*, &c. whose wills shall not

Of Estates, Ancestors, Heirs, &c.

not be good in law: and by the Stat. 29 *Car.* 2. *c.* 3. perpetuated by 1 *Jac.* 2. *c.* 17. *f.* 5. for prevention of frauds, all devises of lands or tenements are to be in writing, signed by the devisor, or some by his express directions, in the presence of three credible witnesses, at least; and no devise in writing shall be revoked, but by some other will in writing, or by cancelling the same by the testator himself, or by his direction, &c. And where nuncupative wills, by word of mouth, are made for the disposition of chattels above 30*l.* value, they must be declared in presence of three witnesses, bid to bear witness, in the last sickness of the party, &c. and the substance of them must be reduced into writing, within six days after the making, &c. Lands entailed are not deviseable by will; only fee-simple lands, and goods and chattels. 32 *H.* 8. *c.* 1. 29 *Car.* 2. *c.* 3. 3 *Rep.* 31. *Co. Lit.* 111, 115.

The construction of wills is more favoured in law than any other deed or conveyance, to fulfil the intent of the testator; because the testator is supposed to be *inops consilii*, and in a hurry, and a devise is not a conveyance by common law, but by the statute: the devises before the statute were by custom, and as custom enabled men to dispose of their estates contrary to the common law; so it exempted this kind of conveyance from the regularity and propriety required in other conveyances; and thus it came to pass that wills upon the statute, in imitation of those by custom, gained such favourable construction. Words in wills are always construed according to the intention of the parties that make them, as near as can be collected; but the words and intent must agree with the law;

and

Of Estates, Ancestors, Heirs, &c.

and if the words are insensible and repugnant, they are void. 3 *Salk.* 127, 128. *Co. Lit.* 25. *Plowd.* 162.

An infant makes his will for lands, and when of age he declares it as his will, yet it is void; but an infant at fourteen years old may make a will of his goods and chattels. Although a feme covert cannot regularly make any will; the husband may bind himself by covenant or bond to permit his wife by will to dispose of legacies, &c. and this will be such an appointment as he will be bound to perform; yet 'tis properly no will, nor ought to be proved in the spiritual court: of things in action, or what she hath as her own as executrix, by her husband's consent, 'tis said she may make a will in law; if in other cases she disposes of any thing by the agreement of the husband, the property passes from him to her legatee, and it is as the gift of husband. A person, when he makes his will, ought not only to have his memory to answer questions, but to have perfect mind and memory; and one must have as good disposing memory when he revokes his will, as when he makes it: but if there be any disagreement of witnesses therein, their testimony is to be preferred, which depose that the testator was of sound memory, for the support of the testament. *Co. Lit.* 89. *Cro. Car.* 219. *Cro. Jac.* 497. *Mod. Rep.* 211. *Swinb.* 67.

If a man bid another make his will, and before it is done he dies, the will is not good: though if it be drawing up in his presence, it may be good for the devises finished. A will was made since the statute 29 *Car.* 2. by which lands were devised, but no name subscribed to it, being sealed in the presence of three witnesses,

was

was adjudged a good will; the will being written by the party himself, and his name in the will, which was held a sufficient signing: and a will may be good to convey lands, altho' it be not sealed; the statute of wills speaking nothing of sealing. *Plowd.* 10, 343. 3 *Lev.* 1. 2 *Danv. Abr.* 542.

A testator devised by will all his lands, tenements and estate whatsoever, whereof he should be possessed at the time of his death; and after this he purchased lands, &c. and it was held, that a devise of personal things was good, tho' the testator had them not at the time of the will; but a chattel real, as a lease for years, doth not pass: and a devise of lands is not good, if the testator at that time had nothing in them. By devise of all a man's lands and tenements, all the lands he hath in possession, and also in reversion, do pass: but where a person, having lands in fee, and other lands for years, devises all his lands and tenements, the fee-simple lands only pass; tho' if he hath only leases for years, by such devise, those leases shall pass to the devisee. *Goulsb.* 93. *Salk.* 237. 2 *Danv. Abr.* 527. 11 *Mod.* 106, 121, 148. *Fitzgib.* 233. *Holt* 750.

The devise of all a man's inheritance carries a fee-simple: also lands given to a person to dispose of at pleasure, makes a fee. If there are no words of inheritance in a will, the devisee hath no more than an estate during life: devise of all a man's estate, &c. passeth an estate for life only, not a fee by implication. So if one wills, that another shall have his lands in *D.* and says not how long, &c. But if a man devises land by will, paying 20 *l.* the devisee hath a fee-simple, altho' the money be not a hundredth part

Of Estates, Ancestors, Heirs, &c.

part of the value of the land: and yet if the devise be to a person, to the intent that he out of the profits pay so much to one, and so much to another, this is said to be but an estate for life. *Hob.* 75. 2 *Nels. Abr.* 745, 837. 4 *Shep. Abr.* 40 *Dyer* 342. *Bridgm. Rep.* 138.

A devise to a man and his heirs male makes an estate-tail; tho' such a gift in any common conveyance would be a fee-simple, it not being said of what body. Devise to one who is heir for life, remainder in contingency, &c. is good; and in these cases of executory devises, the estate descends till the contingency happens: by way of future executory devise, a devise to an infant *in ventre sa mere* shall take place. If a term is devised to *A.* for life, with remainder to *B.* this remainder is good by way of executory devise, for the residue of the term. And a term may be devised to one for life, with remainders to several others for life, when all the persons are *in esse:* though if the devise in remainder be to a person for life, who is not then in being, no limitation of a term may be beyond such estate; as to another and his issue, &c. *Co. Lit.* 27. *Lutw.* 798. *T. Raym.* 28, 164. *Sid.* 451.

In wills a devise may be to one, to the use of another; and the use shall be executed: and devises must be of a thing, and to a person certain. Land given to a man who shall marry my daughter, or to a man and his children, &c. is certain enough: but a condition in a will, that one shall not marry such a person, &c. is unlawful and void: if a legacy or portion is given to a woman, provided she marries not without consent of another, it is only *in terrorem;* unless the portion on such marriage be limited

S over

over to some other person. A man devises 1000*l.* to his daughter, if she attain 21 years, or at that age; if she dies before, the legacy is gone: here in case the legacy had been, to be paid her at the age of 21, then it is *debitum in præsenti & solvendum in futuro*, and her administrator, &c. shall have it, if she die before. If where a legacy is given generally by will, the legatee dies before due, it is extinguished: and legacies are not recoverable at common law; but in the Ecclesiastical Court, Chancery, &c. 2 *Leon. Swinb.* 293. *Mod. Rep.* 300. *Lil. Abr.* 457. 2 *Ventr.* 342.

The last will made by a man shall stand in force; and there can be but one will to take effect, though there may be several codicils to a will. If in a will there are two devises of the same thing, the last devise takes place: and as a latter will doth overthrow a former; so the latter part of a will overthrows the former part of it. But where a devise of lands was to one in fee, and in the same will the same lands were devised to another, this 'twas said made them jointenants; and if a devise is to one person in fee, and to another for life, or years, both devises may stand. *Co. Lit.* 112. *Plowd.* 341. 3 *Leon.* 11. See 3 *Mod.* 204, 207.

A will hath no force 'till after the death of the testator; but then, without any further grant, livery, &c. it gives and transfers estates, and alters the property of lands and goods, as effectually as any deed executed in a man's life-time; and hereby discents may be prevented, estates in fee-simple, fee-tail, for life, years, &c.

^a See Stra. Sel. Cas. of Evid. 59. & 11 Mod. 91. pl. 15. contra.

Of Estates, Ancestors, Heirs, &c.

may be made: and he that takes lands by devise, is in the nature of a purchaser. *Lit.* 167.

Lands may be released to one and his heirs by will; but a man cannot release a debt or duty by his will, tho' he may give and bequeath it. *Ventr.* 39. Devises of lands are deemed void against creditors upon specialties, &c. *Stat.* 3 *W. & M. c.* 14. perpetuated by 6 & 7 *W.* 3. *c.* 14.

A common will *of goods and lands.*

'IN the name of God, *Amen.* I *A. B:* of, &c.
' gentleman, being weak in body, but of
' sound mind and memory (blessed be God) do
' this day of, &c. in the year, &c. make and
' publish this my last will and testament, in
' manner following, (that is to say,) *Imprimis,* I
' give to my son *T. B.* the sum of, &c. *Item,*
' I give and bequeath to my daughter *E. B.* the
' sum, &c. *Item,* I give to my brother *N. B.*
' the sum of, &c. to my sister *M. B.* the like
' sum of, &c. to my grandson *G. B.* the sum,
' &c. And to my cousin, &c. *Item,* I give
' the house I hold by lease from, &c. situate
' and lying in, &c. which I now live in, to my
' said son *T. B. To hold* to him during his life;
' and after his decease, I give the same to my
' daughter *E. B.* during the remainder of my
' estate and interest therein: and all the rest of
' my lands and tenements whatsoever, whereof
' I shall die seised in possession, reversion or re-
' mainder, I give to my said son *T. B.* his heirs
' and assigns for ever. *Item,* all the rest and
' residue of my goods, chattels, and personal
' estate whatsoever, I give to my said daughter
' *E. B. And* I make, constitute and ordain

'my good friends Mr. *C. D.* and *E. F.* to be my executors in trust for my said daughter *E. B.* and it is my will, that they shall put out what monies I have for her use, but so as not to be accountable for any bad debt or debts, that shall be contracted; and that they shall retain all their charges and expences whatsoever, in relation to their said trust; also I give them five guineas a-piece as tokens of my love to them, and for their kindness in accepting this trust. *And I* appoint twenty pounds, and no more, to be expended on my funeral. *In witness* whereof I the said *A. B.* have to this my last will and testament set my hand and seal, the day of   in the   year of the reign, *&c.* and in the year of our Lord 1764.'

Signed, sealed, published and declared by the said testator, as and for his last will and testament, in the presence of us, who at his request, in his presence and in the presence of each other, have subscribed our names as witnesses thereto.

See Stat. 25 *Geo.* 2. *c.* 6. entitled, 'An act for avoiding and putting an end to certain doubts and questions relating to the attestation of wills and codicils, concerning real estates, in that part of *Great Britain* called *England*, and in his majesty's colonies and plantations in *America*,' whereby devisees, creditors and legatees, are made competent witnesses to wills of real estates.

Form

Form of a will, with devise of lands, &c. in the way of settlement.

'IN the name of God, *Amen.* I *A. B.* of,
' *&c.* being in good health, and perfect
' memory, (blessed be God therefore) do this
' day, *&c.* in the fourth year of the reign of
' the lord *George* the Third, *&c.* and in the
' year of our Lord 1764, make and publish this
' my last will and testament, in manner and
' form following, (that is to say:) *Imprimis,* I
' commend my soul into the hands of Al-
' mighty God, Who gave it me; and my body
' to the earth from whence it came, in hopes
' of a joyful resurrection, through the merits of
' my Saviour JESUS CHRIST; and as for that
' worldly estate wherewith it hath pleased God
' to bless me, I dispose thereof as follows: *First,*
' I give to my loving wife *M. B.* the sum of,
' *&c. Item,* I give to my son *H. B.* the sum,
' *&c. Item,* I give to my daughter *F. B.* the
' sum of, *&c. Item,* I give to my brother,
' *&c.* all payable within, *&c.* after my decease.
' *Item,* I give unto my said wife *M. B. All* my
' lands in the parish of, *&c.* which are not set-
' tled upon her for her jointure; *To hold* to her
' during her natural life, she making no spoil,
' waste or destruction thereon; and from and
' after her decease, I give and devise the same
' to my said son *H. B.* for the term of his na-
' tural life; and after his decease, I devise the
' same to my daughter *F. B.* during her natural
' life; and after the determination of that estate,
' I give and devise the same to my loving bro-
' thers *R. B.* and *W. B.* and their heirs, during
' the

'the life of my said daughter *F.* to the intent
'to preserve and support the contingent uses
'and remainders herein after limited: but ne-
'vertheless in trust, to permit my said daugh-
'ter *F.* to receive the rents and profits thereof
'during her life; and from and after her de-
'cease then to remain to the first son of my
'said daughter *F.* and the heirs of the body of
'such first son lawfully issuing; and for default
'of such issue, then to the use and behoof of
'the second, third, fourth, fifth, and all and
'every other son and sons of my said daughter
'*F.* begotten; the elder of such son and sons,
'and the heirs of his body lawfully issuing, to
'be always preferred, and to take before the
'younger of such sons and the heirs of his body;
'and for default of such issue, then to the use
'and behoof of all and every the daughters of
'the body of my said daughter *F.* and the heirs
'of the body of such daughter and daughters,
'as tenants in common, and not as jointenants;
'and for default of such issue, then I give the
'same to my grandson, &c. for and during the
'term of his natural life; and after the deter-
'mination of that estate, then to the use and
'behoof of, &c. and their heirs, during his
'life, and in trust for him, and to the intent
'to support and preserve the contingent uses
'and estates after-mentioned; and after his de-
'cease, to remain to his issue in tail, in such
'manner as I have limited the same to my said
'daughter *F.* and for default of such issue, then
'to remain to, &c. and the heirs male of his
'body begotten, &c. and for default of such
'issue, to remain to my right heirs for ever.
'*Item,* I give to my said wife, during her life,
'the use of all my place and houshold stuff,
'and

'and after her death the same to remain to,
'&c. and for prevention of any embezzlement
'of the said plate and houshold goods, it is my
'will, and I do hereby direct, that a particu-
'lar be taken by my said wife and overseers,
'of all my said plate and houshold goods, and
'that she give her covenant to my said overseers,
'to leave the same to such persons as I have
'hereby given the same at my death, (their rea-
'sonable usage and wearing in the mean time
'excepted.) *Item*, I give to, &c. ten guineas
'a-piece to buy them mourning. *Item*, I give
'to, &c. one guinea a-piece to buy them
'rings, &c. *Item*, I give to my servant man
'and two servant-maids, that shall be living
'with me at the time of my decease, twenty
'pounds a-piece. *Item*, I give to the poor of
'the parish where I shall die, the sum of fifty
'pounds. *Item*, I give all the rest of my goods,
'chattels and personal estate to my said wife
'*M. B.* and I make and ordain her my said wife
'sole executrix of this my will, and my loving
'brothers, &c. and good friend, &c. overseers
'thereof, to take care and see the same per-
'formed, according to my true intent and mean-
'ing; and for their pains herein, I give and al-
'lot to each of them the sum of, &c. *In wit-*
'*ness* whereof I the said *A. B.* have to the first
'sheet of this my last will and testament, con-
'taining two sheets of paper, set my hand, and
'to the last sheet thereof my hand and seal, the
'day and year above-written.

Signed, sealed, published and   A. B.
  declared by the said A. B.
as and for his last will and
testament, in the presence of

*us whose names are here-
under written, who did each
of us subscribe our names
as witnesses at his request,
and in his presence, in the
room where he then was.*

    T. W.
    J. M.
    M. T.

Estates in goods and chattels, with some things thereto relating, and how they may be released, I shall treat of under,

1. Bills of sale of goods.
2. Gifts of goods and chattels.
3. Agreements, contracts and covenants.
4. Bonds and obligations for money.
5. Letters of attorney to receive debts.
6. Releases of debts and actions, &c.

1. A bill of sale is an instrument used for transferring the property of goods and chattels; and it can never be without a consideration.

A person may at any time sell his goods, even though an execution be coming out against him; unless there is a private trust between the parties, and the writ of execution is delivered to the sheriff, &c. And where a bargain is, that one shall give so much for a horse, and he gives one shilling or a penny in earnest, which I accept, this is a perfect sale. *Noy Max.* 87.

Where one agrees for goods sold, the buyer must not carry them away before paid for; except a day of payment is allowed him by the seller. The seller of things is to keep them

for

for a reasonable time, for delivery: but where no time is appointed for the delivery thereof, or for payment of the money, it is generally implied that delivery be made immediately; and payment on the delivery. And on sale of goods in a shop, &c. the seller may not bring an action for the money agreed, 'till the goods are delivered. *Ney* 87. 3 *Salk.* 61.

It hath been held, that on the sale of goods, if earnest be given to the seller, and part of them is taken away by the buyer, he must pay the residue of the money upon fetching away the rest, because no other time is appointed; and the earnest binds the bargain, and gives the buyer a right to demand the goods, but a demand without paying the money is void: and if the buyer doth not take away the goods, and pay the money, the seller ought to require him so to do; and then if he doth not do the same in convenient time, the bargain and sale is dissolved, and the seller may dispose of them to any other person. *Salk.* 113.

A sale of goods upon a *Sunday*, tho' in a fair or market, will not alter the property: and in markets, all contracts for any thing sold there, to make them binding, are to be made as follows: The sale is to be in a place that is open, and in a proper place for such goods; it must be a sale for valuable consideration, and the buyer is not to know that the seller hath a wrongful possession; the sale not to be fraudulently betwixt two, to bar another; there is to be a sale and a contract, by persons able to contract, and the sale may not be in the night, but between sun and sun; and toll must be paid, where required by statute, &c. Also there are toll-takers or book-keepers, who enter the

names

Of Estates, Ancestors, Heirs, &c.

names of buyers and sellers of horses, &c. which are to be rid or stand in the open fair or market one hour; and all the parties to the contract must be present with the horse: the sellers shall likewise produce vouchers of the sale to them, &c. 2 *Inst.* 713. 5 *Rep.* 83. *Stat.* 2 & 3 *P.* & *M. c.* 7. 31 *Eliz.* 12. The buying of cattle, corn and victuals, by the way before brought to a fair or market, &c. is called forestalling, and punishable by imprisonment, loss of goods, &c. 5 & 6 *E.* 6. *c.* 14. perpetuated by 13 *Eliz. c.* 25.

By statute, a contract for the sale of goods for 10 *l.* or upwards, shall not be good, except the buyer receive part of the goods sold; or gives something in earnest to bind the bargain; or some note thereof to be made in writing, signed by the party to be charged with the contract, &c. And where contracts are not to be performed in a year, they must be in writing, or no action can be brought on them; so that a contract for goods under 10 *l.* value, if not to be had in a year, must be in writing, or shall be void: but if no day is set, or the time is uncertain, &c. they may be good without. 29 *Car.* 2. *c.* 3. perpetuated by 1 *Jac.* 2. *c.* 17. *f.* 5.

If a man affirms things sold are of such a value, when they are not, this is not actionable; tho' it is, if he actually warrants them: but where one warrants any thing sold, after the time of sale, it is not good; for 'tis to be at the time of the sale, to be binding. *Cro. Jac.* 4, 386.

A person recommending a stranger to a tradesman, who thereupon sells goods on trust to such stranger; this by the law of merchants may

Of Estates, Ancestors, Heirs, &c.

may make the recommender answerable. *Ibid.* 1. See Ld. *Raym.* 224. 2 Ld. *Raym.* 1085. 12 *Mod.* 250. *Bac. Abr.* 75, 76.

The form of a bill of sale *of goods.*

'KNOW all men by these presents, that I
' *A. B.* of, *&c.* for and in consideration of
' the sum of, *&c.* to me in hand paid, at and
' before the sealing and delivery hereof, by *C.*
' *D.* of, *&c.* the receipt whereof I do hereby
' acknowledge, *Have* bargained and sold, and
' by these presents do bargain and sell unto the
' said *C. D.* all the goods, houshold-stuff and
' implements of houshold and all other goods
' whatsoever, mentioned in the schedule here-
' unto annexed, now remaining and being in,
' *&c. To have and to hold* all and singular the
' said goods, houshold-stuff and implements of
' houshold, and every of them, by these pre-
' sents, bargained and sold unto the said *C. D.*
' his executors, administrators and assigns for
' ever. *And* I the said *A. B.* for myself, my exe-
' cutors and administrators, all and singular the
' said goods, unto the said *C. D.* his executors,
' administrators and assigns, against me the said
' *A. B.* my executors, administrators and as-
' signs, and against all and every other person
' and persons whatsoever, shall and will warrant
' and for ever defend by these presents: of which
' goods I the said *A. B.* have put the said *C. D.*
' in full possession, by delivering him one silver
' tankard, *&c.* at the sealing hereof. *In wit-*
' *ness, &c.*

2. A gift of goods is made either by deed, by word, or in law: and all goods and chattels

tels perſonal may be given without deed, except in ſome ſpecial caſes. *Perk.* 57.

But a general gift of all a man's goods without any exception, though this be by deed, is liable to ſuſpicion as fraudulent, to deceive creditors: and therefore whenever any gift ſhall be made, in ſatisfaction of a debt, it is good to make it in a publick manner before neighbours; that the goods and chattels be appraiſed to the value, and the gift expreſsly made in ſatisfaction of the debt; and that on the gift of the goods the donee take poſſeſſion of them, &c. 4 *Rep.* 80. *Hob.* 230.

As to gifts by word, if a man intending to give a jewel to one, ſay to him, here I give you my ring, with the ruby in it, &c. and with his own hand delivers it to the party, it would be a good gift, notwithſtanding the ring ſhould bear any other jewel, being delivered by the party himſelf to the party to whom given. Here a gift of any thing without conſideration, will be good; but it is revokable before the delivery to the donee of the thing given: and in caſe I give to you one of my horſes in my ſtable, there you ſhall have your election to chuſe which you will. *Bac. Max.* 87. *Jenk. Cent.* 109. *Co. Lit.* 145.

The gift in law is when a man is married to a woman, the law gives all the goods of the wife to the huſband by the marriage; and if a perſon be made executor of a will, on his taking upon him the executorſhip, the law gives and transfers the property of the teſtator's goods to ſuch executor: though in theſe caſes it is as it were conditional; for the huſband is liable to the debts of the wife, and the executor to the debts of the teſtator. *Co. Lit.* 351.

It

Of Estates, Ancestors, Heirs, &c.

It is the same where one takes my goods as a trespasser, and I in action recover damages for them; the law gives him the property of the goods, he having paid for them. 2 *Shep. Abr.* 266.

Form of a gift of goods and chattels.

'TO all people to whom these presents shall
' come, I *A. B.* of, &c. send greeting:
' *Know ye*, that I the said *A. B.* for and in con-
' sideration of natural affection, &c. and for di-
' vers other good causes and considerations me
' hereunto moving, *have* given and granted,
' and by these presents do give and grant unto
' *C. D. all* my blue damask-silk bed, in the best
' chamber in my house at, &c. together with
' all the furniture of that room; or all and sin-
' gular my goods, chattels, plate, jewels, leases,
' and personal estate whatsoever, in whose hands,
' custody or possession soever they be, within
' the kingdom of *Great Britain*, (except, &c.)
' *To have, hold and enjoy* all and singular the
' said goods, chattels, and personal estate afore-
' said, unto the said *C. D.* his executors, admi-
' nistrators and assigns, to the only proper use
' and behoof of him the said *C. D.* his execu-
' tors, administrators and assigns for ever. *And*
' I the said *A. B.* all and singular the aforesaid
' goods, chattels and premisses, to the said
' *C. D.* his executors, administrators and assigns,
' against all persons whatsoever, shall and will
' warrant, and for ever defend by these presents.
' *In witness*, &c.

Livery

Livery and feifin *indorfed thereon.*

'Memorandum, the day, &c. livery and
feifin was delivered by the within named
A. B. unto the faid *C. D.* of one piece of plate,
&c. in the name of all the goods and chattels
within mentioned, to hold to him the faid *C.
D.* his executors, adminiftrators and affigns
for ever, according to the within written deed,
in the prefence of

      E F.
      G. H.

3. Agreement is the mutual confent of parties, or joining together of two or more minds, in any thing done or to be done. A contract is a bargain between two perfons, where one thing is given for another, which is called *quid pro quo*; and if there be not one thing for another, or fome confideration, it is a nude contract and void in law. A covenant is an agreement made by deed in writing, between two or more, to do or not to do fome act agreed upon betwixt them. *Terms de Ley* 32, 459.

Agreements are either executed already at the beginning, or executory, to be performed *in futuro*; and are governed by the intention of the parties: they ought to be perfect, full and complete, fo as to be executed with a recompence, or give an action or other remedy for it. An agreement without fatisfaction is as nothing; and a forced agreement of the party is accounted no agreement; therefore he that did agree to the thing fhall not be compelled to perform it. *Plowd.* 290. 2 *Mod.* 8. *Cro. Car.* 198. *Lil. Abr.* 48.

Any

Any thing under hand and seal, which imports an agreement, will amount to covenant: and a *proviso* by way of agreement amounts to covenant. And a covenant is either in fact, or in law: in fact is that which is expresly agreed between the parties, and inserted in the deed; and in law is that covenant which the law intends and implies, though it be not expressed in words. A servant covenants and agrees to serve me a year, and I covenant to pay him a sum of money for it; here he may have an action against me, although he do not serve me; but then I may oblige him to serve out the time. *Lev.* 155. *Co. Lit.* 204.

A covenant is no duty 'till broken: in covenants the last words, that are general, shall be expounded by the first words which are special and particular: and if some covenants in a deed are good and lawful, and others not; those against law are void, and the other shall stand good. 2 *Ventr.* 218. *Plowd.* 287. 11 *Rep.* 27.

There can be articles of agreement made, to be performed only by the parties; or by them and their executors, &c. wherein both of them are obliged to do something, according to the matter agreed upon.

The form of an agreement *between a master and servant.*

'IT is agreed this day of, &c. in the year of
' our Lord 1764, *Between A. B.* of, &c.
' esquire, and *C. D.* in manner following, viz.
' that he the said *A. B.* shall and will receive
' the said *C. D.* into his house and service, for
' the

'the term of one whole year, from the date hereof; and provide for the said *C. D.* competent and sufficient meat, drink, washing and lodging; and also pay and allow unto him the said *C. D.* the sum or wages of six pounds, he the said *C. D.* continuing in the service of him the said *A. B.* during the said term: *and* the said *C. D.* covenants and agrees with the said *A. B.* that he the said *C. D.* shall and will, for the considerations aforesaid, faithfully serve him the said *A. B.* in the business and service of, *&c.* for and during the said term of one year, without absenting from the same, or embezzling any of the money or goods of the said *A. B.* or any ways disclosing the secrets of his said master. *In witness* whereof the parties aforesaid have hereunto set their hands, *&c.*

4. Bond or obligation is a deed in writing obligatory, whereby one doth bind himself to another, under his hand and seal, to pay a sum of money, or do some other act: a bond contains an obligation with a penalty, *&c.* and a condition, which expresly mentions what money is to be paid, or other thing to be performed, and the limited time for performance thereof; for which the obligation is peremptorily binding. And a bond differs from a bill, which is generally without a penalty or condition, tho' a bill may be obligatory. *Co. Lit.* 172.

A bond or obligation may be made from one to one, or two, three or more; or be from two persons or more, to one, two, three, *&c.* If a bond hath not a date, or hath a false or impossible date, if it be sealed and delivered, it is a good obligation from the delivery: and if one binds himself

himself to pay twenty pounds, but doth not say when it shall be paid, the bond is good, and money due presently. Also in case *A.* binds himself to *B.* in thirty pounds to be paid to *A.* whereas it should be to *B.* the obligation will be good, and the *solvendum* void. 2 *Rep.* 5. *Co. Lit.* 108, 209. 3 *Lev.* 21, 137.

All conditions of bonds must be to do things lawful and possible: and when the matter or thing to be done, or not to be done by a condition, is unlawful or impossible; or the condition is repugnant, insensible or incertain, the condition is void, and in some cases the obligation likewise. And if a thing be possible at the time of making the obligation, and afterwards becomes impossible by the act of God, or of the law, or of the obligee, the obligation is discharged; but sometimes an obligation may remain single, where a condition is impossible, &c. and if money be not paid according to the condition, the obligation becomes single. 10 *Rep.* 120. *Dy.* 51. *Cro. Eliz.* 780. 2 *Lil. Abr.* 252.

A condition of a bond to do any act evil in itself, is void: bonds made by infants, feme coverts, &c. are not good; and if made by women, where prevailed upon by flattery, &c. they may be relieved in chancery. Obligations by duress are void; so are bonds concerning buying and selling offices; made to avoid the debt or duty of others, by fraud; obtained by gaming, &c. by divers statutes. 1 *Rich.* 2. *c.* 13. 5 & 6 *Ed.* 6. *c.* 16. 13 *El. c.* 5. perpetuated by 29 *El. c.* 5. 16 *Car.* 2. *c.* 7. *Lutw.* 160, 484, 487. 2 *Mod.* 54, 279. *Salk.* 344. *Skin.* 572. 8 *Mod.* 57, 187. 10 *Mod.* 336, 337.

T

12 *Mod.*

12 *Mod.* 3, 336, 540. 2 Ld. *Raym.* 1034, 1035. *Stra.* 495. 2 *Stra.* 1159. *Com. Rep.* 4. *Stat.* 9 *Ann. c.* 14. 2 *Stra.* 1048, 1219. 2 *Geo.* 2. *c.* 28. 10 *Geo.* 2. *c.* 19, 22. 12 *Geo.* 2. *c.* 28. 13 *Geo.* 2. *c.* 19. 18 *Geo.* 2. *c.* 34. 25 *Geo.* 2. *c.* 36. perpetuated by 28 *Geo.* 2. *c.* 19. 30 *Geo.* 2. *c.* 24.

And bonds made for more than 5 *l. per Cent. per Annum* interest, are void as usurious; and the receiver shall forfeit treble the value of the money lent. But it is not usury if the interest be higher, where possibly both principal and interest are in danger, upon a contingency, or casualty; or if there is a hazard that one may have less than his principal: and if a person secure both interest and principal, if it be at the will of the party who is to pay; it is no usury. So where a man is to pay a large sum by way of penalty, and in lieu of damages, for non-payment of the principal debt; when he might repay the principal at the time agreed, and avoid the penalty, *&c. Stat.* 12 *Ann. c.* 10. 2 *Inst.* 89. *Cro. Jac.* 268, 677. *Show. Rep.* 8. *Lut.* 273.

A bill obligatory written in a book, with the party's hand and seal to it, is good: and if a bill runs, I have received of *A. B.* the sum of twenty pounds, which I promise to pay, *&c.* Or, I owe to him 20 *l.* or had of him that sum, to be paid at, *&c.* or if the bill be, I shall pay to *C. D.* 10 *l. &c.* these and the like are good bills. *Cro. Eliz.* 613. 2 *Rol. Abr.* 146.

A common bond *from one person to one.*

'KNOW all men by these presents,
'That I *A. B.* of the parish of, *&c.*
'in the county of *S.* gentleman, am held
'and firmly bound to *C. D.* of, *&c.* in the
'county aforesaid, esquire, in one hundred
'pounds of good and lawful money of
'*Great Britain*, to be paid to the said *C. D.*
'or to his certain attorney, his executors,
'administrators or assigns; for which pay-
'ment, well and truly to be made, I bind
'myself, my heirs, executors and adminis-
'trators, firmly by these presents, sealed
'with my seal: dated this day of, *&c.* in
'the eighteenth year of the reign of our so-
'vereign lord *George* the Third, by the
'grace of God, of *Great Britain*, *France*,
'and *Ireland*, king, defender of the faith,
'*&c.* and in the year of our Lord one
'thousand seven hundred and seventy-eight.

'The condition of this obligation is such,
'That if the above bound *A. B.* his heirs, exe-
'cutors or administrators, shall and do well and
'truly pay, or cause to be paid, unto the above
'named *C. D.* his executors, administrators or
'assigns, the full sum of fifty-two pounds and
'ten shillings of lawful money of *Great Bri-
'tain*, on the day of, *&c.* next ensuing the date
'hereof; or which will be in the year, *&c.* then
'this obligation shall be void, or else it shall
'remain in full force and virtue.'

Sealed and delivered in
the presence of

Form of a bond *from two perfons to one.*

'KNOW all men by thefe prefents,
' That we *A. B.* of, *&c.* and *C. D.*
' of, *&c.* in the county, *&c.* are held and
' firmly bound to *E. F.* of, *&c.* gentleman,
' in fifty pounds of good and lawful money
' of *Great Britain,* to be paid to the faid
' *E. F.* or to his certain attorney, his exe-
' cutors, adminiftrators or affigns; and for
' which payment to be well and truly made,
' we bind ourfelves, and each of us by him-
' felf, for and in the whole, our heirs, exe-
' cutors and adminiftrators, and of each of
' us, firmly by thefe prefents, fealed with
' our feals. Dated the day of, *&c.* in the
' year of the reign of the lord *George* the
' Third, by the grace of God of *Great Bri-*
' *tain, France,* and *Ireland,* king, defender
' of the faith, *&c.* the feventeenth, and in
' the year of our Lord 1777.

' The condition of this obligation is fuch,
' That if the above bound *A. B.* and *C. D.* or
' either of them, their or either of their heirs,
' executors or adminiftrators, do and fhall well
' and truly pay or caufe to be paid unto the
' above-named *E. F.* his executors, adminiftra-
' tors or affigns, the full fum of twenty-fix
' pounds and five fhillings, of good and lawful
' money of *Great Britain,* on or before the day,
' *&c.* which will be in the year of our Lord
' one thoufand feven hundred and feventy-eight,
' without fraud or covin: (or if the faid *A. B.*
' and *C. D. &c.* do well and truly pay to the faid
' *E. F. &c.* the full fum of twenty-five pounds,
' with

'with interest for the same, after the rate of
'five pounds *per centum per annum*, or with law-
'ful interest, on the day of, &c.) then this obli-
'gation to be void, or else to remain in full
'force.'

The form of a penal bill for payment of money.

'KNOW all men by these presents, That I
'A. B. of, &c. do owe unto C. D. of, &c.
'gentleman, the sum of one hundred pounds,
'of lawful *British* money, to be paid unto the
'said C. D. his executors, administrators or as-
'signs, on, &c. next ensuing the date hereof;
'for which payment, well and truly to be made,
'I bind myself, my heirs, executors and admi-
'nistrators, to the said C. D. his executors, ad-
'ministrators and assigns, in the penalty of two
'hundred pounds, firmly by these presents. *In
'witness,* &c.'

Form of a single bill for money.

'KNOW all men by these presents, That
'I A. B. of, &c. do owe and am indebted
'to C. D. of, &c. in the sum of thirty pounds
'of lawful money of *Great Britain*, which I pro-
'mise to pay unto the said C. D. his executors,
'administrators or assigns, at or upon the day
'of, &c. next ensuing the date of these presents.
'*In witness* whereof I have hereunto set my
'hand and seal the tenth day of *October, Anno
'Dom.* 1778.'

5. A letter of attorney is a writing authorizing an attorney to do any lawful act for another;

other; in like manner as the party authorizing might do the same. And what a man may do by himself, he may generally do by another person. *West. Symb. par.* 1.

The nature of this instrument is to give the attorney the full power and authority of the maker, to accomplish the act intended to be performed: and sometimes these writings are revocable, and sometimes not so; but when they are revocable, it is usually a bare authority only, and they are irrevocable when debts, &c. are assigned to another, in which case that word is inserted. *Plowd.* 475.

In cases of common letters of attorney, the power given must be strictly pursued, or the act of the attorney shall be void; and a man may limit his authority as strictly as he pleases. If the attorney does less than the authority mentions, it is void; but if he doth more, it may be good for so much as he hath power to do: and notwithstanding the ancient opinions for pursuing authorities with great strictness; yet in case of delivering livery and seisin of lands, they have been always favourably expounded of latter times; unless where it hath appeared that the attorney's power was not followed at all. *Co. Lit.* 258. 2 *Mod.* 79.

Letters of attorney are either general or special; and said to be revocable in their nature, tho' they are otherwise made: and by the death of the party giving it, the power given by letter of attorney generally determines. 8 *Rep.* 82.

The form of a general letter of attorney *to receive and recover debts.*

'KNOW all men by these presents, That
' I *A. B.* of, *&c.* for divers good causes
' and considerations me hereunto moving, have
' made, ordained, authorized and appointed, and
' by these presents do make, ordain, authorize
' and appoint *C. D.* of, *&c.* my true and lawful
' attorney, for me, and in my name, and to my
' use, to ask, demand, sue for, recover and re-
' ceive of *E. F.* of, *&c.* all such sum and sums
' of money, debts and duties whatsoever, which
' now are due and owing unto me the said *A. B.*
' by and from the said *E. F.* And to have, use
' and take all lawful ways and means in my
' name or otherwise, for recovery thereof, by
' attachment, arrest, distress or otherwise, and
' to agree and compound for the same, and ac-
' quittances, or other discharges for the same, for
' me and in my name to make, seal and deliver;
' and to do all other lawful acts and things
' whatsoever, concerning the premisses, as fully
' in every respect as I myself might or could do,
' if I were personally present; and attornies one
' or more under him, for the purposes aforesaid,
' to make, and at his pleasure to revoke: ratify-
' ing and allowing all and whatsoever my said
' attorney shall in my name lawfully do, or cause
' to be done in and about the premisses, by virtue
' of these presents. *In witness,* &c.'

The form of a letter of attorney *to receive rents, and take distresses.*

'KNOW all men, &c. That I *A. B.* of, &c. have made, ordained, constituted and appointed, and by these presents do make, &c. *C. D.* of, &c. my lawful attorney, for me and in my name, and for my use, to ask, demand and receive of and from *E. F. G. H. I. K.* &c. all such rents and arrearages of rents which now are, or hereafter shall grow due, from the said *E. F. G. H. I. K.* &c. or either or any of them, of and for all those my messuages and lands at, &c. and upon receipt thereof, to give acquittances, or other discharges for the same; and in default of payment of the said rents, or any part thereof, to my said attorney, I do hereby authorize and impower him my said attorney, into and upon the said lands and premisses to enter and distrain, and the distress and distresses there found and taken, to dispose of according to law, for the speedy recovering and obtaining my said rents and arrears, or otherwise to proceed by action of debt for the recovery of the same, as to him my said attorney shall be thought fit; hereby ratifying and confirming all and whatsoever he shall do in the premisses. *In witness,* &c.

Form of a seaman's letter of attorney.

'KNOW all men, &c. that I *A. B.* of,
' &c. mariner, have made, ordained,
' constituted and appointed, and by these pre-
' sents do make, &c. my loving wife *M. B.*
' my lawful attorney, for me and in my name,
' and for my use, to ask, demand and receive
' of and from all and every person and persons
' whatsoever, as well all such sum and sums of
' money as now are, or which shall for may at
' any time hereafter become due and owing to
' me for wages from the ship, &c. or any other
' ship or ships, to whom I now do or may be-
' long; as also all other monies now due, or to
' become due and owing to me by any other
' ways or means whatsoever. And upon non-
' payment thereof, the said person or persons, his,
' her or their executors or administrators, for me
' and in my name to sue, arrest, imprison, im-
' plead and prosecute for the same, and upon
' such suit to proceed to judgment and execu-
' tion; and thereupon the said person and per-
' sons, their or either of their executors and
' administrators, in prison to hold, detain and
' keep until payment thereof be made with all
' costs and damages sustained by occasion of
' the detaining the same: and on payment
' thereof, the said person or persons, their exe-
' cutors and administrators, forth of prison to
' discharge, and acquittances for the same, or
' any part thereof, for me and in my name to
' make, seal and deliver; and also to do, per-
' form and execute all and every other lawful
' and reasonable acts and things whatsoever, for
' the obtaining and releasing of the same, as
' shall

'shall be needful and necessary to be done;
giving and by these presents granting unto my
said attorney my full and absolute power in
the premisses, and ratifying and holding firm
all and whatsoever my said attorney shall lawfully do, or cause to be done, in or about the
premisses, by virtue of these presents. *In
witness*, &c.'

Note; it was usual at the end of a sailor's letter of attorney to add his will, but now 'No will of any seaman contained in the same instrument, paper or parchment, with a letter
of attorney, shall be good in law. *Stat.* 9 &
10 *Will.* 3. *c.* 41. *f.* 6. And further, that

'No letter of attorney made by any inferior
officer or seaman in the service of his majesty,
or by the executors or administrators of any
such officer or seaman, to impower any person to receive any wages or allowances of
money due for such service, shall be good,
unless such letter of attorney be declared to be
revocable by the express words thereof; and
unless such letter of attorney, if made by any
such officer or seaman then in the service of
his majesty, be signed before and attested by
the captain or commander, and one other of
the signing officers of the ship to which such
inferior officer or seaman belongs, or by the
clerk of the cheque at some of the dock-
yards; and unless such letter of attorney,
if made by any officer or seaman discharged from the service of his majesty, be
signed before and attested by the mayor or
chief magistrate of the town or place where
such officer or seaman then resides; or if
made by the executors or administrators of any

'such

'such officer or seaman, unless such letter of
'attorney be signed before and attested by the
'minister and churchwardens (or in *Scotland*
'by the minister and two elders) of the parish
'where such executors or administrators respec-
'tively reside.' *Stat.* 31 *Geo.* 2. *c.* 10. *sect.* 21.

6. Release is an instrument extending not
only to the giving up or discharging a right in
lands, &c. but also to goods and chattels, and
the releasing debts, duties and actions. *Lit.* 492.

Releases are likewise express by deed, or implied by law; as when an obligee in a bond makes the obligor executor, or a feme obligee takes the obligor to husband, &c. these are releases in law. A release by deed of a right or action may not be for a time; if made but for an hour, it will be good for ever: and a man cannot release a personal thing upon condition, but the condition will be void, and the release enure to him who made it for ever. If a duty be uncertain at first, to be made certain after, being in the mean time but a mere possibility, it can't be released: but a duty certain may be released before the performance of it. *Co. Lit.* 264. 8 *Rep.* 136. 10 *Rep.* 11. *Cro. El.* 580.

All debts and duties may be released, before or after due, by apt words. A release of all manner of actions bars and discharges all real, personal and mixt actions, subsisting at the time of the release, and bonds, statutes, &c. But not executions or writs of error; tho' a release of all suits, will be a bar to an execution: the release of all actions may not discharge a covenant before broken; but by release of covenants, a covenant not broken may be released. Release of all quarrels, &c. amounts to a release of all actions.

actions. *Lit.* 406. *Co. Lit.* 285, 292. *Ref.* 112. 4 *Rep.* 63.

By a release of all debts, debts upon specialties, executions, &c. are discharged: and a release of all duties discharges all personal actions, judgments, executions and obligations; but release of all dues will not bar a writ of account, there being nothing due before account made up. A release of all actions may be a good bar in account. By release of all demands, all rights and titles to lands, conditions before broken or after, covenants broken, rents, annuities, debts, duties, contracts, obligations, recognizances, statutes, judgments, executions, &c. all manner of actions real and personal, are barred and discharged; for this is the best release of all, and includes in it most of the others. 2 *Rol. Abr.* 404. *Co. Lit.* 291. 8 *Rep.* 153. *Dy.* 56.

The release of all demands, altho' so extensive, is no bar in a writ of error, to reverse an outlawry, nothing being demanded by such writ: it must be released by special words. A future act may not be released by release of all demands; and a release before any rent due, of all demands that the relessor had or should have against the relessee, hath been adjudged not to release the accruing rent. An obligation subsequent is not discharged or avoided by this release: though where a man is bound in a bond to pay money at a time to come, a release before will be a good bar; as it is a debt presently, though payable afterwards. 8 *Rep.* 152. *Co. Lit.* 291. *Lev.* 99. 2 *Lev.* 210.

A release to one person, where there are several jointly bound, &c. discharges the others: and an acknowledgment under hand and seal that a debt is satisfied, is a good release of such debt, 2 *Rol. Abr.* 410. 9 *Rep.* 52.

Form of a release of personal actions.

'KNOW all men by these presents, That
' I *A. B.* of, &c. have remised, released
' and quit-claimed, and by these presents do for
' me, my heirs, executors and administrators,
' and every of them, remise, release, and for
' ever quit-claim unto *C. D.* of, &c. his heirs,
' executors and administrators, and every of
' them, all and all manner of personal actions,
' suits, debts, duties, sum and sums of money,
' claims and demands personal whatsoever, from
' the beginning of the world until the day of the
' date hereof. *In Witness,* &c.'

The form of a general release of all demands.

'KNOW all men by these presents, That I
' *A. B.* of, &c. have remised, released,
' and for ever quit-claimed, and by these pre-
' sents do, for me, my heirs, executors and ad-
' ministrators, remise, release, and for ever
' quit-claim unto *C. D.* of, &c. his heirs, exe-
' cutors and administrators, all and all manner
' of action and actions, cause and causes of ac-
' tion and actions, suits, bills, bonds, writings,
' obligations, debts, dues, duties, reckonings,
' accounts, sum and sums of money, judgments,
' executions, extents, quarrels, controversies,
' trespasses, damages and demands whatsoever,
' both at law and in equity, or otherwise what-
' soever, which against him the said *C. D.* I ever
' had,

Of Estates, Ancestors, Heirs, &c.

'had, now have, or which I, my heirs, exe-
'cutors and administrators, shall or may have,
'claim, challenge or demand, for or by reason
'or means of any act, matter, cause or thing,
'from the beginning of the world to the
'day of the date of these presents. *In Wit-*
, *ness,* &c.'

I now come to *Tenures* and holdings of lands, by the common law, which are,

1. In fee-simple.
2. In fee-tail.
3. In tail, after possibility of issue.
4. By the curtesy,

Tenant
5. In dower.
6. For term of life.
7. For term of years.
8. At will, &c.

1. Tenant in fee-simple is, where one hath lands and tenements of inheritance, to hold to him and his heirs for ever: to have fee is to have an inheritance; and to have fee-simple implies, that it is without limitation to what heirs; but to heirs generally. And a man cannot have a greater estate. *Co. Lit.* 1, 2.

The word *Heirs* makes the inheritance: and an estate granted, to hold to a man for ever, or to him and his assigns for ever, is only for life, the words *his heirs* being wanting. A gift to one and his children, and their heirs, is a fee simple to all jointly that are alive: though if lands be given to a man and his heirs, in the singular number, it is but for life; and the heir cannot take by discent, he being but one, and therefore shall take nothing. Where lands are given or granted to a man and his successors, this creates no fee-simple; except it be to a corporation, when it doth. *Co. Lit.* 8, 9.

A fee-

A fee-simple determinable upon a contingency is a fee to all intents; tho' not so durable as an absolute fee: and there are said to be three sorts of fee-simple: fee absolute to a man and his heirs for ever: fee simple conditional, when the estate is defeasible by not performing a condition; and a qualified fee, which may be defeated by a limitation, &c. But a fee conditional or qualified are not properly fee-simple. A rent or annuity is granted to one and his heirs, this is a fee-simple personal. *Vaugh.* 273. *Co. Lit.* 2, 18. 10 *Rep.* 87.

At the Common Law, all estates were fee-simple; and all other estates are derived out of it, so that there must be a fee at last in some body: but a fee-simple cannot be limited upon a fee-simple: nor may any remainder, as it is an absolute estate, and nothing can be after it. Although fee-simple is the most ample estate, it is subject to many incumbrances, &c. 4 *Inst.* 206. *Dy.* 33.

In pleading estates in fee-simple, it may be generally alledged; but estates-tail, &c. are to be particularly shewn. 1 *Inst.* 11, 303.

2. Tenant in tail is when a man hath an estate of inheritance, limited to him and the heirs of his body begotten, or to be begotten. Here the word *Body* makes the estate-tail, which may be restrained to males or females of the body; and there must be the word *Heirs*. *Co. Lit.* 20.

All lands of inheritance, and inheritances favouring of the realty, may be entailed; rents, profits, uses, offices, &c. which concern lands, or certain places, &c. But where the grant of an inheritance is meerly personal, or exercised with chattels, and not issuing out of land, no

entail

entail may be made: and a leafe for years to a man and the heirs of his body, will be void; becaufe the chattel cannot be turned into an inheritance: but it may be affign'd in truft to permit the iffue in tail, &c. to receive the profits. It is incident to the eftate of a tenant in tail, to be difpunifhable of wafte; that the wife of the donee fhall be endowed; and the hufband of a feme donee be tenant by the curtefy; that the tenant in tail may fuffer a common recovery; and that fuch tenants may levy a fine to bar iffues, &c. alfo they may make leafes according to the ftatute 32 H. 8. and by cuftom grant lands by copy, &c. *Co. Lit.* 19, 224. 4 *Inft.* 87. 10 *Rep.* 38.

The tenure in fee tail is general, where any lands or tenements are given to a man and the heirs of his body begotten, or to a woman and the heirs of her body begotten; or it is fpecial when lands and tenements are given to a man and his wife, and to their heirs of their two bodies begotten. In the firft cafe, whatever woman the man takes to wife, or whatever man the woman takes to hufband, the iffue by any of them may inherit one after another; but in the laft cafe, none fhall inherit but thofe that are begotten by the man and his wife particularly named. And with refpect to thefe eftates it is held, that a general tail and fpecial tail may not be created at one and the fame time; if they are, the general, which is greater, will fruftrate the fpecial. *Co. Lit.* 20, 28.

Where lands are given to the hufband and wife, and the heirs of their bodies, both of them have an eftate in fpecial tail: if lands and tenements are given to a man and his wife, and to the heirs of the body of the man, the hufband

band hath an estate in general tail, and the wife an estate for life; because the word *Heirs* relates generally to the body of the husband. And if the estate is made to the husband and wife, and to the heirs of the body of the wife, there the wife hath an estate in special tail, and the husband for term of life only; the word *Heirs* relating to the body of the wife to be begotten by that particular husband. If an estate be limited to a man's heirs which he shall beget on his wife, it creates a special tail in the husband, but the wife will be entitled to nothing. *Co. Lit.* 22.

An estate-tail may be by implication; where a man gives lands to his son for life, and after his decease, to the issue of his body, &c. and for want of such issue, remainder over: and in this case it was held, that a recovery by the son was well suffered. Lands given to persons that are unmarried, and the heirs of their bodies, is a good estate-tail; so if given to a married man, and another man's wife, for the possibility that they may intermarry. *Co. Lit.* 25. 10 *Rep.* 50. 3 *Salk.* 296.

Intails are generally created upon marriage settlements; and were introduced by the statute of *Westm.* 2. 13 *Ed.* 1. And if tenant in tail die without issue, the donor or his heirs may enter as in reversion. *Lit.* 18.

3. Tenant in tail after possibility of issue extinct is, where any lands, &c. are given to a man and his wife in special tail, and either of them dies without issue had betwixt them, the survivor hath an estate in tail after possibility of issue, &c. *Lit.* 32.

None can have his estate but the donee in special tail; on a general tail it cannot be, by reason of the possibility of issue: and if the donees in special tail have issue, and the issue die without issue, so that there is none left which may inherit by force of the intail; the survivor of the donees will have an estate-tail after possibility of issue. And these tenants are not punishable for waste, like unto tenants for life, &c. *Co. Lit.* 27, 29.

If one gives land to a man and his wife, and the heirs of their two bodies, and they live till each of them are one hundred years old, and have no issue; yet do they continue tenant in tail, for that the law seeth no impossibility of having children: but when a man and his wife are tenants in special tail, if the wife die without issue, there the law seeth an apparent impossiblity, that any issue that the husband can get should inherit the estate. *Co. Lit.* 28.

Estates in tail after possibility of issue, &c. now seldom happen, such accidents being guarded against by settlements.

4. Tenant by the curtesy is when a man taketh a wife seised in fee-simple, or in fee-tail general of lands or tenements, or seised as heiress in special tail, and hath issue by her male or female, born alive, which by any possibility may inherit, and then the wife dies; the husband shall hold the land during his life, by the curtesy of *England*, being a privilege not allowed in any other kingdom. *Co. Lit.* 29.

If a woman tenant in tail general takes a husband, and hath issue by him, which issue dieth, and the wife also some time afterwards dies in the life-time of the husband, without having any further issue, here the husband shall be tenant by the curtesy; for though the estate-tail be determined, yet the husband is intitled by

the

the first issue before the estate was spent. And four things are requisite to estate by the curtesy; marriage, seisin, and issue and death of the wife: and this ought to begin by the issue, and be consummate by the wife's death; and the estate of tenant by the curtesy should avoid the immediate discent. *Terms de Ley* 206. *Co. Lit.* 30.

Where lands descend to the wife, after issue by her, the husband shall be tenant by the curtesy: but if lands be given to a woman, and the heirs male of her body, and she hath issue by her husband a daughter, and then dies; the husband shall not be tenant by the curtesy, for this issue cannot possibly inherit the lands. *Co. Lit.* 29.

And of a bare right, title, use, or of a reversion or remainder expectant, a man may not be tenant by the curtesy; nor of a seisin in law; though of a rent in fee, or of an advowson, if the wife die before rent is due, or the church becomes void, the husband may be tenant by the curtesy; because it was out of his power to procure any other seisin. *Co. Lit.* 30. *F. N. B.* 149.

5. Tenant in dower is where a man is sole seised of lands and tenements in fee-simple, fee-tail general, or as heir in special tail, and marries a wife, and dies; the wife, by the common law, after the death of her husband, shall have a third part of such lands and tenements, as were her husband's, at any time during the coverture, to hold during her life, whether she hath issue by him or not: and 'tis not necessary that seisin should continue to the death of the husband; for if he aliens the land, &c.

the wife shall nevertheless be endowed. *Co. Lit.* 30, 32.

A wife may have dower of the principal messuage, (not being a castle) lands, tenements, &c. And of a third part of a reversion, expectant on a term for years, and the rent reserved thereupon; but not upon a reversion on a lease for life, &c. The wife shall have her dower, where lands were recovered against the husband by default or covin: and it is much favoured in law, being for the benefit of widows. A wife of one *Non compos*, of an idcot, outlaw, or a man attainted of felony, may be endowed: though not of one attainted of treason, nor the wife of an alien, &c. And if a wife commit treason or felony, she shall forfeit and lose her dower. *Co. Lit.* 35. 2 *Inst.* 435.

To entitle to dower there must be three things, marriage, seisin, and death of the husband: at common law, dower is assigned by the sheriff, by virtue of the king's writ; or by the heir, &c. by agreement among themselves. By statute, the widow shall immediately after her husband's death have her marriage inheritance, and remain in his chief house forty days, in which time she shall have her dower, &c. *Co. Lit.* 32, 392. 9 *H.* 3. *c.* 7.

If a woman be deforced of her dower, she shall recover damages, *viz.* the value thereof from her husband's death: but where the wife levies a fine with her husband, it bars dower. 13 *Ed.* 1.

6. Tenant for term of life is where a man lets lands to one for his own, or another person's life: and the lessee is called a freehold tenant;

but

but this is understood to be the least estate of freehold. *Lit. Ten.* 28.

If a man makes a grant of lands, tenements, &c. to another, and therein expressed no estate, it hath been held, that the lessee or grantee has thereby an estate during life: and if a lease or grant be made to a man during the lives of two others, and doth not say of the survivor of them; by construction he hath a freehold during the life of the survivor. Also where a man grants an estate for so long as the grantee shall dwell in such a house, or any like uncertain time; the lessee hath in judgment of law an estate for life determinable, if livery be made: and he may plead, that by force thereof he was seised generally for term of life. 5 *Rep.* 9. *Co. Lit.* 42.

A lease is made to a man and his assigns, to hold to him during life, and the lives of two other persons; here is no merger of the lives of the others; for the lessee hath but one estate, by one and the same deed, with this limitation, *viz.* during his and the other two lives: and though the lessee can have it no longer than his own life, yet his assignee shall have the benefit of it so long as the other two are living. But where a person seised in fee demised and granted to one, to hold to him, and also to two others for their lives, and the life of the successive longer liver; it was held, that none should take but the first person, because he was only party to the deed, and the rest not named but in the *Habendum:* so that they could not take but by way of remainder; which here could not be joint, because of the word successive, &c. nor in succession, it not being said successively, as named in the deed. *5 Rep. 13. T. Raym. 143. Hob. 313.*

The grant of a manor of lands with livery, that at the time of the lease of grant made are worth twenty pounds *per annum*, until a hundred pounds are paid, is an estate for life determinable upon levying the money, the annual profits being uncertain: but if a man grants a rent of twenty pounds a year, until one hundred pounds are paid, there the grantee hath an estate but for five years. *Co. Lit. 42.*

If tenant for life shall remain beyond the seas, or elsewhere absent himself by the space of seven years together, and no sufficient proof be made of his life; in any action to be brought by the lessor or reversioner, such person shall be accounted dead: and the judges, on any such action brought, shall direct the jury to give their verdict, as if the party was dead. But if such person shall return from abroad, or be made appear to be living; he shall recover the profits of the land with interest, from the time he hath been kept out of the same. *Stat. 19 Car. 2. c. 6.*

And by a statute since made, persons in remainder or reversion of any estate, after the death of another, on affidavit in the court of Chancery, that they have cause to believe such other person dead, and his death concealed, *&c.* may move the lord chancellor to order such person to be produced; and if he be not produced, he shall be taken as dead, and those in reversion may enter upon the estate. *6 Ann. c. 18.*

7. Tenant for term of years is when lands or tenements are let to another person for a certain term or number of years to come, and the lessee enters on the lands by virtue of this lease,

then

then he is called tenant for term of years. *Co. Lit.* 24.

A term is granted to a man for eighty years, if he lives so long; this term determines by his death: and a lease for one thousand years is not a freehold, or of so high a nature as an estate for life. If tenant for life, and he in remainder in fee, make a lease for years by indenture, rendering rent; it is, during the life of the tenant for life, the lease of tenant for life, and the confirmation of him in remainder; and after the death of tenant for life, it is the lease of him in remainder: and in an action brought upon such lease, during the life of tenant for life, the declaration must be on a lease made by him only, &c. *Co. Rep.* 153. *Co. Lit.* 45. *Cro. Car.* 154. *Dy.* 235.

Where a man had a term for years in the right of his wife, made a lease thereof to commence after his death; he died, and the wife survived, and this was held good against the wife: for the husband during his life might have sold the whole term which his wife had in it, or any part of the term; but the wife shall have so much thereof as is undisposed of by the husband. If a man is seised of any estate in fee-simple, or fee-tail, in right of his wife, or jointly with her; the wife is to join with the husband in leases to be good against her heirs, as is directed by Stat. 32 *H.* 8. *c.* 28. *Co. Lit.* 44, 46. *Poph.* 5.

One possessed of a term for forty years grants to another so many of the years as shall be to come at the time of his death; it is void for uncertainty: but if the land had been demised, to hold after the death of the lessor for twenty years,

years, &c. it had been good. *Co. Rep.* 155. 2 *Rep.* 36.

8. Tenant at will is where lands are let to hold at the will of the lessor; here the lessor may put out the lessee when he pleaseth: but if the lessee sows the land, and before the corn is ripe the lessor puts him out; yet the lessee shall have the corn. *Lit.* 63.

If a man enters into land by consent of the owner, he is tenant at will; so where a man is in possession, and has paid any rent to the landlord, tho' but a quarter's rent, and altho' there was no agreement between the owner of the land and the tenant, this may be a good tenancy at will; for it shall be presumed the rent was received upon some private contract. *T. Raym.* 147. 2 *Lil. Abr.* 151.

A lease at will ought regularly to be at the will of both parties; and the lessor and lessee, where the estate is at will, may determine the will when they please: but if the lessor doth it within a quarter, he shall lose that quarter's rent; and if the lessee doth it, he must pay a quarter's rent; he should determine his will on the very day of payment of the rent. If a man makes a lease at will, and dies, the lease is determined; and if the tenant continues in possession, he is tenant at sufferance. *Co. Lit.* 55, 57. 2 *Salk.* 413. Ld. *Raym.* 707.

Words spoken off from the land by the lessor will not determine the will, until the lessee hath notice thereof: but an actual entry in the absence of the lessee will determine it. And the lessor may come upon the land, and forbid the lessee to hold any longer; or he may enter thereupon, in the presence of witnesses, and say, *I do here enter and take possession of this my land*, &c.

&c. and so oust the tenant at will. *Co. Lit.* 56, 57.

Tenant at will is not bound to repair, as tenant for years is; but if he commit voluntary waste, action of trespass may be had against him: though for permissive waste there is no remedy. *Co. Lit.* 57. 5 *Rep.* 13.

But now the doctrine of tenancy at will seems almost entirely exploded, for it is held by an opinion of the first authority, that there is no such tenure subsisting at this day; for the nature of the tenure depends upon the agreement for payment of rent; for instance, if it be payable quarterly, the agreement is a lease for a quarter of a year, and cannot be determined by either party without a quarter's notice, and so for any other given time.

Tenants for term of life, and term of years, *vide* more of under title *Lease.*

In this place I shall take some notice of *Copyhold* and *Customary* tenures, which I shall divide into,

1. Copyhold estates held for lives.
2. Copyholds in fee, and their qualities.
3. Copyholder's widow's estate.

1. Tenant by copy or court-roll, or copyhold tenant, is such who holds lands or tenements of his lord for life, or in fee, by copy of court-roll, made by the steward of the lord's court: and a copyholder in former times had but an estate at will, in judgment of law; but now by the custom of the manor, these estates are descendible, and the heirs of the tenants shall inherit. *Lit. Ten.* 40.

Of Estates, Ancestors, Heirs, &c.

This tenure is called *Base-Tenure*, because held at the will of the lord: but the estate of a copyholder is not merely at the lord's will, but *ad voluntatem domini secundum consuetudinem manerii*; so that the custom of the manor is essential to copyhold estates; for without a custom, or if copyholders break their custom, they are subject to the will of the lord; and as a copyhold estate is created by custom, so 'tis guided by it. 4 *Rep.* 21.

Copyhold land cannot be made at this day; for the pillars of a copyhold estate are, That it hath been demised time out of mind by copy of court-roll; and that the tenements are parcel of or within the manor. A manor is lost where there are no customary tenants or copyholders: and if a copyhold comes into the hands of the lord, and he leases it for one year, or half a year or for any certain time, it can never be granted by copy after; and if a copyholder bargains and sells his copyhold to a lessee for years, &c. his copyhold is extinguished. *Co. Lit.* 58. 4 *Rep.* 24. 2 *Danv. Abr.* 176, 205.

These copyhold estates are most commonly for three lives: and when any copyholder for life refuseth to pay his rent, or upon summons refuses to come to court and be sworn of the homage, or to make presentment; if he commits voluntary waste, or cuts down timber on his copyhold lands, except it be for reparations, they are forfeitures of his copyhold: but a copyholder for life committing waste shall not forfeit the estate of him in remainder: and action of the case lies for him in remainder against copyholder for life that commits waste. A copyholder may make a lease for one year of his estate, by the general custom, and no more, without

Of Estates, Ancestors, Heirs, &c.

without incurring a forfeiture; but he may make such a lease for a year, and covenant with the lessee, that after the end of that year, he shall have the same for another year, and so during the space of seven years, &c. *Cro. Eliz.* 880. *Cro. Car.* 7. 3 *Lev.* 128. *Cro. Jac.* 300. 6 *Mod.* 468.

The grant of copyhold estates regularly passeth by surrender and admittance: a copyholder cannot transfer his interest to a stranger, otherwise than by surrender to the lord, to the use of him that is to have the estate. By the common custom of copyhold estates, copyholders may surrender in court, and need not alledge any particular custom for it: though if they surrender out of court, into the hands of the lord by customary tenants, &c. particular custom must be pleaded; surrenders may be made by attorney, but not admittances. Copyholder for life pleaded a custom, that every copyholder for life might in the presence of two other copyholders appoint who should have his estate after his death, without any surrender to his use; and that those copyholders might assess a fine, &c. and it was adjudged a good custom. And by the custom of some manors, where copyhold lands are granted to two or more persons for their lives; the person first named in the copy may surrender all the lands. *Co. Lit.* 58, 59. 9 *Rep.* 75. *Rol. Abr.* 500. 4 *Leon.* 238. *Nelf. Abr.* 497.

A custom to compel a lord to make a grant, is against law; though it may be good to admit a tenant. On admittances, a fine is paid to the lord; and fines may be due on every change of the lord or tenant, and are either certain by custom or uncertain; but must be reasonable:

In

In case of surrender, it is said the lord may make what fine he pleases. A heriot is due to the lord of the best beast, or other thing, upon the death of a copyholder for life, or in fee; and is distinguished into heriot-custom and heriot-service; for the first the lord may seize any beast of the tenant any where, and for the last may distrain on the land, &c. And a lord may take a distress of any man's beasts which are upon the lands, and retain them until the heriot is satisfied. *Moor* 788. 4 *Rep.* 27, 28. *Coke Copyhold* 24, 31. *Plowd.* 96.

2. A copyhold estate in fee is copyhold of inheritance, to hold to a man and his heirs. Where there is tenant for life, remainder in fee of a copyhold; he in remainder may surrender his estate: the admittance of copyholder for life is an admittance of him in remainder; and the remainder man may, after the death of tenant for life, surrender without being admitted. *Cro. Eliz.* 504, 3 *Leon.* 329.

In admittance of copyhold tenants upon voluntary grant, the lord is proprietor; but in admittance upon surrender, or by discent, he is only an instrument of conveyance: on a surrender, the person making it, continues tenant till the admittance of the surrenderee; but he cannot pass away the land, or subject it to any other incumbrances than at the time of the surrender: and till admittance, which is the giving of possession, the tenant hath not an estate therein which he may surrender. But the heir of a copyholder may enter, and bring trespass, before admittance, he being in my discent; and may surrender before his admittance, though he is not a complete tenant, to be sworn of the homage jury, or maintain a plaint in the lord's court.

A surren-

A surrender out of court is to be presented at the next court; and if the surrenderor or surrenderee die before presentment, it is held a presentment afterwards makes it good: tenants refusing to present are compellable in the lord's court: and the lord not doing right may be compelled to it in chancery. 4 *Rep.* 21, 22. *Compl. Cop. Sect.* 39. *Lit. Rep.* 234. *Cro. Eliz.* 90.

If the heir of a copyholder in fee, being of age, do not come in and be admitted, upon three solemn proclamations, made at three several courts, if the death of his ancestor be presented, he may forfeit his estate: but if an infant come not in to be admitted, it is no forfeiture; so one beyond sea, &c. And by particular custom these forfeitures may be mitigated, and the copyholder only amerced. No infant, or feme covert, shall forfeit any copyhold lands for their neglect to come to court to be admitted, or refusal to pay any fine; but on their defaults, the lord or his steward may name a guardian or attorney, and so admit them; and enter on the land, and receive the rents, &c. till the usual fine is paid. 4 *Rep.* 27. *Stat.* 9 *Geo.* c. 29.

Some statutes extend to copyhold lands, and some not; the statutes of fines bar copyhold estates; and they are within the statutes of limitation, and the acts against bankrupts: but copyholds are not within the statute of jointures, or of uses; nor shall be extended in execution. *Sav.* 67. *Gilb. Ten.* 160, 185, 242. *Rol. Abr.* 888. *Cro. Car.* 44. *Hardr.* 433. *O. Benl.* 163. 3 *Co.* 9. 6 *Vin. Abr.* 169. *pl.* 4. 3 *Read. Stat. Law* 123. 2 *Inst.* 396. *Co. Cop.* 149. A copyhold cannot be entailed by statute, but by custom it may; and as copyholds may

Of Estates, Ancestors, Heirs, &c.

may be entailed by custom, so by custom may the tail be cut off by surrender: and a surrender may be to the use of a man's will, &c. A plaint may be made in the court of the manor, in nature of a real action; and a recovery shall be had thereon against tenant in tail, which shall be a discontinuance to the estate-tail. *Cro. Eliz.* 879. 4 *Rep.* 22. *Co. Lit.* 60. *Brownl.* 121. *Stat.* 18 *Ed. β.* 4. 32 *H.* 8. *c.* 2. 13 *El. c.* 7.

Copyholds descend according to the rules and maxims of the common law: but copyhold inheritances have no collateral qualities, which do not concern the discent; as to make them assets, to bind the heir; or whereof the wife may be endowed, &c. Tho' by particular custom, a husband may be tenant by the curtesy, and the wife be tenant in dower, &c. *Cro. Eliz.* 148, 361.

3. The copyholder's widow's estate is created by custom; and in some manors every man's life hath a widow's estate annexed to it, and in others only those lives that are purchasers.

As this tenure during widowhood arises out of the husband's estate; therefore his admittance is the admittance of her: and she who hath a widow's estate by the custom of the manor, on the death of her husband is not obliged to pay a fine to the lord, &c. her estate being only a branch of the husband's. Also when a custom is, that the wife of every copyholder shall have her *Free-Bench*, after the death of the husband, the law casts the estate upon the wife, so that she shall have it before admittance, &c. *Hut.* 18. *Hob.* 181. 2 *Danv. Abr.* 184.

But

Of Estates, Ancestors, Heirs, &c.

But where a wife is entitled to her *Free-Bench* by custom, and a copyholder in fee surrenders to the use of another, and then dies, it hath been adjudged that the surrenderee should have the land, and not the wife: because the wife's title doth not commence 'till after the death of her husband; but the surrenderee's title begins by the surrender, and the admittance relates to that. *Co. Lit.* 59. *Salk.* 185. 12 *Mod.* 49.

A married woman may receive a copyhold estate by surrender from her husband, because she comes not in immediately by him; but by the admittance of the lord according to the surrender. A feme covert is to be secretly examined by the steward, on her surrendering her estate. 4 *Rep.* 29. 1 *Inst.* 49.

If any copyholder, paying the services due, be ejected by the lord, he or she shall have trespass against him. 4 *Rep.* 21.

Form of a grant *of a copyhold estate.*

Manor of B. ———.
' AT a court baron of *J. P.* esquire, lord of the manor aforesaid, held for the said manor, the day of, &c. in the fourth year of the reign of the lord *George* the third, by the grace of God, king of *Great Britain, France,* and *Ireland,* defender of the faith, &c. and in the year of our Lord 1764. before *T. M.* gentleman, steward there, it was inrolled among

Of Estates, Ancestors, Heirs, &c.

' among other things, as fol-
' lows:

'AT this court came *A B.* and took of the
' lord of the manor aforesaid, by the de-
' livery of the steward aforesaid, one messuage
' or tenement, and thirty acres of land, mea-
' dow and pasture, with their appurtenances,
' within the aforesaid manor, late in the tenure
' of *C. D.* deceased : *To have and to hold* the said
' tenement, and thirty acres of land, with all
' and singular the appurtenances, unto the afore-
' said *A. B.* and also to *E.* and *W.* his sons, for
' the term of their lives and the life of either of
' them longest living successively, at the will of
' the lord, according to the custom of the ma-
' nor aforesaid; By the rent of six shillings and
' eight-pence by the year, and for a heriot when
' it happens, twenty shillings, and by all other
' rents, works, suits, customs and services there-
' fore due, and of right accustomed; and for
' such estate and entry so in the premisses had,
' the aforesaid *A. B.* gives to the lord for a
' fine seventy-five pounds beforehand paid, and
' so he is admitted tenant thereof, and does
' his fealty, but the fealties of the others are
' respited until, &c. *Dated* by copy of the
' rolls of the aforesaid court, the day and year
' abovesaid.'

Examined with the rolls
  of the said court,

      By me T. M. *steward there*

The

The form of a surrender and new grant of copyhold lands.

'AT this court came *E. B.* who claims to
' hold for the term of his life, and the life
' of *T.* his son, by copy of court-roll of the ma-
' nor there, bearing date, &c. one tenement called,
' &c. with the appurtenances, within the manor
' aforesaid; and all and singular the premisses,
' and the whole estate thereof, right, title, in-
' terest, possession, reversion, claim and de-
' mand of him the said *E. B.* and *T.* his son (the
' said *E.* being sole purchaser of the premisses)
' together with a copy thereof made now to be
' cancelled, into the hands of the lord in the
' aforesaid court he hath surrendered, that the
' said lord may do therewith according to his
' will, from whence there accrues to the lord a
' heriot, which is included in the fine here un-
' derwritten; *whereupon* to this same court came
' the aforesaid *E. B.* and *T.* his son, and took of
' the lord in the said court, by the delivery of
' the steward, the aforesaid premisses, with the
' appurtenances: *To have and to hold* the tene-
' ment and premisses aforesaid, with all and sin-
' gular the appurtenances, to the aforesaid *E. B.*
' and *T. B.* and also to *M. B.* daughter of the said
' *E. B.* for the term of their lives, and of the
' life of the longest liver of them successively, at
' the will of the lord, according to the custom
' of the manor aforesaid; by the rent therefore
' by the year of 18 *l.* 9 *s.* and one heriot, when
' it shall happen, and by all other rents, bur-
' dens, works, suits, customs and services for-
' merly due, and of right accustomed; and the

X ' aforesaid

Of Estates, Ancestors, Heirs, &c.

'aforesaid *E.* and *T.* to have such estate, and
'entry on the premisses, give to the lord for a
'fine 100 *l.* before-hand paid; and so the afore-
'said *E.* is admitted tenant thereof, and doth
'his fealty to the lord, but the fealties of the
'said *T.* and *M.* are respited, until, *&c.*'

The several other heads of the chapter relate particularly to,

1. Ancestors and the laws concerning them.
2. Heirs to persons dying seised of lands.
3. Executors appointed by will.
4. Administrators by statute.

1. Ancestor signifies as much as a predecessor, or one that has gone before in a family: but the law makes a difference between what we commonly call an ancestor, and a predecessor; the one being applied to a natural person and his ancestors, and the other to a body politick and their predecessors.

A prepossessor of an estate hath been called ancestor; and there is homage ancestrel, and some writs that are called ancestrel, *&c. Homage Auncestrel* is where a man and his ancestors have time out mind held their land of the lord by homage, or service of submission; and such lord is obliged to acquit the tenant against all other lords above him, and if the tenant is impleaded, shall warrant the land, *&c.* But there must be a double prescription for it; so that the same tenant and his ancestors, whose heir he is, is to hold the same land of the same lord and his ancestors also, whose heir the lord is, time out of memory, *&c. Terms de Ley* 392. *Lit. Sect.* 85. *F. N. B.* 269.

The

The writs anceſtrel are the aſſiſe of *Mort d' Anceſtor*, and *Darrein Preſentment*; where a man's anceſtor dies ſeiſed of lands, or preſented to a church, &c. to recover the ſame from an abator or diſturber. *Reg. Orig.* 223, 30.

2. An heir is one that ſucceeds by diſcent, to lands, tenements and hereditaments, being an eſtate of inheritance: and a perſon cannot be heir 'till after the death of the anceſtor; for in his life-time, he is only heir apparent, or at law. *Co. Lit.* 8.

The word *Heirs* comprehends heirs of heirs *in infinitum*: if lands are given to a man and his heirs, all his heirs are ſo totally in him, that he may give his lands to whom he will. But a baſtard; an alien, though born in lawful wed-lock; perſons attainted of treaſon or felony, whoſe blood is corrupted, may not be heirs. An ideot or lunatick, one excommunicated, an outlaw in debt, treſpaſs, perſons attainted in a *Præmunire*, &c. may be heir to a man. *Co. Lit.* 9, 21.

An anceſtor could not, by the common law, convey away lands by will from his heirs at law, without conſent of the heir; but by the Stat. 32 *H.* 8. of wills, the law is altered in that point. The heir being very much favoured at law, dubious words in a will ought to be inter-preted for his benefit; and not to diſinherit him: an heir ſhall enforce an adminiſtrator to pay debts with the perſonal eſtate, to preſerve the inheritance: he is not bound in the bond of his anceſtor, unleſs expreſly bound; in a bond if a man binds his heir, but not himſelf, it is void. A man ſhall never bind his heir to warranty, where he himſelf was not bound: a grant of an annuity muſt be for a man and his heirs, to bind the heir, though there be assets; and if named, an heir shall not be bound, except there be assets, as lands, &c. by discent. 2 *Lil. Abr.* 11. *Noy* 185. 2 *Saund.* 136. *Co. Lit.* 386, 144. *Canc. Rep.* 7, 280.

Where *Cestuy que Trust* dies, leaving a trust in fee simple to descend to the heir; this trust will be assets by discent to the heir's hands, and be liable to the obligation of his ancestors: and 'tis said, when assets descend, a *Scire facias* for debt lies against the heir of an heir, to the tenth degree. Heirs and executors are both chargeable upon specialties: but if the heir is sued for the debt of his ancestor and pays it; he shall be reimbursed by the executor of the obligor, who hath personal assets. 29 *Car.* 2, 3. perpetuated by 1 *Jac.* 2. *c.* 17. *f.* 5. *Noy* 56. *Dy.* 303. *Chanc. Rep.* 74.

An heir may bring an action against one that injures the monument, &c. of his ancestor, And the coffin and shroud of the deceased are the executor's or administrator's; but the dead body belongs to no one: tho' in all cases where taken away, actions and prosecutions may be had. 2 *Inst.* 202. See *Action of debt*, &c.

3. Executor is he to whom the execution or performance of a man's will is committed after his death. All persons that are capable of making a will may be executors; and so may some others; as an infant may be executor, but not act till seventeen years of age: a woman covert may be appointed executor; so may any excommunicate or outlawed person, &c. But popish recusants convict cannot be executors. 4 *Inst.* 335. 5 *Rep.* 29. 6 *Rep.* 67.

If a man who is neither executor or administrator, acts as an executor; as when he takes

into

into his hands the goods of the deceased, and converts them to his own use, or alters the property by sale, &c. or if he delivers the goods to creditors or legatees; receive any debt due to the deceased, &c. he is executor in his own wrong, and shall be sued as executor: but every taking of the deceased's goods, is not an acceptance to make one chargeable; for if a man take away his own goods in the house of the deceased; or use some of the goods of the deceased; in the necessary occasions of his family; bury the deceased, and sell his goods for that purpose, &c. these will not make a man executor in his own wrong. 5 *Rep.* 31. 8 *Rep.* 135. 9 *Rep.* 39. *Dy.* 166. *Noy's Max.* 103.

Executors legally appointed may accept or refuse the executorship: and if there are many, and one proves the will, and takes upon him the executorship; it will do for all; but the rest may at any time after join with him, and intermeddle with the estate; but in case they all refuse, none of them ever after will be admitted: here the ordinary, or where an executor dies before the will is proved, grants administration with the will annexed. In the eye of the law all who take upon them the executorship, are but as as one executor; and most acts done by or to any one of them, are acts done by or to all: actions are to be brought by executors, in the name of all of them, altho' some refuse the executorship; though he or those only that administer shall be sued, in actions against them. 9 *Rep.* 37. *Perk.* 485. *Co. Lit.* 113. *Rol. Abr.* 924, 918.

As an executor hath his power wholly by the will, he may take the goods himself, or authorize

rize another to seize them for him; or may release an action, debt or duty, or do any thing as executor, before probate of the will, so as he afterwards proves it; unless it be bringing of actions for debts, &c. to maintain which, he must shew the testament proved. His office is to bury the testator in a decent manner, according to his rank, and with regard to the estate left: he is to make an inventory of all the goods and chattels of the deceased, with their value, and all debts due to the testator; then prove the will in common form before the ordinary, by his own oath, or by witnesses, if required; and being exhibited in the register's office of the ecclesiastical court, a copy in parchment is delivered the executor, under the ordinary's seal, which is the probate: and when all this is done, an executor must pay all debts, before legacies, in the order following, *viz.* After the funeral charges, the king's debt is to be preferred; then debts on judgments and statutes; debts on mortgages, bonds and other specialties; rent, servants wages, debts on shopbooks, &c. *Plow.* 277. *Co. Lit.* 292. 5 *Rep.* 28, 1. *Rol. Abr.* 917, 926. *Perk.* 486.

Amongst debts of equal degree, the executor may pay himself first: but if he pays the debts in any other order, he is answerable for the debts of a higher degree, altho' it be out of his own estate. Those debts, that are first sued for, shall be first paid; and where no suit is begun, the executor may pay the whole debt to any one creditor in equal degree, though there be no assets left to satisfy another any part of his debt. Where there are two executors, and one dies, debt is to be brought against the surviving executor; not the survivor and the executor of the deceased;

fed;

sed: but in equity, the testator's goods are liable in whosesoever hands they are. And by statute, executors of executors shall answer for goods, as the first executor: also they may bring actions of debt, account, &c. and executors shall have the like writs, actions and process, as the testator might have had, and trespass and damages for wrong done to him. *Noy Max.* 104. *Leon. Ca.* 304. *Canc. Rep.* 57. *Stat.* 4 *Ed.* 3. *c.* 7. 25 *Ed.* 3. *fl.* 5. *c.* 5.

After the debts are paid by the executor, he is to pay the legacies; in payment whereof he may prefer a legacy to himself: then he may pay what legacies he pleases first; or pay each legatee a part in proportion, if there be not enough to pay every one his whole legacy; and he is not bound to order, as in case of debts due from the testator. But if there be a specifick legacy, as of a silver tankard, &c. this must be delivered before any other legacy; if there be assets: and where there is enough to pay all the legacies, they shall be paid; but when there is not enough to pay debts, or more, the legatees must lose their legacies. If an executor pays out the assets in legacies, and afterwards debts appear, of which he had no notice, which he is obliged to pay; the executor by will may force the legatees to refund. *Plowd.* 545. *Offic. Exec.* 204, 217. 2 *Ventr.* 358. *Canc. Rep.* 136.

All the goods and chattels, which belong'd to the testator at the time of his death come to the executor as assets, and make him liable to the debts and legacies of the creditors and legatees: goods, chattels, debts, &c. recovered by the executor, by action after the death of the testator, shall be accounted assets; not before recovered.

vered. If an obligee makes his obligor executor, this is a release in law of the debt: but it shall be assets in his hands; and where an executor hath a bond, and releases the debt, tho' without consideration, it will be assets. On a *Scire facias* against an executor, he cannot plead fully administered; but must plead specially, that no goods of the testator are come to his hands: special bail is not required of heirs, executors, &c. in any action brought for the debt of the testator; and executors and administrators shall pay no costs. 6 *Rep.* 47. *Co. Lit.* 374. 8 *Rep.* 136. *Lil. Abr.* 568. 24 *H.* 8. *c.* 8.

4. An administrator is one who hath the goods of a man dying intestate, without making any will, committed to his charge by the ordinary: who must make an inventory of the goods of the deceased, in the presence of two creditors the next of kin, or two neighbours, and deliver it upon oath to the ordinary.

The ordinary of every diocese is to appoint administrators, to gather up and dispose of the goods of the deceased; account for them, &c. by the Stat. *West.* 2. 13 *Ed.* 3. *c.* 19. And on granting administration, bond with sureties are taken for faithful discharge of trust, and rendering accounts. 22 & 23 *Car.* 2. *c.* 10. perpetuated by 1 *Jac.* 2. *c.* 17. *f.* 5. Widows, and the nearest of kin, are to be appointed administrators; and the mother shall have administrators; and the mother shall have administration of goods of a child, before a brother or sister, &c. The husband shall be administrator of the wife's goods, and the wife of the husband's; and if there be no husband or wife left on the death of either, then is administration granted to children, sons or daughters; if

no

no children alive, to father or mother; and if none such, to brother or sister; and then to next of kin, as uncle, aunt, cousin. 21 *H.* 8. *c.* 4, 5. 4 *Rep.* 51. *Ventr.* 217. *T. Raym.* 93.

A person of the half blood, is in equal degree of kindred, to have letters of administration, as one of the whole blood: and administrators are to distribute equally between whole blood and half blood. A creditor or other person, may be made administrator; and where administration is neglected, the ordinary may grant to a stranger letters to gather the goods of the intestate; or may take them into his own hands, to pay the deceased's debts, in such order as an executor or administrator ought to do it. Where administration is granted, it shall not be revoked without just cause; though if granted where not grantable, may be repealed by delegates: if an administrator die, his executors are not administrators; but new administration shall be had. *Lil. Abr.* 40. 2 *Lev.* 173. 8 *Rep.* 136. *Lev.* 157, 186.

The estates of persons dying intestate, are to be distributed by administrators, one third to the wife, and the residue equally amongst the children, and their representatives; if no children, one moiety of the personal estate is to go to the wife, and the rest equally to the next of kin: and if no wife, but children, it shall be distributed amongst the children; and if no children nor wife, to go to the next of kin in equal degree. But this is not to extend to estates of feme coverts, &c. And where children die after their father, without wife or child, the mother, and every brother and sister, and their representatives, shall have equal shares in their estates. No representatives shall be allowed after brothers and

and sisters children; and children advanced in the intestate's life-time, are excepted by the statute 22 & 23 *Car.* 2. *c.* 10. 14 *Geo.* 2. *c.* 20. *f.* 9. 29 *Car.* 2. *c.* 3. *f.* 25. perpetuated by 1 *Jac.* 2. *c.* 17. *f.* 5.

Against an administrator, and for him, action will lie, as for and against an executor; and he shall be charged to the value of goods, and no further, unless he waste the goods of the intestate: but an administrator can do nothing 'till administration is granted. *Vent.* 307.

Of the Laws relating to Marriage, Bastardy, Infants, Ideots, Lunaticks.

MARRIAGE signifies the lawful conjunction of man and woman in a constant society and agreement of living together, 'till the contract is dissolved by death or breach of faith, or some notorious misbehaviour, destructive of the ends for which it was intended: and mutual consent between parties 'tis said makes the marriage, before consummation. I shall divide this subject of marriage into divers parts or branches, as,

1. How marriages are solemnized.
2. What persons may marry.
3. Contracts of marriage.
4. Rights of husband and wife.
5. Marriage settlements and jointures.

1. Mar-

Of Marriage, Bastardy, &c.

1. Marriage was instituted in a state of innocence, for preservation thereof, and is one of the rights of human nature; and as to the solemnization of marriage, this is a civil right, regulated by the laws and customs of the kingdom or country where we reside; and every state allows such privileges to the parties as it deems expedient, and denies legal advantages to those who refuse to solemnize their marriage in the manner it requires: but they cannot dissolve a marriage celebrated in another manner, marriage being of divine institution, to which only a full and free consent of the mind is necessary. *Moor* 170.

There is a marriage in right or in possession; and marriage *de facto*, or in reputation, as among Quakers, &c. which is allowed to be sufficient to give title to a personal estate: tho' in the case of a *Dissenter*, who was married to a woman by a minister of the congregation, not in orders, it was held, that when a husband demands a right due to him as husband by the ecclesiastical law, he ought to prove himself a husband by that law to intitle him to it: yet this marriage was not a mere nullity, because by the law of nature the contract is binding. Marriages by *Romish priests*, whose orders are acknowledged by the church of *England*, will have the effect of a legal marriage in some instances; as in the case of Mr. *Fielding*, who was married by a *Romish* priest to Mrs. *Wadsworth*: this was held to be such a marriage, as to make it felony in him to marry afterwards to the dutchess of *Cleveland*. 4 Read. Stat. Law 200. 2 Burn's Eccles. Law 30. but marriages should be solemnized according to the rites of the church of *England*, for the parties to be intitled to the privileges attend-tending marriage here; as dower, thirds, &c. *Leon.* 53. *Wood's Inst.* 59. *Salk.* 119.

To guard against private marriages, it is ordained, that parsons, vicars or curates, marrying any persons, or employing other ministers to do the same, without publishing the banns of matrimony according to law, or without a licence for the marriage first had and obtained, shall forfeit 100 *l.* the persons so married 10 *l.* and parish-clerks, &c. assisting, knowing it to be so, 5 *l.* by the statute 7 & 8 W. 3. c. 35. And before this statute an information was exhibited against a person for combination, in procuring a clandestine marriage in the night, without banns or licence, between a maid-servant and a young gentleman, who was heir to an estate; and the parson being in liquor was fined 100 marks, and ordered to be committed 'till paid: but it does not appear that the marriage could be made void. *Cro. Car.* 557.

By the ordinances of our church, when persons are to be married, the banns of matrimony shall be published in the parish church where they dwell three several sundays or holidays, in the time of divine service; and if at the day appointed for their marriage, any man do alledge any impediment, as precontract, consanguinity, or affinity, parents not consenting, where under age, &c. why they should not be married, and become bound with sufficient sureties to prove his allegation; then the solemnization must be deferred, until such time as the truth is tried: and no minister shall celebrate matrimony between any persons without a faculty or licence, except the banns have been first published, as directed by the book of common prayer, upon pain of suspension for three years; nor shall any
minister,

minister, under the like pain, join any persons in marriage who are so licensed, at any unseasonable times, or in a private place, &c. *Rubrick, Canon* 62.

And on granting of licences for marriage, *affidavit* or oath is to be first made before one of the doctors of the commons, by the man, that he and the woman live at such a place, &c. and are willing to marry each other; that there is no impediment of precontract, consanguinity, &c. or any suit depending in any ecclesiastical court, touching any contract of marriage of either of the parties with any other, &c. And then a *bond* is entered into, to the like effect, as to there being no impediment of precontract, or any suit depending, &c. that neither of the parties are of better estate than suggested; and that the marriage be openly solemnized in the church mentioned, in canonical hours, between eight and twelve in the morning, &c. Licences to the contrary shall be void; and the parties marrying are subject to punishment as for clandestine marriages. *Can.* 102.

There are some things disused on granting *Licences*; as the testification of witnesses of the consent of parents; and celebrating the marriage in the parish-church where one of the parties dwelleth, &c. and notwithstanding the canons, marriages of persons of quality are frequently in their own houses, out of canonical hours, in the evening; and often solemnized by others in other churches, &c. which things are dispensed with, in regard to the substance of the marriage, to make the same good without all the ceremonies. But now

All

'All banns of matrimony shall be published in an audible manner in the parish-church, or in some publick chapel, in which banns of matrimony have been usually published, belonging to such parish or chapelry wherein the persons to be married dwell; according to the form prescribed by the rubric prefixed to the office of matrimony in the book of common prayer; upon three *Sundays* preceding the solemnization of marriage, during the time of morning service, (or of evening service, if there be no morning service, in such church or chapel upon any of those *Sundays*) immediately after the second lesson: and when the persons to be married dwell in diverse parishes or chapelries, the banns shall be published in the church or chapel belonging to such parish or chapelry wherein each of them dwell; and where both or either of the persons to be married dwell in any extraparochial place, having no church or chapel wherein banns have been usually published, then the banns shall be published in the parish-church or chapel belonging to some parish or chapelry adjoining to such extraparochial place: and where banns shall be published in any church or chapel belonging to any parish adjoining to such extraparochial place, the parson, vicar, minister or curate, publishing such banns, shall under his hand certify the publication thereof, in such manner as if either of the persons to be married dwelt in such adjoining parish, and all other rules prescribed by the said rubrick, concerning the publication of banns, and the solemnization of matrimony, not hereby altered, shall be observed: and in all cases where banns shall have been published, the marriage shall be

'be solemnized in one of the parish churches
'or chapels where such banns have been pub-
'lished.' *Stat.* 26 *Geo.* 2. *c.* 33. *f.* 1.

'No parson, vicar, minister or curate shall
'be obliged to publish the banns of matrimony
'between any persons, unless the persons to be
'married shall seven days before the time re-
'quired for the first publication of such banns,
'cause to be delivered to such parson, &c. a
'notice in writing of their christian and sur-
'names, and of their respective abodes within
'such parish, chapelry or extraparochial place,
'and of the time during which they have dwelt
'in such houses respectively.' *Id. sect.* 2.

'No parson, &c. solemnizing marriages be-
'tween persons, both or one of whom shall be
'under the age of 21 years, after banns pub-
'lished, shall be punished by ecclesiastical cen-
'sures, for solemnizing such marriages without
'consent of parents or guardians, whose con-
'sent is required by law, unless such parson, &c.
'have notice of the dissent of such parents or
'guardians. And in case such parents or guar-
'dians, or one of them, publickly cause to be
'declared, in the church or chapel where the
'banns shall be so published, at the time of
'such publication, their dissent to such mar-
'riage, such publication of banns shall be void.'
Id. sect. 3.

'No licence of marriage shall be granted, by
'any person having authority to grant such li-
'cences, to solemnize any marriage in any other
'church or chapel, than in the parish-church
'or public chapel belonging to the parish or
'chapelry, within which the usual place of
'abode of one of the persons to be married
'shall have been for four weeks, immediately
'before

'before the granting such licence; or where
'both or either of the parties to be married
'dwell in any extraparochial place, having no
'church or chapel wherein banns have been usu-
'ally published; then in the parish-church or
'chapel belonging to some parish or chapelry
'adjoining to such extraparochial place.' *Id.
sect. 4.*

'All parishes where there shall be no parish-
'church or chapel, or none wherein divine ser-
'vice shall be usually celebrated every *Sunday*,
'may be deemed extraparochial places for the
'purposes of this act.' *Id. sect. 5.*

'Nothing herein contained shall deprive the
'archbishop of *Canterbury* and his officers, of
'the right which hath hitherto been used, in
'virtue of 25 *Hen.* 8. *c.* 21. of granting special
'licences to marry at any convenient time or
'place. *Id. sect. 6.*

'No surrogate deputy by any ecclesiastical
'judge, who hath power to grant licences of
'marriage, shall grant any such licence, before
'he hath taken an oath before the said judge,
'faithfully to execute his office according to law
'to the best of his knowledge, and hath given
'security by his bond in the sum of 100 *l.* to
'the bishop of the diocese, for the faithful exe-
'cution of his office. *Id. sect. 7.*

'If any person shall solemnize matrimony in
'any other place than a church or public cha-
'pel, where banns have been usually published,
'unless by special licence from the archbishop
'of *Canterbury*; or shall solemnize matrimony
'without publication of banns, unless licence
'of marriage be first obtained from some per-
'son having authority to grant the same; every
'person wilfully so offending and convicted,

'shall

' shall be adjudged guilty of felony, and shall
' be transported to some of his majesty's planta-
' tions in *America*, for 14 years, according to
' the laws for transportation of felons. And all
' marriages solemnized in any other place than
' a church or such publick chapel, unless by
' special licence as aforesaid, or without publi-
' cation of banns, or licence of marriage from a
' person having authority to grant the same,
' shall be void.' *Id. sect.* 8.

' All prosecutions for such felony shall be
' commenced within three years after the offence
' committed.' *Id. sect.* 9.

' After the solemnization of any marriage un-
' der a publication of banns, it shall not be ne-
' cessary in support of such marriage, to give any
' proof of the dwelling of the parties in the re-
' spective parishes or chapelries wherein the banns
' were published; or where the marriage is by
' licence, it shall not be necessary to give any
' proof that the usual place of abode of one of the
' parties, for four weeks as aforesaid, was in the
' parish or chapelry where the marriage was so-
' lemnized; nor shall any evidence in any of the
' said cases be received to prove the contrary in
' any suit touching the validity of such marriage.'
Id. sect. 10.

' All marriages solemnized by licence, where
' either of the parties, not being a widower or
' widow, shall be under the age of 21 years,
' which shall be had without the consent of the
' father of such of the parties so under age, if
' living, or if dead, of the guardians of the per-
' son of the party so under age, or one of them;
' and in case there be no such guardian, then of
' the mother, if living and unmarried; or if there
' be no mother living and unmarried, then of
' a guardian

'a guardian of the person appointed by the court
'of *Chancery*, shall be void.' *Id. sect.* 11.

'In case any such guardian or mother or any
'of them, whose consent is made necessary,
'shall be *non compos mentis*, or beyond the seas,
'or shall refuse their consent to the marriage, it
'shall be lawful for any person desirous of mar-
'rying in any of the before mentioned cases,
'to apply by petition to the lord chancellor,
'who is hereby impowered to proceed upon
'such petition in a summary way; and in case
'the marriage proposed appear proper, the lord
'chancellor shall judicially declare the same to
'be so by an order of court, and such order
'shall be deemed as good as if the guardian or
'mother of the person so petitioning, had con-
'sented to such marriage.' *Id. sect.* 12.

'The churchwardens and chapelwardens of
'every parish or chapelry shall provide books
'of vellum, or durable paper, in which all mar-
'riages and banns of marriage respectively, there
'published or solemnized, shall be registered:
'and every page thereof shall be marked at the
'top, with the number of such page, begin-
'ning at the second leaf with number one; and
'every leaf or page so numbered, shall be ruled
'with lines at proper and equal distances: and
'all banns and marriages published or celebra-
'ted in any church or chapel, or within any such
'parish or chapelry, shall be registred, print-
'ed or written upon, or as near as may be to
'such ruled lines; and shall be signed by the
'parson, vicar, minister or curate, or by some
'other person in his presence, and by his direc-
'tion; and such entries shall be made on or
'near such lines in successive order, where the
'paper is not damaged or decayed, until a new
'book shall be necessary; and then the direc-
'tions

'tions aforesaid shall be observed in every such
'new book. And all books provided as aforesaid, shall belong to every such parish or chapelry respectively, and shall be carefully preserved for publick use.' *Id. sect.* 14.

'All marriages shall be solemnized in the
'presence of two witnesses, besides the minister who shall celebrate the same. And immediately after the celebration of every marriage, an entry thereof shall be made in such
'register; in which it shall be expressed, that
'the said marriage was celebrated by banns or
'licence; and if both or either of the parties
'married by licence be under age, with consent of the parents or guardians, as the case
'shall be; and shall be signed by the minister
'with his proper addition, and also by the parties married, and attested by such two witnesses." *Id. sect.* 15.

'If any person shall, with intent to elude this
'act, wilfully insert, or cause to be inserted, in
'the register book of such parish or chapelry,
'any false entry of any thing relating to any
'marriage; or falsely make, alter, forge or
'counterfeit, or cause to be falsely made, &c.
'or assist in falsely making, &c. any such entry in such register; or falsely make, &c. or
'cause to be falsely made, &c. or assist in falsely
'making, &c. any such licence of marriage as
'aforesaid, or publish as true any such false, altered, forged or counterfeited register, or a
'copy thereof, or any such false, &c. licence
'of marriage, knowing such register or licence
'of marriage respectively to be false, &c. or
'if any person shall wilfully destroy, or cause
'to be destroyed, any register-book of marriages, or any part of such register-book, with
'intent to avoid any marriage, or to subject any

' person to any of the penalties of this act;
' every person so offending, and being convic-
' ted, shall be adjudged guilty of felony, and
' shall suffer death. *Id. sect.* 16.

' This act shall not extend to the marriages of
' any of the royal family.' *Id. sect.* 17.

' Nothing in this act shall extend to *Scotland*,
' nor to any marriages amongst *Quakers*, or
' amongst persons professing the *Jewish* reli-
' gion, where both the parties to such marriage
' shall be *Quakers*, or persons professing the
' *Jewish* religion; nor to any marriages solem-
' nized beyond the seas.' *Id. sect.* 18.

The proof of a marriage may be by witnesses who were present at the solemnization; by cohabitation of the parties; by publick fame and reputation; by confession of the married persons themselves, altho' their acknowledgment might only be to avoid the punishment of fornication; and by divers other circumstances; which if they amount to half a proof, ought to be extended in favour of marriage rather than contrary to it. *Wood Civ. L.* 122. 2 *Burn's Eccles. Law* 36. *pl.* 5.

Entry of names of persons, as married, in a church book is not positive evidence of the marriage, unless the identity of the persons be proved; or that it be strengthened with proof of cohabitation, or allowance of parties. 15 *Vin. Abr.* 254. *pl.* 6. 2 *Eq. Caf. Abr.* 585. *pl.* 3. *Gr. & Rud. Law & Eq.* 206. *pl.* 3.

The form of a faculty *or* licence *for marriage.*

EDMUND *by divine permission lord bishop of* London; *to our well beloved in*
' *Christ*

Chrift A. B. *of*, &c. *batchelor, and* C. D. *of* &c. *spinfter, fendeth greeting. Whereas you are, as is alledged, determined to enter into the holy ftate of matrimony, and are very defirous of obtaining your marriage to be folemnized in the face of the church, we are willing that fuch your honeft defires may more fpeedily have their defired effect, and therefore that you may be able to procure fuch marriage to be freely and lawfully folemnized in the parish church of*, &c. *by the rector, vicar or curate thereof, at any time of the year, without publishing of banns, provided that by reason of any precontract, confanguinity, affinity or any other lawful caufe whatfoever, there be no lawful impediment in this behalf, and that there be not at this time any action, fuit, plaint, quarrel or demand moved or depending before any judge ecclefiaftical or temporal for or concerning any marriage contracted by or with either of you, and that the faid marriage be openly folemnized in the church above-mentioned, between the hours of eight and twelve in the forenoon, and without any prejudice to the minifter of the place where the faid woman is a parishoner: we do hereby, for good caufes, give and grant our licence or faculty, as well to you the parties contracting, as to the rector, vicar or curate of the faid church where the faid marriage is intended to be folemnized, to folemnize the fame in manner and form above fpecified, according to the rites and ceremonies prefcribed in the book of common prayer, in that behalf published by authority of parliament. Provided always, that if hereafter any fraud shall appear to have been committed at the time of granting this licence,*

either

either by false suggestions or concealment of the truth, then this licence shall be void to all intents and purposes in law, as if the same had never been granted; and in that case, we do inhibit all ministers whatsoever, if any thing of the premisses shall have come to their knowledge, from proceeding to the celebration of the said marriage, without first consulting us, or our vicar general. Given under the seal (which we use in this behalf) the day of, &c. in the year of our Lord, &c.

The usual fees and charges of taking out this licence, under the bishop's seal which is signed, by the register, with the affidavit and bond, amount to about 1 *l.* 5 *s.* and altho' but one parish-church is named, ministers of almost all other * churches in the diocese will marry the parties by virtue of the licence.

2. As to what persons may marry; in former times priests were restrained from marriage, and their issue accounted bastards, *&c.* but on the reformation, laws were made, declaring that the marriage of priests should be lawful; though the preambles to those statutes set forth, that it would be better for priests to live chaste, and separate from the company of women, that they might the better attend their religious duty. *Stat.* 5 *& 6 Ed.* 6. *c.* 23.

All persons who are of the age of consent to marry, *viz.* the man at fourteen, and the woman at twelve, (not prohibited by the Levitical degrees, or otherwise by God's Law,) may lawfully marry: but marriages made within the degrees are incestuous and unlawful. A son of a father by another wife, and daughter of a mother

by

---

* But now they cannot. See the above statute of 26 *Geo.* 2. *c.* 33. *sect.* 4.

by another husband, cousin germans, &c. may marry with each other: a man may not marry his brother's wife, or wife's sister, an uncle his niece, an aunt her nephew, &c. Though if one takes his sister to wife, they are baron and feme, and the issue are not bastards 'till a divorce. A sister's bastard daughter is said to be within the Levitical law of affinity; it being morally as unlawful to marry a bastard as one born in wedlock: and if a bastard doth not fall under the prohibition, a mother may marry her bastard son; and there are persons within the reason of the prohibition of marriage, though not mentioned, and must be prohibited; as the father from marrying his daughter, the grandson from marrying his grandmother, &c. *Co. Lit.* 24. *Levit. c.* 18, 20. *Rol. Abr.* 394. 5 *Mod.* 168. *Vaugh.* 321.

By the statute 32 *Hen.* 8. *c.* 38. The temporal courts are to determine what marriages are within, or without the Levitical degrees; and prohibit the spiritual courts, if they impeach any persons for marrying without those degrees: and it has been held, if it were not for that statute, we should be under no obligation to observe the Levitical degrees. In case of perpetual impotency, fear, or imprisoment, so that there can be no consent; or where persons are precontracted; a man or woman have a wife or husband living, &c. here the marriages are to be adjudged void, as prohibited by God's Law. And loyalty or lawfulness of marriage is to be tried by the bishop's certificate; on inquisition taken before him, and examination of witnesses, &c. But where the right of marriage is not in question, whether a woman is married, or she is the wife of such a one, is triable by jury at

Common

Common Law. 2 *Ventr.* 9. *Co. Lit.* 235. 2 *Inst.* 687. 7 *Rep.* 23. *Dy.* 303. *Lev.* 41. 3 *Salk.* 64.

If any persons are married before the age of consent, they may at that age disagree, and marry again, without any divorce: but if they once give consent when at age, they cannot afterwards disagree; and where they are married before, there needeth not a new marriage, if they agree at that age. A man being of the age to consent, and the woman not; or the woman of age and the man not; he or she may disagree to the marriage, at the other's coming of age to consent, as well as the other, for there is a mutual power of disagreement: where after disagreement of the parties, at the age of consent they agree to the marriage, and live together as man and wife, the marriage hath continuance, notwithstanding the former disagreement; though if that had been before the ordinary, they could not after agree again to make it good. *Co. Lit.* 33. 2 *Inst.* 182. 3 *Inst.* 88. 6 *Rep.* 22. *Danv. Abr.* 699.

A woman cannot disagree within her age of twelve years, 'till which the marriage continues; and before, her disagreement is void: Though if a man marries a woman under that age, and afterwards she within her age of consent disagrees to the marriage, and at her age of twelve years marries another; now the first marriage is dissolved, so that he may take another wife: for although the disagreement within the age of consent was not sufficient, yet her taking another husband at that age, and cohabiting with him, affirms the same, by which the first marriage will be avoided. *Danv. Abr.* 699. *Moor* 575, 764.

Infants, Incots.

3. Contracts of marriage, where either party is not seven years of age, are absolutely void: but marriages of princes made by the state in their behalf, at any age, are held good; though many of these contracts have been broke through by those great persons.

Where there is a mutual contract of marriage in words of present time, and it can be proved, the ecclesiastical courts will compel the parties to solemnize their marriage; although either or both of them are married elsewhere, and children have been the fruits of it: but if the contract is made in words of future time, and this is not carried into execution by consummation, &c. and the parties marry others, such marriage is good. For a contract of marriage in the present time, when it is said, *I marry you*; or, *You and I are man and wife*, &c. is not releaseable; though the marriage contract of future time, where 'tis said, *I will marry you*, or *I promise to marry you*, &c. may be released. 4 *Read. Stat. Law* 192.

If a man promise a woman to marry her by promise *de præsenti*, as, *I do take thee to my wife*, or the wife make the like promise to the husband; such promise cannot be dissolved, but they are reputed husband and wife in respect of the substance and indissoluble knot of matrimony: and therefore, if either of them should marry with any other person, consummating the same by carnal copulation and procreation of children; this matrimony is to be dissolved as unlawful; the parties marrying are to be punished as adulterers, and their children in danger of bastardy. *Swinb.* 9, 10.

Upon a promise of future marriage, if the parties afterwards lie together, it has been adjudged,
the

the contract passes thereby into a real marriage, in construction of law: and by *Holt* Ch. Just. If a contract be in words of future time, as *I will take thee*, &c. and the man does take her accordingly, and cohabit with her, 'tis a marriage, and the spiritual court cannot punish them for fornication. A man contracts to marry with *A.* and after marries *B.* whereupon *A.* sues him in the spiritual court, and sentence is given that he shall espouse *A.* and live with her, which he doth and they have issue; such issue shall inherit, though there was no divorce from the marriage of *B.* 2 *Salk.* 477. *Danv. Abr.* 700.

When the words of a contract of marriage are, *I will take thee from henceforth*, &c. They are as much as, I do take thee, and an absolute marriage: and if it is demanded of a man, whether he shall take the woman to his wife, and he answers, I will; or it is demanded of the woman, if she will take the man to her husband, and she says, I will; by this marriage, and not spousals only, is contracted. And it is not necessary that both parties use the same words; for if one say, I will marry thee, and the other answers, I am content, &c. hereby spousals *de futuro* are contracted: also where a man says to a woman, I promise to marry thee, and if thou art contented to have me, kiss me, or give me thy hand; if the woman do kiss, or give her hand, by this spousals will be contracted between them. *Swinb.* 220.

If a father or mother promise marriage for their daughter, her silence, she being present at hearing the same, hath been held a consent to the contract: and where the promise of the man is proved, but no actual promise on the woman's side;

side; if she carry herself as one consenting and approving the promise of the man, it is evidence that the woman likewise promised. In case a ring be solemnly delivered by a man, and put on the woman's fourth finger; if she accepts and wears the ring, without any words, they are presumed to have mutually consented to marriage; here, as his consent appears, so her's is implied. *Swinb.* 69, 210. 3 *Salk.* 16.

In marriage contracts, it is not absolutely required, that the parties do it at the same instant, by answering one another; but if there be some distance of time betwixt the promise of the man and the woman, the contract may be good, if the party first promising continues in the same mind until the other party hath promised: but where the parties are under age to consent, it is not matrimony, but spousals, if it be either; and when the words of contract are only conditional on one side, and on the other absolute; or if spoken in jest, they are not obligatory.

A contract of marriage may be made by absent parties, by their proctors, by messengers, or letters; when by proxy, it is by special power of attorney, to contract matrimony or spousals for the party in his name, with such a woman, &c. And in this case, the proctor says, *That such a man doth contract matrimony with thee, by me his proctor,* &c. To which the woman answers, *I do take him to my husband, by thee being his proctor;* and both parties are to continue of the same mind till the contract is finished; for before that the proctor may be revoked, and then the contract will be void. *Ibid.*

But now in no case shall any suit or proceeding be had in any ecclesiastical court, to compel the celebration of any marriage *in facie ecclesiæ*, by reason of any contract of matrimony, whether *per verba de presenti*, or *per verba de futuro*, entered into after 25 *March* 1754. *Stat.* 26 *Geo.* 2. *c.* 33.

On a promise of marriage, damages may be recovered at law, if either party refuses to marry; but the promise must be mutual on both sides to ground the action: and by statute 29 *Car.* 2. *c.* 3. no action shall be brought upon an agreement on consideration of marriage, except it be put in writing, and signed by the party to be charged, &c. A promise by letter is sufficient within this statute. Contracts and bonds for money to procure marriage between others, have been held void in chancery. *Salk.* 24. 3 *Lev.* 41. 2 *Vent.* 361. 2 *Eq. Caf. Abr.* 248. Ld. *Raym.* 387. *Stra.* 34.

4. By marriage with a woman, the husband is intitled to all her estate real and personal; and the effects of marriage are, that the husband and wife are accounted one person, and he hath power over her person as well as estate, &c. Where there is no settlement to the contrary, by the marriage a man gaineth a freehold, &c. in his wife's right, if she have fee: he also gains a chattel real, as a term of years, &c. All chattels personal, in possession of the wife in her own right, are the husband's. The husband shall be tenant by the curtesy of the wife's land after her death, where issue is born between them: and the wife shall have dower in her husband's lands, after the death of her husband, &c. And if she survives him, shall have her term for years, or other chattels real again, if the husband hath not altered the property,

perty. *Co. Lit.* 351, 46. *Dr. & Stud. c.* 7. *Lit.* 35, 36.

Agreements between husband and wife, before marriage, are commonly extinguished by the marriage: a man cannot grant lands, &c. to his wife, nor covenant with her; but he may covenant with others for her use, &c. and may devise to her by will. The wife is so much under the power of her husband, as to be disabled to contract without his consent; and though she may use his goods, yet she may not dispose of, or pawn them: in strictness, a wife cannot bind her husband by contract for necessaries without his assent; but generally, if she buys goods for herself, as apparel, &c. or for her family, the contracts are allowed; and the husband is bound to maintain his wife in necessaries, according to his degree and estate: though if he makes the wife allowance for clothes, &c. which is constantly paid, he shall not be charged. *Co. Lit.* 112, 187. 2 *Rep.* 713. *Rol. Abr.* 350. *Mod. Rep.* 129.

As a man is not bound by his wife's contract, without notice and assent; so 'tis said he is not bound by the wife's receipt. If a woman married enters into bond for money, as a feme sole; and she is sued as such, she may plead *non est factum*, and the coverture will avoid her bond. Where a woman sole indebted takes husband, it is then the debt of husband and wife, and both must be sued; though after the wife's death, the husband is not liable, except there be a judgment against both during the coverture; a husband is bound for the appearance of his wife, where a writ is served on her; he only shall be imprisoned for want of bail, to action brought for debt of the wife, for he must find bail for her

her and himself: but if action is brought against a single woman, who pending the action marries, the plaintiff may proceed to judgment and execution against her. *Noy Max.* 94. *Leon.* 320. *Cro Car.* 376. *Lev.* 216.

A wife may not bring an action for wrong to her, without the husband; and when they join in an action, damage is to be laid only to the husband. But by the custom of *London*, a feme covert trading in the city as a sole merchant, may sue and be sued as a feme sole: a wife in other places cannot be sued without the husband. For trespass and scandalous words, &c. of or against the wife, husband and wife are to sue and be sued; and execution awarded against him; though, for her own offence, a wife may be indicted, without her husband; and be fined, &c. and in Court Christian she may sue and be sued, without the joining of her husband. *Co. Lit.* 182. 11 *Rep.* 62. 9 *Rep.* 72. 2 *Rol. Abr.* 298.

In all cases where the wife shall not have the thing recovered, and for a promise or personal duty to the wife, the husband only may bring the action; and a husband is intitled to the fruits of his wife's labour, for which he may bring a *Quantum Meruit*. If a person takes any thing from the wife, the husband is to bring the action for it, who has the property: where an injury is done to the wife alone, action cannot be maintained by the husband without her; but for a loss and injury to the husband, in depriving him of the conversation and service of his wife, he alone may bring an action; and these actions are laid for assault and detaining the wife, *per quod consortium amisit*, &c. Rol. Rep. 160. Salk. 114. Cro. Jac. 538.

If a husband suffers banishment for any crime, it is in law a civil death; and the wife of such a person may bring actions, or be impleaded during the natural life of the husband, which she may not do in any other case. The wife cannot be a witness either for or against her husband, nor he against her; unless it be in cases of high treason: but if a man threaten to beat or kill his wife, she may make him find surety of the peace, &c. *Co. Lit.* 133. *F. N. B.* 80.

A husband is not to alien the wife's lands, but by fine wherein she joins; if he doth, she may recover them by the writ *cui in vita* after his death: if the husband and wife acknowledge a deed to be inrolled, or a statute, &c. this will not be binding to the wife; because she is not examined by writ, to bar her, as on levying a fine. The husband may make leases of his wife's land for 21 years, or three lives, &c. provided she be a party, and the rent is reserved to husband and wife, and her heirs. *Stat.* 32 *H.* 8. *c.* 28.

5. Marriage settlements are usually made of the estate of the husband, &c. To the husband for life, and after his death to the wife for life, and to their issue in remainder, with limitations to trustees to support contingent uses, and leases for terms of years, to raise daughters portions, &c. and they are made several ways, as by lease and release, fine and recovery, &c. These settlements the law is ever careful to preserve, especially that part of them which relates to the wife, of which she may not be devested, but by her own fine.

If a woman about to marry a man, to prevent his disposing of her lands, convey the same to friends in trust, and the trustees with the husband

band after marriage make sale thereof; in this case the court of Chancery will decree the purchaser to reconvey the lands to the wife. And where a man and a woman, intending to marry, enter into articles of marriage, by which the intended husband agrees to settle such lands upon her, &c. and thereupon she marries him; if he die before any settlement made, in pursuance of those articles of agreement, in equity the widow shall have the articles executed, and hold the lands during her life, &c. *Totbil* 43. 2 *Vent.* 242.

There are settlements of personal estates, in trustees on marriage, and of money in funds, &c. as well as settlements of lands. And if a man before marriage gives bond and judgment to leave the wife worth 1000 *l.* at his death, if she shall survive him, in consideration of a marriage portion; this shall be made good out of the husband's estate, and be satisfied before any debt; so if a person covenant, that if the intended wife shall marry him, and shall happen to survive, he shall leave her worth 500 *l.* after his death, action may be brought against his administrator for the money; for here the debt arises by the death of the husband. *Palm.* 99. 2 *Sid.* 58.

A jointure is a particular settlement of lands made by a man to a woman, in consideration of marriage; which must be to take effect for the life of the wife, in possession or profit, presently after the husband's death, and be made to herself, and none other for her; it must be expressed to be in full of her dower, and in satisfaction thereof; and it may be made before, or after marriage: but if it be made after the marriage, the wife may wave it, and claim her dower.

dower. And all other settlements, in lieu of jointure, are jointures at common law, and no bars to dower. *Co. Lit.* 36. 4 *Rep.* 1. *Stat.* 27 *H.* 8. *c.* 10.

Of things whereof a wife shall be endowed, she may have jointure; and if lands, &c. are settled upon her before marriage, in part of her jointure and after marriage other lands in full; she may take her first jointure lands and dower together, she not having her full jointure till after marriage. Though where a jointure is made of lands according to the statute, before coverture; and after the husband and wife alien them by fine, she shall not have dower in any other lands of her husband; but 'tis otherwise when the jointure is made after marriage. 3 *Rep.* 3. *Co. Lit.* 36, 46.

An estate in fee conveyed to a woman for her jointure, and in satisfaction of dower, is a jointure within the statute 27 *H.* 8. An estate for life, upon condition, may bar the wife, if she accepts it; and so if an estate be made *durante viduitate*. And after the death of the husband, the wife may enter into her jointure, and is not driven to a real action, as she is to recover dower: nor shall her jointure be forfeited by the treason of her husband; as in case of dower. 4 *Rep.* 3. *Co. Lit.* 36, 37.

If a woman conceals her jointure, and brings dower, she is barred of her jointure: but if she be evicted of part of her jointure: she shall have dower *pro tanto*. Married women committing crimes may incur forfeiture of their jointures; and being convict of recusancy, forfeit two parts in three of their jointures and dower. *Co. Lit.* 31. *Stat.* 3 *Jac. c.* 5. *f.* 13.

An infant is bound by her jointure made on her before marriage, so that she cannot wave it, and claim dower; and resolved by the house of peers on an appeal from lord chancellor *Northington*'s decree, on *Thursday* 26 *May* 1762.

The form of a common *marriage settlement* of an estate in lands.

THIS *indenture tripartite, made the day of &c. in the year, &c. Between A. B. of the first part, C. D. E. F. and G. H. of the second part, and J. D. daughter of the said C. D. of the third part,* Witnesseth, *that the said A. B. for and in consideration of a marriage intended (by God's permission) shortly to be had and solemnized between the said A. B. and the said J. D. and of the sum of* 3000 l. *to be had and received by the said A. B. as a marriage portion with the said J. and that a competent jointure may be had, made and provided for the said J. D. (in case the said marriage shall take effect) and for the settling and assuring of the messuages, lands, tenements and hereditaments herein after mentioned, to and upon the several uses, intents and purposes herein after limited and declared, pursuant to the agreement made upon the contract of the said intended marriage; he the said A. B.* Hath *granted, bargained and sold, released and confirmed, and by these presents doth grant, bargain and sell, release and confirm unto the said C. D. E. F. and G. H. (in the actual possession now being, by virtue of a bargain and sale to them thereof made for one whole year, &c.) and*

and to their heirs and assigns for ever, All that messuage or tenement called, &c. with the appurtenances, and all other the messuages, lands, tenements and hereditaments of the said A. B. *situate, lying and being in,* &c. *in the county of* S. *and all houses, buildings, gardens, orchards, lands, tenements, meadows, pastures, feedings, ways, waters, water-courses,* &c. *to the said messuages or tenements belonging, or in any wise appertaining,* &c. *and also the reversion and reversions, remainder and remainders,* &c. *and all the estate, right, title,* &c. *of him the said* A. B. *of, in and to the same premises, and of, in and to every part and parcel thereof, with the appurtenances:* To have and to hold *all and singular the messuages, lands, tenements and hereditaments above mentioned, and every part and parcel thereof, with the appurtenances, unto the said* C. D. E. F. *and* G. H. *their heirs and assigns, to and for the several uses, intents, trusts and purposes herein after mentioned, limited, expressed and declared, (that is to say) To the use and behoof of the said* A. B. *and his heirs, until the marriage between him and the said* J. D. *his intended wife, shall be had and solemnized, and from and after the solemnization thereof, to the use and behoof of the said* A. B. *and his assigns, for and during the term of his natural life, without impeachment of waste; and from and after the determination of that estate, by forfeiture or otherwise, to the use and behoof of the said* C. D. E. F. *and* G. H. *and their heirs, for and during the natural life of the said* A. B. *in trust to preserve and support the contingent remainders herein after limited, from being defeated and destroyed, and for that purpose to make entries, and bring actions, as the case shall require; yet nevertheless in trust, to permit and suffer the said A. B. and his assigns, to receive and take the rents, issues and profits thereof, to his and their own proper use and benefit, during his natural life; and from and after the decease of the said A. B. to the use and behoof of the said J. D. (intended wife of the said A. B.) and her assigns, for and during the term of her natural life, for her jointure, and in full satisfaction and bar of her dower or thirds, which she may claim to have in any lands, tenements or hereditaments, whereof or wherein he the said A. B. shall at the time during his life be seised of any estate of inheritance; and from and after the decease of the survivor of them, the said A. B. and J. his intended wife, to the use and behoof of the heirs male of the body of the said A. B. on the body of the said J. D. lawfully to be begotten; (or to the use and behoof of the first son of the body of the said A. B. on the body of the said J. D. lawfully begotten, and the heirs male of the body of such first son lawfully issuing; and for want of such issue, then to the use and behoof of the second son of the body of the said A. B. on the body of the said J. D. lawfully to be begotten, and the heirs male of the body of such second son lawfully issuing; and for default of such issue, then to the use and behoof of the third son of the body of the said A. B. on the body of the said J. D. lawfully to be begotten, and the heirs male of the body of such third son lawfully issuing; and for want of such issue, then to the use and behoof of the fourth, fifth, sixth, seventh, eighth, ninth and tenth,*

and

and all and every other the son and sons of him the said A. B. begotten on the body of the said J. D. severally and successively one after another, as they shall be in seniority of age and priority of birth, viz. the elder of such son and sons, and the heirs male of his body, always to be preferred and take before the younger and the heirs of his body;) and for default of such issue, to the use and behoof of the said C. D. E. F. and G. H. their executors, administrators and assigns, for and during the term of 500 years thence next following, and fully to be compleat and ended, upon the trust, and to and for the ends, intents and purposes herein after declared, of and concerning the same term; and from and after the expiration, or other sooner determination of that term; to the use and behoof of the said A. B. his heirs and assigns for ever. Provided always, and it is hereby declared and agreed, by and between the said parties to these presents, that the said term of 500 years, so limited to them the said C. D. E. F. and G. H. their executors, administrators and assigns, as aforesaid, is upon this condition; That if the said A. B. shall happen to die without issue male by him begotten on the body of the said J. or shall leave issue male, and such issue shall happen to die before he shall attain the age of twenty-one years, without issue male; and that in either of the said cases, there shall happen to be one or more daughter or daughters of their bodies begotten, that then and in such case, if the heirs or assigns of the said A. B. do and shall well and truly pay or cause to be paid to such daughter or daughters respectively, at her and their respective ages of

Z 3 twenty-one

twenty-one years, or days of marriage, the several portions following, (that is to say) if it shall happen there shall be but one such daughter, then the sum of 2500 l. for the portion of such daughter, to be paid to her at the age of twenty one years, or day of marriage, which shall first happen, with interest in the mean time after the rate of 5 l. per Cent. per Annum; and if it shall happen, that there shall be two or more such daughters, then the sum of 3000 l. &c. for the portions of such two or more daughters to be equally divided between them, share and share alike, and to be paid to them respectively at their respective ages of twenty-one years, or days of marriage, which shall first happen, with interest therefore in the mean time, &c. And if any such daughter or daughters shall happen to die unmarried, before her or their portion or portions shall become payable as aforesaid, then the portion or portions of her or them so dying shall go and be paid to the survivors and survivor of them, equally to be divided among them, share and share alike (to be paid at the same time as the original portions should or ought to become payable as aforesaid, in case they have been living;) so as no one such daughter shall have for her portion, by survivorship or otherwise, by virtue of the said term of 500 years, above the sum of 2500 l. And in case there shall be no such daughter, who shall live to be married, or attain the age of twenty-one years, that then and in either of the said cases so happening, the said term shall cease, determine, and be void; any thing herein contained to the contrary notwithstanding. Provided also and it is hereby further declared

red and agreed, that it shall and may be lawful to and for him the said A. B. during his life, and after his death for the said J. his intended wife, during her life, in case the said intended marriage shall take effect, by any writing or writings, under his or her hand and seal respectively, attested by two or more credible witnesses, to make any lease or leases, demise or grant, of all or any part or parts of the said messuages and lands, to any person or persons whatsoever, for the term of twenty-one years, or for any term or number of years, not exceeding twenty-one years, so as such leases, demises or grants for years be made to commence and take effect in possession within one year after the date thereof; and so as upon all and every such lease or leases, demises or grants to be made by the said A. B. and J. his intended wife respectively, there be reserved payable yearly, during the continuance thereof, the best and most improved yearly rents, which, at the time of making thereof, can or may be gotten for the same; and so that in every such lease or leases there be contained a clause of re-entry for non-payment of the rent or rents thereby reserved; and so as the lessee and lessees, to whom such lease and leases shall be made, do seal and deliver counterparts of such lease and leases. And the said A. B. for himself, his heirs and assigns, doth covenant and grant to and with the said C. D. E. F. and G. H. their heirs and assigns, that the said messuages, lands, tenements, hereditaments and premisses above-mentioned, shall and may from henceforth, for ever hereafter be, remain and continue to, for and upon the several uses, intents, trusts and purposes, and

under

under and subject to the several limitations, proviso's and agreements herein before mentioned and expressed, concerning the same, according to the true intent and meaning of these presents: And also, *that be the said* A. B. *and his heirs, and all and every other person and persons and his and their heirs, any thing having or claiming in the said messuages, lands, tenements and premisses above-mentioned, or any part thereof, by, from or under him, them or any of them, shall and will, at all times hereafter, upon the reasonable request of the said* C. D. E. F. *and* G. H. *their heirs and assigns, make, do and execute, or cause or procure to be made,* &c. *all and every such further and other lawful and reasonable grants, acts and assurances in the law whatsoever, for the further, better and more perfect granting and assuring of all and singular the said messuages, lands, tenements, hereditaments and premisses above-mentioned, with the appurtenances, to and for the several uses, intents, trusts and purposes above declared, limited and appointed, and according to the true intent and meaning of these presents, as by the said* C. D. E. F. *and* G. H. *and their heirs, or their or any of their counsel learned in the law, shall be reasonably devised, or advised and required.* And further, *it is covenanted, granted, concluded and agreed upon by and between the said parties to these presents, and the true meaning hereof also is, and it is hereby so declared, that all and every fine and fines, recovery and recoveries, assurance and assurances, conveyance and conveyances in the law whatsoever already had, made, levied, suffered, executed or acknowledged, or at any time here-*
after

after to be had, made, &c. of the said messuages, tenements, lands and premisses above-mentioned, or any part thereof, either alone, or jointly with any other lands, tenements or hereditaments, by or between the said parties to these presents, or by or between them, and any other person or persons, as for and concerning all and singular the said messuages, lands, tenements, hereditaments and premisses above-mentioned, and every part thereof, with the appurtenances, shall be and enure, and shall be adjudged, esteemed and taken to be and enure to and for the several uses, intents and purposes above-mentioned, limited, expressed and declared, according to the true intent and meaning of these presents, and to and for no other use, intent or purpose whatsoever. In Witness, &c.'

Form of a *marriage settlement* of South-sea stock.

THIS Indenture tripartite, made, &c. Between A. B. of, &c. of the first part, C. D. of, &c. of the second part, and E. F. G. H. and J. K. of, &c. of the third part. Whereas a marriage, by God's permission, is intended shortly to be had and solemnized between the said A. B. and C. D. with whom the said A. B. is to receive a considerable marriage portion: And whereas the said A. B. is intitled to the sum of 2000 l. capital stock in the stock of the governor and company of merchants of Great Britain trading to the South Sea, commonly called South-Sea stock: Now this indenture witnesseth, that in consideration of the said intended marriage, and to the intent that the

said

Of Marriage, Bastardy.

said stock, and the dividends and profits thereof, may be secured and applied upon the trusts, and to and for the uses, intents and purposes hereafter mentioned; he the said A. B. doth for himself, his heirs, executors and administrators, covenant, promise and agree, to and with the said E. F. G. H. and J. K. their executors and administrators, that he the said A. B. shall and will within one and twenty days next ensuing the date of these presents, in due form, well and sufficiently transfer and assign in the books kept for that purpose, the said sum of 2000 l. South-Sea stock to the said E. F. G. H. and J. K. their executors, administrators and assigns. And it is hereby declared, concluded and agreed, by and between the said parties to these presents, that the said stock, when so transferred and assigned, and all the dividends and profits thereof, shall be and remain in the said E. F. G. H. and J. K. their executors, administrators and assigns, upon and under and subject to the several trusts, uses, intents, purposes, conditions and agreements herein after expressed, (that is to say) In trust for the said A. B. his executors, administrators and assigns, until the said marriage shall be solemnized; and from and immediately after the solemnization of the said intended marriage, then that they the said E. F. G. H. and J. K. their executors, administrators and assigns, shall permit and suffer the said A. B. and his assigns, during the term of his natural life, to have, receive and take, to his and their own proper use and behoof, all the dividends, interests and other profits, which shall, during his life, accrue, arise or be made by or from the said stock, or any part thereof; and from and immediately after the decease of the said A. B.

A. B. then and upon trust, (in case the said C. D. shall survive the said A. B.) to permit and suffer the said C. D. and her assigns, during the term of her natural life, to receive and take, to her and their own proper use and behoof, all the dividends, interest, &c. And upon this further trust and confidence, that they the said trustees, their executors and administrators, shall and do, after the deaths of the said A. B. and C. D. transfer, assign, pay, apply or dispose of the said stock, and the dividends, interest and other profits thereof, unto and amongst all and every the sons and daughters of the said A. B. on the said C. D. begotten and their children, in case any of them shall be then dead leaving issue, in such parts and proportions, and at such time or times, and in such manner as the said A. B. by his last will and testament in writing, or any other writing duly executed, shall limit, direct or appoint the same; and in default of such limitation, direction and appointment, then unto and amongst all and every the son and sons, daughter and daughters of the said A. B. on the said C. D. lawfully to be begotten, as aforesaid, and the children of such sons and daughters, (in case any of them shall happen to be dead leaving issue) in equal shares and portions, equally to be divided among such children, if there be more than one, and if but one child, then wholly to that one. And upon this further trust and confidence, that in case the said A. B. shall survive the said C. D. and there shall be no such son or daughter, nor any issue of such son or daughter, living at the time of her decease; or if the said C. D. shall survive the said A. B. and there shall be no such son *or daughter, nor any issue of such son or daughter, living at the time of the decease of the said A. B. and the said C. D. shall not then be enfient of a child which shall be afterwards born; then that the said trustees, their executors and administrators, do and shall in either of the said cases, (after the decease of the said C. D.) transfer, assign, pay, apply and dispose of the said stock, and the dividends, interest and profits thereof to the said A. B. (if he survives the said C. D.) or the executors, administrators or assigns of the said A. B. after the decease of the said C. D. in case she happens to survive him as aforesaid: Provided always, and it is agreed and declared by and between all the said parties to these presents, that in case the said A. B. shall be minded or desirous to have the said stock or any part thereof sold, and the money arising by the sale thereof invested in any other stock or fund, or placed out upon any security, or laid out in the purchase of lands, tenements or hereditaments; or to have the said money, after it shall have been so invested or placed out, in or upon any other stocks, funds or securities, called in again and disposed of in any other manner, and shall signify such his mind or desire by writing under his hand, signed in the presence of two or more credible witnesses; that then the said trustees, their executors and administrators, shall accordingly sell and dispose of the said stock, or any part thereof, and invest, place, lay out or dispose of the money arising by the sale thereof, in such other stocks, funds or securities, or in the purchase of such lands or tenements, or in such other manner, as the said A. B. shall by such writing, or any other writing*

ing or writings, to be subscribed and attested as aforesaid, direct, limit or appoint; which said other stocks so to be bought with the said money, when so invested or placed out upon any such funds or securities, and such lands and tenements, when purchased, shall be transferred, assigned, conveyed, settled and assured so and in such manner, as that the same, with the dividends, interests, rents and profits thereof, may remain, continue, and be applied and disposed of, to, for and upon the same trusts, uses, intents and purposes, as the said South-Sea stock, and the dividends, interest and profits thereof are herein before directed, limited and appointed, to go, be applied and disposed of, or as near the same as may be, and that in all respects according to the true intent and meaning of these presents: And it is agreed by and between all the said parties to these presents, that the said trustees, their executors and administrators, shall or lawfully may in the first place deduct and retain out of the said stock so intended to be transferred or assigned as aforesaid, or out of such other stocks, &c. purchased, all such sum and sums, of money, costs, charges, expences and damages which they or any of them shall pay, expend, lay out, sustain, or be put unto, for or by reason or means of this present trust, or any act, matter or thing which shall or may be done or happen in, about or relating to the execution thereof, or touching or concerning the same: And also that the said trustees, their executors or administrators, shall not be chargeable or accountable for more money than what they or any of them shall respectively and actually receive by virtue of these presents,

nor

nor shall the one of them be answerable or chargeable for or with the act, receipt or default of the other of them, but each for himself and his own act, receipt or default only; and in case any loss shall happen of the said stock, or the money arising by the sale thereof, or any part thereof, or of the dividends, interest or proceed thereof, without the neglect or default of them the said trustees, their executors, &c. or some of them, then they the said trustees, or any of them, their or any of their executors or administrators, shall not be charged or chargeable with such loss, or be liable to answer or make good the same or any part thereof. In Witness, *&c.*

Articles of agreement on marriage, *in nature of a settlement of personal estate.*

Articles of agreement tripartite, indented, made, concluded and agreed upon, the day of, *&c.* in the year, *&c. Between A. B. of, &c* of the first part, *E. D.* daughter of *T. D.* of, *&c.* of the second part, and the said *T. D.* of the third part.

WHEREAS *a marriage is intended shortly to be had and solemnized between the said* A. B. *and* E. D. *upon which said marriage be the said* A. B. *will be intitled to, and is to receive of and from the said* T. D. *the sum of* 600 l. *or the value thereof, as and for the marriage portion of the said* E. D. *Now it is hereby agreed by and between the said parties to these presents; and* First, *in consideration of the said intended marriage, and of the said sum of* 600 l. *which the said* A. B.
will

Infants, Idiots.

will be intitled to, and is to receive, by and upon the said marriage, in case the same takes effect; he the said A. B. for himself, his executors and administrators, doth covenant, promise, grant and agree, to and with the said T. D. his executors and administrators, in manner following, (that is to say) That in case the said intended marriage shall take effect, and the said E. D. shall happen to die within the space of five years next after the solemnization thereof, having no child or children living at the time of her decease, and he the said A. B. surviving her; that then the said A. B. shall and will pay or cause to be paid unto the said T. D. his executors, administrators or assigns, the sum of 200 l. part of the marriage portion aforesaid, within six months next after the decease of her the said E. D. so dying as aforesaid.

'Item, it is agreed, and for the considerations aforesaid, he the said A. B. for himself, his executors and administrators, doth further covenant, promise, grant and agree, to and with the said T. D. his executors and administrators, by these presents; that in case the said intended marriage shall take effect, and the said E. D. shall happen to survive him the said A. B. her said intended husband, he dying without issue by her, that then the executors and administrators, of the said A. B. shall permit and suffer the said E. D. to have and enjoy her rings, jewels, wearing apparel, and furniture of her chamber; or if the same, or any part thereof, shall be out of her possession, shall upon request deliver the same unto her: and also, that the executors and administrators of the said A. B. shall and will pay or cause to be

paid

paid unto her the said E. D. her executors, administrators or assigns, the full sum of 700 l. of lawful money, &c. within six months after the decease of the said A. B. But if at the time of the death of the said A. B. the said E. D. surviving him, be the said A. B. shall have any child or children then living, that then the executors and administrators of the said A. B. shall permit and suffer the said E. to enjoy her rings, jewels, wearing apparel, and furniture of her chamber as aforesaid; and also, upon reasonable request in that behalf, shall and will account, pay and deliver over to her the said E. D. her executors, administrators or assigns, one full moiety or half-part of all the personal estate of him the said intended husband, his debts and funeral expences being first discharged.

Lastly, the said T. D. for the considerations aforesaid, doth hereby declare, that the said sum of 600 l. to be by him paid, as and for the marriage portion of the said E. his daughter as aforesaid, is not intended to be the full, sole and absolute provision, part and portion of her the said E. of and in the estate, goods and chattels of the said T. D. But the said T. D. doth for himself, his executors and administrators, covenant, promise, grant and agree, to and with the said A. B. his executors and administrators, by these presents, that after the decease of him the said T. D. she the said E. shall have and receive of and from the executors and administrators of the said T. D. so much more out of his estate, goods and chattels, as shall make the said marriage portion or sum of 600 l. to amount to as much, and be equal in value with whatsoever be the said

T. D.

' *T. D.* shall in his life-time, or at the time
' of his decease, give or bequeath unto, *&c.*
' the other daughter of the said *T. D. In*
' *Witness,* &c.

Having now gone through the large titles of marriage, I proceed to some smaller heads concerning it:

1. Elopements of married women.
2. Divorces between husband and wife.
3. Felony in stealing and marrying women.

1. Elopement is where a woman that is married, of her own accord goes away and departs from her husband, and lives with an adulterer.

A woman thus leaving her husband is said to elope; and in this case the husband is not obliged to allow her any alimony or maintenance out of his estate; nor shall he be chargeable for necessaries for her, as wearing apparel, diet, lodging, *&c.* And where the same is notorious, whoever gives her credit, doth it at his peril: but on an elopement, the putting a wife in the *Gazette,* or other news-papers, is no legal notice to persons in general not to trust her; tho' personal notice to particular persons given by the husband will be good, not to be chargeable to them. *Rol. Abr.* 350. *Vent.* 42.

If a woman elopes, and the husband gives publick notice of it, and declares he will not pay any debts of hers she contracts; it hath been held, that if persons trust her afterwards, the husband is not liable to satisfy the debt: yet according to the opinion of chief justice *Holt,* if a wife run away from her husband, and contract

A a   debts,

debts, and afterwards the husband comes after her and lies with her, tho' but for a night; that will make him chargeable for the debts of the wife. *Sid.* 109. *Mod. Rep.* 124. 6 *Mod.* 171.

Where the wife goes away from her husband, and liveth in adultery with another, she shall lose and forfeit her dower; unless the husband of his own free will suffer her to cohabit with him, and be reconciled to his wife. But to prove the reconciliation, on such an elopement, lying together several nights, at several places, it is said shall not avail; if they are not resident or abiding in one house together, &c. If after the elopement of the wife, her husband and she demean themselves as husband and wife, it is evidence of reconciliation. *Dy.* 170, 196.

If a man grants his wife with her goods to another man, and the wife by virtue of the grant lives with the grantee during the life of the husband, this shall incur forfeiture of dower; for she lived in adultery, notwithstanding the grant. 2 *Inst.* 435. 2 *Danv. Abr.* 662.

2. Divorce is a separation of two persons married together, made by law: and there are many divorces mentioned in our books, but they are usually of two kinds, *i. e. a Mensa & Thoro*, from bed and board; and *a Vincula Matrimonii*, from the very bond of marriage. *Co. Lit.* 235.

The divorce *a Mensa & Thoro* dissolves not the marriage; for the cause of it is subsequent, and supposes the marriage to be lawful: it may be by reason of adultery in either of the parties, for cruelty of the husband, &c. and as it doth not dissolve the marriage, so it debars not the woman of her dower; nor bastardizes the issue;

or

or makes void any estate for the life of husband and wife, &c. A woman under this divorce may sue her husband in her own name for alimony, and others by her next friend, &c. The divorce *a Vinculo Matrimonii* absolutely dissolveth the marriage, and makes it void from the beginning, the causes thereof being precedent to the marriage; as precontract with some other person, consanguinity or affinity, impotency, &c. On this divorce, dower is gone; and if by reason of precontract, consanguinity or affinity, the children begotten between them are bastards. *Co. Lit.* 235. 3 *Inst.* 89. 2 *Inst.* 93. 7 *Rep.* 43.

In these last kind of divorces, the wife, 'tis said, shall receive all again that she brought with her, because the nullity of the marriage arises through some impediment, and the goods of the wife were given for her advancement in marriage, which now ceaseth: but here it is where the goods are not spent, and in case the husband gives them away during the coverture, it shall bind her. If she knows her goods unspent, she may bring action of detinue for them; and for money, &c. which cannot be known, she must sue in the spiritual court: by this divorce an estate-tail of baron and feme, it has been held, may be extinct. *Dy* 62. *Nel. Abr.* 675. *Godb.* 18.

If after a divorce *a Mensa & Thoro*, either of the parties marry again, the other being living, such marriage is merely void; and as in this case the marriage continues, marrying again hath been adjudged within the statute 1 *Jac.* 1. of felony; where a woman was so divorced, and inhibited, by the sentence not to marry during her husband's life: On a divorce *a Vinculo Matrimonii*, the parties may marry again; and in divorces for adultery, several acts of parliament have allowed the innocent party to marry again. 2 *Leon.* 173. *Cro. Car.* 333.

If a marriage is voidable by divorce, yet if the husband dies before any divorce, the wife *de facto* shall be endowed: and where there is a divorce, the children of a second marriage may inherit until the sentence is repealed. Sentence of divorce must be given in the Spiritual Court, in the life of the parties, and not afterwards; but it may be repealed there after their deaths. *Co. Lit.* 33. 2 *Leon.* 207.

3. Where any persons married do marry any other person, the former husband or wife being alive, it is felony: but if a husband or wife are abroad beyond sea, &c. seven years, the one not knowing the other to be living; or there be a divorce of the husband and wife, &c. they are excepted out of the act. As the latter marriage makes this crime; if the first marriage were beyond sea, and the second in *England*, the party may be indicted for it here: though if the first marriage be in *England*, and the latter beyond sea, the offender cannot be indicted there. *Stat.* 1 *Jac. c.* 11. *Kel.* 79, 80. *Sid.* 171. *II. H. P. C.* 693, 694. 3 *Inst.* 89.

To steal or take away any woman, having an estate in lands or goods, or that is heir apparent, against her will, and marry or defile her, is felony by statute: and it is the same, if the taking be against her will, though the marriage was with her consent. And not only the takers, but the procurers, abetters and receivers of the woman before the fact, so taken away, knowing the same, shall be deemed principal felons. 3 *H.* 7. *c.* 2. 39 *Eliz. c.* 9.

Taking away any woman child under the age of sixteen years and unmarried, out of the custody and against the will of the father, guardian, &c. the offender shall suffer fine and imprisonment. And an Information shall lie for seducing a young man or woman from their parents, against their consents, in order to marry them, &c. Stat. 4 & 5 P. & M. c. 8. T. Raym. 473.

The court granted an information for taking away a *natural* daughter under 16, under the care of her putative father; being of opinion it was within sect. 3. of this statute. 2 Stra. 1162.

I shall conclude this chapter with the laws and statutes relating to the particular titles of,

1. Bastardy.   } Heads. { 3. Ideots.
2. Infants.   4. Lunaticks.

1. Bastardy signifies a defect of birth, objected to one born out of wedlock: for a bastard is he that is born of any woman not married, so that his father is not known by the order of law; and therefore he shall not be heir, or of kin to any person; he being the first of his family, nor shall he have heirs, but of his own body.

A woman is with child by a man, who afterwards marries her, and then the child is born; this child is not a bastard: but if a man hath issue by a woman before marriage, and after they marry, the issue is a bastard by our law; but legitimate by the civil law. In case one marries a woman grosly big with child by another, and within three days after she is delivered, in our law the issue is no bastard; 'tis otherwise by the spiritual law:

law: and where a child is born within a day after marriage between parties of full age, if there be no apparent impossibility that the husband should be the father of it, the child is not a bastard, but supposed to be the husband's child. 2 *Inst.* 96. *Danv. Abr.* 729. *Rol. Abr.* 358.

But if the husband be but eight or nine years of age, or if he be within the age of fourteen, the issue is a bastard: so where a husband is gelt, or hath lost his genitals, &c. which shews an impossibility to get a child; but it must be by special matter. By the Common Law, if the husband be within the four seas, so that by intendment he may converse with his wife, and the wife hath issue, the child will not be a bastard: but he is a bastard who is born of a woman when her husband is over sea, at and from the time of the begetting to the birth of such child. Where a woman lives in adultery with another, her children by such other are bastards; for they are born out of the limits of matrimony; though if husband and wife consent to live separate, the children born after such separation shall be taken to be ligitimate, and not bastards, because the access of the husband shall be presumed. Issue of a second wife or husband, the first being living, is a bastard. *Co. Lit.* 244. *Danv. Abr.* 729. *Salk.* 122. 2 *Salk.* 483. *Ld. Raym.* 395. *Carth.* 469. 2 *Stra.* 925, 940. *Andr.* 9. 2 *Stra.* 1076. *Andr.* 8. *Andr.* 10. *Sess. Cas.* 235. 2 *Sess. Cas.* 286. *pl.* 175. 3 *Will. Rep.* 276. *Fortesc. Rep.* 315. 11 *Mod.* 106. 2 *Burn, qto.* 123.

It hath been held, that if a woman hath a child forty weeks and eight days after the death of her husband, it shall be legitimate; the law having appointed no exact certain time for the birth

birth of legitimate issues. And here, if a woman great with child by a former husband, shall marry another man after his death, the child shall be the lawful child of the first husband; but if the woman be privily with child, it shall belong to the second husband. Where any woman says she is with child by a deceased husband, and with-holds lands from the heir, a writ *Ventre inspiciendo* is to be granted to search her, and try it by a jury of women: and if it be found, she shall be kept in custody 'till delivered, &c. *Dawv. Abr.* 721. See 2 *Will. Rep.* 593. *Moseley Rep.* 391.

Bastards having gotten names by reputation, may purchase by such names to them and their heirs: and a limitation to them when *in esse*, and known, is good, but not before they are born: they may not take by the name of issue, which must be lawful; nor shall a use be raised to such a reputed son, &c. Special bastardy is triable by the country, in the temporal courts: but general bastardy, whether a person is a bastard or not, and was born in lawful matrimony, &c. upon some question of inheritance, is try'd by the bishop's certificate; after issue joined in a court of law, it is to be transmitted to the ecclesiastical court, to be examined and certified, &c. But the judges shall not award a writ to the ordinary to certify bastardy, 'till proclamation is issued for all persons having interest therein to make their objections before him against the party, &c. *Co. Lit.* 3. 6 *Rep.* 65. *Dy.* 374. *Hob.* 117. *Kitcb.* 64. *Stat.* 9 *H.* 6. c. 11.

By statutes the two next Justices of peace may take order for punishing of the mother and father of a common bastard, and for relief of

Of Marriage, Bastardy,

the parish where born, by a weekly payment, &c. And the father and mother not obeying the order, shall be imprisoned. And where a bastard child is born, churchwardens may seize goods of the reputed father and mother, to discharge the parish: the justices are to send lewd women, having bastards, to the house of correction; but persons able to keep them are not within the statute; and a mother discharging the parish shall not be punished. It is esteemed murder to conceal the death of a bastard child, when born alive. *Stat.* 18. *Eliz. c.* 3. 7 *Jac. c.* 4. 13 & 14 *Car.* 2. *c.* 12. perpetuated by 12 *Ann. Seff.* 1. *c.* 18. 2 Ld. *Raym.* 858. 3 *Salk.* 66. 21 *Jac. c.* 27. 2 *Hawk. Pl. Cur.* 438. *H. H. P. C.* 433.

2. An infant is a person under the age of 21 years; whose acts are in many cases either void or voidable. *Co. Lit.* 171.

If an infant bargain and sell lands by deed indented and inrolled, he may avoid it: and where such infant makes a feoffment, he may enter and avoid it; and if he dies, his heir may enter, &c. An infant makes a deed, and delivers it within age, though he afterwards deliver it again when at full age, this second delivery and deed are void; for the deed must take effect from the first delivery. All gifts and grants, &c. of any infant, which do not take effect by delivery of his hand, will be void; and if made to take effect by delivery of his own hand, are voidable by himself and his heirs, and those who shall have his estate. But if an infant make a lease, paying rent, and after his coming of age he accepts the rent; by this the voidable lease is made good. 2 *Inst.* 673. *Co. Lit.* 247. 3. *Rep.* 35. 8 *Rep.* 43.

An

Infants, Ideots.

An infant may purchase land, being intended for his benefit; but, at his full age, he may either agree to and confirm it, or wave or disagree to it; and if he agrees not when at age, his heirs after him may disagree: a lease made to an infant may be avoided, by waving the land before the rent-day. Infants ought not to be received to levy fines of lands; but if they are admitted, 'twill be good and unavoidable, unless reversed during their minority: a common recovery suffered by an infant by guardian shall bind him; conditions annexed to lands, whether the estate come by grant or descent, are binding to infants; and laches shall prejudice an infant, if he presents not to a church in six months, &c. *Co. Lit.* 2, 172, 380. *Cro. Car.* 307.

If an infant enters into bond, pretending to be of full age, though he may avoid it by pleading nonage, he may be indicted for a cheat: An infant may voluntarily bind himself apprentice; but his bond for service shall not bind him: he may bind himself to pay for necessaries, as to eating, drinking, apparel, &c. Though an infant is not obliged to pay for cloaths, except it be averred to be for his own wearing, and that they were convenient and necessary for him to wear, according to his estate. Money laid out for necessaries for an infant hath been allowed, when money lent for that purpose hath not: the infant may buy, but cannot borrow money to buy necessaries; for the law will not trust him with money, but at the peril of the lender, who must see it thus laid out. *Cro. Car.* 179. 2 *Inst.* 483. *Cro. Jac.* 560. 5 *Mod.* 368. *Salk.* 386. 10 *Mod.* 66. 12 *Mod.* 197.

Of Marriage, Bastardy,

In the prosecution of actions, an infant is to sue by *Prochein Amy*, or guardian; but always defend by guardian; and he is not to appear by attorney in his own right. If an infant, &c. commit a trespass against the person or possession of another; he must answer for the damage in a civil action: but infants, under the age of fourteen years, are not generally punishable for crimes; although if they are of that age, which is of the age of discretion, or under those years, having maturity of discretion, they may be punished as felons. *Co. Lit.* 135. 2 *Saund.* 112.

A father by deed in his life-time, or by will, may dispose the custody of his infant child under twenty-one years of age, and not married, during the minority, to any persons, not popish recusants, he thinks fit; who may maintain actions of trespass, &c. against unlawful takers away of such children, and take into custody their lands. A guardian in socage at common law not thus appointed, continues till the minor accomplishes the age of fourteen years; and then he may chuse his guardian before a judge at his chamber, or in court, or in chancery: and these guardians shall make no waste, or sale of the inheritance, but keep it safely for the heir; they are to take the profits of the minor's lands, &c. to his use, and on accounting for the same, shall have allowance of costs and expences; and if they are robbed, &c. without any default or negligence, they shall be discharged thereof. *Stat.* 12 *Car.* 2. *c.* 24. *Lil. Abr.* 655. 2 *Lev.* 262. *Co. Lit.* 89.

Where there hath been some doubt of the sufficiency of a guardian to an infant, the chancery hath required security to be given: and action

Infants, Ideots.

tion of account lies against executors, &c. of guardians. 2 *Mod.* 177. 4 *Ann. c.* 16.

Form of a common election of a guardian *by a minor.*

'KNOW all men by these presents, That I
' *A. B.* son and heir of *T. B.* of, &c. esq;
' deceased, being now about the age of seven-
' teen years, *Have* elected and chosen, and by
' these presents do elect and chuse *C. D.* of,
' &c. gentleman, to be guardian of my person
' and estate, until I shall attain the age of twenty-
' one years; and I do hereby promise to be ruled
' and governed by him in all things touching
' my welfare; and I do authorize and impower
' the said *C. D.* to enter upon and take possession
' of all and every my messuages, lands, tene-
' ments, hereditaments and premisses whatsoever,
' situate, lying and being in, &c. in the county
' of, &c. or elsewhere, whereunto I have or may
' have any right or title, and to let and set the
' same, and receive and take the rents, issues and
' profits thereof, for my use and benefit, during
' the term aforesaid; giving and hereby grant-
' ing unto the said *C. D.* my full power in the
' said premisses, and whatsoever he shall law-
' fully do or cause to be done in the said premis-
' ses, by virtue hereof, I do hereby promise to
' ratify and confirm. *In witness*, &c.

9. An ideot is used in our law for one who is a natural fool, from his birth: and the king shall have the custody of the lands of an ideot, taking the profits during his life, without committing waste, and finding him and his family

necessaries;

necessaries; and after his death, shall render the lands to the right heir. This is by statute; and by the common law the king shall also have the custody of the body, goods and chattels of ideots, after office found, &c. 17 *Ed.* 2. *c.* 9. *Dy.* 302.

But where a person hath once understanding, and becomes a fool by chance or misfortune; the king shall not have the custody of him: and if one have so much knowledge, as to measure a yard of cloth, number twenty pence, or rightly name the days of the week, &c. he shall not be accounted an ideot by the laws of the realm. On a writ returnable in chancery, one may be examined whether ideot or not; and there is a writ *Idiota inquirendo vel examinando*, directed to the sheriff to call before him the party represented to be an ideot, and examine him, and inquire by a jury whether he be of sufficient understanding to manage his estate, and to certify the same into the chancery: after which he may be examined by the lord chancellor. 4 *Rep.* 124. 9 *Rep.* 31. *N. F. B.* 232, 233.

By his prerogative the king hath the lands from the time of the inquisition, and 'tis said, the sole interest in granting the estate of an ideot, but not of a lunatick. The use of the ideot's lands is in the king; but the freehold is in the ideot: if he alien the land, the king may have a *scire facias* against the alienee, and reseise the same into his hands, and the inheritance shall be vested in the ideot; though this must be after he is found by inquisition to be an ideot. *Dy.* 302. 5 *Rep.* 125.

Ideots not having understanding are incapable to make a will; their deeds, grants and conveyances are voidable, or may be made void:

but

Infants, Ideots.

but what they do concerning lands, &c. in a court of record, shall bind themselves, and all others claiming under them. If an ideot contracts matrimony, it shall bind him; and ideots shall be bound to pay for necessaries, in the same manner as infants: a discent may take away an entry of an ideot, &c. Though where an heir is ideot, any man may make a tender for him; and ideots, &c. ought not to be prosecuted for any crime; because they want knowledge to distinguish good and evil. *Co. Lit.* 247. 4 *Rep.* 111. 2 *Inst.* 483. *Rol. Abr.* 357. 3 *Inst.* 208.

An ideot cannot appear by attorney; when he sues or defends any action he must appear in person, and the suit is to be in his name, but followed by others. 2 *Sid.* 112, 335.

4. A lunatick is defined to be a person who is sometimes of good and sound memory and understanding, and sometimes not: and so long as he hath not understanding, he is *non compos mentis*. A commission of lunacy shall issue out of chancery, to examine whether the person be lunatick, or not; and to make inquests of his lands, &c. *Dy.* 25.

It is ordained by statute, that the king shall provide that the lands of lunaticks be safely preserved, and they and their families maintained by the profits; and the residue shall be kept for their use, and be delivered to them when they come to their right mind, the king taking nothing to his own use, &c. Here the king hath the guardianship of the lands of lunaticks; but not the custody of their lands or bodies: and the guardian of a lunatick is accountable to him, his executors, &c. As a lunatick may recover his understanding, and have discretion enough to govern himself and his lands; therefore the king shall not have the custody of him and his lands; for after he hath recovered his memory, he is to have his estate at his own disposal. *Stat.* 17 *Ed.* 2. *c.* 10. 4 *Rep.* 124.

By the ancient common law, a dangerous madman may be kept in prison, 'till he recover his senses: lunaticks or madmen wandering may be apprehended by a justice's warrant, and locked up and chained; or be sent to their last legal settlement, &c. A lunatick without memory understands not what he does, so that he cannot lawfully promise or contract for any thing: Every deed made by a lunatick, who is *non compos*, is voidable; and his deeds may be avoided by his heir, except he levy a fine, or do any other act of record, &c. But the deed of a lunatick shall not be voidable by himself; he shall not be allowed to work his own disability, by making himself a madman. *Co. Lit.* 247. 4 *Rep.* 126. *Stat.* 17 *Geo.* 2. *c.* 5.

In criminal cases, the acts of a lunatick shall not be imputed to him; unless he kill, or offer to kill the king, when by our old books he may be guilty of treason; but this is now contradicted: and it is said, if one who has committed a capital offence, become lunatick, and *non compos* before conviction, he shall not be tried, and if after conviction, that he shall not be executed. Though if a person feigns himself mad, and refuses to answer for a crime, he shall be taken as one that stands mute, &c. *Co. Lit.* 247. 3 *Inst.* 46. *Hawk. Pl. Cr.* 2. *Hale's Pl. Cr.* 10.

If a lunatick sue an action, it must be sued in his own name; and if an action be brought against a lunatick, he is to appear by attorney,

if

Infants, Ideots.

if of full age, and by guardians, if he be under age. *Co. Lit.* 135.

Ideots and lunaticks feifed of eftates in truft, &c. by order of the chancery may make conveyances thereof. *Stat.* 4 *Geo.* 2. *c.* 10. may furrender leafes in *Chancery* or *Exchequer*, in order to renew the fame. *Stat.* 29 *Geo.* 2. *c.* 31.

Of the Liberty of the Subject, Magna Charta, and other Statutes.

The Statute of Magna Charta, *or the Great Charter made in the ninth Year of King* Henry 3.

'HENRY, by the grace of God, king of
' England, lord of *Ireland*, duke of *Nor-*
' *mandy* and *Guyan*, &c. To all archbifhops,
' bifhops, earls, barons, fheriffs, provofts, of-
' ficers, and to all bailiffs, and other our faith-
' ful fubjects, who fhall fee this prefent charter,
' greeting: Know you, that we unto the honour
' of Almighty God, and for the falvation of the
' fouls of our progenitors and fucceffors, kings
' of *England*, to the advancement of holy church,
' and amendment of the realm, of our mere
' and free will, have given and granted to all
' archbifhops, bifhops, earls, barons, and all
' freemen of this our realm, thefe liberties fol-
' lowing, to be kept in our kingdom of *England*
' for ever.

CHAP.

CHAP. I.

A confirmation of liberties.

' *First*, We have granted to God, and by
this our present charter have confirmed, for us
and our heirs for ever, that the church of *England* shall be free, and have all her whole
rights and liberties inviolable. We have granted also, and given to all the freemen of our
realm, for us and our heirs for ever, the liberties under-written, to have and to hold to
them and their heirs for ever.'

CHAP. II.

The relief of the king's tenant of full age.

' If any of our earls or barons, or any other
which hold of us in chief by knight's service
die, and at the time of his death his heir be
of full age, and oweth to us a relief, he shall
have his inheritance by the old relief, that is
to say; the heir or heirs of an earl, for a
whole earldom, by one hundred pounds; the
heir or heirs of a baron, for a whole barony,
by one hundred marks; the heir or heirs of
a knight, for one whole knight's fee, one hundred shillings at the most: and he that hath
less shall give less, according to the old custom
of the fees.'

CHAP.

CHAP. III.

The wardship of an heir within age.

'But if the heir of any such tenant be within
'age, his lord shall not have the ward of him
'nor his land, before that he hath taken of him
'homage: and after such an heir hath been in
'ward, when he is come to full age, (that is to
'say, to the age of twenty one years) he shall
'have his inheritance without relief, and with-
'out fine: so that if such heir being within age
'be made a knight, yet nevertheless his land
'shall remain in the keeping of his lord, unto
'the term aforesaid.'

CHAP. IV.

No waste shall be made by a guardian in ward's lands.

'The keeper of the land of such an heir,
'being within age, shall not take of the lands
'of the heir but reasonable issues, reasonable
'customs, and reasonable services, and that
'without destruction and waste of his men and
'his goods. And if we commit the custody of
'any such land to the sheriff, or to any other,
'who is answerable unto us for the issues of the
'same land, and he make destruction or waste
'of those things that he hath in custody, we
'will take of him amends and recompence
'therefore. And the land shall be committed
'to two lawful and discreet men of that fee,

'who shall answer unto us for the issues of the
'same land, or unto him whom we will assign.
'And if we give or sell to any man the custody
'of any such land, and he make therein des-
'truction or waste, he shall lose the same cus-
'tody: and then it shall be assigned to two
'lawful and discreet men of that fee, who also
'in like manner shall be answerable to us, as
'aforesaid.'

CHAP. V.

*Guardians shall maintain the inheritance of their
wards: and of bishopricks.*

'The keeper, so long as he hath the custody
'of the land of such an heir, shall keep up the
'houses, parks, warrens, ponds, mills and other
'things pertaining to the same lands, with the
'issues of the said land: and he shall deliver to
'the heir, when he cometh to his full age, all
'his land stored with ploughs, and all other
'things, at the least as he received it. All these
'things shall be observed in the custody of
'archbishopricks, bishopricks, abbies, priories,
'churches and dignities vacant, which pertain
'to us; except this, that such custody shall not
'be sold.'

CHAP. VI.

Heirs to be married without disparagement.

'And heirs shall be married without any dis-
'paragement.'

CHAP. VII.

A widow shall have her marriage inheritance and quarentine. The king's widow.

'A widow, after the death of her husband, without any difficulty, shall have her marriage, and her inheritance: and shall give nothing for her dower, marriage or inheritance, which her husband and she held the day of the death of her husband. And she shall tarry in the chief house of her husband, by forty days after the death of her husband; within which time her dower shall be assigned her, if it were not assigned before, or that the house be a castle; and if she depart from the castle, then a competent house shall be forthwith provided for her, in the which she may honestly dwell, until her dower be to her assigned, as is aforesaid; and she shall have in the mean time her reasonable estovers of the common. And for her dower shall be assigned unto her the third part of all the lands of her husband, which were his, during the coverture; except she were endowed of less at the church door. No widow shall be distrained to marry herself: Nevertheless she shall find surety that she shall not marry without our licence and assent, (if she hold of us); not without the assent of the lord, if she holds of another.'

CHAP. VIII.

How sureties shall be charged to the king.

'We or our bailiffs shall not seize any land or rents for any debt, so long as the present goods and chattels of the debtor do suffice to pay the debt, and the debtor himself be ready to satisfy therefore: neither shall the pledges of the debtor be distrained, as long as the principal debtor is sufficient for the payment of the debt. And if the principal debtor fail in the payment of the debt, having nothing therewith to pay, or will not pay where he is able, the pledges shall answer for the debt. And if they will, they shall have the lands and rents of the debtor until they be satisfied of that which they before paid for him, except that the debtor can shew himself to be acquitted against the said sureties.'

CHAP. IX.

The liberties of London, *and other cities and towns, confirmed.*

'The city of *London* shall have all the old liberties and customs which it hath been used to have. Moreover, we will and grant, that all other cities and boroughs, towns, and the barons of the five ports, and all other ports, shall have all their liberties and free customs.'

CHAP.

CHAP. X.

None shall distrain for more service than due.

'No man shall be distrained to do more service for a knight's fee, nor for any freehold, than therefore is due.'

CHAP. XI.

The common pleas shall not follow the king's court.

'Common pleas shall not follow our court, but shall be holden in some place certain.'

CHAP. XII.

Where and before whom assises shall be taken. Adjournment for difficulty.

'Assizes of *Novel Disseisin* and of *Mortdancestor* shall not be taken but in the shires, and after this manner. If we be out of the realm, our chief justices shall send our justices through every county once in the year; which, with the knights of the shire, shall take the said assises, in those counties. And those things that at the coming of the aforesaid justices, being sent to take those assises in the counties, cannot be determined, shall be ended by them in some other place in their circuit. And those things, which for difficulty in some articles cannot be determined by them, shall be referred to our justices of the bench, and there be ended.'

CHAP. XIII.

Assises of darrein presentment.

'Assises of darrein presentment shall be always taken before our justices of the bench,
and there shall be determined.'

CHAP. XIV.

How men of all sorts shall be amerced, and by whom.

'A freeman shall not be amerced for a small
fault, but after the manner of the fault: and
for a great fault after the greatness thereof,
saving to him his contentment: and a merchant likewise, saving to him his merchandize. And any other's villein than ours shall
be likewise amerced, saving his wainage, if he
fall into our mercy. And none of the said
amerciaments shall be assessed, but by the oaths
of honest and lawful men of the vicinage.
Earls and barons shall not be amerced, but by
their peers, and after the manner of their offence. No man of the church shall be amerced
after the quantity of his spiritual benefice, but
of his lay tenement, and after the quantity of
his offence.'

CHAP. XV.

Making of bridges, and banks.

'No town or freeman shall be distrained to
make bridges or banks, but such as of old time
and of right have been accustomed to make
them

' them, in the time of king *Henry* our grand-
' father.'

CHAP. XVI.

Defending of banks.

' No banks shall be defended from henceforth
' but such as were in defence in the time of
' king *Henry* our grandfather, by the same places
' and the same bounds, as they were wont to be
' in his time.'

CHAP. XVII.

Holding pleas of the crown.

' No sheriff, constable, escheator, coroner
' nor any other our bailiffs, shall hold pleas of
' the crown.'

CHAP. XVIII.

The king's debtor dying, the king shall be first paid.

' If any that holdeth of us lay-fee shall die,
' and our sheriff or bailiff do shew our letters
' patents of our summons for debt, which the
' dead man did owe to us; it shall be lawful for
' our sheriff or bailiff, to attach and inroll all
' the goods and chattels of the dead, being found
' in the said fee, to the value of the same debt,
' by the sight and testimony of lawful men, so
' that nothing thereof be taken away, until we
' be clearly paid off the debt. And the residue
' shall remain to the executors, to perform the
' testament of the dead. And if nothing be
' owing

'owing to us, all the chattels shall go to the use
of the dead, saving to his wife and children
their reasonable parts.'

CHAP. XIX.

Purveyance for a castle.

'No constable nor his bailiff, shall take corn
or other chattels of any man, if the man be
not of the town where the castle is; but he shall
forthwith pay for the same, unless that the will
of the seller was to respite the payment. And
if he be of the same town, the price shall be
paid unto him within forty days.'

CHAP. XX.

Doing of castle-ward.

'No constable shall distrain any knight to
give money for keeping of his castle, if he himself will do it in his proper person, or cause it
to be done by another sufficient man, if he may
not do it himself for a reasonable cause. And
if we do lead or send him in an army, he shall
be free from castle-ward for the time that he
shall be with us in fee in our host, for the
which he hath done service in our wars.'

CHAP. XXI.

Taking of horses, carts, and woods.

'No sheriff nor bailiff of ours, nor any other,
shall take the horses or carts of any man to
make carriage, except he pay the old price
limited.

'limited. No demesne cart of any spiritual
' person or knight, or any lord, shall be taken
' by our bailiffs: nor shall we, nor our bailiffs,
' or any other, take any man's wood for our
' castles, or other our necessaries, but by the
' licence of him whose wood it is.'

C H A P. XXII.

How long felons lands shall be holden by the king.

' We will not hold the lands of them that be
' convict of felony but one year and a day, and
' then those lands shall be delivered to the lords
' of the fee.'

C H A P. XXIII.

In what places wears shall be put down.

' All wears from henceforth shall be utterly
' put down by *Thames* and *Medway*; and thro'
' all *England* but only by the sea-coasts.

C H A P. XXIV.

In what case a Præcipe in capite *is not grantable.*

' The writ that is called *Præcipe in Capite*, shall
' be from henceforth granted to no person of
' any freehold, whereby any freeman may lose
' his court.

CHAP.

Of the Liberty of the Subject.

CHAP. XXV:

There shall be but one measure throughout the realm.

' One measure of wine shall be through our
' realm, and one measure of ale and a measure
' of corn, that is to say, the quarter of *London*.
' And one breadth of died cloth, russets, &c.
' that is to say, two yards within the lists. And
' it shall be of weights as it is of measures.'

CHAP. XXVI.

Inquisition of life and member.

' Nothing from henceforth shall be given for a
' writ of inquisition, nor taken of him that pray-
' eth inquisition of life or member, but it shall
' be granted freely, and not deny'd.'

CHAP. XXVII.

Tenure of the king in socage, and of another by knight's service. Petit serjeanty.

' If any do hold of us by fee-farm, or by so-
' cage or burgage, and he holdeth lands of an-
' other by knight's service, we will not have the
' custody of his heir, nor of his land, which is
' holden of the fee of another, by reason of that
' fee-farm, socage or burgage: neither will we
' have the custody of such fee-farm, socage or
' burgage, except knight's service be due unto
' us out of the same. We will not have the
' custody of the heir, or of any land, by occasion

'casion of any petit sergeanty that any man
holdeth of us by service, to pay an arrow, or
the like.'

CHAP. XXVIII.

Wager of law shall not be without witness.

'No bailiff from henceforth shall put any man
to his open law, nor to an oath, upon his own
bare saying, without faithful witnesses brought
in for the same.'

CHAP. XXIX.

None shall be condemned without trial. Justice shall not be sold or deferred.

'No freeman shall be taken or imprisoned, or
disseised of his freehold, or liberties, or free
customs, or be outlawed or exiled, or any otherwise destroyed, and we will not pass sentence
upon him, nor condemn him, but by lawful
judgment of his peers, or by the law of the
land. We will sell to no man, we will not
deny or defer to any man either justice or
right.'

CHAP. XXX.

Merchant Strangers, coming into this realm, shall be well used.

'All merchants (if they were not openly prohibited before) shall have their safe and sure
conduct to depart out of *England*, to come into
England, to tarry in and go through *England*,

Of the Liberty of the Subject.

' as well by land as by sea, to buy and sell
' without any manner of evil tools, by the old
' and rightful customs, except in time of war.
' And if they be of a land making war against
' us, and be found in our realm at the beginning
' of the wars, they shall be attached without
' harm of body and goods, until it be known
' unto us or our chief justice, how our merchants
' are treated there in the land making war against
' us; and if our merchants be well treated there,
' theirs shall be likewise with us.'

C H A P. XXXI.

Tenure of a barony, coming into the king's hand by escheat.

' If any man hold of any escheat, as of the
' honour of *Wallingford*, *Nottingham*, *Boloign*,
' or of any other escheats which be in our hands,
' and are baronies, and die, his heir shall give
' no other relief, nor do any other service to us,
' than he should to the baron, if it were in the
' baron's hand. And we in the same wise shall
' hold it as the baron held it, neither shall we
' have, by occasion of any barony or escheats,
' any escheat or keeping of any of our men, un-
' less he that held the barony or escheat, other-
' wise held of us in chief.'

C H A P. XXXII.

Lands shall not be aliened to the prejudice of the lord's service.

' No freeman from henceforth shall give or sell
' any more of his land, but so that of the residue

Of the Liberty of the Subject.

' of the lands the lord may have the services
' due to him, which belong to the fee.'

CHAP. XXXIII.

Patrons of abbies shall have the custody of them in the time of vacation.

' All patrons of abbies, who have the king's
' charter of *England*, of advowson, or have old
' tenure or possession in the same, shall have the
' custody of them when they fall void, as it hath
' been accustomed, and as it is before declared.'

CHAP. XXXIV.

In what case only a woman shall have appeal of death.

' No man shall be taken or imprisoned upon
' the appeal of a woman, for the death of any
' other but her husband.'

CHAP. XXXV.

At what time shall be kept a county-court, sheriff's turn, and a leet.

' No county court from henceforth shall be
' holden, but from month to month; and where
' greater time hath been used, there shall be
' greater. Nor shall any sheriff or his bailiff keep
' his turn in the hundred, but twice in the year:
' and no where but in the due place and accus-
' tomed, that is to say, once after *Easter*, and
' again after the feast of St. *Michael*. And the
' view of frank-pledge shall be likewise at the
' feast

Of the Liberty of the Subject.

'feast of St. *Michael* without occasion ; so that
every man may have his liberties which he had,
or used to have in the time of king *Henry* our
grandfather, or which he hath purchased since.
The view of frank-pledge shall be done, that
our peace may be kept; and that the tithing
be wholly kept, as it hath been accustomed.
And that the sheriff seek no occasions, and that
he be content with so much as the sheriff was
wont to have for his view making in the time
of king *Henry* our grandfather.'

CHAP. XXXVI.

No land shall be given in mortmain.

'It shall not be lawful from henceforth for
any one to give his lands to any religious house,
and to take the same land again to hold of the
same house. Nor shall it be lawful for any
house of religion to take the lands of any one,
and to lease the same to him of whom he
received it: if any from henceforth give his
lands to any religious house, and thereupon be
convict, the gift shall be utterly void, and the
land shall accrue to the lord of the fee.'

CHAP. XXXVII.

A subsidy in respect of this charter, and the charter of the forest, granted to the king.

'Escuage from henceforth shall be taken like
as it was wont to be in the time of king *Henry*
our grandfather; reserving to all archbishops,
bishops, abbots, &c. earls, barons, and all
persons as well spiritual as temporal, all their
'free

'free liberties and free customs which they
'have had in time past, and all these customs
'and liberties aforesaid, which we have granted
'to be holden within this our realm, as much
'as appertaineth to us and our heirs, we shall
'observe: and all men of this our realm, as well
'spiritual as temporal (as much as in them is)
'shall observe the same against all persons in like
'wise. And for this our gift and grant of these
'liberties, and of others contained in our char-
'ter of liberties of our forest, the archbishops,
'bishops, earls, barons, knights, freeholders,
'and other our subjects, have given unto us the
'fifteenth part of all their moveables. And we
'have granted to them on the other part, that
'neither we nor our heirs shall procure or do
'any thing, whereby the liberties in this char-
'ter contained shall be infringed or broken. And
'if any thing be procured contrary to the same,
'it shall be had of no force or effect.'

Charta de Foresta, *or the charter of the forest, granted in the ninth year of* king
Hen. III.

I. 'ALL forests that were afforested by king
  Henry the second, shall be viewed by
'lawful men; and if he hath afforested any other
'woods than his own demesne, whereby any is
'prejudiced, they shall be disafforested: saving
'common of herbage and other things within
'the forest, to such as have been accustomed to
'enjoy them.'

II. *Cap.* 2. 'None dwelling out of the forest
'shall come before the justices of our forest by
'common summons, unless they be impleaded
                                        'there,

'there, or be sureties for others that are attached
'for the forest.'

III. *Cap.* 3. "All woods made forest by K.
'*Richard* I. or king *John*, shall be disafforested,
'except they be our demesne woods.'

IV. *Cap.* 4. 'All freeholders having woods
'in forests, shall enjoy them as they did at the
'time of the coronation of K. *Henry* II. acquit-
'ted of all purprestures, wastes and assarts made
'before the second year of *Henry* III. and they
'that make them henceforward shall be answer-
'able to the king for the same.

V. *Cap.* 5. 'Rangers of the forest shall exer-
'cise their office as it was used at the corona-
'tion of *Henry* II. and not otherwise.

VI. *Cap.* 6. 'The lawing of dogs shall be made
'in forests from three to three years by the view
'and testimony of lawful men, and not other-
'wise; and he that hath not his dog lawed
'shall be amerced 3 *s.* and it shall be done by
'the usual assise, *viz.* Three claws of the fore-
'feet to be cut off by the skin: howbeit, such
'lawing shall not be but where it hath been used
'from the coronation of *Henry* II.

VII. *Cap.* 7. 'No forester or beadle shall
'make scotal, or gather garb, oats, corn, lamb
'or pig, but by the sight and oath of the twelve
'rangers, when they shall make their range:
'and there shall be so many rangers assigned for
'the keeping of forests, as shall seem reasonable
'and sufficient for the same.

VIII. *Cap.* 8. "There shall be only three
'swain-motes in the year, *viz.* one court fifteen
'days before *Michaelmas*, another about *Martin-
'mas*, and the third fifteen days before *Mid-
'summer*, at the first two of which none shall ap-
'pear by distress but the foresters, verderors

'and

' and Geft-takers, and at the other only the fo-
' reftors and verderors: but the forefters and
' verderors fhall meet every forty days, to fee
' the attachments of the forefts, as well for green-
' hue as hunting; and the fwain-motes fhall not
' be kept but in the counties where they have
' been ufed to be kept.

IX. *Cap.* 9. ' Every one having a wood in the
' foreft may agift it, and take his pawnage there
' at his pleafure: he may alfo drive his hogs
' through the king's woods, or elfewhere, for
' that purpofe; and if they lie all night in the
' foreft, he fhall not be queftioned for it.

X. *Cap.* 10. ' None fhall lofe life or member
' for killing of deer, but fhall be fined for it, if
' he have any thing; if not, he fhall be imprifoned
' a year and a day, and (if he can find good
' fureties) fhall then be delivered; but for want
' of fureties he fhall abjure the realm.'

' XI. *Cap.* 11. ' A peer of the realm, being
' fent for by the king, in coming and returning
' may kill a deer or two in the foreft through
' which he paffeth: howbeit, it muft not be done
' privily, but by the view of the forefter, if pre-
' fent; and if abfent, by caufing one to blow a
' horn for him, left otherwife he feem to fteal
' the deer.

XII. *Cap.* 12. ' Every freeman may within
' the foreft (upon his own ground) make a mill,
' fpring, pool, marl-pit, dike, or arable land,
' without inclofing fuch arable, fo it be not to
' the nufance of any of his neighbours.'

XIII. *Cap.* 13. ' Every freeman may have
' his aviaries of hawks, eagles and herons, and
' alfo honey found in his woods within the fo-
' reft.'

'XIV. *Cap.* 14. 'No chiminage or toll shall be taken in forests but by a forester in fee, that farms his bailiwick, and only of such as buy their bushes, timber, bark or coal, to sell it again, *viz.* 2 *d.* for a cart, and 1 *d.* for a horse, to be taken half-yearly; and it shall only be taken where it hath used to be so taken, and not elsewhere; neither shall any chiminage be taken of such as carry burthens of bushes, bark or coal, although they sell them, unless they take them out of the king's demesne woods.'

XV. *Cap.* 15. 'All persons outlawed for trespass in forests since *Henry* III. shall be released, finding sureties to offend no more.

XVI. *Cap.* 16. 'No constable, castellain or bailiff shall hold pleas of forests for green-hue or hunting, but the forester shall attach such pleas, and present them to the verderors of the provinces; who shall inrol them, and present them inclosed under their seals unto the chief justice of the forest, when he comes into those parts to hold pleas of the forest, to be determined before him.'

XVII. 'These liberties of the forest the king grants to all men; saving to persons the liberties and free customs in forests, warrens, and other places, which they have formerly enjoyed.'

And by the *Statute* of 1 *Ed.* 3. *c.* 8.

'None shall be taken or imprisoned for vert or venison, unless he be taken with the manner, that is trespassing in the forest, or else duly indicted; and then the warden of the forest shall let him to mainprize until the eyre of the forest, without taking any thing for his deliverance; and if the warden will not so do,

'he

'he shall have a writ out of the chancery of old
'ordained for persons indicted, to be bailed 'till
'the eyre.'

'If the warden after the writ served deliver
'not the person so indicted to mainprise, the
'party may have another writ out of chancery
'directed to the sheriff to attach the warden to
'answer his default before the king at a certain
'day; and then the sheriff (the verderors being
'called to him) shall deliver the person indicted
'by good main-prise, in the presence of the said
'verderors, and shall deliver the names of the
'mainpernors to the same verderors to answer
'in the eyre before the justices.

'If the chief warden be thereof attainted, he
'shall be awarded to pay treble damages to the
'party grieved, committed to prison, and ran-
'somed at the king's will.'

The statute De Tallagio non concedendo,
  in the time of K. Edward I.

'NO tax, tallage or aid shall be levied by
'us or our heirs, without the will and
'assent of the archbishops, bishops, earls, ba-
'rons, knights, burgesses, and other free com-
'mons of our realm.'

'And all persons shall have their laws, liber-
'ties and free customs, as largely as they have
'used to have them when they had them best:
'and if any statutes or customs have been made
'or brought in by us or our predecessors, or
'any article in this charter be found contrary
'thereunto, they shall be void.'

'There is the form of a writ to be directed
'to the sheriff, to permit all men to enjoy all
'such

'such Liberties as they had before; and a pro-
'clamation may issue, that such as claim liber-
'ties, shall shew to the justices (at the first as-
'sises, when they shall come into those parts)
'how they hold them, for which they shall have
'forty days summons; but if they appear not,
'their liberties shall be seized in the name of a
'distress: also there may be another proclamation,
'that such as complain of the king's officers shall
'shew their grievances to the said Justices.'

This last clause is by the statute *de quo warranto*, 30 *Ed*. 1.

The Habeas Corpus *statute made in the* 31*st year of* K. Charles II.

'THERE having been great delays used
'by sheriffs, gaolers, and other officers,
'to whose custody the king's subjects had been
'committed, in making returns of writs of *Ha-
'beas Corpus*, &c. whereby many persons had
'been long detained in prison, in such cases
'where by law they were bailable; for preven-
'tion thereof, and the more speedy relief of all
'persons imprisoned for any criminal matters,
'it is enacted,

I. 'That whensoever any writ of *Habeas Cor-
'pus* shall be brought and served upon any of-
'ficer, or other person, for any one in his cu-
'stody, or shall be left at the gaol with any of
'the under officers, the said officers or their
'keepers or deputies, within three days after
'that, (unless the commitment were for treason
'or felony plainly expressed in the warrant of
'commitment) on payment of the charges of
'bringing

'bringing the prisoner, or tender thereof, to be
ascertain'd by the judge or court that awarded
' the writ and endorsed on the same, not ex-
' ceeding 12 d. per mile, and upon security given
' by the prisoner's own bond to pay charges of
' carrying them back, if he be remanded by the
' court, and that he will not make any escape
' by the way, shall make return of such writ of
' *Habeas Corpus*, and bring the body of the
' party committed before the judges or barons
' of the court from whence the writ shall issue,
' or to such persons before whom the writ is re-
' turnable; and shall certify the true causes of his
' detainer or imprisonment: but if the place of
' imprisonment be beyond twenty miles, and
' not above one hundred miles off, then ten days
' are allowed for the same; and if further, it shall
' be within twenty days, and no longer.'

II. 'And persons committed or detained for
' any crime (unless for treason or felony expres-
' sed in the warrant as aforesaid) in the vacation-
' time, may complain to the lord chancellor or
' keeper, or any judge, who upon view of the
' copy of commitment, or oath of its being de-
' nied, shall upon request by such persons, or
' any in their behalf, attested and subscribed
' by two witnesses, grant a *Habeas Corpus* under
' the seal of their respective courts, returnable
' immediately; and on service thereof, the of-
' ficer within the times before limited is to
' bring up such prisoner before the said lord
' chancellor or judges, before whom the writ is
' made returnable, with the causes of his com-
' mitment; and thereupon, within two days
' after he shall be brought up, the prisoner
' shall be discharged from his imprisonment, on

' entering

'entering into recognizance with one or more
'sureties to appear in the court of king's bench
'the term following, or at the next assises, ses-
'sions or general gaol delivery, or such other
'court for the county where the offence is cog-
'nizable; into which court the writ, return
'and recognizance aforesaid, shall be certified;
'unless it shall appear that the party is detained
'upon a legal process or warrant, for such mat-
'ters or offences which are not bailable by law.

III. 'Provided always, that if any person shall
'neglect to pray a *Habeas Corpus* for his inlarge-
'ment, by the space of two terms after he is
'committed, he shall not have any such writ in
'time of vacation, in pursuance of this act.

IV. 'If any officer or officers shall refuse to
'make their returns, or to bring the body of
'the prisoner as aforesaid, according to the com-
'mand of the writ, within the times aforesaid;
'or upon demand made by the prisoner, or any
'in his behalf, shall refuse to deliver a true copy
'of the warrant or commitment, within six
'hours after demanded, such officers, gaolers,
'&c. in whose custody the prisoner shall be de-
'tained, shall forfeit for the first offence 100 *l.*
'and for the second offence 200 *l.* to the party
'grieved, and be rendered incapable to hold their
'offices: the penalties to be recovered by action
'of debt, bill, plaint or information, in any of
'the king's courts at *Westminster*, wherein no
'essoin, &c. or stay of prosecution shall be ad-
'mitted or allowed.

V. 'And no person, who shall be delivered
'and set at large by *Habeas Corpus*, shall be
'again imprisoned for the same offence, by any
'person other than by legal order and process

of

Of the Liberty of the Subject.

'of such court, wherein he shall be bound by
'recognizance to appear, or other court having
'jurisdiction of the cause: and if any other
'persons shall knowingly imprison again the
'person delivered or set at large, they shall for-
'feit to the prisoner 500 *l.* to be recovered as
'aforesaid.'

VI. 'Persons committed for high treason or
'felony, plainly and especially expressed in the
'warrant, upon prayer in open court the first
'week of the term, or first day of the sessions
'of *Oyer & Terminer* or gaol-delivery, to be
'brought to trial; if they are not indicted the
'next term, sessions of *Oyer & Terminer*, or
'gaol-delivery after such commitment, the
'judges upon motion made in court the last
'day of the term or sessions, shall set them at
'liberty upon bail, unless it appear upon oath,
'that the king's witnesses could not be pro-
'duced that term or sessions: and if any such
'persons committed as aforesaid, upon such
'prayer aforesaid, shall not be indicted and tried
'the second term or sessions after commitment,
'they shall be discharged from their imprison-
'ment.'

VII. 'But nothing in this act shall extend to
'discharge out of prison any person charged in
'debt or other action, or with process in any
'civil cause, but that after his acquittal for his
'crime, he shall be kept in custody for such
'other suits.

VIII. 'If any person or persons, subjects of
'this realm, shall be committed to any prison,
'or be in custody of any officer, for any cri-
'minal matter, the said person shall not be re-
'moved from the said custody into the custody
'of any other officer; unless it be by *Habeas*
  'Corpus,

'*Corpus*, or some other legal writ, or where the
prisoner is delivered to the constable to be carried to goal, &c. or when any person is sent by
order to the house of correction, or removed
from one prison to another in the same county,
in order to a trial or discharge: or in case of
sudden fire, infection or other necessity. And
persons making out and signing any warrants
for removal, contrary hereto, or counter signing the same, and the officers obeying or executing them, shall incur the forfeitures before
mentioned, both for the first and second offence,
to the party grieved.'

IX. 'And any prisoner may move for and obtain his *Habeas Corpus*, as well out of the *Chancery* or *Exchequer*, as out of the courts of *King's
Bench* or *Common Pleas*; and if the lord chancellor or any judge or baron, shall deny any
writ of *Habeas Corpus* required to be granted as
aforesaid, they shall forfeit to the party grieved
500 *l*. recoverable in manner aforesaid.'

X. 'And it is declared, that writs of *Habeas
Corpus* may run into any county palatine, the
cinque ports, and other privileged places of
England, and into the isles *Jersey* or *Guernsey*.

XI. 'No subject of this realm shall be sent
prisoner into *Scotland*, *Ireland*, or into any
parts beyond the seas, which are or may be
within or without the dominions of his majesty, his heirs or successors: and if any of the
said subjects be so imprisoned, it is illegal, and
every such person shall for such imprisonment
have an action of false imprisonment against
him by whom he shall be committed, detained, imprisoned, sent prisoner or transported, and against all persons that shall frame,
contrive, write, seal or countersign any warrant

'rant for such commitment, or shall be advis-
'ing, aiding or assisting in the same; and shall
'have judgment to recover treble costs, besides
'damages, which damages shall not be less than
'500 l. in which action no delay or stop of pro-
'ceedings, nor no injunction, protection or pri-
'vilege, &c. shall be allowed; and the person
'or persons so offending as aforesaid, being law-
'fully convicted thereof, shall be disabled to
'bear any office of trust or profit within the
'realm, or dominions thereunto belonging, and
'incur the pains, penalties and forfeitures or-
'dained by the statute of *Præmunire* made in
'the 16th year of *Richard* II. and be incapable
'of any pardon from the king, his heirs or suc-
'cessors.'

XII. 'This act shall not extend to any per-
'son who by contract in writing shall agree
'with any merchant or owner of a plantation,
'&c. to be transported, and shall have received
'earnest upon such agreement: nor to persons
'convicted of felony, and praying to be trans-
'ported beyond the seas, who may be so trans-
'ported into any parts notwithstanding this sta-
'tute; nor to the imprisonment of any person
'before the time limited for the commencement
'of the act, or any thing thereto relating; nor
'to persons resident in this realm, that shall
'have committed any capital crime in *Scotland*
'or *Ireland*, &c. but that such persons may be
'sent to receive trial as before this act.'

XIII. 'And persons offending against this act
'shall not be impleaded for any offence, unless
'the same be done within two years at most
'after the offence was committed, in case the
'party grieved shall not be then in prison; and
'if

Of the Liberty of the Subject.

'if he shall be in prison, then within two years
'after his delivery out of prison or decease.'

XIV. 'After the assizes proclaimed for any
'county, no person shall be removed from the
'common gaol upon any *Habeas Corpus*, pursu-
'ant to this act, but shall be brought thereupon
'before the judge of assize in open court: but
'after the assizes are ended, any person detained
'may have a *Habeas Corpus*, according to the
'direction and intention of the act.'

XV. 'If any information, suit or action, be
'brought against any person or persons for of-
'fences against this law, the defendants may
'plead the general issue, and give the special
'matter in evidence; and the said matter shall be
'as available to all intents, as if they had plead-
'ed or alledged the same matter in bar or dis-
'charge of such information, suit or action.'

XVI. 'Persons appearing to be committed as
'accessary before the fact, to any petit treason
'or felony, or upon suspicion thereof, which
'shall be specially expressed in the warrant of
'commitment, shall not be removed or bailed
'by virtue of this act, or in any other manner
'than they might have been before the making
'of the same.'

Two things I shall observe upon this statute:

1. That altho' the constable by his own authority, without any warrant of commitment,
may carry an offender to gaol, and this was the
method of securing prisoners, before that there
were any justices of the peace; yet since the institution of that magistrate, it is better that they

be carried before him to be sent by him to gaol by warrant of commitment; otherwise they have a right to be bailed upon this act, whatever the offence may be.

2. That the warrant of commitment ought to set forth the cause specially: that is to say, not for treason or felony in general, but treason *for counterfeiting the king's coin*, or felony *for stealing the goods of such a one to such a value*, and the like; that so the court may judge thereupon, whether or no the offence is such, for which a prisoner ought to be admitted to bail. *Burn's Just. qto.* 104.

Of the King and his Prerogative, and the Officers and Ministers of Justice under him.

THE king is he who hath the highest rule over the whole land. Our king being above all others, he hath therefore many singular privileges and preheminences in him beyond all other persons: and he, for the excellency of his person and greatness of his office, has ascribed to him by law some of the attributes even of God; as sovereignty and power, omnipresence, immortality, verity and justice, &c. But this is to be understood in his publick or political capacity, for, in his private or natural capacity, the law looks on him as mortal, and subject to the infirmities of other men. 3 *Shep. Abr.* 44.

Of the King and his Prerogative.

As to the prerogatives of the king, they are called *Jura Regalia*, or *Insignia Coronæ*, and are inseparably annexed to the crown, so that none but the king himself may have and use them: and the particular power and prerogative of the king hath its exercise in these things,

1. As the king is head of the state.
2. As he is supreme head of the church.
3. As lord paramount of all lands; and grants of the king.
4. His debts how paid, and acts construed in civil cases, *&c.*

1. It is the king's royal prerogative to make war or peace; to send and receive embassadors, and make leagues and treaties with foreign states: and, as head of the state, he calls, continues, prorogues and dissolves parliaments; and all statutes are to have his royal assent, which he may refuse to give to a bill; but his denial is that he will advise upon it, and not an express negative. *Co. Lit.* 110.

In calling or dissolving parliaments, declaring war and peace, *&c.* his proclamation has the effect of a law; though he cannot by proclamation introduce new laws; yet he may thereby inforce old statutes discontinued; and he may dispense with a penal statute, wherein his subjects have not any interest. The king may take the benefit of any statute, although he be not named; but acts of parliament do not bind the king, if he is not specially named, unless they concern the commonwealth, suppress wrong or fraud, *&c.* in which cases they are binding to him. 3 *Inst.* 162. 2 *Inst.* 743. 5 *Rep.* 14. 7 *Rep.* 32.

Of the King and his Prerogative.

It is his prerogative alone to dispose and govern the militia of the kingdom: and he hath the command of all forts, and places of strength, &c. Also authority in the making and casting of ordnance. He gives commissions for levying men and arms, by sea and land; and disposes of all magazines, ammunition, castles, fortresses, ships of war, and publick money: the king may lay embargoes on shipping, but then it must be *pro bono publico*; he may, if he see cause, open or shut the sea-ports, and forbid the passage of his subjects over sea, without licence, &c. The ports he may not grant to a subject, but shall appoint officers for the custody thereof, under him. 12 *Rep.* 34. 11 *Rep.* 86. *Salk.* 32.

He hath power to make an alien free-born; and to grant letters of safe conduct to foreign parts: he can put a value upon the coin which is made by his authority, and make foreign coin current by proclamation; and to make money, the law gives the king all mines of gold and silver; or where the gold and silver in mines is of the greater value, which are called royal mines. *Plowd.* 314.

All writs and processes, commissions, &c. are in the king's name; and he may erect courts of justice, which shall proceed according to the common law: he may make and create universities, colleges, counties, boroughs, fairs, markets, &c. And no forest, chase, or park can be made, or castle built, without the king's leave. The king by his prerogative may incorporate a whole city, parish, &c. or part of it, and grant and annex to such corporations divers franchises; though they may not under colour thereof set up a monopoly which is against law. *Jenk. Cent.* 285. 4 *Inst.* 294. *Noy* 182.

The

Of the King and his Prerogative.

The king is the fountain of honour, and has the sole power of conferring dignities and honourable titles; as to make dukes, earls, barons, knights of the garter, &c. And he names, creates, makes and removes the great officers of the government: he determines rewards and punishments; moderates laws, and pardons offenders. But the king cannot pardon murder, where appeal is brought by the subject; and pardons of felony, &c. shall be granted only, where the king may lawfully do it, according to his coronation oath. *Co. Lit.* 165. 2 *Inst.* 316. *Stat.* 14 *Ed.* 3.

And altho' the king hath an interest in every subject, and a right to his service, he cannot discharge the right of a subject, or hinder him of a remedy the law gives him. *Salk.* 168.

2. As supreme head of the church, our king hath power to call a national or provincial council; and by his royal assent the canons made in convocation have the force of laws: and to him the last appeal is made. 4 *Inst.* 325. *Danv. Abr.* 73.

The king hath this prerogative in the convocation of the clergy; that when it is called, it is by his writ; it may not make any canons without his licence; if the king pleases he may sit there, as he doth in the parliament; and he hath a negative voice, as he hath in parliament. The archbishop of *Canterbury*, who is president, prorogues and dissolves it by the king's direction; and the clergy called to the convocation shall have the same privileges as members of parliament. *Crompt. Jur.* 4. *Stat.* 8 *H.* 6. *c.* 1. *Eq. Caf. Abr.* 349. (*A.*) *pl.* 1. 3 *Chanc. Rep.* 22. *fol. edit.* 1736. 4 *Pryn. Reg. Writs* 644.

By

Of the King and his Prerogative.

By his prerogative, the king hath the supreme right of patronage all over *England*; and is the founder and patron of all bishopricks, &c. so that none can be made a bishop but by his nomination: and the election of bishops is to be by the king's *Conge d' Eslire*, or licence to elect the person named by the king; and if the dean and chapter fail to make election, the king may nominate, &c. by letters patent. But the dean and chapter having made their election, certify it to the king, and the archbishop, &c. and then the king gives his assent under the great seal. *Co. Lit.* 96. 25 *H.* 8. *c.* 20.

The king has not only the choice and making of all bishops, but of deans, and the like clergymen: and he may licence a new bishop to retain his old parsonage in *Commendam*; and where a bishop may hold the profits of a benefice for a time, by way of *Commendam*, this cannot be done without the king's licence. The custody of the temporalities of every bishop and archbishop, during the vacancy of these sees, belongs to the king, and he may grant it away: and the king may present to a void advowson, when the temporalities are in his hands. *Davis* 75. *F. N. B.* 34. *Co. Lit.* 398.

He may now make any bishop, or other person in holy orders, a privy counsellor, justice of oyer and terminer, justice of peace, &c. or give them power to execute any temporal authority. The king, according to the statutes, may dispense with plurality of benefices, and non-residence of clergymen, where there are two or more benefices with cure: appropriations of church benefices, made by consent of the patron and ordinary, must be with the king's licence. When the patron of a church neglects to present to the

same

Of the King and his Prerogative.

same in six months; the bishop of the diocese, on his default, the archbishop is to collate within the like time; and he not doing it, the king shall present to the church. *Cro. Jac.* 552. 11 *Rep.* 10. 2 *Rol. Abr.* 360.

Churches are founded by the king, and he licenses others to found them, exempt from the ordinary's jurisdiction; and he hath the tithes of forests and places extraparochial, which he may grant by letters patent: also the king shall pay no tithes, &c. *Cro. Eliz.* 511.

3. The king is lord paramount of all the lands in *England*; and all estates for want of heirs, or by forfeiture, escheat to him: he shall have the lands of felons, &c. convict; and the goods of felons and fugitives; goods and chattels of pirates; wreck of the sea, &c. *Stat.* 17 *Ed.* 2. 4 *Inst.* 136.

All lands are said to be holden of the king; lands in the king's possession are free from tenure; and the king may not be jointenant with any one: where the title of the king and of a common person concurs, his title shall be preferred. No distress can be made upon the king's possession; but he may distrain out of his fee in other lands, &c. and may take distresses in the highway. Goods and chattels may go in succession to the king, though they may not to any other sole corporation. *Co. Lit.* 1, 30, 90; *Finch* 83. 2 *Inst.* 131.

The king may grant a thing in action, which another cannot; and reserve a rent to a stranger, &c. But he cannot grant or take any land, (not cast upon him by discent) but by matter of record: and the king may not grant an annuity to charge his person, which is not chargeable like the person of a subject; though he may grant it

out

Of the King and his Prerogative.

out of the revenue of the excise, &c. The grant of the king is taken favourably for him, and most strongly against another; and he may avoid his own grant for deceit. 4 *Rep.* 54. 2 *Inst.* 186. *Plowd.* 243. *Salk.* 58.

The king's grant is good for himself and successors, though his successors are not named: but if a grant is made by the king, and a former grant is in being of the same thing, if it be not recited, the grant will be void; yet there may be a *non obstante* to a former grant, if the king is deceived in his grant, as where it contains more than was intended to be granted, &c. it is void: and the king's grants may be void by reason of incertainty; where debts and duties are granted, without saying in particular what duties, &c. Though when there is a particular certainty preceeding, they shall not be destroyed by any incertainty or mistake which follows it. *Yelv.* 13. *Dyer* 77. 5 *Rep.* 94. 12 *Rep.* 46. *Mod. Rep.* 195.

A grant of the king to a corporation, that they shall not be impleaded for any cause arising there, elsewhere than before themselves, &c. this binds not the king, where he is party: and the king may not by his grant exclude himself from prosecuting pleas of the crown; for it concerns the publick government. *Kelw.* 88. *Dy.* 376.

4. The king's debt shall be satisfied before that of a subject, for which there is a prerogative writ; and until his debt be paid he may protect the debtor from the arrest of others. But by statute a common person may sue the king's debtor, notwithstanding he hath a protection, and recover judgment against him; tho' he cannot have execution, unless he gives security to pay the king's debt. If a debtor hath

not a writ of protection, he may be in execution for a common person, as well as the king: and the debt of the king ought to be in equal degree with that of his subject, to have preference. *Co. Lit.* 130. *Stat.* 25 *Ed.* 3. *c.* 19. 33 *H.* 8. *c.* 39. *Cro. Car.* 283.

In whose soever hands the goods of the king come, their lands are chargeable, and may be seized for the same: and the king is not bound by sale of his goods in open market. No prescription of time runs against the king; he is not within the statute of limitation of actions: he may sue in what court he pleases, and cannot be nonsuit, as he is supposed to be present in all his courts; the king may have such process in his suit, as no other person but himself can have, in any case: and in his pleading he need not plead an act of parliament, though a subject is bound to do it. 2 *Inst.* 713. 11 *Rep.* 74. *Finch* 82, 476. 4 *R. p.* 75.

Action lies not against the king, but a petition to him in chancery instead thereof: and it is lawful for any subject to petition the king for redress, where he finds himself grieved by any sentence or judgment. The king's title is not to be tried, without warrant from the king, or assent of the attorney-general: there are no costs allowed against the king; no entry will bar him; and no judgment is ever final against him, but with a *salvo jure regis*; and in the case of others, the king may issue a command to the judges, not to proceed 'till he is advised, where his right may be prejudiced, &c. 2 *Inst.* 187, 424. *Hob.* 220. *Finch* 460.

The king's only testimony of any thing done in his presence is of as high a nature and credit as any record; whence it is that in all writs or
pre-

Of the King and his Prerogative.

precepts sent out for the dispatch of justice, he useth no other witnesses than himself, as *Teste meipso*, &c. The king cannot be a minor or under age; and in him the law will see no defect, negligence or folly. *Co. Lit.* 41, 57.

These prerogatives and others arise to the king, from the reason of the common law; which allows that to be law almost in every case for the king, which is not so for the subject: but the king's prerogative doth not extend to any thing injurious to his subjects; for the king by our law can do no wrong. *Finch* 85.

The king or queen may make laws, by authority of parliament to bind the crown, &c. Kings of *England* are to be Protestants, and join in the communion of the church of *England*: and the king's coronation oath is settled by statute. *Stat.* 1 *W. & M. st.* 2. *c.* 2. *f.* 10.

The oath of the king *at his coronation, administered by the archbishop,* &c.

'HE solemnly promises and swears, that he
' will govern the people of this kingdom
' of *England*, and the dominions thereunto be-
' longing, according to the statutes in parlia-
' ment agreed on, and the laws and customs of
' the same; that he will to his power cause law
' and justice, in mercy, to be executed in all his
' judgments; that he will to the utmost of his
' power maintain the laws of God, the true
' profession of the gospel, and the protestant
' reformed religion established by law: and
' preserve unto the bishops and clergy of this
' realm, and to the churches committed to their
' charge, all such rights and privileges, as by
' law

Of the King and his Prerogative.

'law do or shall appertain unto them, or any
'of them. All which things, put to him by
'way of question, the king promises to perform
'and keep, laying his hand upon the holy gos-
'pels, and then kissing the book.'

Prerogative of the queen and prince.

THE queen in our law is either she that holds the crown of this realm by right of blood, or who is married to the king; the first of which is called *Queen Regnant*, and the last *Queen Consort*: she who holdeth by blood is, in construction of law, the same with the king, and hath the like regal power and authority; but the queen consort is inferior to the king, and his subject. *3 Inst.* 7. *1 Mar. cap.* 1.

By the common law the queen, as the king's wife, partakes of several prerogatives above other women: she is a publick person, exempt from the king; and capable of lands or tenements of the gift or grant of the king her husband, which no other feme covert is: and she is of ability, without the king, to purchase or grant lands, and make leases; she may have in herself the possession of personal things, during her life, &c. But both her real and personal estate goes to the king after her death; if she do not in her lifetime dispose of them, or devise them away by will. *Co. Lit.* 3, 31, 133. *Rol. Abr.* 912.

The queen may sue and be sued alone, in her own name only, by *præcipe*, not by petition; and no writ of right is to be directed to her, but to her bailiff: she shall not find pledges in an action; or be amerced as another shall be. In a writ of *Quare Impedit* brought by the queen,

on

on her being disturbed in presenting to a church, some say plenarty is no plea against her: acts of parliament relating to her need not be pleaded; for the court must take notice of them, as they do those that concern the king, because she is a publick person. *Finch* 86. 2 *Inst.* 361. 8 *Rep.* 28.

In case a tenant of the queen aliens part of his land to one, and part of it to another; the queen may distrain in any one part of the whole, as the king may do: and she is not bound by the statute of *Marlbridge* against driving of a distress out of the county. If the king take an alien to wife, she shall have the queen's dowry; and the queen shall pay no toll, &c. 4 *Rep.* 23. *Plowd.* 124, 231. *Co. Lit.* 133.

As for the *Prince of Wales*, to plot his death is high treason. He is not restrained by the statute 1 *Hen.* 4. *cap.* 6. concerning the king's grants: the judges are to take notice of an act of parliament made for him, whether pleading it, and the like. 8 *Rep.* 28.

And the king's other children have some privileges more than other men's children: being born beyond sea, they are inheritable to land here, &c. 4 *Rep.* 23. 1 *Inst.* 132.

A *Provision* not only for the king's houshold, is settled by parliament; but is ordained also for the queen. *Stat.* 1 *Geo.* 3. *c.* 1. 2 *Geo.* 3. *c.* 1.

The privileges of the nobility.

THE nobility and peerage of this kingdom is created by the king, either by writ or letters patent. The calling up a lord by writ is the most ancient way, and gives a fee-simple in a barony, to him and his heirs, without words of inheritance; but the king may limit it to heirs male, or the heirs of the body; and if he dies before he sits in parliament, his blood is not ennobled: but the creation by letters patent is good, and makes the peerage sure, though he never sits in parliament; and his heirs shall inherit the honour, pursuant to the words of the patent. *Co. Lit.* 16. 2 *Inst.* 48. 4 *Bac. Abr.* 229. 3 *Seld.* 1478, 1726. *Styl.* 222, 253. *Mo.* 767.

All peers of the realm are looked upon as the king's hereditary counsellors; the king and whole kingdom have an interest in the peerage of every lord: and the privileges belonging to our nobility, beyond other men, are very great. The person of a peer, as well out as in parliament time is privileged from all arrests, unless for treason, felony or breach of the peace, &c. and this privilege is so extensive in respect of his person, that the king may not restrain any peer of his liberty, without order of the house of lords, except it be in cases of treason, &c. 6 *Rep.* 52. 5 *Bac. Abr.* 228, 231. 2 *Ld. Raym.* 1297.

Peers are not to be arrested upon mesne process, or on execution for debt or trespass, because they are presumed not only to attend the king and the publick affairs; but the law doth presume they have sufficient lands, in which they may be distrained: but they may be apprehended in criminal cases. And tho' a peer may not be arrested in his body, his estate may be sequestred for debt, &c. upon a prosecution after a dissolution and prorogation of parliament, or adjournment for above fourteen days, when he refuses to appear and answer, on a bill of complaint exhibited

Of the King and his Prerogative.

hibited in the Chancery, Exchequer, &c. 6 *Rep.* 53. *Stat.* 12 & 13 *W.* 3. *c.* 3.

Suits may be brought against any peer, or member of parliament, or their menial servants, &c. in the intervals of parliament, or of sessions, being above fourteen days; and the courts, after dissolutions, or prorogations, may give judgment, and award execution: and where any plaintiff shall be stayed from prosecuting his suit, he shall not be nonsuited, but upon the rising of the parliament may proceed to judgment, &c. Also no proceedings in law against the king's debtor, shall be delayed under colour of any privilege: only the person of a peer shall not be arrested, or imprisoned thereupon, &c. 11 *Geo.* 2. *c.* 24.

Every lord of parliament is allowed his clergy in all cases, where others are excluded by the Stat. 1 *Ed.* 6. *c.* 12. except for wilful murder: and it is said the lord *Morley*, who was tried for murder, and found guilty of manslaughter, was discharged without clergy. For treason committed by a peer of the realm, he shall be tried by his peers, lords of parliament: and if a nobleman be indicted of murder or felony, his trial shall be by his peers; but on an appeal of felony, which is the suit of the party, he shall be tried by an ordinary jury of twelve men. *S. P. C.* 130. *Sid.* 277. 2 *Inst.* 49. *Stat.* 9 *H.* 3. *c.* 29.

In many cases the protestation of honour shall be sufficient in noblemen; as in trials of peers, they proceed upon their honour, not on oath: and if any peer is a defendant in a court of equity, he shall put in his answer upon his honour (tho' formerly it was to be on oath): and in action of debt upon account, the plaintiff being a peer, it shall suffice to examine his attorney

upon

upon oath, and not himself: tho' where a peer is to make an affidavit, or to be examined as a witness, he must be upon his oath like another person. 9 *Rep.* 49. 3 *Inst.* 29. 2 *Salk.* 512. *Wil. Rep.* 1462. *Mod.* 99. 3 *Keb. Rep.* 631. *Freem. Rep.* 422. *pl.* 566. 16 *Vin. Abr.* 293. *pl.* 3. 4 *Bac. Abr.* 237.

A writ of *subpoena* shall not be awarded against a peer out of Chancery in a cause; but a letter from the lord chancellor in lieu thereof. No *capias* or exigent can be sued out against peers of the realm, in actions of debt or trespass; and no essoin lies against them: in any trial where a peer is plaintiff or defendant, there must be returned on the jury at least * one knight, or it shall be cause of challenge; but peers on the trial of a peer may not be challenged, as jurors may in case of a common person. A peer may not be impanelled upon any inquest, though the cause hath relation to two peers. *Gilb. Chanc.* 65. *Har. Chanc. Pract.* 50. 4 *Bac. Abr.* 237, 238. 2 *Hawk. Pl. Cr. chap.* 43. *f.* 4, 11.

If any person shall divulge or tell false tales of any lord of parliament, by which dissention may happen, or any slander arise, the offender shall be imprisoned, *&c.* and such lord may bring his action of *Scandalum Magnatum* in the name of the king, and in his own name, and recover large damages; and the defendant shall be otherwise punished. *Stat.* 12 *R.* 2. *c.* 11.

* Lord Ch. Just. *Holt* said, the reason a knight was to be on a jury, when a peer was concerned, was for the security of the commons, *for a knight was presumed to be a man of courage, and not afraid to look a peer in the face.* 11 Mod. 102. However this challenge is now taken away by Stat. 24 *Geo.* 2. *c.* 18. *f.* 4.

Of the King and his Prerogative.

No peer can be assessed towards the militia, but by assessment made by six or more peers: and the houses of peers shall not be searched for conventicles, but by warrant under the sign manual, or in the presence of the lord lieutenant of the county, or one deputy lieutenant and two justices of the peace, &c. 9. *H.* 3. 13 & 14 *Car.* 2. *c.* 3.

It was lawful by the Common Law for any peer to retain as many chaplains as he would; but by statute their number is limited, *viz.* a duke to have six chaplains, a marquis or earl five, vicount four, baron, three, &c. *Stat.* 31 *H.* 8. *c.* 10.

Now I come to the officers and ministers of justice under the king, which I shall treat of in the order following:

1. Of the judges of the law.
2. Of sheriffs of counties.
3. Of coroners and their duty.
4. Of justices of the peace.
5. Of constables, &c.

1. A judge is a chief magistrate, in the law, to try civil and criminal causes, and punish offences: and our king hath the nomination and appointment of judges. *Co. Lit.* 56.

The king in all cases doth judge by the judges; and judges are to give sentence according to law, that which by law they know to be right, and what is alledged and proved: a judge ought not to judge in his own cause, or in pleas wherein he is party. *Co. Lit.* 71. 7 *Rep.* 27. *Stat.* 18 *Ed.* 1.

Of the King and his Prerogative.

If a judge is doubtful or mistaken in matter of law, a stander-by may be allowed to inform the court, as *Amicus Curiæ*. But no judge shall generally be excepted against, or challenged, or have any action brought against him for what he does as judge. And to kill a judge of either bench, or of assise, &c. in their places administring justice, is treason: also drawing a weapon only upon a judge in any of the courts of justice, the offender shall lose his right hand, forfeit his lands and goods, and suffer perpetual imprisonment. 2 *Inst.* 178, 422. *Co. Lit.* 294. 25 *Ed.* 3. *c.* 2.

The judges are freed from all prosecutions whatsoever, except in the parliament, where they may be punished for any thing done by them as judges: and there bribery in a judge, which is a very high offence, is punishable by loss of office, fine and imprisonment. If a judge, who hath no jurisdiction of the cause, give judgment of death, and award execution, which is executed, such judge is guilty of felony; and also the officer who executes the sentence. Though judges are not in any way punishable for a meer error of judgment. 12 *Rep.* 24. *Vaugh.* 138. *Cro. Jac.* 65. *H. P. C.* 35. 2 *Hawk.* 4.

Judges of the Common Law have no ordinary jurisdiction to examine witnesses at their chambers; though by consent of parties and rule of court they may on interrogatories; and some things done by judges at their chambers, in order to proceedings in court, are accounted as done by the court. They are to have a paper of the causes which are to be spoken to in court; and where special matter arises upon reading the record of a cause, so that the judges are not for the present satisfied of the law, they order paper-books

Of the King and his Prerogative.

books to be made and delivered them, containing copies of the record, &c. that they may the better consider of the matters in contest. 2 *Lil. Abr.* 90, 91.

Our judges are to execute their offices in proper person, and cannot act by deputy, as the judges of ecclesiastical courts may: yet where there are divers judges of a court of record, the act of every one of them is effectual, especially if their commission do not expresly require more; but what a majority rules when present, is the act of the court. 1 *Roll. Abr.* 382. 2 *Hawk.* 3.

A judge of *B. R.* cannot be made by a writ, but by commission under the great seal; but he may be discharged by writ *sub magno sigillo*: a judge at his creation takes the following oath. 8 *Rep.* 18. 18 *Ed.* 3. *c.* 1.

The oath of a judge *of the law.*

'THE judge swears, that he will well and Stat. 18 Edw.
' truly counsel the king, and take no re- 3. st. 4.
' ward for doing of justice; that he will advise
' no man where the king is party, maintain no
' plea, and deny no man right, but in all things
' execute the laws: that he will administer ju-
' stice and right indifferently to all men; and
' this he shall not forbear or delay to do, though
' the king, under the great seal, or privy seal,
' or by any order or message command the
' contrary, &c. And in such case he shall
' proceed, as if no such writ, order, message,
' or other commandment were come to him:
' and he shall be answerable in body, lands and
' goods.'

2. A sheriff

2. A sheriff is the chief officer, under the king, of a shire or county, for keeping of the peace, and execution and service of writs and processes, &c. At Common Law, sheriffs were chosen by the county, as knights of parliament now are; but by statute, they are to be made by the king; and the chancellor, treasurer and barons of the exchequer, &c. nominate three persons yearly for each county, out of which the king chuses one: and by statute they are to have sufficient lands in the county where chosen, to answer the king and his people. *Stat.* 9 *Ed.* 2. *st.* 2. 14 *Ed.* 3. *c.* 9.

The power of a sheriff is judicial, and ministerial: his judicial authority consists in trying and determining causes in his county courts; and in preserving the peace of the county, he being by the Common Law the principal conservator of the peace there; and he is to assist the justices of peace, and raise the *Posse Comitatus* to suppress riots, &c. Though his judicial power, as conservator of the peace, is seldom used; being commonly executed by justices of peace. His ministerial power relates to executing writs out of the king's courts; and herein he is not to dispute the validity of any writ, but must execute it: for he must not let a person escape, tho' taken on an erroneous process; but shall be excused by reason thereof, in false imprisonment. *Co. Lit.* 174. 2 *Inst.* 193, 452. 5 *Rep.* 64.

Besides their ministerial office to execute process, &c. Sheriffs are to proclaim statutes; return juries, for trials in civil and criminal cases; make returns of writs for electing knights of the shire, &c. And they are to collect the rents of the king, seise profits of lands forfeited, goods of felons, &c. To levy the king's debts, and

Of the King and his Prerogative.

be accountable to the king for all issues and profits of their counties; for which they are to give up their accounts in the exchequer: by statute, sheriffs shall have allowance on their accounts, for executing the king's writs, levying estreats &c. Their accounts shall not be delayed; and 4000 *l.* yearly is set apart at the exchequer, and allowed the sheriffs of the several counties, to help pass their accounts. Also they are to see that criminals be executed, and observe the order of law in putting them to death. *Dr. & Stud. cb.* 41. 23 *H.* 6. *c.* 9. 3 *Geo. c.* 15.

The officers under the sheriff are an under-sheriff, bailiff, gaoler, &c. for whom he is answerable. As to the under sheriff, his power is the same with that of the high sheriff, he acting in his stead: but all returns by the under sheriff are in the name of the high sheriff; the under sheriff is removeable at pleasure, and some say but in nature of a general bailiff errant to the sheriff in the whole county, as other bailiffs are over particular districts. The under sheriff is to file a warrant of attorney for his high sheriff in all the courts of *Westminster*, by an attorney of each court; and ought always to have his deputy attendant in courts, to receive and execute their commands, give account of business, &c. And sheriffs shall not take any money or reward for the places of under-sheriff, gaoler, bailiffs, &c. 4 *Inst.* 114. 2 *Lil. Abr.* 511, 513. *Stat.* 3 *Geo. c.* 15.

If a sheriff do not make a return of writs, or making a false return, he shall be amerced; or the party may bring action of the case against him: sheriffs shall let persons to bail upon reasonable sureties; and where a sheriff takes bail-bond of two good men of visible estates at the
time

time of taking it, if they afterwards become insolvent, the sheriff shall be excused. When any sheriff is chargeable in his life-time for a personal tort; there the action for it dieth with the person; but if a sheriff levies money on a *fieri facias*, and dies, action may be brought against his executors for the money, being a duty: and if an under-sheriff procure goods taken in execution to be appraised at under value, and deliver them to the plaintiff accordingly; for this oppression of the defendant indictment will lie. Sheriffs are not to take above 1 *s.* in the pound where under a 100 *l.* nor more than 6 *d. per* pound if above that, for levying an extent or execution; and 1 *s.* in the pound of the yearly value of lands, for executing a writ of *Habere facias Possessionem*, &c. where the whole exceeds not 100 *l. per Annum*, and 6 *d.* if above. 10 *Rep.* 70. *Cro. Eliz.* 808. *Cro. Car.* 539. *Cro. Jac.* 426. 29 *Eliz. c.* 4. 3 *Geo.* 15.

Sheriffs may not continue in their offices above one year; which also extends to under-sheriffs: and no sheriff is to act as a justice of peace of the county, during his shrievalty; nor an under-sheriff, &c. be attorney in any of the king's courts, so long as he bears the office; though such as are attornies may practice in the name of others. No sheriff, at assize time, shall keep a table for any but those of his own retinue; nor make a present to any judge, &c. or have above forty servants in liveries, or under twenty attending him. On the deaths of sheriffs, under-sheriffs are to act in their names 'till others are appointed, and be answerable. *Stat.* 14 *Ed.* 3. *c.* 7. 42 *Ed.* 3. *c.* 9. 1 *M. c.* 8. 1 *H.* 5. *c.* 4. 13 *&* 14 *Car.* 2. *c.* 21. perpetuated by 1 *Jac.* 2. *c.* 17. *s.* 4. 3 *Geo. stat.* 2. *c.* 15.

The

Of the King and his Prerogative.

The oath of a sheriff *by statute:*

'I *A. B.* do swear, that I will well and truly
' serve the king's majesty, in the office of
' sheriff of the county of, &c. and promote his
' majesty's profit in all things that belong to
' my office, as far as I legally can or may; and
' I will truly preserve the king's rights, and all
' that belong to the crown, and will not assent
' to decrease, lessen or conceal the king's rights,
' or the rights of his franchises; and whensoever
' I shall have knowledge that the rights of the
' crown are concealed or withdrawn, be it in
' lands, rents, franchises, suits or services, or
' in any other matter or thing, I will do my ut-
' most to cause them to be restored to the
' crown; and if I may not do it myself, I will
' certify and inform the king thereof, or some of
' the judges; I will not respite or delay to levy
' the king's debt for any gift, promise, reward,
' or favour, where I may raise the same without
' great grievance to the debtors; I will do right,
' as well to poor as to rich, in all things be-
' longing to my office; I will do no wrong to
' any man for any gift, reward or promise, nor
' for favour or hatred; I will disturb no man's
' right, and will truly and faithfully acquit at
' the *Exchequer,* all those of whom I receive
' any debts or duties belonging to the crown;
' I will take nothing whereby the king may
' lose, or whereby his right may be disturbed,
' injured or delayed; I will truly serve, and
' truly return all the king's writs, according to
' the best of my skill and knowledge; I will
' take no bailiffs into my service, but such as I
' will

'will answer for, and will cause each of them to take the like oaths as I myself do, in what belongs to their business and occupation; I will truly set and return reasonable and due issues of them that be within my bailiwick, according to their estates and circumstances, and make due panels on juries of persons able and sufficient, and not suspected or procured, as is appointed by the statutes of this realm; I have not sold or let to farm, nor contracted for, nor have I granted or promised for reward or benefit, nor will I sell or let to farm, or contract for, or grant for reward or benefit by myself, or any other person for me, or for my use, directly or indirectly, my sheriffwick, or any bailiwick thereof, or any office belonging thereunto, or the profits of the same, to any person or persons whatsoever; I will truly and diligently execute the laws and statutes of this realm; and in all things well and truly behave myself in my office, for the honour of the king, and the good of his subjects, and discharge the same according to the best of my skill and power.'

The *Oath* of an under-sheriff, is to the like purpose, and almost *verbatim* the same with that of the high-sheriff. And the particular sums to be paid the sheriffs of the several counties to bear the expences of the patents for their offices, pass their accounts in the exchequer, and obtain their *Quietus's*, &c. by the Stat. 3 *Geo*. 1. c. 16. are as follow, *viz.*

Allowances

Of the King and his Prerogative.

Allowances *to the sheriffs of counties.*

To the sheriff for the county of *Bedford*, ninety-three pounds and six shillings; for the county of *Berks*, ninety-six pounds; for the county of *Bucks*, ninety-six pounds; for the counties of *Cambridge* and *Huntingdon*, ninety-five pounds and ten shillings; for the county of *Chester*, sixty-two pounds five shillings; for the county of *Cornwall*, one hundred and two pounds and sixteen shillings; for the county of *Cumberland*, ninety pounds and two shillings; for the county of *Derby*, ninety-three pounds and nineteen shillings; for the county of *Devon*, one hundred and six pounds nine shillings; for the county of *Dorset*, one hundred and one pounds six shillings; for the county of *Essex*, one hundred and eight pounds ten shillings; for the county of *Gloucester*, ninety-eight pounds and ten shillings; for the county of *Hereford*, ninety-four pounds and six shillings; for the county of *Hertford*, ninety-three pounds; for the county of *Kent*, one hundred and eight pounds ten shillings; for the county of *Lancaster*, sixty-seven pounds and seven shillings; for the county of *Leicester*, ninety-four pounds and six shillings; for the county of *Lincoln*, one hundred and one pounds and three shillings; for the county of *Middlesex*, one hundred and nineteen pounds three shillings; for the county of *Monmouth*, eighty-nine pounds and three shillings; for the county of *Norfolk*, one hundred and one pounds and fifteen shillings; for the county of *Northampton* ninety-six pounds; for the county of *Northumberland*, ninety one pounds; for the county of *Nottingham*, ninety-five pounds and thirteen shillings; for the county of *Oxon*, ninety-seven pounds seven shillings; for the county of *Rutland*, sixty nine pounds and eleven shillings; for the county of *Salop*, ninety-eight pounds and three shillings: for the county of *Somerset*, one hundred and twelve pounds nineteen shillings; for the county of *Southampton*, one hundred and one pounds and three shillings; for the county of *Stafford*, ninety five pounds and ten shillings; for the county of *Suffolk*, one hundred and two pounds twelve shillings; for the county of *Surrey*, ninety pounds and two shillings; for the county of *Sussex*, ninety pounds and five shillings; for the county of *Warwick*, ninety-three pounds and ten shillings; for the county of *Wilts*, one hundred and four pounds and ten shillings; for the county of *Worcester*, ninety-eight pounds and three shillings; for the county of *York*, one hundred and fifty pounds; for all the twelve counties of *Wales*, thirty pounds each: and for the county of *Westmoreland*, forty pounds six shillings.

3. A coroner is an ancient officer of this realm, that deals wholly for the king and crown. There are generally four coroners in a county; in some counties fewer, and in some but one, according to usage: and they are elected at the county court, in full county, by the freeholders, upon the king's writ.

Coroners are to be men of good ability, and have lands in fee in the county where chosen, to answer all people; and if insufficient, the county shall answer for them: there are also special coroners, within divers liberties, as well as the ordinary officers in every county; as the coroner of *the Verge*, which is a certain compass about the king's court, &c. and some corporations

Of the King and his Prerogative.

tions and colleges are licensed by charter to appoint their coroners within their own precincts. 2 *Inst.* 174. 4 *Inst.* 271.

Their authority, like that of sheriffs, is judicial and ministerial; judicial, where one comes to a violent death, and to take and enter appeals of murder, pronounce judgment upon outlawries, &c. And they are to inquire of the lands and goods and escapes of murderers; of treasure trove, wreck of the sea, * deodands. &c. The ministerial authority is where coroners execute the king's writs, on exception to the sheriff, as being party to a suit, kin to either of the parties, and on default of the sheriff, &c. And as ministers, coroners must all join in their acts; but as judges, they may divide and act separate. On the defaults of sheriffs, coroners are to impanel juries; and in case of two coroners, if one is challenged, the other may execute the writ, &c. yet both make but one officer. 4 *Inst.* 271. 4 *Rep.* 79. 9 *Rep.* 11, 93. *Lev.* 399. *Salk.* 144.

As the sheriff in his turn might inquire of all felonies by the Common Law, saving the death of a man; so the coroner can inquire of no felony but of the death of a person, and that *super visum corporis*. When the coroner hath notice given him of a person slain, or suddenly dead, he is to go to the place where, and shall by his warrant to the bailiffs, constables, &c. summon a jury out of the four or five neighbouring towns or villages, to make inquiry upon view of the body; and the coroner and jury are to inquire into the manner of killing, and all circumstances

---

* Not much countenanced in *Westminster* hall. *Foss. Cr. Law* 165, 166.

that occasioned the party's death; as who were present, whether the dead person was known, where he lay the night before, &c. and examine the body, if there be any signs of strangling about the neck, or of cords about the members, &c. Also all wounds must be viewed, and inquiry made with what weapons given. *Stat.* 4 *Ed. st.* 2. 4 *Inst.* 271.

And to discover the truth, the coroner may send his warrant for witnesses, and take their examination in writing; and if any appear guilty of the murder, he shall inquire what goods and lands he hath, and then the dead body is to be buried: a coroner may likewise commit the person to prison, who is by his inquisition found guilty of the murder; and the witnesses are to be bound by recognizance to appear at the next assizes, &c. When the jury have brought in the verdict, the coroner is to inrol and return the inquisition, whether it be of murder, manslaughter, &c. to the justices of the next gaol-delivery of the county; or certify it unto *B. R.* where the murderer shall be proceeded against. If a coroner doth not come to inquire, having notice of the death of any person, he may be fined and imprisoned by the justices; and he shall be fined and imprisoned for not certifying his recognizances, and the evidence and inquisition taken before him, to the court where they ought. 2 *Rol. Abr.* 32. *Cro. Eliz.* 135. *Stat.* 1 & 2 *P. & M. c.* 13.

The coroner is to sit on the body of every prisoner that dies in prison, and inquire if he died by the duress and ill usage of the gaoler, which is murder: and the coroner's inquisition being final, he ought to hear counsel, and evidence on both sides. If the body of a dead person is buried before

before the coroner comes, he may in convenient time take up the same, in order to view it, and in such case the town shall be amerced; as it shall be if the body is suffered to lie so long that it stinks, or cannot be judged how it came by his death, &c. A coroner may find any nusance by which the death of a man happens: and the township may be amerced: if one is slain in the day-time, and the murderer escapes, the town where done shall be amerced, and the coroner is to inquire thereof on view of the body. 3 *Inst.* 91. *Bro. Coren.* 167. 2 *Danv. Abr.* 209. *Nels. Abr.* 536. *Stat.* 3 *Hen.* 7. *c.* 1.

If a body is drown'd, and cannot be found to be viewed, the inquisition must be taken by justices of the peace, on examination of witnesses, &c. A coroner's inquest may be quashed, whereupon he is to make a new one; and for mismanagement of the coroner, filing of the inquisition may be stopp'd: if he hath been guilty of bribery, &c. Commissioners may be ordered to take a new inquisition, on the testimony of witnesses. By statute, coroners concealing felonies, &c. are to be fined, and suffer one year's imprisonment: they shall not take above 13 *s.* 4 *d.* fee, of the goods of the murderer, or out of the amercement of the vill for the escape, if he be gone; and where a person is slain by misadventure, the coroner is to take no fee, on pain of 40 *s.* 9 *Rep.* 110. *Mod. Rep.* 82. 3 *H.* 7. *c.* 1. 1 *Hen.* 8. *c.* 7. and see now *Stat.* 25 *Geo.* 2. *c.* 29. concerning his fees and punishment.

The oath of a coroner *administred by the sheriff.*

'YOU shall swear, that you will well and
'truly serve our sovereign lord the king
'and his people in the office of a coroner, and
'as one of his majesty's coroners for this county
'of *S.* and therein you shall diligently and faith-
'fully do and execute all and every thing and
'things belonging to your said office, according
'to the best of your knowledge and power, both
'for the king's profit and the good of the peo-
'ple within the said county; according to the
'direction of the statutes, or acts of parliament
'in that case made; taking such fees as you
'ought, and without taking any bribes or fees
'more than the said acts do allow.'

So help you God.

4. A justice of peace is a person appointed by the king's commission to keep the peace of the county where he dwells; but these persons are rather commissioners of the peace, of whom some of the greatest quality are of the *Quorum*, because business of importance cannot be done without the presence of one of them.

And a justice of the peace is a judge of record, for he may take a recognizance of the peace, which none but a judge of record can do; and hence they are called justices, being before the 1 *Ed.* 3. called conservators of the peace. The power of appointing justices of peace is only in the king, tho' they are generally made at the discre-

discretion of the lord chancellor, by the king's leave; and the king may appoint in every county of *England* as many as he shall think fit. *Dalt. Just.* 8. *Lamb.* 186.

The general commission of the peace, by statute, began 1 *Ed.* 3. tho' before that time there were conservators and particular commissioners of the peace in certain places, but no commission throughout *England*: at first the number of justices was not above three or four in a county; afterwards they were limited to six in every county, whereof two were to be knights, and two men of the law. But by stat. 14 *R.* 2. *c.* 11. eight justices of peace were to be assigned in every county; and the number of justices has greatly increased since their first institution, they being now without limitation. *Co. Lit.* 174. *Dalt. c.* 5. 1 *Ed.* 3. *c.* 16.

Justices of peace are to be resident in the county where appointed; and to keep their sessions four times a year, *viz.* the first week after *Michaelmas*, the *Epiphany*, *Easter*, and S*t. Thomas* the martyr, called *Becket*. They are to be the most sufficient persons within the county, and of the best reputation; and they must have certain estates in lands to qualify them: no steward of any lord shall be in the commission of peace. And justices of the peace were formerly to be allowed 4 *s.* a day during their attendance at the quarter-sessions, to be paid by the sheriffs of counties, &c. Now the qualification of justices is 100 *l.* a year estate, freehold or copyhold, in possession for life, or greater estate, or certain term of twenty-one years, above incumbrances; or acting as justices shall forfeit 100 *l.* And attornies, &c. are incapable to be justices of peace.

Stat.

Stat. 2 H. 5. st. 1. c. 4. 18 H. 6. c. 11. 13 R. 2. c. 11. 5 Geo. 2. c. 18. 18 Geo. 2. c. 20.

By virtue of one *Assignavimus*, or clause in their commission, every justice of peace hath a separate power, and may do all acts concerning his office apart and by himself; and even may commit a fellow justice upon treason, felony or breach of the peace: and this is the ancient power which conservators of the peace had at Common Law: but it has been held, that one justice of peace cannot commit another justice, for breach of the peace; though the justices in sessions may do it. By virtue of another *Assignavimus*, or clause in the commission, two or more justices of the peace (one of the *Quorum*) have a joint power to inquire by jury of all offences mentioned in their commission; to take indictments, grant process, &c. and to hear and try the offences, which are matters to be transacted at the quarter sessions: and by the statutes, in many cases they are empowered to act where their commission doth not reach, the statutes themselves being a sufficient commission. *Lamb. Just.* 385. *Jenk. Cent.* 174. *Wood's Inst.* 80.

The statutes of [*] 4 *Hen.* 7. c. 12. 33 *Hen.* 8. c. 10. and 37 *H.* 8. c. 7. give a further general power to justices of peace, than is expressed either in their commission or any particular statute. The particular statutes are to be executed as they direct; wherein if no express power is given to any one justice, he can admonish only; and if not obeyed, may make presentment of the offence upon the statute, and with his fellow justices hear and determine it in sessions; or he may bind the offender to the peace, or the good

---

[*] *Qu.* If in force since the death of king *Henry* 7.

Of the King and his Prerogative.

behaviour: some statutes impower one justice of peace alone to act; some require two, three or four justices, &c. And where a special authority is given to justices of peace, it must be exactly pursued; or the acts of the justices will not be good. 2 *Salk.* 475.

A justice of peace has no need to shew his commission, when he justifieth the doing things as a justice; for the commission remains with the *Custos Rotulorum* of the county, and he is called by commission in open assise, or sessions. Where the statutes refer a trial to the justice's discretion, it is said he may examine upon oath: and in some cases the testimony of a justice of peace is of as great force, and sometimes greater than an indictment of twelve men on oath, *viz.* in case of presentment of highways, force and riots. A justice certifying into the *King's Bench*, that such a one broke the peace in his presence, the party shall be put to his fine, without a traverse to the same. *Crompt.* 120, 132. *Lamb.* 387. *Dalt.* 9.

Justices in their sessions, might originally hear and determine felonies; but they at this time only try petty larcenies, other felonies being of course tried at the assises: but out of sessions they commit all felons in order to trial; and it is incident to the office of justices of peace, to commit offenders; they also bind over prosecutors, to the assises, take and certify examinations and informations, recognizances, &c. and if they neglect their duty herein, they shall be fined. A justice may commit a person that doth a felony in his own view, without warrant; but if it be on the information of another, he must make a warrant under hand and seal for that purpose: and if a justice issues his warrant to arrest a felon, tho'

Of the King and his Prerogative.

tho' the accusation be false, the justice is excused where a felony is committed; but in case there be no accusation, action will lie against the justice. *Dalt. c.* 11. 2 *Leon.* 187.

Where a justice of peace acts to compel another to perform any thing required by law, as if he commands one to be imprisoned, &c. he cannot act out of the jurisdiction of his county; but he may take informations any where, to prove offences in the county where committed, and he principally resides, or take a recognizance to prosecute. Justices have a discretionary power of binding to the good behaviour, on breaches of the peace, &c. and may require recognizance with great penalty of a dangerous person, for keeping the peace; and for default of sureties, they may be committed to prison: but a man giving security in the court of *B. R.* may have a *Supersedeas* to the justices; so on giving it to other justices, &c. *Cro. Car.* 213. 2 *Lil. Abr.* 131.

Surety of the peace, and binding to the good behaviour, a justice may grant at the request of any person, or demand, *ex officio:* when granted on request of another, he that demands it is to make oath of blows given, or that he goes in fear of his life, or some bodily harm, &c. And persons doing any thing tending to the breach of the peace, by affrays, assaults, fighting or quarrelling, barretors, rioters, &c. may be required to enter into recognizances with sureties to keep the peace, and be of the good behaviour; so persons of ill fame and suspected to break the peace, and who live a scandalous life, by frequenting gaming-houses, &c. Night-walkers, common drunkards, common whores, cheats, those that live idly, &c. But misbehaviours must

relate

relate to the publick peace; and abusive language, as calling one rogue, rascal, lyar, &c. are not breaches of it. *Dalt.* 263, 268, 292. 4 *Inst.* 191.

If one makes an assault upon a justice, he may apprehend the offender, and send him to a gaol till he finds sureties for the peace: and where a man abuseth a justice by words before his face or behind his back, in relation to his office, he may be bound to the good behaviour; and if the justice of peace be abused in the execution of his office, the offender may be indicted and fined. To say of a justice of peace, he doth not understand law, &c. is indictable; and contempts against justices are punishable by indictment and fine at the sessions. *Cromp.* 149. 4 *Rep.* 16. 3 *Mod.* 139.

Justices have power to grant warrants to bring persons before them; for arresting and apprehending criminals; levying penalties on offenders against statutes; and making commitments, &c. And if complaint and oath be made by a person of goods stolen, and that he suspects they are in such a house, and shews the cause of his suspicion; the justice of peace may grant his warrant to a constable, &c. to search in the place suspected, and to attach the goods and party in whose custody they are found, and bring them before him or some other justice to give an account how he came by them, and further to abide such order as to law appertains: but a general warrant to search all places, is not safe or strictly lawful. 2 *Hale's Hist. P. C.* 113, 114.

A justice may make a warrant to bring a person before him only, and it will be good; though it is usual to bring offenders before him, or any other justice of the county, &c. If a justice

grants

Of the King and his Prerogative.

grants any warrant beyond his authority, the officer must obey; but not if it be where the justice hath no authority; justices may not intermeddle with property; if they do, it is actionable. But justices of peace may make and persuade an agreement in petty quarrels and breaches of the peace, where the king is not intitled to a fine: though they may not compound offences, or take money for making agreements. 5 *Reg.* 60. *Noy* 103. 3 *Salk.* 217.

Justices shall not be regularly punished for any thing done by them in sessions as judges: and if a justice of peace be sued for any thing done in his office, he may plead the general issue, and give the special matter in evidence; and if a verdict goes for him, or the plaintiff be nonsuit, he shall have double costs. Though justices of peace may be indicted for taking money, or any corrupt practice: and if a justice of peace is guilty of any misdemeanor in his office, information lies against him in *B. R.* where he shall be punished by fine and imprisonment. Also for contempt of laws, &c. Attachment may be had against justices of peace out of the King's Bench, on motion of the attorney-general, &c. *Stat.* 21 *Jac.* 6 12. *Keb.* 727. *Sid.* 192. 24 *Geo.* 2. *c.* 44.

The particular power of justices by the statutes relates to alehouses, apprentices, artificers, badgers, bail, bakers, bankrupts, bastards, behaviour, brewers, bricks, and tiles, bridges, buggery, burglary, burials, burning of houses, butchers, callico, candles, carriers, *certiorari's*, church and church-wardens, clipping and coining, clothiers, coals, coffee, constables, conventicles, corn, cottages, county-court, curriers, customs, deer-stealers, dissenters, distillers, drunkenness, dyers,

Of the King and his Prerogative.

dyers, excise, false tokens, felony, fish, forcible entry, forestallers, fuel, game and gaming, gaols, goldsmiths, gunpowder, hackney coaches, hawkers and pedlars, hay, hedge-breakers, highways, hops, horse-stealing, houses of correction, hue and cry, informers, juries, labourers, leather, lights, Lord's day, lotteries, malt, nonconformists, oaths, papists, parliament, perjury, pewter, plague, poor, post-letters, purveyance, quakers, rapes, recognizances, recusance, religion, riots, robbery, sacrament, salt, scavengers, schoolmasters, seamen, servant, sewers, ships, shoemakers, silkthrowers, soldiers, squibs, stamp duty, swearing, taxes, taylors, tithes, tobacco, treason, trophy money, vagrants, victuallers, wages, warrants, watch, watermen, weights and measures, windows, wine, woodstealers, wool, wrecks, &c. See *Burn's Justice.*

And there are justices of peace within liberties, who are such in *Cities,* and other *Corporate Towns,* as the others are for the county; and their authority is all one within their several territories and precincts, having besides, the assise of ale and beer, wood, victuals, &c. 27 *H.* 8. c. 25.

But the king, notwithstanding his charter to the mayor and others to be justices of peace within a city, may grant a commission of the peace especially in that city or county, to have jurisdiction with the justices by charter: and if all the justices of a corporation are concerned in a force, and will not inquire thereof, the next justices of the county shall do it; for the denying it, is a forfeiture of their exemption from the county. 2 *Hale's Hist. P. C.* 47. 6 *Mod.* 164.

If a justice dwell in any city, which is a county of itself within the county at large, he may grant warrants, &c. at his dwelling-house, though out of his county for which he is a justice. The judgments of justices of peace in their sessions, shall not be removed into *B. R.* without entering into recognizance of 50 *l.* to prosecute with effect, and pay costs if affirmed. 9 *Geo.* c. 7. 5 *Geo.* 2. c. 19.

The oath of a justice of peace.

'YOU shall swear, That in the office of a
' justice of peace, in and for the county
' of, &c. in all and every the articles in his
' majesty's commission, enjoined and to you di-
' rected, you will do equal right to the rich and
' poor, according to your knowledge, and the
' laws and statutes of this realm; you shall not
' be counsel to any person, in any quarrel de-
' pending before you; you shall hold your ses-
' sions according to the directions of the statutes
' in that case made; and you shall cause to be
' entered the issues, fines and amercements that
' shall happen to be made, and all forfeitures,
' without any concealment, and send an account
' of them to the king's exchequer; you shall not
' spare any one for gift or other cause, nor take
' any thing for doing the business of your of-
' fice, but the fees and allowances accustomed,
' and fixt by acts of parliament, &c. and in all
' things you shall well and truly do and execute
' the office of a justice of peace.'

So help you God.

5. A con-

5. A constable is an officer over a hundred or in a parish, for preservation of the peace; there being two sorts of these officers, high constables, and petty constables.

The statute of *Winchester*, 13 *Ed.* 1. *c.* 6. appoints for conservation of the peace, two constables in every hundred, called high constables; and continuance of time, and increase of people and offences, hath under these made others necessary in every town, called petty constables; which are of like nature, but of inferior authority to the others, and are as it were assistants to them: also there are other officers in towns and parishes, as headboroughs, tithingmen, &c. and where there is no constable, their duty is the same; but they seem generally to be for particular boroughs, tithings and villages. *Dalt.* 3.

It is said, constables were conservators of the peace before justices of peace were made; but some of our law books mention that constables were only subordinate officers to the conservators of the peace, as they are now to the justices. In places where headboroughs are appointed, they are a kind of constables, though constables are the principal officers; and there are some things which a constable has power to do, that headboroughs and tithingmen cannot intermeddle with: indeed in the absence of the constable, they are chiefly to attend the service of the office; and in a town or parish, having no other parish officer, the tithingman, &c. is in effect the constable of the place. *Dalt.* 3. *Owen* 105.

Anciently high and petty constables were appointed by the sheriff in his tourn, and sworn there, as well as in the leet: a constable of common right is to be chosen by the jury in the

court-

court-leet; and if he be present, and refuse to be sworn in his office, the steward may fine him: if he is absent when elected, he shall be sworn before justices of peace; and then if such constable refuse to be sworn, and to take upon him the office, the homage must present his refusal at the next court, and there he shall be amerced. At the court-leet a high constable may be chosen by the steward, on presentment of the jury, where custom warrants it: but where such courts are not kept, or there is a neglect in chusing him, the justices at their quarter-sessions may chuse and swear a high constable: and he may be sworn out of sessions, by warrant from thence. *Salk.* 175.

If constables, headboroughs, &c. die, or go out of the parish, or in case of refusal to serve the office, two justices of peace are to swear new ones, 'till the lord of the manor hold a court-leet, or until the next quarter-sessions, and then the steward or justices may either approve of them, or appoint others to continue in for one year; and if any of them continue above a year, the justices of peace may discharge them, and put in others until the lord of the manor holds a court. *Stat.* 13 & 14 *Car.* 2. *c.* 12.

All constables are appointed yearly: the high constables are now generally chosen and sworn by the justices at their sessions; and petty constables and tithingmen, in each town, parish or vill, and choice of them properly belongs to the court-leet; but they may be elected by the parishioners, and sworn by a justice, &c. who on just cause may remove them. A village having no constable, the justices of peace, by order of sessions, appointed one to serve there; for justices

Of the King and his Prerogative.

stices have always exercised a power of appointing constables: and they are officers to the justices of peace, as the sheriff is to the court of King's Bench. 4 *Inst.* 267. *Salk.* 175, 176.

The persons elected to this office ought to be men of honesty, knowledge and ability; not infants, lunaticks, &c. and they are to be men of substance, and not of the meaner sort, also shall be resident where chosen; and if they be not thus qualified, upon complaint, two justices may appoint other persons. But physicians, apothecaries, &c. are excused by statute from bearing the office of constable, or other parish offices; and justices of peace, attornies and officers of the courts at *Westminster*, barristers at law, &c. are privileged from serving this office; and poor, old, sick and decrepit persons, are exempted from it. 8 *Rep.* 41. 5 *Mod.* 96. 2 *Hawk. P. C.* 63.

A constable may make a deputy; but the constable is answerable for him, and the deputy must be sworn: and constables may appoint a deputy, or person to execute a warrant, when by reason of sickness, &c. they cannot do it themselves. Dissenters chosen to the office of a constable, &c. scrupling to take the oaths, are to make deputies for the execution of the office, who shall comply with the law in this behalf: and a woman made constable, by virtue of a custom, that the inhabitants of a town shall serve by turns, on account of their estates or houses, may hire one to execute the office for her, and the custom is good. *Sid.* 355. 2 *Hawk.* 63. 1 *W. & M. c.* 18.

The office of *High Constable* consists in these things: he hath the direction of the petty constables,

stables, headboroughs and tithingmen within his hundred. In general, his duty is to keep the peace, and apprehend felons, rioters, &c. He is to make hue and cry after felons, and take care that the watch be duly kept in his hundred; and that the statutes for punishing rogues and vagrants be put in execution. He ought to present unlawful gaming, tippling and drunkenness, bloodshed, affrays, &c. He is to execute warrants and precepts directed to him by justices of the peace; and make returns to the sessions of the justices to all the articles contained in his oath, or that concern his office: and he is to issue his precept to the petty constables, to make presentments of offences, and cause them to make their returns; also to prepare lists of jurors, levy gaol-money, &c. *Dalt. c.* 28.

He shall return all victuallers and alehouse-keepers that are unlicensed; and such persons as entertain inmates in houses, who are likely to be chargeable to parishes: he must present the defaults of petty constables, headboroughs, &c. that neglect to apprehend rogues, vagrants and idle persons, whores, night-walkers, mothers of bastard children like to be a charge to their parishes, &c. And also all defects of highways and bridges, and the names of those who ought to repair them; scavengers that neglect their duty; and all common nusances in streets and highways; bakers who sell their bread under weight; brewers selling beer to unlicensed alehouses or victualling-houses; forestallers of markets, ingrossers and regrators, &c. At every quarter-sessions high constables are to pay to the collectors appointed, and the treasurer of the county, all such money as hath been levied and received by them of the churchwardens of parishes

rishes for the relief of the poor in prisons and hospitals, &c. *Dalt.* 28. *Lamb.* 125. *Stat.* 43 *Eliz. c.* 2.

By an old statute, the high constable may determine complaints of clothiers and their spinners, and other labourers relating to not paying wages in ready money, &c. which is liable to a forfeiture of three times the value of the wages; and he may enter into any place to search for tenters and ropes, &c. for stretching of cloth; and if he finds any, he may seize and deface them, &c. And persons resisting the constable, to forfeit 10 *l. Stat.* 4 *Ed.* 4. *c.* 9. 39 *Eliz. c.* 20.

The duty and office of *Petty Constables*, in their several towns, parishes, &c. is generally much the same as the high constable's in his hundred: these officers are to keep the peace; and as conservators thereof, they may command affrayers to depart, &c. and not ceasing, but making resistance may put them in the stocks, 'till they can carry them before some justice, or to the gaol; and may break into a house to see the peace kept; make fresh pursuit into another county, &c. They may command all persons to assist them, to prevent a breach of the peace; justify beating another, if assaulted; and if they happen to be killed doing their duty, it will be taken to be premeditated murder: they may without any warrant from a justice of peace, take into custody any persons whom they see committing a felony, or breach of the peace; though if it be out of their sight, as where a person is seized by another, &c. they may not do it without a justice's warrant. And a constable cannot detain a man at his pleasure, but only stay him to bring him before a justice, to be examined and committed

mitted, &c. *Dalt. c.* 1, 8. *Lamb.* 126, 141. *II. P. C.* 135. 8 *Leon.* 307.

If any offence be done, for which the constable may arrest without warrant, he may convey the offender to the sheriff or gaoler of the county; and a constable by his original authority, for breach of the peace, and some misdemeanors that are not felony, may imprison a man. But 'tis safest and best, to bring offenders to a justice, who, as the cause shall require, will either bail or commit them to prison. Constables may not lawfully take up night-walkers, on bare suspicion only of their being of ill fame; if they are not found breaking the peace, or doing some unlawful act, &c. And in *London* they ought to be cautious, what persons they send to the compter, taken up at night, for fear of actions for false imprisonment. 2 *Hale's Hist. Pl. C.* 88, 89, 90.

One part of the office of constables is attendance upon justices of assize, justices of peace at their general and special sessions, and other meetings, to execute warrants, and present offences upon oath; and they must attend at courts-leet, and on coroners, for executing warrants, &c. Petty constables are to execute the warrants of justices, and not dispute it where the justice hath jurisdiction and the warrant is lawful: and being sworn officers, they need not shew their warrants when they come to arrest any one. But if the justice's warrant doth not set forth the special matter therein, it is unlawful; and if a justice of peace sends a warrant to a constable to take up one for slander, &c. the justice having no jurisdiction in such cases, the constable ought not to execute it; if he does, he is liable to an action

of

of false imprisonment. 10 *Rep.* 67. 2 *Inst.* 297. 2 *Danv. Abr.* 148.

As the constable is the proper officer to a justice of peace, and bound to execute his lawful warrant; if a warrant be directed to any constable by name, commanding him to execute the same, though he is not compellable to go out of his own parish, yet he may if he will, and execute it in any place in the county, and shall be justified by the warrant for his so doing; but if the warrant is directed to all constables, &c. generally, no constable can make execution of it out of his precinct. *Salk.* 175.

By warrant from a justice, a constable shall sell the goods of an offender apprehended to discharge the expence of carrying him to gaol: if he hath no goods, then the town where he was taken, must be at the expence, and the constable, with three or four of the principal inhabitants, may impose a tax on every inhabitant, &c. which being allowed by a justice of peace, the constable by his warrant may levy it: and if the inhabitants refuse to make a *Rate*, two justices may by their warrant compel them to it. *Stat.* 3 *Jac. c.* 10.

Constables, headboroughs, &c. having laid out money in their offices, they and the inhabitants may tax all persons chargeable by the 43 *Eliz. c.* 2. concerning the poor, as every occupier of land, &c. which rate being confirmed by two justices, the constables may levy it by distress and sale of goods, &c. Constables sued may plead the general issue, and give the special matter in evidence, for any thing done in their offices. And if a constable doth not his duty, he may be indicted and fined by the justice of peace.

21 Jac. c. 12. 13 & 14 Car. 2. c. 12. 24 Geo. 2. c. 44.

And the duty of constables under particular heads, extends to affrays, alehouses, arms, arrests, artificers, bakers, bastardy, bawdy-houses, bridges, butter, buttons, carriages, cattle, clothiers, coals, conventicles, customs, deer-stealing, deserters, distillers, distress, drunkenness, dyers, escapes, excise, felons, fish, forcible entry, forestallers, game, gaming, gaol and gaolers, gunpowder, hawkers, hay-market, hedge-breakers, highways, horses, hue and cry, inns, juries, labourers, land-tax, malsters, measurers, militia, night-walkers, orchards robbed, physicians, plague, popish recusants, post-letters, presentments, prisons, prisoners, riots, rogues, robbery, sabbath, servants, shoemakers, soldiers, swearing, taylors, tithes, tobacco, vagrants, watch, warrants, weights, wreck, &c.

Under all which heads above, the constable's business is chiefly in serving warrants, making commitments, and levying penalties, &c. by order of justices.

There is a long form of a constable's oath in *Dalton*, which is adopted by Mr. *Barlow*, expressing his duty in many instances; but as that form nevertheless doth not contain the hundredth part of the constable's duty, nor indeed the most material instances thereof, it may be more eligible (as no particular form is directed by any statute) to swear him to the due execution of his office in general, than to descend to those particulars; lest by mentioning some parts of his duty, and not others, he may be induced to think, that those others are not so necessary. *Burn's Just.* q10. 256. pl. 11.

Constable's Oath.

'YOU shall well and truly serve our sovereign lord the king, (and the lord of this leet, if sworn in a couet-leet) in the office of constable, for the township of   for the year ensuing (or, until you shall be lawfully discharged therefrom; or, until another shall be sworn in your place.) You shall well and truly do and execute all things belonging to the said office, according to the best of your skill and knowledge.'

So help you God.   *Burn 263.*

The ancient oath *of a* petty constable, *&c.*

'YOU shall swear, that you will well and truly execute the office of a petty constable, (tithingman or headborough) of and for the parish of, *&c.* His Majesty's peace you shall keep, and see it kept by others, as much as in you lieth; in the presence of the high constable, you shall be aiding and assisting to him; and in his absence you shall exercise his office, according to your power and knowledge, 'till another be chosen in your place, or you be legally discharged.'

So help you God.

Of publick Offences committed against the King and the People, and their Punishment.

AN offence is a crime or fault laid to a man's charge, which may affect the life, fortune or poffeffions of another; or it is an act committed againft a law, and punifhable by it: and offences are various and many; but the moft common and publick ones are thefe,

Crimes.
1. High treafon.
2. Petit treafon.
3. Murder.
4. Felony.
5. Burglary.
6. Robbery.
7. Rape.
8. Sodomy.
9. Forgery.
10. Perjury, &c.

Treafon is defined to be an offence committed againft the fecurity of the king and kingdom: at common law there were different opinions concerning high treafon, and before the ftatute 25 *Ed.* 3. it was a very uncertain crime; for the killing of the king's brother, or even his meffenger, was taken to be included in it; fo when acts tending to diminifh the dignity of the crown, and where a man grew popular, this was conftrued to be incroaching royal power, and held to be treafon: but fince the making that act there can be no conftructive treafon. *Hawk. Pl. Cr.* 34.

The treasons by the above-mentioned statute I shall divide into,

1. High treason against the king and queen's person, &c. and the crown. See *Fost. Cr. Law* 193.
2. Treason in levying war against the king in his realm. *Id.* 208.
3. By adhering to the king's enemies, within the realm, or aiding them elsewhere.
4. In violating or deflowering the queen, or the king's eldest daughter.
5. By counterfeiting the king's great or privy seal, or his money.

1. By the statute 25 *Ed.* 3. *st.* 5. *c.* 2. To compass or imagine the death of the king, queen, or their eldest son and heir, is high treason: though it must be manifested by some overt act; as by providing arms to do it, consulting to levy war against him, writing letters to excite others to join therein, assembling persons in order to imprison or depose the king, or to get him into their power, &c. these acts are sufficient to prove that one compassed or imagined the death of the king, and to make a man guilty of high treason. 3 *Inst.* 6, 12.

It was formerly held that compassing by bare words, is not an overt-act to make this crime treason; but it hath been adjudged, that words are an overt act: such deliberate words as shew a direct purpose against the king's life, will amount to an overt act of compassing or imagining the king's death; for as the compassing or imagining the death of the king is the treason, words are the most natural way of expressing the imagination of the heart, and may be good evidence of it: and any external act, which may be a manifestation of such imagination, is an overt-act. But if words are set down in writing, and kept privately in a man's closet, they are no overt-act of treason, except the words are published. *Cro. Car.* 242. *Hawk. P. C.* 40, 41. *Kel.* 20.

Words of persuasion to kill the king, are overt-acts of compassing his death; and it is held, that he who intendeth by force to prescribe laws to the king, and to restrain him of his power, doth intend to deprive him of his crown and life; that if a man be ignorant of the intention of those who take up arms against the king, if he joins in any action with them, he is guilty of treason: and that the law judges every rebellion to be a plot against the king's life, and a deposing him; because a rebel would not suffer that king to reign and live, who will punish him for rebellion. *Moor* 620.

Under the head of compassing and imagining the king's death, intention of treason proved by circumstances is punished as high treason; and men's actions are governed by their intentions, &c. 5 *Mod.* 206.

2. To levy war against the king in his realm is high treason, by the statute of *Ed.* III. and was so at common law. But, as, in cases of treason, there must be an overt-act; a conspiracy or compassing to levy war is no overt-act, unless a war is actually levied; though if a war be levied, then the conspirators are all traitors, although they are not in arms: and a conspiracy to levy war, will be evidence of an overt-act for compassing the king's death; but if the charge in an indictment be for levying war only, it must be proved that a war was levied, to bring

the

the offender under this clause of the statute. 3 *Inst.* 8, 9. *H. P. C.* 14.

Persons raising forces for any publick end or purpose, and putting themselves in a posture of war, by chusing leaders, and resisting constables, or the guards, &c. is high treason: and those who make an insurrection in order to redress a publick grievance, whether it be a real or pretended one, are said to levy war against the king, though they have no direct design against his person. Where great numbers by force endeavour to remove certain persons from the king, or to lay violent hands on a privy counsellor, or revenge themselves against a magistrate for executing his office; or to deliver men out of prison or reform religion, or the law, to pull down all bawdy houses, or throw down all inclosures in general, &c. these acts will be high treason: but where a number of men rise to remove a grievance to their private interest; as to pull down a particular inclosure, &c. they are only rioters. *Sid.* 358. 5 *Inst.* 9. *Kel.* 75. *Hawk. Pl. Cr.* 37.

If two or more conspire to levy war, and one of them alone raises forces; this shall be adjudged treason in all. And not only such as directly rebel and take up arms against the king; but also those who in a violent manner withstand his lawful authority, or attempt a reformation of his government, do levy war against him: and therefore to hold a fort or castle against the king's forces; to keep together armed men in great numbers, against the king's express commands, have been held treason. *Dy.* 98. 3 *Inst.* 10.

But

Of publick Offences.

But, if where a rebellion is broke out, persons join themselves to rebels, &c. for fear of death, and return the first opportunity, they are not guilty of this offence. *Kel.* 76.

3. To adhere to the king's enemies within his realm, or give them aid in the realm, or elsewhere, is treason by the statute: here adherence may be proved by giving the king's enemies comfort or relief, or being in counsel with others to levy any seditious wars; and the delivery or surrender of the king's castles or forts, by the captains thereof, to the king's enemy, within the realm or without, for reward, &c. is an adhering to the king's enemies and high treason by 25 *Ed.* 3.

It has been adjudged, that adhering to the king's enemies is an adhering against him; and this adhering to the enemies of the king out of the realm will be treason: one who was beyond sea, having solicited a foreign prince to invade the kingdom, was held guilty of high treason, and triable by the Stat. 35 *H.* 8. *c.* 2. But adherence out of the realm must be alledged in some place in *England.* 3 Inst. 10. H. P. C. 14. Dyer 298.

Subjects of the king, in open war, or rebellion, are not the king's enemies, but traitors; and if a subject join with a foreign enemy, and come into *England* with him: if he be taken prisoner, he shall not be ransomed, or proceeded against as an enemy, but as a traitor to the king: but an enemy coming in open hostility into this kingdom and taken, shall be either executed by martial law, or ransomed; for he cannot be indicted of treason, because he never was within the allegiance of the king. 3 *Inst.* 11.

When

When one knows that another hath committed treason, and doth not reveal it to the king, or his privy council, or some magistrate, that the offender may be secured, &c. it is high treason by our ancient law: but there must now be an assent to some outward act, to make concealing it treason. *3 Inst.* 138.

4. To violate and deflower the king's wife, or eldest daughter unmarried, or the wife of the king's eldest son, are treason within the statute of king *Edw.* III. Also violating the queen's person, &c. was high treason at common law, because it destroyed the certainty of the king's issue, and consequently raised contention about the succession. *H. P. C.* 16.

Not only violating the queen consort is high treason, but also her yielding and consenting to it is treason in her; but this doth not extend to a queen dowager: so likewise violating the wife of the prince, is treason only during the marriage. And the eldest daughter of the king is such a daughter as is eldest not married at the time of the violation, which will be treason, although there was an elder daughter than her, who died without issue; for now the elder alive has a right to the inheritance of the crown, upon a failure of issue male. *3 Inst.* 9.

The treason against the queen's life, mentioned in the statute, must be also during the coverture; and it extendeth not to a dowager queen. *Ibid.*

5. To counterfeit the king's great seal, privy seal, or his money; or bring false money into this kingdom counterfeited like the money of *England*, to make payment therewith in deceit of the king and his people, these are high treason by the statute of *E*6. 3.

Of publick Offences.

As to counterfeiting the king's seal, it was treason by the common law; and the statute 25 *Ed.* 3. mentions only the great seal and privy seal; for the counterfeiting of the sign manual, or privy signet, is not treason within that act; but by 1 & 2 *P. & M. c.* 11. Those who aid and consent to the counterfeiting of the great seal, are equally guilty with the actors; but an intent or going about to counterfeit the great seal, if it be not actually done, is not treason; there must be an actual counterfeiting, and it is to be like the king's great seal. 3 *Inst.* 15. *H. P. C.* 18.

And the fixing the great seal to a patent, without warrant, or rasing any thing out of a patent, and adding new matter therein; or taking off the wax impressed by the great seal from one patent, and fixing it to another, are not within this law: but here, though this be not a counterfeiting, it has been adjudged a misprision of treason of the highest degree. 3 *Inst.* 16. *Kel.* 80.

At common law, *Forging of the king's money* was treason; as counterfeiting it is by the Stat. 25 *Ed.* 3. And forging or counterfeiting foreign money made current here by proclamation, is likewise high treason by 1 *Mar. sess.* 2. *c.* 6. And as those persons that coin money without the king's authority, are guilty of treason; so are those who have authority to do it, if they make it of greater alloy, or less weight, than they ought. In case of bringing counterfeit money into this kingdom, it must be actually counterfeited, according to the likeness of *English* money, and is to be knowingly brought over from some foreign nation, not from any place subject

Of publick Offences.

ject to the crown of *England*, and must be uttered in payment. 3 *Inst.* 17. *H. P. C.* 20.

All *Trials* for high treason shall be according to the course of the Common Law, and not otherwise: but treasons committed out of the realm, may be tried in *B. R.* as if the offence had been done in the county of *Middlesex*; also they may be inquired of and tried in such county as the king thinks fit, &c. Persons indicted for treason are to have a copy of the indictment five days before trial, to advise with counsel; and shall be admitted to make a full defence, by counsel, witnesses, &c. and there must be two lawful witnesses to the same overt-act, or two acts of the same treason, produced face to face, to make out the treason against them. *Stat.* 35 *H.* 8. *c.* 2. 1 & 2 *P. & M. c.* 10. 7 *W.* 3. *c.* 3. See *Fost. Cro. Law.* 221. touching this act, and Stat. 20 *Geo.* 2. *c.* 30.

Petit Treason is where one out of malice takes away the life of a subject to whom he owes special obedience; and is called petit treason, in respect to high treason, which is against the king: it may be committed where a servant kills his master, a wife her husband, or a secular or religious person killeth his prelate or superior. And aiders, abettors and procurers are within the act: but if the killing is upon a sudden falling out, or *se defendendo*, &c. it is not petit treason. 25 *Ed.* 3. *st.* 5. *c.* 2. 3 *Inst.* 20. *H. P. C.* 24.

This is a crime committed against the head, tho' not against the supreme head; and if a servant kills his mistress, or the wife of his master, she is master within the letter of the statute, and it will be petit treason. A servant intending to kill

kill his master, laid in wait for that purpose while he was his servant, but did not do it 'till he had been a year out of his service; it was adjudged petit treason: and if a servant procure another person to kill his master, and he kills him in the servant's presence; this is petit treason in the servant, and murder in the other; but if the servant be absent, he will be only accessary to the murder. *3 Inst.* 20. *Moor* 91. *H. P. C.* 23.

If a wife and a stranger kill the husband, it is petit treason in the wife, and murder in the stranger: and where a wife and her servant conspire to kill the husband, and the servant alone in the wife's absence killeth him, it shall be petit treason in both. If the wife procure a servant to kill her husband, both are guilty of petit treason; and if a stranger procures a wife or servant to kill the husband or master, he may be indicted as accessary to petit treason. *Dalt.* 337. *Cromp.* 41. *Dyer* 128, 332.

A maid servant and a stranger conspired to rob the mistress, and in the night the servant opened the door, and let in the stranger into the house, who killed her mistress, she lighting him to her bed, but neither saying nor doing any thing, only holding the candle; and this was held murder in the stranger, and petit treason in the servant. *Dyer* 128.

By our law petit treason implies murder, and is the highest degree thereof: and it is said that in petit treason two witnesses are required to the indictment; but not to the trial of it, for it is not within the statute 7 *W.* 3. *c.* 3. 2 *Hawk. Pl. Cr.* 258.

Murder is a wilful and felonious killing of a man upon malice forethought; so as the party wounded

wounded or hurt die within a year and a day: and if one dies in that time, through diforderly living, it fhall be no excufe, the wounds will be judged the principal caufe of his death. 3 *Inft.* 53. *H. P. C.* 55.

There are many ways of committing this crime of murder; as by weapon, poifon, crufhing, bruifing, fmothering, ftrangling, ftarving, &c. which I fhall here treat of under,

1. Murder done out of malice prepenfed. *Foft. Cr. Law* 307.
2. Manflaughter or killing without malice. See *ib.* 290.
3. Homicide or killing juftifiable and excufable.

1. In murder 'tis malice makes the crime; which is either exprefs, where it may be evidently proved there was former ill-will, and the killing is with a fedate mind, and formed defign of doing it; or it is implied by law, when one kills another fuddenly, having nothing to defend himfelf, as going over a ftile, and the like. He who doth a cruel and voluntary act, whereby death enfues, doth it of malice prepenfed and forethought, in the efteem of the law: and if a perfon in cool blood malicioufly and deliberately beats another in fuch a manner, beyond any apparent intent of chaftifement, that he dieth; it is murder by exprefs malice. So where a man executes his revenge, on a fudden provocation, in fuch a cruel manner, with a dangerous weapon, as fhews a malicious intention to do mifchief, and death follows, 'tis malice exprefs from the nature of the fact. 2 *Inft.* 51. *H. P. C.* 47, 49. *Kel.* 64, 127.

Of publick Offences.

If one lays poison to kill a certain person, and another takes it, and dies; or if having malice to a man, strikes or shoots at him, but misseth him and kills another person; these are murder: and by poisoning, and where one killeth another without provocation, malice is implied. If one resolves to kill the next man he meets, and does kill him, it is murder, though he knew him not; here malice is implied against mankind. Where two persons meet and fight on a precedent quarrel, and one is killed; or if a person upon a sudden quarrel appears to be master of his temper, and kills another, it will be murder: for when persons fight after a former quarrel, it shall be presumed to be out of malice; and if two men fall out in the morning and meet and fight in the afternoon, if one of them be killed, this is murder; their after-meeting is of malice. If two persons fight a *duel*, upon some quarrel precedent, and one of them be killed, both principal and seconds are guilty of murder. 3 *Inst.* 51. 52. *Kel.* 27. *Plowd.* 578. *H. P. C.* 51. *Hawk. Pl. Cr.* 81.

A man being provoked by words or gestures, makes a push at a person before his sword is drawn, and thereupon a fight ensues, wherein he who made the assault kills the other, this will be murder; but if he had made no push 'till the other's sword was drawn, it would have been only manslaughter in the person killing. And if one upon a quarrel with another tell him that he will not strike first, but will give such other a pot of ale to strike him, and thereupon the other strikes him, and he kills the other, he is guilty of murder; this being only a covert to his malicious intention. *Kel.* 55, 61. *H. P. C.* 48.

Where

Of publick Offences.

Where a person assaults another with malice, altho' he be afterwards driven by the other to the wall, and kill him there in his own defence, it is murder in respect of his first intent: but if the party assaulted fly to the wall, and being still pursued kills the other, it is only manslaughter in his own defence. If two having malice fight, and the servant of one of them, not knowing of the malice, killeth the other, this is murder in the master, and but manslaughter in the servant; though when there is a conspiracy to kill a man, but no malice against his servant, if the servant be slain, the malice against the master shall be construed to extend to his servant, and killing a man's servant is murder. *H. P. C.* 47. *Kel.* 58, 129. *Dyer* 128.

If two or more persons come together to do any unlawful act, as to beat a person, rob a park, &c. and one of them kills a man, it is murder in all that are present, aiding and assisting, or that were ready to aid and assist: all will be said to intend the murder, and such persons adjudged to be present that are in the same house, though in another room, or in the same park, though half a mile off: when persons are doing an unlawful act, the law presumes malice: and so it is if death happens, where several persons intend only a breach of the peace, &c. 3 *Inst.* 56. *Dalt.* 344. *Kel.* 87, 116, 127.

In case any magistrate or minister of justice is killed in the execution of his office; a sheriff, constable or watchman, in doing of their duty, or any other that comes in aid of the king's officer; and if a watchman be killed in staying of night-walkers, it is said to be murder: and here a person shall not come off by alledging that what he did was in a sudden affray, &c. Also where a bailiff is killed in executing a lawful warrant, it is murder; but if the bailiff doth that which is unwarrantable, as if he break open a door, or window of a house, &c. to make any arrest in a civil case; and where he hath no authority, it is no murder to kill him. *3 Inst.* 51. *Kel.* 60, 128. *H. P. C.* 46. *Cro. Jac.* 280. *Cro. Car.* 372. *Hawk. Pl. Cr.* 84, 86.

Killing a person endeavouring to part others fighting, tho' without any evil intention against him, is murder: and if one who sees a murder committed, doth not his best endeavours to apprehend the murderer, or if where two are fighting and others looking on do not endeavour to part them, if one is killed, the lookers on may be indicted and fined. *5 Inst.* 53. *Noy* 50.

2. Manslaughter is the unlawful killing a man, without any prepensed malice; as when two persons meet, and upon some sudden falling out, the one kills the other. And this crime is felony, but for the first time admits of clergy.

It must be on a sudden quarrel, where the party guilty doth not appear to be master of his temper; by talking calmly upon the quarrel, or afterwards in other discourse, whereby the heat of blood may be presumed to be cooled: therefore if two persons meet together, and in striving for the wall one of them kills the other, this is manslaughter; so it is, if upon a sudden occasion they had gone into the fields and fought, and one had killed the other; for all is one continued act of passion, on the first sudden occasion. *Kel.* 56. *3 Inst.* 51, 54. *H. P. C.* 48.

In manslaughter the killing is to be upon an immediate falling out, or on just provocation; and as to provocations, no trespass, breach of a

man's

man's word, or affront by words, &c. will be thought a just provocation to excuse the killing of another; though if upon ill words, as calling another son of a whore, &c. both the parties suddenly fight, and one of them kill the other, it will be but manslaughter; being done in a present heat. And if one upon angry words assault another, by pulling him by the nose, and he that is assaulted draws his sword, and immediately kills the other party, this is only manslaughter; for the peace was first broken by the party killed, and here an indignity was offered to the slayer, from whence he might apprehend that there might be some farther design against him. If a man is taken in adultery with another person's wife, and the husband presently kills the adulterer; it is a just provocation, and makes it manslaughter. *Kel.* 55, 131, 135. *Hawk. Pl. Cr.* 82. *Ventr.* 158.

If it appears that one hath killed another, it shall be intended that he did it maliciously; unless he can prove the contrary, that he did the fact upon just provocation, *Fost. Cr. Law* 255. And there is a manslaughter punishable as murder by the statute 1 *Jac. c.* 8. which ordains, that if any person shall stab another, not having then a weapon drawn, or not striking first, so that he dies within six months, although it were not of malice or forethought, it is felony without benefit of clergy: but this doth not extend to persons stabbing others by misfortune, &c. with no intent to commit manslaughter; and the act relates to the party only that actually gave the stroke, or stabbed the other, and not to those who were aiding or abetting. *H. P. C.* 58, 266. *H. H. P. C.* 467. *Hawk. Pl. Cr.* 77. *f.* 4. *Gilb. Evid.* 272. *Al.* 43, 44, 47. 2 *H. H. P. C.* 292.

292. *Law Evid.* 277. *pl.* 39. *Kel.* 33, 35. *Bulſtr.* 87. *W. Jones* 220. *Foſt. Cr. Law Diſc.* 2. *chap.* 6. *p.* 297. 7 *Mod.* 133. 2 Ld. *Raym.* 845.

A blow given, or weapon drawn at any time during the quarrel, before the thruſt or ſtab, is within the words of the ſtatute; and drawing out a piſtol, and levying it at the party killing, or throwing a pot, bottle, &c. are within the equity of the words, *having a weapon drawn*: and the perſon ſtabbing muſt be ſpeedily indicted upon the ſtatute, to be ouſted of clergy; though even then it is ſaid the jury may find manſlaughter generally. 3 *Lev.* 255, 266.

If a man ſhoots off a gun in a city, or publick highway, which muſt endanger the life of ſome perſon, and one is killed, it is manſlaughter by the common law: and if a perſon throw a ſtone over a wall in a place where people often reſort, or at another in play, and kill any one, if it be done without an evil intention, it is manſlaughter; if with an evil intention to hurt, murder. A man ſhoots at the tame fowl of another, which is an unlawful act, and kills a ſtander by, it is murder: if he be ſhooting at wild fowl, hare, &c. and not qualified to keep a gun or to kill game, 'tis manſlaughter; and where he is qualified to keep a gun, it is only chancemedley. 3 *Inſt.* 56, 57. *H. H. P. C.* 475, 476.

3. There is a *Homicide* or killing juſtifiable; as if a perſon attempt to commit murder, robbery, or other felony, a man or any of his ſervants, may lawfully kill him: and where one in poſſeſſion of a room in a publick houſe, kills another who attempts to turn him out of it; the killing the aſſailant hath been held to be juſtifiable. Alſo if a woman kill a man attempting to raviſh her,

Of publick Offences.

her, it is juftifiable to do it. 2 *Inft.* 316. *H. P. C.* 32. *Kel.* 51. *Hawk. P. C.* 83.

Thofe who are engaged in a riot, &c. ftanding in oppofition to a juftice's command, or lawful warrant, or if trefpaffers in a foreft, or park, will not furrender, but defend themfelves; if a felon will not fuffer himfelf to be arrefted, and refufes to obey an arreft on lawful warrant; or if a felon purfued upon hue and cry, flies for it; where a prifoner affaults thofe that conduct him to gaol, or his gaoler in endeavouring to efcape; or a perfon arrefted refifts the fheriff, &c. the killing thefe is juftifiable: but this is underftood when an offender on an arreft cannot be taken without killing, &c. 3 *Inft.* 56, 221. *H. P. C.* 57. *Kel.* 28.

The *Homicide*, or killing excufable, is where a man kills another merely in his own defence; and this muft be upon an unavoidable neceffity, when it is called *se defendendo*. Here malice is not to be coloured under pretence of neceffity, if it be, it is murder. 3 *Inft.* 220. *Bac. Max.* 25.

Trials for murder are to be in the county where this fact was committed, by the common law: though on an indictment being found againft a perfon in the proper county; by fpecial commiffion it may be heard and determined in any other county. And offenders for murder, and acceffaries being indicted, may be arraigned at any time within the year, at the king's fuit; and if the principal or acceffary be acquit, yet the juftices fhall not fuffer them to go at large, but either remand them to prifon, or let them be bailed, until a year and a day be out, allowed for an appeal. *Cro. Car.* 247. 3 *Inft.* 27. 3 *H.* 7. *c.* 1.

Of publick Offences.

And an *Appeal* of murder is always at the suit of the subject, brought by a party interested in the person killed; and may be had by the heir male for the death of his ancestor, or by a wife for the death of her husband, &c. *Co. Lit.* 287; 2 *Inst.* 318.

Felony is a crime committed with a fell, fierce or bitter mind; and was anciently every capital offence, perpetrated with an evil intention: for all capital crimes by the common law came generally under the title of felony. We now account any offence felony, that is in degree next petit treason; and this crime I shall reduce to the heads of,

1. Felony by the common law.
2. Larceny and felony in stealing goods.
3. Felonies by statutes.

1. Felony by the common law, is against the life of a man; as murder, manslaughter, *Felo de se, Se defendendo,* &c. Against a man's goods, such as larceny and robbery; against his habitation, as burglary, arson or house-burning; and against publick justice, as breach of prison. Piracy, robbery or murder upon the sea, are felonies punishable by the civil law; and likewise by statute; and felonies are said to be of a publick or private nature; hurtful to the people in general, or to some particular persons. *Co. Lit.* 391. 3 *Inst.* 15.

Where persons are to undergo judgment of life and member for any crime, it is felony, whether the word *Felony* be mentioned or not. And of felonies in general, there are two sorts; one which for the first offence is allowed clergy, and another

another that is not; but clergy is granted where it is not expresly taken away by statute: and by statute, all felons are to have clergy, except for murder, burglary, robbery, horse-stealing, &c. Rapes and stealing of women, &c. *Hawk. Pl. Cr.* 107. 23 *H.* 8. *c.* 1. perpetuated by 32 *H.* 8. *c.* 3. *f.* 2. *c.* 12. 1 *Ed* 6. 4 *& 5 P. & M. c.* 4.

If a person to whom goods are delivered, on a pretended buying them, runs away with them, it is felony; and a guest stealing plate set before him at an inn, &c. 'tis felony; also persons who have the charge of things, may be guilty of felony: and the least removing of a thing, in common attempts of felony, is felony, tho' it be not carried off. But things must not be of a base nature, or *Feræ Naturæ*, as dogs, deer, hares, &c. tho' if these last are made tame, 'tis felony to steal them; and so it is of turkeys, geese, poultry, fish in a trunk or pond, &c. if they are taken away. 3 *Inst.* 308, 309, 310. *T. Raym.* 275.

A married woman cannot be guilty of felony in stealing the goods of her husband; but if she deliver them to an adulterer, and he receives them, it is felony in him: and if a feme covert commits felony against any one in company with her husband, it shall be presumed to be done by his command, and she shall be excused; though 'tis otherwise where the wife steals goods alone. 3 *Inst.* 310.

2. Larceny is a private felony, against the goods of a man, in his absence; and in respect of the things stolen, is either great or small: grand larceny is a felonious taking and carrying away the personal goods of another, above the value of 12 *d.* not from the person, or by night, in the

Of publick Offences.

the houfe of the owner; and petit larceny is when the goods ftolen do not exceed the value of 12 d. *H. P. C.* 69.

The difference between grand and petit larceny is only the value of the goods: and if two perfons fteal goods to the value of 13 d. it is grand larceny in both; and in cafe one at diffrrent times fteals divers parcels of goods from the fame perfon, which together exceed the value of 12 d. they may be put together in one indictment, and the offender found guilty of grand larceny; though this is very feldom done: but on the contrary, the jury fometimes, where it is an offender's firft offence, &c. find it fpecially, as they may, that the goods are but 10 d. value; fo as to be only petit larceny, though the offender be indicted for ftealing things of the value of 30 or 40 s. 3 *Inft.* 109. *H. P. C.* 70. *Heil. Rep.* 66.

To make the crime larceny, there muft be a felonious taking, or an intent of ftealing the thing, when it comes firft to the hands of the offender, at the very time of the receiving. If a man hath poffeffion of goods once lawfully, though he afterwards carry them away with an ill intention, it is no larceny: where a taylor imbezils cloth delivered to him, to make a fuit of clothes, &c. it is no felony; nor is it where a fervant goes away with his mafter's goods delivered to him, which is only a breach of truft, by reafon of the delivery; (but by ftatute they are to be under 40 s. value:) and I lend a man a horfe to go to a certain place, and he goes there, and then rides away with the horfe, it is not larceny. 3 *Inft.* 107. *Dalt.* 367, 369. 5 *Rep.* 13. *H. P. C.* 61.

As

As in these cases, there is a lawful possession by the delivery of the goods, that extenuates the offence; but if one intending to steal goods, gets possession of them by ejectment, replevin, or other process at law unduly obtained, by false oath, &c. is a felonious taking. And a man may commit larceny, by taking away his own goods, in the hands of another; where the owner delivers goods to a carrier, and afterwards secretly steals them from him, with an intent to charge him for them, &c. because the carrier had a special property for a time. 3 *Inst.* 108, 64, 110. *Kel.* 43, 44. *Dalt.* 373.

All felony includes in it trespass, so that if the party offending be guilty of no trespass in taking the goods, he cannot be guilty of felony or larceny in carrying them away. *Hawk. P. C.* 89.

3. Felonies by statutes, are very numerous: as imbezzling armour to the value of 20 *s.* Acknowledging bail in the name of another; bankrupts not surrendering or not discovering their estates; stealing bonds, bills, notes, &c. buggery with man or beast; burning of houses or barns with corn, &c. Destroying any cattle; breaking into shops to destroy cloth in the loom; paying away coin that is counterfeit; acknowledging deeds inrolled in the name of another; or a fine in the name of another person; forgery of deeds, or any bond, &c. also of bank-notes, exchequer-bills, lottery orders, stamps, &c. A person helping another to goods stolen for reward, and not apprehending the felon; maliciously cutting hop-binds on poles; stealing of horses; house-robbery in the day time, and taking to the value of 5 *s.* unlawful hunting in forests, &c. armed and disguised; acknowledging

Of publick Offences.

a judgment in the name of another person; stealing lead from houses, or iron bars or rails fixed thereto or in gardens; and stealing linen from whitening grounds of 10*s.* value; maiming any one maliciously, so as to disable any limb, &c. Persons marrying a second husband or wife, the first living; maliciously setting any mine, or pit of coal on fire; imbezzling munition, naval stores, ordnance, &c. Pickpockets taking above 12 *d.* from the person *clam & secrete*; setting out or trading with pirates; poisoning a person of malice; those who receive or relieve priests and jesuits knowingly; who attempt to kill, or do strike a privy counsellor in the execution of his office; rapes of women, and carnally knowing them under ten years of age; acknowledging of a recognizance or recovery, in the name of another; rioters to the number of twelve, not dispersing within an hour of proclamation; persons assaulting others with intent to rob on the highway; robbery of churches or sacrilege; servants purloining their masters goods to the value of 40 *s.* Ships casting away and destroying; soldiers departing from their colours, without licence; and persons inlisting themselves soldiers, or others procuring it to go beyond sea to serve any foreign prince, without leave; persons receiving stolen goods from felons; cutting out the tongue, &c. of any person; wilfully or maliciously pulling down turnpikes; woollen cloth stolen from tenters in the night-time; women-stealing, having lands or goods, or being heirs apparent; woods, underwoods, maliciously burning, &c. All these and many other offences are made felony by statute. See the second *Appendix* annexed.

Any

Of publick Offences.

Any perſon convicted of felony or larceny, within the benefit of clergy, may be ordered by the court by whom convicted, to be tranſported to the plantations for ſeven years, inſtead of being burnt in the hand or whipped; and for any felony excluded clergy, the offenders may be pardoned, and tranſported for fourteen years. But if any felon thus under tranſportation ſhall return before the end of the time limited, he ſhall ſuffer death; though the king may pardon the tranſportation, &c. *Stat.* 4 *Geo. c.* 11. 6. *Geo. c.* 23.

Beſides this general power of tranſporting, the puniſhment of felony, is ſometimes particularly made *Tranſportation*; as where three or more are aſſembled and armed, to be aſſiſting in running goods: perſons to the number of five, that in a riotous manner aſſemble, to beat or wound informers againſt diſtillers, and unlawful retailers of ſpirituous liquors: and hindering the exporting of corn, a ſecond offence, entering granaries, or boats, &c. and taking away or ſpoiling it, &c. ſuſpicion of ſtealing cloth, or woollen goods, &c. on tenters, &c. third offence; conveying into gaols diſguiſe for making eſcape or aiding therein; ſtealing linen, &c. to 10 s. value; vagrants eſcaping out of houſes of correction: entering lead mines with intent to ſteal the lead; reſcuing body of a murderer from ſheriff or ſurgeon; ſolemnizing matrimony in other place than a church, or without banns; buying or receiving lead, &c. knowing it to be ſtolen or unlawfully come by, &c. counterfeiting the franking of letters. So in ſeveral other caſes. See 9 *Geo.* 2. *c.* 35. 11 *Geo.* 2. *c.* 22 & 26. 15 *Geo.* 2. *c.* 27. 16 *Geo.* 2. *c.* 31. 18 *Geo.* 2. *c.* 27. 17 *Geo.* 2. *c.* 5. *ſ.* 9. 24 *Geo.* 2. *c.* 40. *ſ.* 28.

f. 28. 25 *Geo.* 2. *c.* 10. *c.* 37. *f.* 10. 26 *Geo.* 2. *c.* 33. *f.* 8. 29 *Geo.* 2. *c.* 30. 4 *Geo.* 3. *c.* 24. *f.* 8. See the second *Appendix* annexed.

In felony there are *Accessaries* before or after the fact; before where one advises, abets or procures the felony, but is absent when done; after, when a man receives, relieves, assists, &c. knowingly any one that hath committed felony: and persons furnishing others with weapons; finding a felon a horse for his journey: or relieving him with money, victuals, &c. will make them accessary. Accessaries before the fact, in petit treason, murder, robbery, burglary, &c. Clergy is taken away from, by statute. *Co. Lit.* 57. *H. P. C.* 218, 219. 23 *H.* 8. *c.* 1.

Private persons may arrest felons; and every person is bound to assist an officer to take them: but one ought not to be taken upon suspicion of felony, except there be probable cause shewed for the ground of it. If a man be committed to prison for one felony, the justice of gaol-delivery may try him for another for which he was not committed; and a felon refusing to plead, and put himself upon his trial, shall be put to the penance of *peine fort & dure*, and be pressed to death; but if he stands mute by the act of God, it shall be inquired of, &c. 2 *Hawk. Pl. Cr.* 75. *Lil. Abr.* 602, 603. *Stat. Westm.* 1. *c.* 12. 2 *Inst.* 178.

Burglary is where a man in the night-time breaketh and entereth into the house of another, to the intent to commit felony, whether the intention be execute or not. In its natural signification, it is nothing but the robbing of a house; but our law restrains it to robbing houses by night, or breaking in with an intent

to

to rob, or do some other felony: and the like offence committed by day is called house-breaking, to distinguish it from burglary. 4 *Rep.* 493.

It is an offence excluded the benefit of clergy; but the house must be a mansion-house, and the out-buildings, as barns, stables, *&c.* adjoining to it, 'tis burglary to break; tho' not a barn, *&c.* at a distance; Where part of a house is divided from the rest, with a door of its own to the street, it is mansion; but a chamber wherein any person lodges as an inmate is not, in which if burglary be committed, it must be laid in the mansion-house of him that let it. A chamber in an inn of court is mansion; because every one there hath several property. 4 *Rep.* 40. *H. P. C.* 82. *Kel.* 84. 3 *Inst.* 65. *Fost. Cr. Law* 76, 77.

There may be a burglary committed in a mansion-house, though all the family are absent: and if a man hath two houses, and lives sometimes in one, and sometimes in another; and the house he doth not inhabit is broken in the night, it is burglary. If a servant draws the latch of his master's chamber, to rob, *&c.* 'tis a breaking; and if he open a window for a thief to come in, it is burglary in the stranger, and robbery in the servant: if a person do not break a house, as if he be within and steal the goods, and then open the house on the inside, and go out with the goods, this is burglary: so where one comes down a chimney to rob a house, *&c. Poph.* 52. 4 *Inst.* 64. *Kel.* 682. *H. P. C.* 83. *Fost. Cr. Law* 108, 109. *Stra.* 481. *H. H. P. C.* 562. *Kel.* 30, 67. *Hut.* 20, 33. 2 *Stra.* 881. See *H. H. P. C.* 552.

If

Of publick Offences.

If thieves pretend business to get into a house by night, &c. and thereupon the owner opens his door, and they enter and rob the house, this will be burglary; where a thief breaks the glass of windows; makes a hole in the wall; or unlocks any door, &c. to rob, it is a breaking the house: and not only setting a foot over the threshold, but putting a hand, hook or pistol within the window or door, is an entry to make it burglary. Though if a door, &c. be open, or a hole made in the wall before, and the thief enters and steals, or draws out goods; this is not burglary by the Common Law. *H. P. C.* 81, 82. *Kel.* 42, 62. *Fost. Cr. Law* 107, 109.

Robbery in a booth or tent in a fair or market, the owner being within the same, is punished as burglary: and by statute, taking away goods from a dwelling-house, any person being therein; or breaking any shop, warehouse, &c. in the day-time, and taking goods of 5 s. value, no person being therein, is burglary; also such stealing privately, 'tho there be no breaking, in night or day, is excluded clergy. And a reward of 40 l. is given, for apprehending a burglar, and prosecuting him to conviction, &c. *Stat.* 5 & 6 *Edw.* 6. c. 9. 3 & 4 *W.* & *M.* c. 9. perpetuated by 6 & 7 *W.* 3. c. 14. 10 & 11 *W.* 3. c. 23. 8 *Mod.* 165. *Fost. Cr. Law* 77. 5 *An.* c. 31. 6 *Geo.* c. 23.

Robbery is a felonious taking away of money or goods, of any value, from the person of another on the highway, in a violent manner, thereby putting him in fear: and this robbery on the highway is felony of death, though the

sum

sum taken is under twelve-pence, or be but one penny. *H. P. C.* 73. *Fost. Cr. Law* 121.

Where any thief bids the party deliver his money, &c. either with or without weapon drawn, and he gives it him; or a person with sword or pistol in his hand demands my money, and afterwards prays me to give him alms, and I give it accordingly; or if a thief compels one by fear to swear that he will fetch him a sum of money, which he doth, and the thief receives it: these are a taking, to make it robbery. And so when a thief takes the purse of a person, which in a fright he casts into a bush; and where a man endeavouring to escape from a robber drops his hat, &c. which the highwayman takes up, it is a taking from the person: and in case a thief cuts a man's pocket, whereby his purse falls to the ground, if he takes up the same, tho' he lets it fall again, it is robbery. 3 *Inst.* 60. *Dalt.* 363. *H. P. C.* 73.

If a robber having taken a person's purse, finding little in it, delivers it back with all the money to the party; 'tis notwithstanding a felonious taking, because he had it in his possession, and the continuance of his possession is not required by law. A person who hath assaulted me, drives my cattle in my presence out of my pasture; or robs my servant of money or other thing before my face, he may be indicted as having taken such things from my person; for when a servant is robbed, in the sight of his master, of his master's goods, it is adjudged a robbery of the master. Not only the taking away a horse, which a man is actually riding, is robbery; but if the horse be standing by him, and taken against his will, it is in law a taking from the person; and to claim a property, without colour for it will not excuse it: but if one leaves his horse tied, and steps aside; or if a carrier follows his horses at a distance, and they are taken away, this is not such a taking as to be robbery. 3 *Inst.* 69. *S. P. C.* 27. *Dalt.* 364. *Pult.* 129. *Styles* 156.

All that are in company to commit a robbery are principals, and esteemed to take away, tho' one only doth it, in respect to that encouragement which they give one to another; and if one of the gang rides from the rest, and robs another person not intended in the same highway, without their knowledge and consent, out of their view, and returns to them afterwards, all are guilty of the robbery. He, who apprehends and prosecutes a robber on the highway to conviction, shall receive of the sheriff of the county where the robbery was done 40 *l.* (producing the certificate of the judge before whom the offender was convicted) with his horse, furniture, arms, &c. And if any person out of prison, having committed any robbery, discovers two or more robbers, so as they are convicted, he shall be intitled to a pardon *Crompt.* 34. *H. P. C.* 72. *Stat.* 1 *W. & M. c.* 8. *f.* 7.

The hundred where a robbery is committed on the highway is chargeable and answerable for it, if done in the day-time of any day, except * *Sunday*; but notice must be immediately given of it to some of the inhabitants of the village near the place, to the intent they may make *Hue and Cry*, to apprehend the robbers: and if any of the robbers are taken within forty days

---

* Stra. 406 Com. Rep. 345.

and convicted, the hundred shall be excused; if not, the party robbed is to make oath before a justice of peace of the county, of the time and place of the robbery, and of what he was robbed, and that he knew none of the robbers; and that in twenty days he may bring his action against the hundred, by original writ, &c. *Stat.* 27 *Eliz. c.* 13. *Cro. Car.* 37, 41, 211, 379. 3 *Salk.* 184. 2 *Stra.* 1247.

Process is to be served on the high constable of the hundred, &c. and the party robbed in twenty days to give publick notice in the *Gazette*, describing the robber and circumstances of the robbery; and no hundred shall be charged, if any of the robbers are apprehended in forty days after such notice given; also a reward of 10*l.* shall be paid by the hundred for taking any robber on the highway. 8 *Geo.* 2. *c.* 16. 2 *Stra.* 1170. not to receive above 200*l.* Stat. 22 *Geo.* 2. *c.* 24.

Persons who with offensive weapons assault, or in a forcible manner demand money, &c. of any person with an intent to commit robbery, shall be guilty of felony, and be transported for seven years, by the statute 7 *Geo.* 2. *c.* 21.

Rape is an unlawful and carnal knowledge of a woman, by force and against her will: a ravishment of the body, and violent deflowering her, which is felony by the common and statute law. There must be penetration and emission, to make this crime; otherwise an attempt to ravish a woman, though it be never so outrageous, will be an assault only. *Co. Lit.* 124.

In rapes, it is no excuse or mitigation of the crime, that the woman at last yielded to the violence, and consented either after the fact or before,

before, if such her consent was forced by fear of death, or of imprisonment; or that she was a common strumpet, for she is still under the protection of the law, and may be forced: but it is said by some to be evidence of a woman's consent, that she was a common whore. And it is a strong presumption against a woman, that she made no complaint in a reasonable time after the fact; if she conceals it for any long time, it may argue a consent. *Co. Lit.* 123. *H. P. C.* 117. *Hawk. P. C.* 108. 3 *Nelf. Abr.* 45. *H. H. P. C.* 633. 5 *Read. Stat. Law* 49.

It was formerly adjudged not to be rape to force a woman who conceived at the time; because if she had not consented, she could not conceive: though this opinion hath been since questioned, by reason the previous violence is no way extenuated by such a subsequent consent. And it was a question before 18 *Eliz. c.* 7. Whether a rape could be committed on a child of the age of six or seven years? by that statute, whosoever shall carnally know and abuse any woman child under the age of ten years, he shall suffer as a felon, without benefit of clergy, and here it is not material whether such child consented, or were forced, but it must be proved that the offender entered her body, &c. 2 *Inst.* 190. *Dalt.* 393.

Though a woman ravished may prosecute, and be a witness in her own cause; yet a woman's positive oath of a rape, without concurring circumstances, is seldom credited: if a man can prove himself to be in another place, or in other company, at the time she charges him with committing the fact, this will invalidate her oath: so if she is wrong in the description of the place where done, or swears the fact to be committed
in

in such place, to which it was impossible the man could have access at that time; as if the room was then locked up, and the key in the keeping of another person, &c. *3 Rep.* 37. *Dalt.* 107.

The aiders and abettors in committing a rape may be indicted as principal felons, whether men or women: and there is an *Appeal* of rape, which a feme covert may bring without her husband. If a woman ravished afterwards consents to it, her husband, if she have any, or a father, or next of kin, there being no husband, may prosecute this appeal; also the criminal in such case, may be attainted at the suit of the king: and if a woman consent after, she is disabled to challenge any inheritance, dower, &c. 6 *R*. 2. *c*. 6. 3 *Inst.* 30, 131.

Sodomy, or buggery, is a carnal knowledge of the body of a man or beast, against the order of nature: and it may be committed by a man with man, which is the common crime; or by man with woman; or a man or woman with a beast. 3 *Inst.* 58.

This sin against God, nature and law, it is said, was in ancient time punished with burning; though others say with burying alive: but at this day it is felony excluded clergy; and punished as other felonies. It is felony both in the agent, and patient consenting, unless the person on whom committed be within the age of discretion; and then 'tis felony in the agent only, not him: and he that doth the act is not only a principal, but those that are present aiding and abetting him are principals. 12 *Rep.* 36. *H. P. C.* 117. 25 *H.* 8. *c.* 6. perpetuated by 5 *El. c.* 17. *H. H. P. C.* 670.

Some kind of penetration and emission must be proved, in acts of sodomy, but any the least degree is sufficient. See *Fortesc. Rep.* 91.

Forgery by the common law is a fraudulent making or altering of a deed or writing, to the prejudice of another man's right, whether it be matter of record, or any other writing, deed, or will. 3 *Inst.* 169.

Where one makes a false deed; or if he makes any fraudulent alteration of a true deed, in a material part of it; if he alters a bond, &c. for 500l. expressed in figures, to 5000l. by adding a new cypher, these are forgery: so it is if a man finding another's name at the bottom of a letter, at a considerable distance from the other writing, causes the letter to be cut off, and a general release to be written above the name, &c. And where one being directed to draw up a will for a sick person, inserts some legacies therein falsely of his own head; or if he omits a bequest to a certain person, which causes a material alteration in the limitation of an estate to another, it will be forgery by the common law. *Hawk. P. C.* 182, 183. *Noy* 118. *Moor* 760.

A person knowingly falsifies the date of a second conveyance, which he hath no power to make, in order to deceive a purchaser, &c. he is said to be guilty of forgery: and if a feoffment be made of land, and livery and seisin is not indorsed when the deed is delivered, and afterwards, on selling the land for a valuable consideration to another, livery is indorsed upon the first deed; this hath been adjudged forgery both in the feoffor and feoffee, being done in deceit of an honest purchaser: but there can be no forgery, where none can be prejudiced by the act but the

person

person doing it. 3 *Inst.* 170. *Hawk. P. C.* 182. *Moor* 665. *Salk.* 375. Ld. *Raym.* 530.

By statute, if any person shall falsely forge or make, or cause to be forged, or assent to the forging of any deed, or writing sealed, or will, &c. to the intent that the freehold and inheritance of lands may be defeated or charged, or the title troubled, &c. or shall publish or give such forged writing in evidence as true, knowing of the forgery; and shall be convicted thereof, by action on this statute, or by bill, &c. he shall pay double costs and damages to the party grieved, be set on the pillory, and have both his ears cut off and his nostrils slit; and shall forfeit to the king the issues and profits of his lands during life, suffer perpetual imprisonment, &c. And if any one shall forge or falsely make any lease for years of lands, or a grant of an annuity, an obligation, acquittance, release or other discharge of any debt or personal demand; or publish, or give in evidence the same knowingly, he shall pay to the party injured double costs and damages, stand in the pillory, and lose one of his ears, and be imprisoned for a year. And the second offence is felony, without benefit of clergy. *Stat.* 5 *Eliz.* c. 14. 2 *Stra.* 901. *Barnard. K. B.* 168. *Fitzgib.* 57.

The forgery of a deed of gift of chattels is not within the words of this statute: and forging an assignment of a lease is not within the act, because it doth not charge the lands, but only transfers an interest, which was in being before. The king may pardon the corporal punishment of this offence; but the plaintiff cannot release it: if he releases the judgment, &c. it shall only discharge the costs and damages; and the judges shall proceed to judgment upon the residue of the pains, and award execution on the same. But in a very extraordinary case, a forgery hath been compounded; and the defendant discharged on paying a fine. 3 *Leon.* 170. 5 *Rep.* 50. 3 *Salk.* 172.

Forging or counterfeiting any deed, will, bond, note, acquittance, &c. for money, or uttering or publishing as true, knowing them to be false, is felony (for every offence) excluded clergy: but the attainder not to make corruption of blood, &c. by statute 2 *Geo.* 2. *c.* 26. perpetuated by 2 *Geo.* 2. *c.* 18. See 7 *Geo.* 2. *c.* 22. *Foſt. Cr. Law* 116.

Perjury is a crime committed by wilful and false swearing, in any judicial proceedings, in what is material to the issue or cause in question, by a man's own act, or the subornation of others. 3 *Inſt.* 194.

To make an offence perjury, it must be wilful and deliberate, and not committed through surprize, inadvertency or mistake of the question; and the deposition is to be direct and absolute, for nothing which the party offers upon his belief is assignable for perjury: it must be false in express words or intention; and if one knows not what he swears, it is a false oath in him, so that a person may swear the truth, and yet be perjured. 3 *Inſt.* 167, 266. 2 *Roll. Abr.* 77.

Where an oath is taken before a person that hath no authority to give it, or when a court hath not power to hold plea of the cause; there perjury cannot be committed; and if an oath be given by him who hath lawful authority, if it be not in a judicial proceeding, but in a private affair, it is not punishable as perjury. The forswearing

swearing must be in something material to the issue: and therefore if what a witness swears be not of any consequence in deciding the cause, it may not be punished as perjury; but if a false oath be given by a man, attended with such circumstances, that the jury are thereby induced in the giving of a verdict, he may be guilty of perjury. 3 *Inst.* 164. 4 *Inst.* 278. *Rol. Abr.* 41, 78.

A person may be indicted at Common Law for a false affidavit taken before a master in chancery; but not on the statute, because this is not perjury in a matter relating to the proof of what is in issue: perjury by the Common Law may be in an immaterial thing, in an answer in chancery; but if one swear false to an interrogatory, in a thing not materially charged therein, it is not perjury. The statute made against perjury extends to no other persons than witnesses; but persons perjuring themselves in their answers in Chancery, or in the Exchequer, or by swearing the peace against another, &c. may be punished for the perjury or subornation thereof at the Common Law; by fine, imprisonment, pillory, &c. *Bulst.* 322. *Sid.* 274. 3 *Inst.* 166.

By the statute, persons committing wilful and corrupt perjury, in any cause depending concerning lands or goods, &c. in any of the courts of record, shall forfeit 20 *l.* and be imprisoned six months; and their oath shall not be received in any court of record, until the judgment is reversed; and if the offenders have not goods or chattles to pay the forfeiture, they shall be set on the pillory in some market-place, and have both their ears nailed thereto, and for unlawful and corrupt procuring and suborning a witness to give false testimony in any court of record, &c. the offender shall forfeit 40 *l.* and if he be not worth that,

that, he shall suffer six months imprisonment, and stand in the pillory in some open market near the place where the offence was committed; and shall not be received as a witness, 'till such judgment be reversed: but in case the judgment is reversed, the party grieved shall recover damages against the prosecutor, in action on the case, &c. 5 *El. c.* 9. perpetuated by 29 *El. c.* 5. 21 *Jac. c.* 28. *f.* 8.

It hath been adjudged, that if a man be convicted of a perjury at Common Law, a pardon will restore the party to his testimony; but not in a conviction on the statute, for there he must reverse the judgment before he can be restored, and disability is part of the judgment. Perjury, or subornation, in proceedings on an indictment, is not within the statute, which mentions only suits, by writ, plaint, &c. Though where a witness for the king swears falsly, he may be indicted at the Common Law; and it is not material whether the oath were at all credited, or the party be any way grieved by it, or not; as this is not a prosecution grounded on the damage of the party, but on the abuse of publick justice. And if a person procure another to take a false oath amounting to perjury, but he doth not take it, though the person who incited him is not guilty of subornation of perjury, he is punishable by fine. 2 *Salk.* 512. 3 *Inst.* 164. 3 *Leon.* 230.

The court, before whom any person is convicted of wilful perjury or subornation, besides the punishment already inflicted by law, shall order the offender to be sent to the house of correction for seven years, there to be kept to hard labour, or be transported for the like term as felons, by Stat. 2 *Geo.* 2. *c.* 25. perpetuated by 9 *Geo.* 2. *c.* 18.

The

The punishments and forfeitures of criminals are as follow, viz.

Punishment for *high treason*.
IF a peer commit treason he shall be only beheaded, which is part of the judgment, and the king commonly pardons the rest. The judgment in all cases of high treason (except for counterfeiting the coin) is that the offender shall be drawn on a hurdle or sledge to the place of execution, and there be hang'd by the neck, to be cut down alive, his privy members cut off, his bowels ript up, taken out and burnt before his face, his head severed from his body, and his body divided into four quarters, which are to be disposed of as the king shall think fit.

Punishment in *petit treason*.
For counterfeiting the coin, the offender is to be drawn and hang'd: and the judgment in petit treason is for a man to be drawn and hang'd; and for a woman to be drawn and burnt.

Forfeiture.
The criminal for treason shall forfeit all his lands, tenements and hereditaments, which he had at the time of the treason committed, or afterwards, the right of others saved; and all his goods and chattels shall be forfeited from the time of the conviction. Also his blood shall be corrupted, on attainder, and his children be incapable to inherit to him or any of his ancestors.

Punish-

Of publick Offences.

Punishment of *murder and felony*.	For murder, felony and larceny above 12 d. a man or woman is to be hanged by the neck 'till dead; and in extraordinary cases, where a barbarous murder is committed, the body of the offender is usually hanged in chains. And see now St. 25 *Geo.* 2. c. 37.
Forfeiture.	In case of murder, burglary, robbery, and all felonies for which offenders shall suffer death, they shall forfeit all their lands in fee-simple, and goods and chattels. The king shall have goods of felons, and year, day and waste in their lands; which afterwards escheat to the lord of the manor of whom held: for standing mute in cases of felony, goods and chattels are forfeited.
Punishment of *manslaughter*.	For manslaughter, where the offender is admitted to his clergy, he shall be burnt in the hand.
Forfeiture.	In manslaughter, chancemedley, and *se defendendo*, an offender forfeits his goods and chattels; but in the two last he has a pardon of course.
Punishment of *petit larceny*, &c.	Here the punishment is whipping, or transportation for seven years, &c.
Forfeiture.	And in petit larceny, goods are forfeited; so also for flight in felony, &c.

Pro-

Proceedings on an indictment of murder at the assizes.

Indictment and conviction of murder.

Warwickshire, to wit. BE it remembered, that at the sessions of *Oyer* and *Terminer* of the lord the king, holden at *Warwick,* in and for the said county, on *Friday* the twelfth day of *March* in the seventeenth year of the reign of the lord *George* the Third, now King of *Great Britain*, before *William* earl *Mansfield* chief justice of the said lord the King himself, Sir *Henry Gould,* knight, one of the justices of the said lord the King of the bench, and others their fellows; justices of the said lord the King, assigned by letters patent of the said lord the King, under the great seal of *Great Britain,* made to them the aforesaid justices and others, and any two or more of them, (whereof one of them the said *William* earl *Mansfield* and Sir *Henry Gould,* among others in the said letters patent named, the said lord the King would should be one) to inquire fully by the oath of good and lawful men of the county aforesaid, by whom the truth of the matter might be the better known, (and by other ways, methods and means, whereby they might the better know, or be able, as well within liberties as without,) the truth of all treasons, misprisions of treasons, insurrections, rebellions, murders, felonies, manslaughter, killings, burglaries, rapes of women, and other misdeeds, offences and injuries whatsoever, and also the accessaries of the same, within the county aforesaid, as well within liberties as without,

Sessions of Oyer and Terminer.

Commission of

without, by whomsoever and howsoever done, had, perpetrated and committed, and by whom, to whom, when, how, and in what manner; and of other articles and offences in the said letters patent of the said lord the King specified, the premisses and every and each of them howsoever concerning; and to hear and determine the said treasons and other the premisses, according to the law and custom of the realm of *England*; and also keepers of the peace, and justices of the said lord the King, assigned to hear and determine divers felonies, trespasses, and other misdemeanors committed within the county aforesaid; by the oath of Sir *James Thompson*, baronet, *Charles Roper*, *Henry Dawes*, *Peter Wilson*, *Samuel Rogers*, *John Dawson*, *James Philips*, *John Mayo*, *Richard Savage*, *William Bell*, *James Morris*, *Lawrence Hall*, and *Charles Carter*, esquires, good and lawful men of the county aforesaid, impanelled, sworn and charged to inquire for the said lord the King and for the body of the said county, it is presented, That *Peter Hunt*, late of *Birmingham*, in the said county, gent. not having God before his eyes, but being moved and seduced by the instigation of the devil, on the fifth day of *March* in the said seventeenth year of the reign of the said lord the King, at *Birmingham* aforesaid, with force and arms, in and upon one *Samuel Collins*, in the peace of God, and of the said lord the King, then and there being, feloniously, wilfully, and of his malice aforethought, did make an assault; and that the said *Peter Hunt*, with a certain drawn sword of the value of five shillings, which he the said *Peter Hunt* in his right hand then and there had and held, the said *Samuel Collins* in and upon the left side of the belly

Oyer and Terminer.

of the peace.

Grand Jury.

Indictment.

belly of him the said *Samuel Collins* then and there feloniously, wilfully, and of his malice aforethought did strike and thrust; giving unto the said *Samuel Collins* then and there with the sword aforesaid, in and upon the left side of the belly of him the said *Samuel Collins*, one mortal wound of the breadth of one inch, and the depth of nine inches; of which said mortal wound he the said *Samuel Collins* then and there instantly died: and so the said *Peter Hunt* him the said *Samuel Collins* on the aforesaid fifth day of *March* in the year aforesaid, at *Birmingham* aforesaid, in the county aforesaid, in manner and form aforesaid, feloniously, wilfully and of his malice aforethought, did kill and murder, against the peace of the said lord the now King, his crown and dignity. Whereupon the sheriff *Capias.* of the county aforesaid is commanded, that he omit not for any liberty in his bailiwick, but that he take the said *Peter Hunt*, if he may be found in his bailiwick, and him safely keep, to answer to the felony and murder whereof he stands indicted. Which said indictment the said Session of gaol justices of the lord the King above-named after- delivery. wards, to wit, at the delivery of the gaol of the said lord the King, holden at *Warwick* in and for the county aforesaid on *Monday* the sixth day of *August* in the seventeenth year of the reign of the said lord the King, before *George Perrott*, esquire, one of the barons of the exchequer of the said lord the King, Sir *Joseph Yates*, knight, one of the justices of the said lord the King assigned to hold pleas before the King himself, and others their fellows, justices of the said lord the King, assigned to deliver his said gaol of the county aforesaid, of the prisoners therein being, by their proper hands to deliver here in court of record

Arraignment. record in form of law to be determined. And afterwards, to wit, at the same delivery of the gaol of the said lord the King of his county aforesaid, on the said *Monday* the sixth day of *August* in the said seventeenth year of the reign of the said lord the King, before the said justices of the lord the King last above named, and others their fellows aforesaid; here cometh the said *Peter Hunt*, under the custody of *W. B.* esquire, sheriff of the county aforesaid, (in whose custody is the gaol of the county aforesaid, for the cause aforesaid, he had been before committed) being brought to the bar by the said sheriff, to whom he is here also committed: and forthwith being demanded of the premisses aforesaid above charged upon him how he will acquit himself thereof, he saith, that **Plea; not guilty.** he is not guilty thereof; and thereof for good and evil he puts himself upon the country: **Venire.** Therefore let a jury thereupon here immediately come before the said justices of the lord the King last above named, and others their fellows aforesaid, by whom the truth of the matter may be the better known, and who have no affinity to the said *Peter Hunt*, to recognize upon their oath, whether the said *Peter Hunt* be guilty of the premisses in the indictment aforesaid above specified, or not guilty. And the jurors of the said jury by the said sheriff for this purpose impanelled and returned, to wit, *David Williams, John Smith, Thomas Horne, Charles Nokes, Richard May, Walter Duke, Matthew Lyon, James White, William Bates, Oliver Green, Bartholomew Nash,* and *Henry Long,* being called, come; who being elected, tried and sworn, to speak the truth of

the

the premisses, upon their oath say, that the said *Peter Hunt* is guilty of the felony and murder aforesaid, on him above charged in the form aforesaid, as by the indictment aforesaid is above supposed against him; and that the said *Peter Hunt*, at the time of committing the said felony and murder, or at any time since, had no goods or chattels, lands or tenements, to the knowledge of the said jurors; and upon this it is demanded of him, if he hath or knoweth any thing to say, wherefore the said justices ought not upon the premisses to proceed to judgment and execution of him: who nothing further saith, unless as he before had said: therefore it is considered by the said justices here, that the said *Peter Hunt* be hanged by the neck till he be dead. *Black. Anal.* 186.

Conviction of manslaughter.

——— upon their oath, that the said *Peter Hunt* is not guilty of the murder aforesaid, above charged upon him; but that the said *Peter* is guilty of the felonious slaying of the aforesaid *Samuel Collins*; and that he hath no goods or chattels, lands or tenements at the time of the felony and manslaughter aforesaid, or ever afterwards to their knowledge. And immediately it is demanded of the said *Peter*, if he hath or knoweth any thing to say, wherefore the justices here ought not upon the premisses to proceed to judgment and execution of him: who saith that he is a clerk, and prayeth the benefit of his clergy to be allowed him in this behalf: therefore it is considered by the said justices here, that the said *Peter Hunt* be burned in his left hand, and delivered. And immediately he is burned in his left hand, and is delivered, according to the form of the statute. *Id.* 189.

APPEN-

APPENDIX I.

Page 1. AS all wrong may be considered *ante.* as merely a privation of right, the one natural remedy for every species of wrong is the being put in possession of that right, whereof the party injured is deprived. This may either be effected by a specific delivery or restoration of the subject-matter in dispute to the legal owner; as when lands or personal chattels are unjustly with-held or invaded: or, where that is not a possible or at least an adequate remedy, by making the sufferer a pecuniary satisfaction in damages; as in case of assault, breach of contract, &c. to which damages the party injured has acquired an incomplete or inchoate *right*, the instant he receives the injury: tho' such right be not fully ascertained till they are assessed by the intervention of the law. The instruments whereby this remedy is obtained (which are sometimes considered in the light of the remedy itself) are a *diversity* of SUITS and ACTIONS; which are defined by the mirror (*c.* 2. § 1.) to be "THE LAWFUL DEMAND OF ONE'S RIGHT:" or as *Bracton* and *Fleta* express it, in the words of *Justinian, jus prosequendi in judicio quod alicui debetur.*

APPENDIX I.

The *diversity of* suits, or remedial inftruments of juftice, are from the fubject of them diftinguifhed into three kinds; Actions,

PERSONAL, REAL, *and* MIXED.

PERSONAL actions are fuch whereby a man claims a debt, or perfonal duty, or damages in lieu thereof; and likewife whereby a man claims a fatisfaction *in damages* for fome injury done to his perfon or property. The former are faid to be founded on CONTRACTS, the latter on TORTS or wrongs. Of the former nature are all actions upon debt or promifes:—of the latter all actions for trefpaffes, nufances, affaults, defamatory words, and the like.

REAL actions, (or, as they are called in the mirror, *c.* 2, § 6. *feodal* actions) which concern real property *only*, are fuch whereby the plaintiff, here called the demandant, claims title to have any lands or tenements, rents, commons, or other hereditaments, in fee-fimple, fee-tail, or for term of life. By thefe actions formerly all difputes concerning *real* eftates were decided; but they are now pretty generally laid afide in practice, on account of the great nicety required in their management, and the inconvenient length of their procefs: a much more expeditious method of trying titles being fince introduced, by other actions perfonal and mixed.

MIXED actions are fuits partaking of the nature of the other two, wherein fome *real property is demanded*,

APPENDIX I.

manded, and *also personal* DAMAGES *for a wrong sustained.* As for instance, an action of waste: which is brought by him who hath the inheritance, in remainder or reversion, against the tenant for life, who hath committed waste therein, to recover not only the land wasted, which would make it merely a *real* action; but also TREBLE DAMAGES, in pursuance of the statute of *Gloucester,* 6 *Ed.* 1. *c.* 5. which is A PERSONAL RECOMPENSE; and so both, being joined together, denominate it a *mixed* action.

Under these *three* heads may every species of remedy by suit or action in the courts of common law be comprised. But in order effectually to apply the remedy, it is first necessary to ascertain the complaint.

Tho' in the first part of this book, the several kinds of private wrongs, or civil injuries, are in a concise manner enumerated, and their respective natures enquired into; recounting at the same time the respective remedies, which are furnished by the law for every infraction of right, yet it must be remembred, that all civil injuries are of two kinds, the one *without* FORCE or violence, as slander or breach of contract; the other coupled *with force* and violence, as batteries, or false imprisonment. *Finch L.* 184.) which latter species favour something of the criminal kind, being always attended with some violation of the peace; for which in strictness of law a fine ought to be paid to the king, as well as private satisfaction to the party injured. *Finch L.* 198. *Jenk. Cent.* 185.

This distinction of private wrongs, into injuries *with* and *without* force, run thro' all the variety of which we have treated in the former part of this book.

APPENDIX I.

Page 34.—As to actions *on the case*, or, in the true legal term, *a special Action of trespass upon the case.*

For wrongs or injuries unaccompanied by force, there is a remedy in damages by the above action. It is an universal remedy for all personal injuries *without* force; so called, because the plaintiff's *whole* case or cause of complaint is set forth *at length* in the original writ. For tho' in general there are methods prescribed and forms of actions previously settled, for redressing those wrongs which most usually occur, and in which the very act itself is IMMEDIATELY prejudicial or injurious to the plaintiff's person or property, as battery, non-payment of debts, detaining goods, or the like; yet where any special CONSEQUENTIAL damage arises, which could not be foreseen and provided for in the ordinary course of justice, the party injured is allowed, both by common law and the *Stat.* of *Westm.* 2. *c.* 24. to bring a special action *on his own case*, by a writ formed according to the peculiar circumstances of his own particular grievance. For WHEREVER THE COMMON LAW GIVES A RIGHT OR PROHIBITS AN INJURY, IT ALSO GIVES A REMEDY BY ACTION; (1 *Salk.* 20, 6 *Mod.* 54.) therefore, whenever a *new* injury is done, a new method of remedy *must* be pursued. *Cro. Jac.* 478. And it is a settled distinction, (11 *Mod.* 180, Ld. *Raymond* 1402. *Stra.* 635.) that where an act is done which is in *itself* an IMMEDIATE INJURY, there the remedy is usually by an action of trespass *vi et armis:* but where there is *no act done*, but only a culpable omission; or where the act is not immediately injurious, but only BY CONSEQUENCE and collaterally; there no action of trespass *vi et armis* will

will lie, but *an action on the special case*, for the damages consequent on such omission or act.

Page 48.—As to the action of *account*.

It is of late very much disused, since it is found by experience that the most ready and effectual way to settle matters of account is by bill in a court of equity, where a discovery may be had on defendant's oath, without relying merely on the evidence which the plaintiff may be able to produce. Tho' when an account is once stated, nothing is more common than an action upon the implied *assumpsit* to pay the ballance.

Page 59.—Trover.

The freedom of this action from wager of law, and the less degree of certainty requisite in describing the goods, (*Salk.* 654.) gave it so considerable an advantage over the action of *detinue*, that BY A FICTION OF LAW actions of trover were at length permitted to be brought against any man who had in his possession by any means whatsoever the personal goods of another, and sold or used them without the consent of the owner, or refused to deliver them when demanded. THE INJURY LIES IN THE CONVERSION, for any man may take the goods of another into possession, if he finds them; but no finder is allowed to acquire a property therein, unless the owner be for ever unknown: therefore he must not convert them to his own use, which the law presumes him to do, if he refuses to restore them to the owner; for which reason such refusal is, *prima facie*, sufficient evidence of a conversion. 10 *Rep.* 56. The fact of the finding, or *trover*, is therefore now totally immaterial: for the plaintiff needs only to suggest (*as words of form*) that he lost such goods, and that defendant found them; and if he proves that the goods are *his* property, and that the defendant had them in his possession, it is sufficient. But A CONVERSION MUST BE FULLY PROVED: and then in this action the plaintiff recovers damages, equal to the value of the thing converted, but not the thing *itself*; which nothing will recover but an action of *detinue* or *replevin*.

Page 64.—As to the action of slander, it is necessary to observe that, words spoken in derogation of a peer, a judge, or other *great* officer of the realm, which are called *scandalum magnatum*, are held to be more heinous, than words spoken of a common person; (1 *Vent.* 60.) and, tho' they be such as would not be actionable in the case of a common person, yet when spoken in disgrace of such high and respectable characters, they amount to an atrocious injury: which is redressed by an action on the case founded on many antient statutes, (*Westm.* 1. 3 *Ed.* 1. *c.* 34. 2 *Ric.* 2. *c.* 5. 12 *Ric.* 2, *c.* 11.) as well on behalf of the 'crown, to inflict the punishment of imprisonment on the slanderer, as on behalf of the party to recover damages for the injury sustained. Words also tending to scandalize a magistrate, or person in a public trust, are reputed more highly injurious than when spoken of a private man. Lord *Raym.* 1369. It is said, that formerly no actions were brought for words, unless the slander was such, as (if true) would endanger the life of the object of it. 2 *Vent.* 28. But, too great encouragement being given by this lenity to false and malicious slanderers, it is now held, that for scandalous words, which may endanger a man in law, may exclude him from society, may impair

APPENDIX I.

pair his trade, or may affect a peer, a magistrate, or one in public trust, an action on the case may be had WITHOUT PROVING ANY PARTICULAR DAMAGE to have happened, *but merely on the probability that it* MIGHT *happen*. But with regard to words that do not thus apparently, and upon the face of them, import such defamation as will of course be injurious, it is necessary that the plaintiff should aver some *particular* damage to have happened; which is called laying his action with a *per quod*. As if I say that such a clergyman, is a bastard, he cannot for this bring any action against me, unless he can shew some *special loss* by it; in which case he may bring his action against me, for saying he was a bastard, *per quod*, he lost the presentation to such a living. 4 *Rep.* 17. 1 *Lev.* 248. But mere scurrility, or opprobrious words, which neither in themselves import, nor are in fact attended with any injurious effects, will not support an action. So scandals, which concern matters merely spiritual, as to call a man, heretic, or adulterer, are cognizable only in the ecclesiastical court; unless any temporal damage ensues, which may be a foundation for a *per quod*. *Noy* 64. 1 *Freem.* 277. Words of heat and passion, as to call a man rogue and rascal, if productive of no ill consequence, and not of any of the dangerous species before mentioned, are not actionable; neither are words spoken in a friendly manner, as by way of advice, admonition, or concern, without any tincture or circumstance of ill will; for, in both these cases, they are not *maliciously* spoken, which is part of the definition of slander. (*Finch L.* 186. 1 *Lev.* 82. *Cro. Jac.* 91.) The manner of laying the slander or defamation in a declaration for words being, that defendant,

falsely

falsely and MALICIOUSLY, *said, rehearsed, proclaimed and loudly published* the words, &c.

Neither are any reflecting words made use of in legal proceedings, and PERTINENT TO THE CAUSE IN HAND, a sufficient cause for action of slander.

N. B.—No notice being taken of the violation of the right of personal liberty, by *false imprisonment*, the reader who chuses to consult that part of the law, will find it very fully and learnedly treated of by Doctor *Blackstone*, in 3 *Com.* 127, &c.

Page 81.—Ejectment.

A writ of *ejectione firmæ*, or action of trespass in *ejectment*, lieth, where lands or tenements are let for a term of years; and afterwards the lessor, reversioner, remainder-man, or any stranger, doth eject or oust the lessee of his term. *F. N. B.* 220. In this case he shall have this writ of *ejection*, to call the defendant to answer for entering on the lands so demised to the plaintiff for a term that is not yet expired, and ejecting him. And by this writ the plaintiff shall recover back his term, or the remainder of it, with damages.

Since the disuse of real actions, this mixed proceeding is become the common method of trying the title to lands or tenements. It may not therefore be improper to delineate, with some degree of minuteness, it's history, the manner of it's process, and the principles whereon it is grounded.

The writ of covenant, for breach of the contract contained in the lease for years, was antiently the only specific remedy for recovering against the lessor a term from which he had
ejected

ejected his lessee, together with damages for the ouster. But if the lessee was ejected by a stranger, claiming under a title superior (F. N. B. 145.) to that of the lessor, or by a grantee of the reversion, (who might at any time by a common recovery have destroyed the term,) tho' the lessee might still maintain an action of covenant against the lessor, for non-performance of his contract or lease, yet he could not by any means recover the term itself. If the ouster was committed by a mere stranger, without any title to the land, the lessor might indeed by a real action recover possession of the freehold, but the lessee had no other remedy against the ejector but in damages, by a writ of *ejectione firmæ*, for the trespass committed in ejecting him from his farm. *Fitz. Abr. tit. eject. firm.* 2. But afterwards, when the courts of equity began to oblige the ejector to make a specific restitution of the land to the party immediately injured, the courts of law also adopted the same method of doing complete justice; and, in the prosecution of a writ of ejectment, introduced a species of remedy *not warranted* by the original writ *nor prayed* by the declaration (which go only for damages merely, and are silent as to any restitution,) viz. a judgment to recover the term, and a writ of possession thereupon. This method seems to have been settled as early as the reign of *Edward* IV. [*] tho' it hath been said (*F. N. B.* 220.) to have first begun under *Henry* VII. because it

---

[*] 7 *Edw.* IV. 6. *Per Fairfax*; *si home port ejectione firmæ, le plaintiff recovera son terme qui est arere, sibien come in quare ejecit infra terminum; et, si nul soit arere, donques tout in damages.* (Bro. Abr. tit. *quare ejecit infra terminum*, 6.)

probably

APPENDIX I.

probably was *then first* applied to it's present principal use, that of trying the title to the land.

The better to apprehend the contrivance, whereby this end is effected, we must recollect that the remedy by ejectment is in it's original an action brought by one who hath a lease *for years*, to repair the injury done him by dispossession. In order therefore to convert it into a method of trying titles to the freehold, it is first necessary that the claimant do take possession of the lands, to empower him to constitute a lessee for years, who may be capable of receiving this injury of dispossession. For it would be an offence, called in our law MAINTENANCE, to convey a title to another, when the grantor is not in possession of the land: and indeed it was doubted at first, whether this occasional possession, taken merely for the purpose of conveying the title, excused the lessor from the legal guilt of maintenance. 1 *Cb. Rep. Append.* 39.—When therefore a person, who hath right of entry into lands, determines to acquire that possession, which is wrongfully with-held by the present tenant, he makes (as by law he may) a FORMAL entry on the premisses; and being so in possession of the soil, he there, *upon the land*, seals and delivers a lease for years to some third person or lessee: and, having thus given him entry, leaves him in possession of the premises. This lessee is to stay upon the land, till the prior tenant, or he who had the previous possession, enters thereon afresh and ousts him; or till some other person (either by accident, or by *agreement before-hand*) comes on the land, and turns *him* out, or ejects him.

For this injury the lessee is intitled to his action of ejectment against the tenant, or this

casual

casual ejector, which ever it was who ousted him, to recover back his term and damages. But where this action is brought against such a casual ejector as is before mentioned, and not against the very tenant in possession, the court will not suffer the tenant to lose his possession without any opportunity to defend it. Wherefore it is a standing rule, that no plaintiff shall proceed in ejectment to recover lands against a casual ejector, without notice given to the tenant in possession (if any there be) and making him a defendant if he pleases. And, in order to maintain the action, the plaintiff must, in case of any defence, make out four points before the court; viz. TITLE, LEASE, ENTRY, and OUSTER. First, he must shew a good *title* in his lessor, which brings the matter of right entirely before the court; then that the lessor, being seised by virtue of such title, did make him the *lease* for the present term; thirdly, that he the lessee or plaintiff, did *enter* or take possession in consequence of such lease; and then, lastly, that the defendant *ousted* or ejected him. Whereupon he shall have judgment to recover his term and damages; and shall, in consequence, have a *writ of possession*, which the sheriff is to execute, by delivering him the undisturbed and peaceable possession of his term.

This is the regular method of bringing an action of ejectment, in which the title of the lessor comes collaterally and incidentally before the court, in order to shew the injury done to the lessee by this ouster. This method must be still continued in due form and strictness, save only as to the notice to the tenant, whenever the possession is vacant, or there is no actual occupant

occupant of the premises; and also in some other cases. But, as much trouble and formality were found to attend the actual making of the *lease, entry,* and *ouster,* a new and more easy method of trying titles by writ of ejectment, *where there is any actual tenant or occupier of the premises in dispute,* was invented somewhat more than a century ago, by the lord chief justice *Rolle,* who then sat in the court of *upper* bench; so called during the exile of king *Charles* the second. This new method entirely DEPENDS ON A STRING OF LEGAL FICTIONS; no actual lease is made, no actual entry by plaintiff, no actual ouster by defendant; but all are merely ideal, for the sole purpose of trying the title. To this end, in the proceedings (ante 85.) a lease for a term of years is stated to have been made, by him who claims title, to the plaintiff who brings the action; as by *T. B* to *A. B.*; which plaintiff ought to be some real person, and not merely an ideal fictitious one, who has no existence, as is frequently tho' unwarrantably practised: 6 *Mod.* 309. It is also stated that *A. B.* the lessee, entered; and that defendant *C. D.* who is called the *casual ejector,* ousted him; for which ouster he brings this action. As soon as this action is brought, and the complaint fully stated in the declaration, (*ante* 85.) *C. D.* the casual ejector sends a written notice to the tenant in possession of the lands, as *E. E.* informing him of the action brought by *A. B.* and transmitting him a copy of the declaration.—*vide ante* 86. On receipt of this friendly caution, if the tenant in possession does not within a limited time apply to the court to be admitted a defendant in the stead of *C. D.* he is supposed to have no right at all; and, on judgment being had against *C. D.*

the

APPENDIX I.

the cafual ejector, *E. E.* the real tenant will be turned out of poffeffion by the fheriff.

But if the tenant in poffeffion applies to be made a defendant, it is allowed him on this condition; that he enter into a rule of court to confefs, at the trial of the caufe, three of the four requifites for the maintenance of the plaintiff's action; *viz.* the LEASE, of *T. B.* the leffor, the ENTRY of *A. B.* the plaintiff, and his OUSTER by *E. E.* himfelf, now made the defendant inftead of *C. D.* which requifites, as they are wholly fictitious, fhould the defendant put the plaintiff to prove, he muft of courfe be nonfuited for want of evidence; but by fuch ftipulated confeffion of *leafe*, *entry*, and *oufter*, the trial will now ftand on the merits of the *title* only. This done, the declaration is altered by inferting the name of *E. E.* inftead of *C. D.* and the caufe goes down to trial under the name of *A. B.* (the plaintiff) on the demife of *T. B.* (the leffor) againft *E. E.* the new defendant. And therein the leffor of the plaintiff (*T. B.*) is bound to make out a *clear title*, otherwife his fictitious leffee cannot obtain judgment to have poffeffion of the land for the term fuppofed to be granted. But, if the leffor makes out his title in a fatisfactory manner, then judgment and a writ of poffeffion fhall go for *A. B.* the nominal plaintiff, who by this trial has proved the right of *T. B.* his fuppofed leffor. Yet, to prevent fraudulent recoveries of the poffeffion, by collufion with the tenant of the land, all tenants are obliged by 11 Geo. II. c. 19. on pain of forfeiting three years rent, to give notice to their landlords, when ferved with any declaration in ejectment; and any landlord may by leave of the

court

APPENDIX I.

court be made a co-defendant to the action; which indeed *he had a right to demand*, long before the provision of this statute. 7 Mod. 70. Salk. 257. In like manner as (previous to the statute of West. 2. *c.* 3.) if in a real action the tenant of the freehold made default, the remainder-man or reversioner had *a Right* to come in and defend the possession; lest, if judgment were had against the tenant, the estate of those behind should be turned to a naked right. *Bract. l.* 5. *c.* 10. §. 14.

But if the new defendant fails to appear at the trial, and to confess lease, entry, and ouster, the plaintiff *A. B.* must indeed be there nonsuited, for want of proving those requisites; but judgment will in the end be entered against the casual ejector *C. D.*: for the condition on which *E. E.* was admitted a defendant is broken, and therefore the plaintiff is put again in the same situation as if he never had appeared at all; the consequence of which (we have seen) would have been, that judgment would have been entered for the plaintiff, and the sheriff, by virtue of a writ for that purpose, would have turned out *E. E.* and delivered possession to *A. B.* The same process therefore as would have been had, provided no conditional rule had been ever made, must now be pursued as soon as the condition is broken. But execution shall be stayed, if any landlord after the default of his tenant applies to be made a defendant, and enters into the usual rule, to confess lease, entry, and ouster. 11 *Geo.* 2. *c.* 19.

The damages recovered in these actions, tho' formerly their only intent, are now usually (since the title has been considered as the principal question) very small and inadequate; amounting
com-

commonly to one shilling or some other trivial sum. In order therefore to complete the remedy, when the possession has been long detained from him who has right, an action of trespass also lies, after a recovery in ejectment, *to recover the* MESNE *profits* (i. e. the profits arising *between* the time of ejecting the plaintiff, and his recovery in ejectment) which the tenant in possession has wrongfully received. Which action may be brought in the name of either the nominal plaintiff in the ejectment, or his lessor, against the tenant in possession; whether he be made party to the ejectment, or suffers judgment to go by default. 4 *Burr.* 668.

Such is the modern way, of *obliquely* bringing in question the title to lands and tenements, in order to try it in this collateral manner; a method which is now UNIVERSALLY ADOPTED IN ALMOST EVERY CASE. It is founded on the same principle as the ancient writs of assise, being calculated to try the mere POSSESSORY title to an estate; and hath succeeded to those real actions, as being infinitely more convenient for attaining the end of justice: because, the form of the proceeding being intirely fictitious, *it is wholly in the power of the court* TO DIRECT THE APPLICATION *of that fiction, so as* TO PREVENT FRAUD AND CHICANE, AND EVISCERATE THE VERY TRUTH OF THE TITLE.

But a writ of ejectment is not an adequate means to try the title of *all* estates; for on such things whereon an entry *cannot* in fact be made, *no* entry shall be *supposed* by any fiction of the parties. Therefore an ejectment will *not* lie of an advowson, a rent, a common, or other *incorporeal* hereditament; (*Brown.* 129. *Cro. Car.*

K k

492. *Stra.* 54.) except for tithes in the hands of lay appropriators, by the expreſs purview of ſtatute 3 *Hen.* VIII. *c.* 7. which doctrine hath ſince been extended by analogy to tithes in the hands of the clergy. *Cro. Car.* 301. 2 Lord *Raym.* 789. Nor will it lie in ſuch caſes, where the entry of him who hath right is taken away by deſcent, diſcontinuance, twenty years diſpoſſeſſion, or otherwiſe.

This action of ejectment is however rendered a very eaſy and expeditious remedy to landlords whoſe tenants are in arrere, by 4 *Geo.* 2. *c.* 28. which ſee *ante*, 84. 5.

Page 120.—As to controverſies determined, without action at law, or redreſs by the mere act of the parties; they are

1. From the SOLE act of the party injured.
2. From the JOINT act of all the parties.

Of the firſt ſort are, 1. Self defence. 2 Recaption of goods. 3. Entry on lands and tenements. 4. Abatement of Nuſances. 5. Diſtreſs for Rent, or for Damage. 6. Seiſing of Heriots, &c.

Of the ſecond ſort are, 1. Accord. 2. Arbitration.

There is alſo REDRESS by a mere OPERATION of law, which is, 1. Where a creditor is executor or adminiſtrator, and is thereupon allowed to *retain* his own debt. 2. In the caſe of *remitter*; where one, who has a GOOD title to lands, &c. comes into poſſeſſion by a BAD one, and is thereupon *remitted* to his antient good title, which protects his ill acquired poſſeſſion.

APPENDIX II.

CONTAINING

An ANALYSIS of all the STATUTES concerning FELONIES in general, and FELONIES *within* and *without* CLERGY.

1. *Statutes concerning felony in general.*
2. *Felonies within Clergy.*
3. *Felonies without Clergy.*

1. *Statutes concerning felony in general.*

FELONS standing mute shall be put to strong and hard imprisonment, 3 *Ed.* 1. *c.* 12. See *Felonies without clergy.* (mute.)

The goods of felons and fugitives ought to be inventoried and inrolled by the coroner, *Artic. Exon.* 14 *Ed.* 1.

Breaking prison felony, only where the prisoner was in custody for a felony, 1 *Ed.* 2. *st.* 2.

Writs to take felons shall be directed to all the counties, 5 *Ed.* 3. *c.* 11.

Felons goods and lands shall not be seized before conviction, *Stat. de Catall. felon. incerti temp.* 1 *R.* 3. *c.* 3. His chattels shall be forfeited on the return of a *non est inventus*, 25 *Ed.* 3. *f̄.* 5 *c.* 14.

Process against felons, *ibid.*

One charged in the Exchequer with felons goods may charge another over, 31 *Ed.* 3. *ft.* 1. *c.* 2.

Justices of the King's Bench may remand felons into their proper counties, 6 *H.* 8. *c.* 6.

Stolen goods shall be restored upon the attainder of the felon, 21 *H.* 8. *c.* 11.

How foreign pleas pleaded by felons shall be tried, 22 *H.* 8. *c.* 2. & *c.* 14. 1 *Ed.* 6. *c.* 12. *sect.* 11.

No forfeiture for killing a man attempting to commit murder or robbery, 24 *H.* 8. *c.* 5.

The clerk of the assise, &c. shall certify the names of the felons convict into the King's Bench, 34 & 35 *H.* 8. *c.* 14.

Repeal of all felonies made since 1 *H.* 8. 1 *Ed.* 6. *c.* 12. *sect.* 4. 1 *M. ft.* 1. *c.* 1.

All felonies and offences of *præmunire* since 1 *H.* 8. repealed, 1 *M. ft.* 1. *c.* 5.

Persons indicted of felony in embezzling stores may make defence by witnesses, 31 *Eliz.* *c.* 4.

Apprehenders of burglars and shoplifters to have a certificate to discharge them from parish offices, 10 & 11. *W.* 3. *c.* 23. *sect.* 2.

Farther intitled to 40 *l.* reward, on tendring certificate of conviction, 5 *Ann.* *c.* 31.

Burglars and shoplifters discovering their accomplices, &c. to be pardoned, 10 & 11 *W.* 3. *c.* 23. *sect.* 5.

Felons to be burnt in the cheek, 10 & 11 *W.* 3. *c.* 23. *sect.* 6. repealed 5 *Ann.* *c.* 6.

Fee for drawing a bill of indictment settled at two shillings, 10 & 11 *W.* 3. *c.* 23. *sect.* 7.

Offences

APPENDIX II.

Offences committed at sea may be tried as directed by commission, and person standing mute, &c. to suffer death, 1 *Ann. st.* 2. *c.* 9. *sect.* 5.

Felons may be burnt in the hand, and committed to hard labour, 5 *Ann. c.* 6.

Felon discovering and convicting two accomplices, intitled to a pardon, &c. 5 *Ann. c.* 31. *sect.* 4.

Receivers of stolen goods made accessary, 5 *Ann. c.* 31. *sect.* 5.

Judges to settle the rights and shares of persons intitled to certificates, 5 *Ann. c.* 31. *sect.* 7.

Intitled to the same certificate as for apprehending highwaymen, 6 *Geo.* 1. *c.* 23. *sect.* 9.

Proclamation for offenders to surrender to be printed in the Gazette, 9 *Geo.* 1. *c.* 22. *sect.* 4.

Justices to give certificate to persons wounded, or to executors of persons killed in apprehending felons, 9 *Geo.* 1. *c.* 22. *sect.* 12.

Returning from transportation excluded clergy, 25 *Geo.* 2. *c.* 10.

The court may order the expence of prosecuting a felon to be paid by the treasurer of the county, 25 *Geo.* 2. *c.* 36. *sect.* 11. And the expence of the attendance of poor witnesses, 27 *Geo.* 2. *c.* 3. *sect.* 3.

Buying or receiving lead, iron, copper, brass, metal or solder, knowing it to be stolen, to be punished by transportation, 29 *Geo.* 2. *c.* 30. Penalties on having these materials without being able to account for them, 29 *Geo.* 2. *c.* 30. *sect.* 6.

2. *Felon within Clergy.*

Armour. Imbezzling it, 31 *Eliz. c.* 4. See *Felonies without clergy* (armour).

Assault.

APPENDIX II.

Assault. Assaulting persons with intent to tear or spoil their clothes, 6 *Geo.* 1. *c.* 23. *sect.* 11. See *Robbery* under this division.

Bridge. Destroying *London* bridge, 29 *Geo.* 2. *c.* 40. *sect.* 6. See *Felonies without clergy.*

Or *Walton* bridge, 20 *Geo.* 2. *cap.* 22.

Or *Hampton-Court* bridge, 23 *Geo.* 2. *c.* 37. *sect.* 12.

Or *Ribble* bridge, 24 *Geo.* 2. *c.* 36. *sect.* 34.

Or *Sandwich* bridge, 28 *Geo.* 2. *c.* 55.

Or *Wyde* bridge, 24 *Geo.* 2. *c.* 73.

Or *Black Friars* bridge, 29 *Geo.* 2. *c.* 86.

Or *Jeremy Ferry's* bridge, 30 *Geo.* 2. *c.* 59.

Or *Old Brentford* bridge, 30 *Geo.* 2. *c.* 63. *sect.* 19. 31 *Geo.* 2. *c.* 46.

Bail. Personating bail before commissioners in the country, 4 *W. & M. c.* 4. *sect.* 4. See *Felonies without clergy.*

Bigamy. See *Polygamy.*

Blacklead. See *Lead.*

Burning. Farms of timber, 37 *H.* 8. *c.* 6. *sect.* 2. repealed by 1 *Ed.* 6. *c.* 12. 1 *M. sess.* 1. *c.* 1.

Stacks of corn, houses, &c. in the night-time, 22 & 23 *Car.* 2. *c.* 7. *sect.* 2. See *Felonies without clergy.*

Cattle. Killing them in the night, &c 22 & 23 *Car.* 2. *c.* 7. *sect.* 2. See *Felonies without clergy.*

Cloth. Stealing it, or wool, left to dry, off the tenters, &c. the third offence, 15 *Geo.* 2. *c.* 27. See *Felonies without clergy.*

Corn. Destroying granaries, the second offence, 11 *Geo.* 2. *c.* 22. See *Felonies without clergy*; and see *Burning, ante.*

Council. See *King.*

Copper. See *Money, Lead.*

Customs

Customs. Running goods five in company armed, 8 *Geo.* 1. *c.* 18. *sect.* 6. See *Felonies without clergy.*

Assembling armed to the number of three for running goods, 9 *Geo.* 2. *c.* 35. *sect.* 10.

Persons deemed smugglers according to the description of 9 *Geo.* 2. *c.* 35. *sect.* 13.

Harbouring offenders against the laws of customs, 19 *Geo.* 2. *c.* 34. *sect.* 3. See *Felonies without clergy.*

Dikes. Cutting them in marsh land, 22 *H.* 8. *c.* 11. 2 & 3 *P. & M. c.* 19.

Escape. See *Prisoner.*

Fish. Fishing in another's pond with intent to steal, 31 *H.* 8. *c.* 2.

Floodgate. See *Locks.*

Foreign State. Serving it without taking oath of allegiance, 3 *Jac.* 1. *c.* 4. *sect.* 18.

Forgery. Of bank bills, 11 *Geo.* 2. *c.* 9. *sect.* 6.—Of bank notes and indorsements, *ibid.* See *Felonies without clergy.*

Gaoler. Foreign prisoner to become approver, 14 *Ed.* 3. *c.* 10.

Hawk. Stealing one, 37 *Ed.* 3. *c.* 19.

Hunting. In the night or in disguise, 1 *H.* 7. *c.* 7. rescuing such offenders, *ibid.* See *Felonies without clergy,* title *Black act.*

Iron-bars. Stealing them, fixed to buildings, 4 *Geo.* 2. *c.* 32. See *Lead.*

King. Conspiring or imagining to destroy him, or any of his council, 3 *H.* 7. *cap.* 14. See *Felonies without clergy,* title *Privy counsellors.*

Labourers. Confederacies of masons to prevent the statutes of labourers, 3 *H.* 6. *c.* 1.

Lead. Entering mines of black lead with intent to steal, 25 *Geo.* 2. *c.* 10. *sect.* 1.

APPENDIX II.

Stealing it, fixed to buildings, 4 *Geo.* 2. *c.* 32.

Receivers of lead so stolen, *ibid. sect.* 3.

Buying or receiving lead, iron, copper, &c. knowing it to be stolen, 29 *Geo.* 2. *c.* 30.

Locks. Persons guilty of demolishing them, or of sluices or floodgates, 1 *Geo.* 2. *st.* 2. *c.* 19.

Maiming. And after cutting out tongues or putting out eyes, 5 *H.* 4. *c.* 5. See *Felonies without clergy.*

Marriage. Solemnizing it clandestinely, 26 *Geo.* 2. *c.* 33. *sect.* 8. See *Women.*

Mariners. See *Mutiny, Seamen.*

Money. Transportation of silver, or importation of false money, 17 *Ed.* 3. *not printed.*

Multiplication of gold or silver, 5 *H.* 4. *cap.* 4 repealed by 1 *W. & M. st.* 1. *c.* 30.

Coining or bringing in gally-half-pence, suskins or dodkins, 3 *H.* 5 *c.* 1.

Payment of blanks, 2 *H.* 6. *c.* 9. *Obs.*

Blanching copper, or putting off counterfeit money, 8 & 9 *W.* 3. *c.* 26. *sect.* 6.

Mutiny. In mariners, hindering commanders from fighting, 22 *Car.* 2. *c.* 11. *sect.* 9.

Officers, &c. destroying ship, *ibid. sect.* 12. See *Felonies without clergy.*

Officer or soldier upon or beyond the sea raising mutiny, disobeying or resisting superior, 2 & 3 *Ann. c.* 20. *sect.* 35.

Palaces. Entring into King's house with intent to steal, 33 *H.* 8. *c.* 12. *sect.* 27.

Plague. Persons infected with it going abroad, 1 *Jac.* 1. *c.* 31. *sect.* 7.

Polygamy. By 1 *Jac.* 1. *c.* 11.

Prisoner. Assisting one committed for treason or felony (except petty larceny) to attempt an escape, 16 *Geo.* 2. *c.* 31. See *Gaoler.*

Process.

APPENDIX II.

Process. Opposing the execution of it in any pretended privileged place, 9 *Geo.* 1. *c.* 28. 11 *Geo.* 1. *c.* 22. See *Felonies without clergy.*

Purveyors. In some cases by 28 *Ed.* 1 *st.* 3. *c.* 2.

N. B. Purveyance is taken away by 12 *Car.* 2. *c.* 24.

Rape. By 13 *Ed.* 1. *c.* 34. See *Felonies without clergy.*

Records. Withdrawing them, 8 *H.* 6. *c.* 12.

Rescue. Rescuing the body of offender executed for murder from the sheriff or surgeons, 25 *Geo.* 2. *c.* 37. *sect.* 10. See *Felonies without clergy, Hunting, Spirituous liquors.*

Rogues. Incorrigible, breaking out or escaping from house of correction, or offending a second time, 17 *Geo.* 2. *cap.* 5. *sect.* 9.

Adjudged to the gallies returning without licence, 39 *El. c.* 4. 1 *Jac.* 1. *c.* 7. & 25. repealed by 12 *Ann. st.* 2. *c.* 23.

Robbery. Stealing furniture from lodgings (if under 12 d.) 3 *W. & M. cap.* 9. *sect.* 5. See *Felonies without clergy.*

Assaulting with intent to rob, 7 *Geo.* 2. *c.* 21. *sect.* 1.

Seamen. Deserting, 5 *El. c.* 5. *sect.* 27. See *Felonies without clergy.*

Soldiers. Deserting, 18 *H.* 6. *c.* 19. *sect.* 2. See *Felonies without clergy.*

Servants. Taking their master's goods at their death, 33 *H.* 6. *c.* 1. *Q. If in use?*

Assaulting, &c. master wool-comber or weaver, 12 *Geo.* 1. *c.* 34. *sect.* 6.

Imbezilling goods delivered to them to the value of 40 s. 21 *H.* 8. *c.* 7. perp. by 5 *El. c.* 10. Apprentices under 18 excepted, 21 *H.* 8. *c.* 7. *sect.* 2.

Sheep.

APPENDIX II.

Sheep. Exporting them alive, the second offence, 8 *El. c.* 3. *sect.* 2. See *Felonies without clergy.*

Ships. Destroying them, 22 & 23 *Car.* 2. *c.* 11. *sect.* 12. See *Mutiny ante*, and *Felonies without clergy.*

Sluices. See *Locks.*

Smuggling. See *Customs.*

Spirituous liquors. Rescuing offenders against the acts concerning these liquors, 11 *Geo.* 2. *c.* 26. *sect.* 2. 24 *Geo.* 2. *c.* 40. *sect.* 28.

Stamps. Taking off the stamp of any playing cards, 12 *Geo.* 3. *c.* 48.

Stolen goods, Buyers or receivers of them, 5 *Ann. c.* 31. *sect.* 5.

Taking reward to help one to stolen goods (if he do not apprehend offender) in some cases, 4 *Geo.* 1. *c.* 11. *sect.* 4.

Stores. Imbezilling them to 20 *s.* value, 31 *El. c.* 4.

Treason. Anonymous accusation of high treason, 37 *H.* 8. *c.* 10. rep. 1 *Ed.* 6. *c.* 12.

Turnpikes. Destroying them, 5 *Geo.* 2. *c.* 33. See *Felonies without clergy.*

Waterman. Carrying greater number of passengers than allowed, if any passenger be drowned, 10 *Geo.* 2. *c.* 31. *sect.* 9.

Women. Taking them away, and marrying or defiling them, &c. having lands or goods, 3 *H.* 7. *c.* 2. See *Felonies without clergy.*

Woods. Firing them, 1 *Geo.* 1. *st.* 2. *c.* 48. *sect.* 48. 6 *Geo.* 3. *c.* 48. See *Felonies without clergy.*

Wool. Exportation of it, other than to the staple at *Calais,* 18 *H.* 6. *c.* 15.

Transporting of it out of *England, Wales* or *Ireland,* 13 & 14 *Car.* 2. *c.* 18. altered by the 7 & 8 *W.* 3. *c.* 28. See *Cloth*, and *Servants ante.*

By

APPENDIX II.

By Stat. 16 *Geo.* 3. Any male convicted in *England* of any crime punishable by transportation to *America*, may, instead thereof, be kept to hard labour in cleansing the river *Thames*, &c. for any term not less than three, nor more than ten years.

3. *Felonies without clergy.*

Accessaries. Before the fact in petty treason, murder, burglary, robbery in dwelling-houses, or in churches, or in or near the highway, house-burning, or burning of barns where there is corn or grain, 25 *H.* 8. *c.* 1. 5 & 6 *Ed.* 6. *c.* 9. 4 & 5 *P.* & *M.* *c.* 4.

Before and after in horse-stealing, 31 *El. c.* 12. *ſ* 5.

Before the fact in stealing women, having lands or goods, or being heirs apparent, 39 *El. c.* 9. *sect.* 2.

Before the fact in witchcraft, 1 *Jac.* 1. *c.* 12. repealed by 9 *Geo.* 2. *c.* 5.

Before the fact in procuring any fine, recovery, deed inrolled, statute, recognizance, bail or judgment to be acknowledged in the name of another, 21 *Jac.* 1. *c.* 26.

Before the fact in maiming, 22 & 23 *Car.* 2. *c.* 1.

Before the fact in burglary, shoplifting, &c. 3 & 4 *W.* & *M. c.* 9.

Before the fact in robberies in shops, warehouses, coach-houses or stables, 10 & 11 *W.* 3. *c.* 23.

Before the fact in piracy, in some cases, 11 & 12 *W.* 3. *c.* 7. 8 *Geo.* 1. *c.* 24.

APPENDIX II

To forging any deed, will, bond, bill of exchange, note, indorsement or assignment of bill or note, or any acquittance or receipt, 2 *Geo.* 2. *c.* 25. perpetual by 9 *Geo.* 2. *c.* 18.

To forging bills of exchange, accountable receipts, warrants, or orders for payment of money or delivery of goods, 7 *Geo.* 2. *c.* 22.

Before the fact in sheep-stealing, 14 *Geo.* 2. *c.* 6. and see 15 *Geo.* 2. *c.* 34.

Before the fact in stealing cotton, &c. from bleaching grounds, 18 *Geo.* 2. *c.* 27.

Before the fact in thefts to 40*s.* value in any vessel or in any wharf, 24 *Geo.* 2. *c.* 45.

Before the fact in destroying *London Bridge*, 31 *Geo.* 2. *c.* 20. *sect.* 6.

Armour. See *Stores.*

Annuities. See *Forgery.*

Bail. Personating bail, 21 *Jac.* 1. *c.* 26.

Bank. Officer or servant of bank secreting or embezzling any note, &c. 15 *Geo.* 2. *c.* 13. *sect.* 12. See *Forgery, Robbery.*

Banks. Destroying them, 6 *Geo.* 2. *c.* 37. *sect.* 5. perpetual by 31 *Geo.* 2. *c.* 42.

Bankrupt. Not surrendering, or not submitting to be examined, or concealing or embezzling their estates, 5 *Geo.* 2. *c.* 30.

Bastard. Mother concealing the death of a bastard child, 21 *Jac.* 1. *c.* 21. *sect.* 2.

Bedford Level. See *Fens.*

Black act. Hunting armed and disguised, and killing or stealing deer, or robbing warren, or stealing fish out of any river, &c. or any persons unlawfully hunting in his majesty's forests, &c. or breaking down the head of any fish-pond, or killing, &c. of cattle, or cutting down trees, or setting fire to house, barn or wood, or shooting at any person, or sending anonymous letter,

or

or signed with fictitious name, demanding money, &c. or rescuing such offenders, 9 *Geo.* 1. *c.* 72. perpetual by 31 *Geo.* 2. *c.* 42.

Black lead. Offenders committed or transported for entering mines of black lead with intent to steal, escaping or breaking prison, or returning from transportation, 25 *Geo.* 2. *c.* 10.

Black mail. See *Cumberland.*

Bonds. See *Forgery, Robbery.*

Booths. See *Robbery.*

Bridges. Wilful damaging *London Bridge*, 31 *Geo.* 2. *c.* 10. *s.* 6.

Destroying *Westminster Bridge*, 9 *Geo.* 2. *c.* 29. *sect.* 5.

Or *Fulham Bridge*, 12 *Geo.* 1. *c.* 36. *sect.* 3.

Buggery. By 25 *H.* 8. *c.* 6. 2 & 3 *Ed.* 6. *c.* 29. revived by 5 *El. c.* 17.

Burglary. By 1 *Ed.* 6. *c.* 12. 18 *El. c.* 7. 12 *Ann. c.* 7.

Burning. Houses or barns with corn, 23 *H.* 8. *c.* 1. 25 *H.* 8. *c.* 3. 22 & 23 *Car.* 2. *c.* 7. 43 *El. c.* 13. See *Black act, Coals, Fens.*

Breaking prison. See *Black lead, Perjury, Robbery.*

Cattle. See *Black act, Sheep.*

Challenge of jurors. Challenge above twenty, if the indictment be for such offence for which the offender would have been excluded clergy, if convicted or confession, 25 *H.* 8. *c.* 3. 4 & 5 *P. & M. c.* 4. 3 & 4 *W. & M. c.* 9.

Cloth. Stealing it from the rack or tenters, 25 *Car.* 2. *c.* 5. *sect.* 3.

Coals. Firing collieries, 10 *Geo. c.* 32. perpetual 31 *Geo.* 2. *c.* 42.

Corn. Persons transported for destroying granaries returning, 11 *Geo. c.* 23. *sect.* 2. See *Black act, Burning, Cumberland.*

Council.

APPENDIX II.

Council. See *Privy Counsellors.*

Cumberland. Forcibly carrying subjects out of *Cumberland, Northumberland, Westmoreland,* and *Durham,* and taking or giving black mail, burning corn, &c. 43 *El. c.* 13. *sect.* 2.

Notorious thieves, or spoil-takers in *Northumberland* or *Cumberland* (or to be transported at discretion of judge). 18 *Car.* 2. *c.* 3.

Customs. Persons liable to transportation for offences against the customs, offending again, after having taken the benefit of the indemnifying act, 9 *Geo.* 2. *c.* 35. *s.* 7. 18 *Geo.* 2. *c.* 28. *sect.* 7.

Persons convicted of wounding custom-house officers, returning from transportation, 6 *Geo.* 1. *c.* 21. *s.* 35. 3 *Geo.* 2. *c.* 35. *sect.* 28. See *Smuggling.*

Cutpurse. See *Pickpocket.*

Deer. Persons convicted of second offence in hunting and taking them away, or for coming armed into a forest with intent to steal them, 10 *Geo.* 2. *c.* 32. *sect.* 7. See *Black act.*

Deeds Inrolled. Acknowledging them in the name of another, 21 *Jac.* 1. *c.* 26.

Egyptians. Remaining in the realm one month, 1 & 2 *Ph.* & *M. c.* 4. *sect.* 3.

Associating with them one month, 5 *El. c.* 20. *s.* 3.

East-India Bonds, &c. See *Forgery, Robbery.*

Escape. See *Breaking prison, Prisoner.*

Exchequer Order, &c. See *Forgery, Robbery.*

Fens. Destroying, &c. any of the works in *Bedford Level,* 27 *Geo.* 2. *c.* 19. *Vide Marches.*

Fines. Acknowledging them in the name of another, 21 *Jac.* 1. *c.* 26.

Fish. See *Black act.*

Floodgates. See *Turnpikes.*

Forests. See *Black act.*

Forgeries. Of deeds on second conviction, 5 *El. c.* 14. *sect.* 7.

Of testimonial of justices by soldiers or mariners, 39 *El. c.* 17. *sect.* 3.

Of deeds, will, bill of exchange, note, indorsement, or receipt, on first conviction, 2 *Geo.* 2. *c.* 25. *sect.* 1. perpetual by 9 *Geo.* 2. *c.* 18. and see 31 *Geo.* 2. *c.* 22. *sect.* 81.

Of authorities to transfer stock, or personating proprietors, 18 *Geo.* 1. *c.* 22. Extended to funds established since 8 *Geo.* 1. by 31 *Geo.* 2. *c.* 22. *sect.* 80.

Of order for payment of annuities, or personating proprietors, 9 *Geo.* 1. *c.* 12. *sect.* 4. 9 *Geo.* 2. *c.* 34. *sect.* 8.

Of new stamps, or receipts for monies payable on indentures, 8 *Ann. c.* 8. *sect.* 41.

Of the hand of accountant general, register, clerk of the report-office, or any of the cashiers of the Bank, 12 *Geo.* 1. *c.* 32. *sect.* 9.

Of *East-India* bonds, 12 *Geo.* 1. *cap.* 32. *sect.* 9.

Of *South-Sea* common seal, bonds, receipts, or warrants for dividends, 9 *Ann. c.* 25. *sect.* 57. 6 *Geo.* 1. *c.* 4. *sect.* 56. 6 *Geo.* 1. *c.* 11. *sect.* 50. 12 *Geo.* 1. *c.* 32. *sect.* 9. and other subsequent acts.

Of *Mediterranean* passes, 4 *Geo.* 2. *c.* 18.

Of any entry of acknowledgment of bargain or in bargain and sale in the registry of *York*, the second offence, 8 *Geo. c.* 6. *sect.* 31.

Of stamp for marking gold and silver, 31 *Geo.* 2. *c.* 32. *sect.* 15.

Of policies of *Royal Exchange* and *London* assurances, 6 *Geo.* 1. *c.* 18. *sect.* 13.

Of debentures, 5 *Geo.* 1. *c.* 14. *sect.* 10.

Of the marks on leather, 9 *Ann. c.* 11. *sect.* 44. 5 *Geo.* 1. *c.* 2. *sect.* 9.

APPENDIX II.

Of the marks on linen, 10 *Ann. c.* 19. *sect.* 97. 4 *Geo.* 3. *c.* 37. *sect.* 26.

Of register or licence of marriage, 26 *Geo.* 2. *c.* 33. *sect.* 16.

Of the common seal of Bank or Bank notes, 8 & 9 *W.* 3. *c.* 20. *sect.* 36. 11 *Geo.* 1. *c.* 9. *sect.* 6. 15 *Geo.* 2. *c.* 13. *sect.* 11.

Of Exchequer bills, &c. 7 & 8 *W.* 3. *c.* 31. *sect.* 78. 9 *W.* 3. *c.* 2. *sect.* 3. 5 *Ann. c.* 13. 3 *Geo.* 1. *c.* 8. *sect.* 40. 6 *Geo.* 1. *c.* 4. *sect.* 91. 9 *Geo.* 1. *c.* 5. *sect.* 19. 11 *Geo.* 1. *c.* 17. *sect.* 6. 30 *Geo.* 2. *c.* 3. *sect.* 156. 33 *Geo.* 2. *c.* 1. *sect.* 156.

Of lottery orders, 12 *Ann. c.* 2. 5 *Geo.* 1. *c.* 3. and other subsequent lottery acts.

Of stamps, 5 *W. & M. c.* 21. *sect.* 11. 9 & 10 *W.* 3. *c.* 25. *sect.* 59. 9 *Ann. c.* 23. *sect.* 34. 10 *Ann. c.* 19. *sect.* 115, 163. 10 *Ann. c.* 26. *sect.* 72. 5 *Geo.* 1. *c.* 2. *sect.* 9. 6 *Geo. c.* 21. *sect.* 60. 20 *Geo.* 2. *c.* 12. *sect.* 21. 29 *Geo.* 2. *c.* 13. *sect.* 5. 30 *Geo.* 2. *c.* 19. *sect.* 27. 32 *Geo.* 2. *c.* 35. *sect.* 17. 2 *Geo.* 3. *c.* 36. *sect.* 8.

Of the hand of the receiver of the prefines, 32 *Geo.* 2. *c.* 14. *sect.* 9.

Of the acceptance of bills of exchange, or accountable receipts, 7 *Geo.* 2. *c.* 22.

Of any warrant, or order for payment for money or delivery of goods, 7 *Geo.* 2. *c.* 22.

Fustian. Stealing it from the bleaching grounds, 4 *Geo.* 2. *c.* 16. 18 *Geo.* 2. *c.* 27.

Gaol. See *Breaking prison.*

Helping to stolen goods for reward. In some cases, unless the helper apprehends the offender, 4 *Geo.* 1. *c.* 11.

Hops. Cutting hop-binds, 6 *Geo.* 2. *c.* 37. *sect.* 6.

APPENDIX II.

Horse-stealing. By 37 H. 8. c. 8. sect. 2. 1 Ed. 6. c. 12. sect. 10. 2 & 3 Ed. 6. c. 33.

House-breaking. See *Robbery.*

Houses. See *Burning, Black act.*

Hunting. See *Black act.*

Jesuits. See *Priests.*

Judgments, Acknowledging them in the name of another, 21 *Jac.* 1. *c.* 26.

Letters threatning. Sending them, or rescuing such offenders, 27 *Geo.* 2. c. 15.

Letters anonymous, or signed with fictitious name. See *Black act.*

Linen. Stealing it from bleaching grounds, 4 *Geo.* 2. c. 16. 18 *Geo.* 2. c. 27. See *Forgeries* 59.

Breaking into shops, &c. to steal or destroy linen, yarn, or implements, 4 *Geo.* 3. c. 37.

Locks. See *Turnpikes.*

Lotteries. See *Forgery.*

Maid. See *Woman.*

Maiming. Any person maliciously lying in wait, 22 & 23 *Car.* 2. c. 1.

Marshes. Firing engines for draining them, the second offence, 12 *Geo.* 2. c. 34. 14 *Geo.* 2. c. 24. 21 *Geo.* 2. c. 18.

Mariners. Wandering without testimonial of justices, 39 *Eliz.* c. 17. sect. 2. See *Forgery.*

Departing within the year from the service of those who took them, to save them from execution, 39 *El.* c. 17. sect. 4.

Marriage. See *Women.*

Money. Uttering false money the third time, &c. 15 *Geo.* 2. c. 28. sect. 2, 3.

Murder. By 12 H. 7. c. 7. 23 H. 8. c. 1. 25 H. 8. c. 3. 29 H. 8. c. 1. 1 Ed. 6. c. 22.

Mute. Standing mute, or not answering directly, 25 H. 8. c. 3. 1 Ed. 6. c. 12. 4 & 5

APPENDIX II.

Ph. & Mar. c. 4. 3 *& 4 W. & M. c.* 9. 1. *Ann. c.* 9. 12 *Geo.* 3. *c.* 20.

Northumberland. See *Cumberland.*

Notes. See *Forgery, Robbery.*

Ordnance. See *Stores.*

Outlawry. For offences not within the benefit of clergy, 1 *Ed.* 6. *c.* 12. 4 *& 5 Ph. & M. c.* 4. 8 *El. c.* 4. 18 *El. c.* 7. 22 *Car.* 2. *c.* 5. 3 *& 4 W. & M. c.* 9.

Petty Treason. See *Murder.*

Perjury. Person convicted of wilful and corrupt perjury, escaping, breaking prison, or returning from transportation, 2 *Geo.* 2. *c.* 25. *sect.* 2. See *Prisoners.*

Pickpocket. Taking *clam & secrete* from the person above the value of 12 *d.* 8 *El. c.* 4.

Piracy. By 11 *& 12 W.* 3. *c.* 7. 4 *Geo.* 1. *c.* 12. 8 *Geo.* 1. *c.* 24.

Person laying violent hands on his commander, to hinder him from fighting, &c. to suffer as a pirate, 11 *& 12 W.* 3. *c.* 7. *sect* 9.

Trading with pirates, 8 *Geo.* 1. *c.* 24.

Plague. See *Quarentine.*

Poisoning. Of malice prepensed, 1 *Ed.* 6. *c.* 12. *sect.* 13.

Popish recusants. Refusing to abjure, or not departing the realm within a time limited, or returning without the king's leave, 35 *El. c.* 1. *sect.* 3. 35 *El. c.* 2. *sect.* 10.

Priests and jesuits. They who receive, relieve or maintain them knowingly, 27 *El. c.* 2. *sect.* 4.

Prisoners. Taking the benefit of insolvent acts and forswearing themselves, 28 *Geo.* 2 *c.* 13. *sect.* 17. 1 *Geo.* 3. *c.* 17. *sect.* 26. 5 *Geo.* 3. *c.* 41.

Refus-

APPENDIX II.

Refusing to deliver up their effects, or concealing to the value of 20 *l.* 28 *Geo.* 2. *c.* 13. *sect.* 39. 1 *Geo.* 3. *c.* 17. *sect.* 46.

Persons transported for assisting prisoners to escape, and returning, 16 *Geo.* 2. *c.* 31.

Privy Counsellors. They who attempt to kill, or to strike or wound them in the execution of their office, 9 *Ann. c.* 16.

Process. Persons disguised, abetting rioters who oppose the execution of process in pretended privileged places, 9 *Geo.* 1. *c.* 28. *sect.* 3.

Quarentine. Not performing it, 7 *Geo.* 1. *c.* 3. 8 *Geo. c.* 8. 1 *Geo.* 2. *c.* 13. 6 *Geo. c.* 34. 26 *Geo.* 2. *c.* 6.

Masters of ships offending against directions of 26 *Geo.* 2. *c.* 6. *sect.* 2.

Concealing the having infected person on board, 26. *Geo.* 2. *c.* 6. *sect.* 3.

Refusing to perform quarentine, 26 *Geo.* 2. *c.* 6. *sect.* 8.

Sound persons entering lazaret, and escaping before they have performed quarentine, 26 *Geo.* 2. *c.* 6. *sect.* 10.

Superintendant of quarentine neglecting duty, 26 *Geo.* 2. *c.* 6. *sect.* 17.

Concealing or clandestinely conveying letters or goods, 26 *Geo.* 2. *c.* 6. *sect.* 18.

Rape. By 18 *El. c.* 7. *sect.* 1.

Carnally knowing a woman child under the age of ten years, 18 *El. c.* 7. *sect.* 4.

Rebels. Pardoned and returning from transportation, or going into the dominions of *France* or *Spain,* 20 *Geo.* 2. *c.* 46. *sect.* 1.

Persons aiding them to such purposes, 20 *Geo.* 2. *c.* 46. *sect.* 2.

Or holding correspondence with them, or with persons employed by them, by letters or otherwise, 20 *Geo.* 2. *c.* 46. *sect.* 3.

Recognizance. Acknowledging it in the name of another, 21 *Jac.* 1. *c.* 26.

Recovery, Acknowledging it in the name of another, 21 *Jac.* 1. *c.* 26.

Rescue. Rescuing convicts from transportation, 6 *Geo.* 1. *c.* 23. *sect.* 5.

Rescuing any person committed for, or found guilty of murder, or going to execution, or during execution, 25 *Geo.* 2. *c.* 37. *sect.* 9.

Persons transported for rescuing the body of such offenders, after execution, from the sheriff or surgeons, *&c.* and returning, 25 *Geo.* 2. *c.* 37. *sect.* 10. See *Black act, Letter threatning, Turnpike.*

Rioters. Assembled to the number of twelve, and continuing together one hour after proclamation, 1 *Geo.* 1. *st.* 2. *c.* 5. *sect.* 1.

Pulling down buildings, 1 *Geo.* 1. *st.* 2. *c.* 5. *sect.* 4.

Or hindring proclamation being made, 1 *Geo.* 1. *st.* 2. *c.* 5. *sect.* 5. See *Process.*

Robbery. Of churches, or sacrilege, 23 *H.* 8. *c.* 1. 25 *H.* 8. *c.* 3. 1 *Ed.* 6. *c.* 12. 5 *&* 6 *Ed.* 6. *c.* 9 *&* 10.

In or near the highway, 23 *Hen.* 8. *c.* 1. 25 *H.* 8. *c.* 3. 1 *Ed.* 6. *c.* 12.

In booths or tents in any fair or market, 5 *&* 6 *Ed.* 6. *c.* 9.

In dwelling-houses, shops, warehouses, coach-houses, or stables, 23 *H.* 8. *c.* 1. 25 *H.* 8. *c.* 3. 1 *Ed.* 6. *c.* 12. 5 *&* 6 *Ed.* 6. *c.* 9 *&* 10. 39 *El.* *c.* 15. 3 *&* 4 *W.* *&* *M.* *c.* 23. 12 *Ann.* *c.* 7.

On board any vessel, or on any wharf, to the value of 40 *s.* 24 *Geo.* 2. *c.* 45.

Stealing furniture, *&c.* from lodgings, (if above 12 *d.* value) 3 *&* 4 *W.* *&* *M.* *c.* 9. *sect.* 5.

Stealing

APPENDIX II.

Stealing Exchequer orders, tallies or other orders intitling person to annuity or share in any parliamentary fund, or Exchequer bills, bank notes, *South-Sea* bonds, *East-India* bonds, dividend warrants of bank, *South-Sea*, *East-India* or other company, bills of exchange, navy bills or debentures, goldsmiths notes, or other bonds or warrants, bills or promissory notes, &c. is felony the same as if the money secured by such bonds, &c. had been stolen, 2 *Geo.* 2. *c.* 25. *sect.* 3. and see 31. *Geo.* 2. *cap.* 22. *sect.* 81.

Offenders ordered to be transported for assault with intent to rob, breaking gaol or escaping, 7 *Geo.* 2. *c.* 21. *sect.* 2.

Rogue. Branded, and afterwards offending, 1 *Jac.* 1. *c.* 7. repealed by 12 *Ann. st.* 2. *c.* 23.

Sacrilege. See *Robbery*.

Sea. Treasons, robberies, felonies, murders and confederacies done upon the sea, 28 *H.* 8. *c.* 15. *sect.* 3.

Seamen. Personating them to receive their pay, 31 *Geo.* 2. *c.* 10. *sect.* 24.

Sheepstealing. By 14 *Geo.* 2. *c.* 6. extended to bull, cow, &c. By 15 *Geo.* 2. *c.* 34.

Ships. Destroying them wilfully, 22 & 23 *Car.* 2. *c.* 11. *sect.* 12. 1 *Ann. st.* 2. *c.* 9. 4 *Geo.* 1. *c.* 12. 11 *Geo.* 1. *c.* 29. 12 *Geo.* 3. *c.* 24. See *Robbery, Wreck*.

Shooting. See *Black act*.

Sluices. See *Turnpike*.

Smuggling. By 8 *Geo.* 1. *c.* 18.

Assembling armed for running of goods, 19 *Geo.* 2. *c.* 34. *sect.* 1.

Person transported for assisting in running goods, and returning, 9 *Geo.* 2. *c.* 35. *sect.* 10.

Persons convicted of running goods, returning from transportation, 8 *Geo.* 1. *c.* 18. *sect.* 6. See *Customs*.

Soldiers.

APPENDIX II.

Soldiers. Departing without licence, 7 *H.* 7. *c.* 1. 3 *H.* 8. *c.* 5. 2 & 3 *Ed.* 6. *c.* 2. *sect.* 6.

Wandering without testimonial from justices, 39 *El. c.* 17. *sect.* 2. See *Forgery.*

Departing within the year from the service of those who took them to save them from execution, 39 *El. c.* 17. *sect.* 4.

Inlisting or causing others to inlist in foreign service, 9 *Geo.* 2. *c.* 30.

Accepting commission from the *French* King. — Continuing in the *French* service after 29th of *September* 1757. Contracting to inlist in foreign service, 29 *Geo.* 2. *c.* 17.

South Sea company. Officer or servant imbezzling their effects, 24 *Geo.* 2. *c.* 11. *sect.* 3. See *Forgery.*

S. S. bonds. See *Forgery, Robbery.*

Statute. Acknowledging it in the name of another, 21 *Jac.* 1. *c.* 26.

Stolen goods. See *Helping to stolen goods.*

Stores. Embezzling them to the value of 20 *s.* or offending against 31 *El. cap.* 4. concerning embezzlement of stores, 22 *Car.* 2. *c.* 5. *sect.* 3. 12 *Geo.* 3. *c.* 24.

Transported. Felons returning within the time, 4 *Geo.* 1. *c.* 11. 6 *Geo.* 1. *c.* 23. 16 *Geo.* 2. *c.* 15. See *Rescue.*

Trees. See *Black act.*

Turnpikes. Destroying them, or locks, sluices, or floodgates, or rescuing such offenders, 8 *Geo.* 2. perpetual by 27 *Geo.* 2 *c* 16

Warren. See *Black act.*

Wharf. See *Robbery.*

Witchcraft. By 1 *Jac.* 1. *c.* 12. repealed by 9 *Geo.* 2. *c.* 5.

Woods. See *Black act.*

Wool

APPENDIX II.

Wool and woollen manufactures. Unlawful exporters returning after transportation, 4 *Geo.* 1. *c.* 11. *sect.* 6.

Opposing officers of customs, excise, &c. in seising wool, 12 *Geo.* 2. *c.* 21. *sect.* 26.

Destroying woollen goods, or rack, or tools, 12 *Geo.* 1. *c.* 34. *sect.* 7. See *Cloth*.

Women. Stealing them, and marrying or defiling them, having lands or goods, or being heirs apparent, 39 *El. c.* 9.

After conviction of an offence that was within clergy, ousted of it on conviction of any other felony, 3 & 4 *W.* & *M. c.* 9.

Wreck. Making holes in ship in distress, or stealing pump, 12 *Ann. st.* 2. *c.* 18. *sect.* 5.

Plundering shipwrecked goods, or beating, &c. with intent to kill, or otherwise obstructing the escape of any person from such ship, or putting out false lights with intent to bring any ship into danger, 26 *Geo.* 2. *c.* 19. See *Accessary*, *ante*.

THE
TABLE.

Actions and Remedies.

1. OF *Debt*, for money due on a bond, or bill, Page 2
2. For rent due from tenants, 6
3. For goods or money delivered, 7
4. For an attorney's expences, 8
5. For permitting a prisoner to escape, Ibid.
6. Upon a judgment or arbitrament, 9
7. Upon an act of parliament, Ibid.

Proceedings in Actions of Debt.

1. By writs, procefs and arreft, 10
2. By bail and appearance, 18
3. By declarations, pleadings, &c. 25

A bill of *Middlesex*, 16
A latitat, Ibid.
An *Alias* and *Pluries*, Ibid.
A *Copias* in debt in C. B. 18
A *Copias* in action of the cafe, Ibid.

A com-

The TABLE.

A common *Bail-piece*,	Page 22
A special *Bail-piece*,	23
A *Bail-bond* and *Assignment thereupon*,	24, 25
A *Declaration* in debt in *B. R.*	29, 30
A *Plea* in debt,	30, 31
Of pleas and demurrers,	31
A general *Demurrer* to a declaration,	33
——— Joinder in demurrer	33, 34

Action upon the Case.

1. For nonfeazance on promises,	34
2. Malefeazance, or doing what ought not to be done,	35
3. Misfeazance, or misdoing any thing,	37
4. Deceits on contracts, &c.	39
5. Particular nusances,	40
A *Declaration* in case, for goods and merchandizes sold,	42
A *Declaration* in case, for a deceit upon a warranty of goods,	45
A *Declaration* in case, for nusance to a man's water,	45, &c.
A *Plea* in case, of payment in satisfaction of a promise and *Replication*,	47
Plea that the defendant made no such promise, &c.	48
A *Plea* of not guilty in case,	Ibid.

Action of Account.

1. Against a bailiff or receiver of rents and debts,	49
2. Where one was not bailiff or receiver,	Ibid.

3. Before

3. Before auditors assigned, &c. Page 50
A *Declaration* in an action of account, 51, 52

Action of Covenant.

1. Covenant personal for doing a thing, 52
2. Covenant real concerning lands, 53
A *Declaration* in action of covenant, 55
A *Plea* that all covenants are performed, 56

Action of Detinue.

1. For recovery of goods detained, 57
2. For recovery of deeds and charters, 58
A *Declaration* in action of detinue, 59

Action of Trover.

In what case it lies, Ibid.
A *Declaration* in trover, 61
A *Plea* in trover, with a traverse of the conversion, 62

Action of Slander.

1. For charging a man with particular crimes, 64
2. Slander of persons in their offices and professions, 66
3. Slandering a man's title to an estate, &c. 67
4. Of defamation by libels, 69
A *Declaration* in action of slander, 69, &c.
A *Declaration* for slandering a person's title, 72

Action of Assault and Battery.

The nature of this action, and where it lieth, Page 73
A *Declaration* in assault and battery, 76

Action of Trespass.

1. Trespass to a man's lands or goods, Ibid.
2. Where actions are brought, and trespasses continued, 78
3. Actions of trespass by statute, 79
A *Declaration* in trespass, Ibid.
Declaration in action of trespass, for several trespasses, 79, 80
A *Plea* in action of trespass, 81

Action of Ejectment.

In what cases it lieth, the manner of proceeding therein, &c. 81
A *Declaration* in ejectment, 85
A *Notice* for the tenant to appear, &c. 86

Action or writ of Assise.

1. Assise of lands and tenements, 87
2. Of rents, commons and tolls, 88
3. Of an office held for life, &c. 89
A *Declaration* in assise, for a rent, 90

Action

Action of Waste.

1. For any waste done or suffered to houses, Page 92
2. For cutting down timber-trees, or other trees on an estate, 93
3. For plowing up meadow ground, digging mines, destroying deer, &c. 94
4. And who shall bring this action for the land, &c. and damages, 95

A *Declaration* in action of waste, 96
A *Plea*, &c. in this action, 98

Distress for Rent.

The proceedings in it, of what things taken, and manner thereof, 98, &c.
A landlord's warrant to distrain for rent, 109
Appraiser's Oath, to appraise goods distrained, 110
An *Inventory* and *Appraisement* of the goods taken in distress, 111
Notice of the distress to the tenant, Ibid

Replevins on taking Distresses.

Where replevin lies, and how brought, &c. 112, &c.
A *Count* or *Declaration* in replevin, 116
An *Avowry* for arrears of rent, 117

The TABLE.

The Statutes of Limitation of Actions.

In what time real and personal actions are to be commenced, Page 118

Controversies determined without Action.

By award, power of arbitrators, &c. 120
An Award of differences. 123

Of Courts, Juries, Witnesses, Trials.

1. THE high court of Chancery, 126
2. King's Bench, 129
3. The court of Common Pleas, 130
4. The Exchequer, 131
5. The court of Assizes, &c. 132

Inferior Courts in the Country.

1. The County-Court, 134
2. The Court Leet, 135
3. The Court-Baron, 136

Attornies, &c. of Court.

1. By orders of court and the common law, 138
2. By ancient and modern statutes, 140

The TABLE.

In Order to Trials.

1. Of juries to try causes, Page 142
2. Witnesses and other evidence necessary, 150
A writ of *Subpœna* for witnesses to testify, &c. 155
A *Subpœna Ticket* for a witness to appear, *Ibid.*

The Head Trial divided into,

1. Things to be known preparatory thereto, 156
2. The form of trial in the courts at *Westminster*, 158
3. How trials are managed at the assizes, 159
4. Of new trials, &c. 161
A *Record* of an issue and trial of a cause in B. R. 162
Executions and other things *after trials*, 165
A writ of *Capias ad Satisfaciendum*, 166
A writ of *Fieri Facias*, 167
A writ of *Elegit*, 169
How persons relieved by *Auditâ Querelâ*, 170
The writ *Auditâ Querelâ*, 171
Prisoners in execution discharged by statute. *Ibid.*

Writs of Error.

To reverse and set aside judgment and executions. 173
A *Writ of Error* in B. R. 175

Of Estates, Ancestors, Heirs, &c.

1. ESTATES obtained by discent and right of blood, *Page* 176
2. By conveyance, or grant from one man to another, &c. 182
3. Ancient tenures of lands, 269

And lands are conveyed,

1. By feoffment, the nature of it, 182
A deed of *Feoffment*, 184
2. By lease and release, the nature and law thereof, 187
A *lease for a year*, whereon to ground a release, 190
A *Release* and conveyance of the lands, 191
3. By bargain and sale, its nature, &c. 196
A *Bargain and Sale* of land, and *Inrollment*, 199
4. By fine and recovery, the nature of, and laws concerning them, manner of prosecuting, &c. 200
A *Præcipe and Concord* of a fine, 210
A *Fine* by husband and wife, of his land, 211
An *Indenture* to declare the *Uses* of a fine, 212
A *Writ of Entry* sur Disseisin, &c. in order to suffer a recovery, 214
A deed to lead the uses of a *Fine* and *Recovery*, on a purchase, 215
5. By surrender, sorts of, &c. 220
A *Surrender* of lands, &c. 282

6. By

The TABLE.

	Page
6. By gift and grant, the nature and laws thereof,	223
A deed of *Gift* of land,	226
7. By lease, for life, or years,	226
A *Lease* for years of a house,	235
8. By mortgage, the nature of it,	239
A common *Mortgage* of an estate,	242
An *Assignment of a Mortgage* to attend the fee,	248
9. By assignment, the law concerning it, &c.	248
Assignment of a lease,	250
10. By will, the nature and law of, how construed, and devises and legacies,	253
A *Will* of goods and lands,	259
A *Will*, with devise of lands, &c. in the way of settlement,	261

Estates in Goods and Chattels, &c.

1. Of bills of sale of goods, when good and binding, and alter the property,	264
A *Bill of Sale* of goods,	267
2. Gifts of goods and chattels,	267
A *Gift* of goods, with *Livery and Seisin*,	269, 270
3. Agreements, contracts and covenants,	270
An agreement between a master and a servant,	271
4. Bonds and obligations for money;	272
A common *Bond* from two persons to one,	275
A bond from one person to one,	276
A penal *Bill* for payment of money,	277
A single *Bill* for money,	Ibid.
5. Letters of attorney to receive debts,	Ibid.
A general *Letter of attorney*,	279
A *Letter of Attorney* to receive rents and take distresses, &c.	280

M m

A sea-

A seaman's *Letter of Attorney*, Page 281
6. Releases of debts and actions, &c. 283
A *Release* of personal actions, 285
A *General Release* of all demands, *Ibid.*

Tenures and holdings of lands.

1. Tenant in fee-simple, 286
2. In fee-tail, general and special, 287
3. In tail, after possibility of issue, 289
4. By the curtesy, 290
5. In dower, 291
6. For term of life, 292
7. For term of years, 294
8. At will, &c. 296

Copyhold Tenures.

1. Copyhold estates held for lives, 297
2. Copyholds in fee, and their qualities, 300
3. Copyholder's widow's estate, 302
A *Grant* of a copyhold estate, 303
A *Surrender* and *New Grant* of copyhold lands, 305

Other Heads of this Chapter.

1. Ancestors, and the laws relating to them, 306
2. Heirs to persons dying seised of lands, 307
3. Executors appointed by will, 308
4. Administrators by statute, 312

The TABLE.

Of Marriage, Bastardy, Infants, Ideots.

1. HOW marriages are solemnized, Page 315
2. What persons may marry, 326
3. Contracts of marriage, 329
4. Rights of husband and wife, 332
5. Marriage settlements and jointures, 335
A faculty or *Licence* for *Marriage*, 324
A common *Marriage Settlement* of an estate in lands, 338
A *Marriage Settlement* of *South-Sea* Stock, 345
Articles of agreement of *Marriage*, in nature of a settlement of personal estate, 350

Smaller Heads concerning Marriage.

1. Elopements of married women, 353
2. Divorces between the husband and wife, 354
3. Felony in stealing and marrying women, 356

Laws and Statutes relating to,

1. Bastardy and bastards, 357
2. Infants under age, and their guardians, 360
An *Election of a Guardian* by a minor, 363
3. Ideots or fools, Ibid.
4. Lunaticks and madmen, 365

The TABLE.

Of the Liberty of the Subject.

THE statute of *Magna Charta*, or great charter, made in the 9th year of king *Henry* III. Page 367
Charta de Foresta, or the charter of the forest, granted in the 9th year of *Hen.* III. 383
The statute *De Tallagio non concedendo*, in the time of king *Edw.* I. 387
The statute *De quo Warranto* 30 *Edw.* I. 388
The *Habeas Corpus* statute, made in the 31st year of king *Cha.* II. Ibid.

Of the King and his Prerogative, &c.

1. AS the KING is head of the state, 396
2. As he is supreme head of the church, 398
3. As lord paramount of all land, and grants of the king, 400
4. His debts how paid, and acts construed in civil cases, &c. 401

The *Oath of the King* at his coronation, 403
Prerogative of the *QUEEN* and *Prince*, 404
The privileges of the nobility, 405

Officers

The TABLE.

Officers and Ministers of Justice.

1. The judges of the law, Page 409
2. Sheriffs of counties, 412
3. Coroners and their duty, 418
4. Justices of peace, 422
5. And constables, &c. 431
The *Oath* of a *Judge* of the law, 411
The *Oath* of a *Sheriff* by statute, 415
Allowances to the sheriff of counties, 417
The *Oath of a Coroner*. 422
The usual *Oath* of a *Constable*, 439
The ancient *Oath* of a *Petty Constable*, Ibid.

Of publick Offences.

1. HIGH treason against the king and queen's person, &c. and the crown, 441
—— Treason in levying war against the king in his realm, 442
—— By adhering to the king's enemies within the realm, or aiding them elsewhere, 444
—— In violating or deflowering the queen, or the king's eldest daughter, 445
—— By counterfeiting the king's great or privy seal, or his money, Ibid.
2. Petit treason against a master, husband, &c. 447
3. Murder done out of malice prepensed, 448

The TABLE.

——— Manslaughter, or killing without malice, Page 452
——— Homicide, or killing justifiable and excusable, 455
4. Felony by the common law, 456
——— Larceny and felony in stealing goods, 457
——— Felonies by statutes, 459
——— Accessaries to felony, 462
5. Burglary or robbing houses, &c. Ibid.
6. Robbery on the highway, 464
7. Rapes of women, 467
8. Sodomy or buggery, 469
9. Forgery, by the common law, and by statute, 470
10. Perjury, at common law, and by statutes. 472

Punishments and Forfeitures

Punishments for high treason, 475
——— In petit treason, Ibid.
Forfeiture therein, Ibid.
Punishment of murder and felony, 476
Forfeiture for these crimes, Ibid.
Punishment of manslaughter, Ibid.
Forfeiture therein, Ibid.
Punishment of larceny, &c. Ibid.
And forfeiture, Ibid.
An indictment and conviction of murder, 477
Conviction of manslaughter 481

INDEX.

INDEX.

A.
Accessaries,	Page 1
Account,	49
Actions,	2, &c.
Act of Parliament,	9
Administrators,	312
Agreements,	270, 271, 350
Ancestors,	306
Appearance,	18, 155
Appraiser,	110
Arbitrament,	9, 120
Arrest,	10
Assault,	73
Assignment,	25, 245, 248, 250
Assize,	87, 132, 159
Attorney,	8, 138
Auditâ Querelâ,	170
Auditors,	50
Avowry,	117
Award,	123

B.
Bail,	18, 22, 23
Bail Bond,	24
Bailiff,	49
Bargain and Sale,	Page 196, 199
Bastards,	357
Battery,	73
Bill,	2, 277
Bill of *Middlesex*,	16
Bill of Sale,	264, 267
Bonds,	2, 272
Buggery,	469
Burglary,	462

C.
Capias,	18
Ca. Sa.	166
Chancery,	126
Charters,	58
Common Bail-piece,	22
Common Pleas,	130
Commons,	88
Constables,	431, 439
Contracts,	39, 270
Controversies,	120
Conveyance,	182, 191
Copyhold,	297
Coronation,	403
Coroners,	418
County Court,	134
Court Baron,	136

Court

INDEX.

Court Leet, Page 135
Curtesy, 290
Covenant, 52, 270

D.

Debt, 2, 10
Deceit, 39, 45
Declarations, 25, 29, 30, 42, 45
Deeds, 58
Deer, 94
Defamation, 69
Demurrer, 31, 33, 34
Detinue, 57
Devises, 253, 261
Discent, 176
Distress, 98, 280
Divorces, 354
Dower, 291

E.

Ejectment, 81
Elegit, 169
Elopement, 353
Error, 173, 175
Escape, 8
Evidence, 150
Exchequer, 131
Execution, 165, 173
Executors, 312

F.

Faculty, 324
Fee simple, 286
—Tail, 287
Felony, 456
Feoffment, 182, 184

Fieri facias, Page 167
Fine, 200, 210, 211, 212, 215
Fools, 363
Forest, 385
Forfeiture, 475
Forgery, 470

G.

Gift, 223, 226, 267, 269
Grant, 182, 223, 305
Guardians, 362

H.

Habeas Corpus, 388
Heirs, 307
Homicide, 454
Husband and Wife, 332, 354

I.

Ideots, 363
Indictment, 477
Infants, 360
Inferior Courts, 134
Inventory, 111
Jointures, 335
Issue, 162
Judges, 409
Judgment, 9, 173
Juries, 142
Justices of Peace, 422

K.

King, (the) 396, &c.
King's Bench, 129

L.

INDEX.

L.

Landlord,	Page 109
Larceny,	457
Latitat,	16
Lease,	187, 228, 235, 250
Leet,	135
Legacies,	253
Letters of attorney,	277
Libel,	69
Licence,	324
Limitation,	118
Livery and Seisin,	270

M.

Madman,	365
Magna Charta,	367
Malefeazance,	35
Manslaughter,	452
Marriage,	315, 32
Master,	271
Meadow,	94
Merchandize,	42
Mines,	94
Minors,	353
Misfeasance,	37
Mortgage,	239, 242, 245
Murder,	448

N.

New Trial,	161
Nobility,	405
Nonfeazance,	34
Not guilty,	48
Notice,	86, 111
Nusances,	40, 45

O.

Oath,	Page 110, 403, 422, 430, 439
Obligations,	272
Office,	66, 98
Orders of Court,	138

P.

Payment,	47
Perjury,	472
Pleadings,	25
Pleas,	31, 47, 48
Prerogative,	396, 404
Prince,	404
Prisoner,	8, 171
Privileges,	405
Profession,	66
Process,	10
Punishment,	475

Q.

Queen,	404
Quo Warranto,	380

R.

Rapes,	467
Record,	162
Recovery,	200, 214, 215
Release,	187, 191, 283
Rent,	6, 49, 88, 109, 280
Replevin,	112, &c.
Replication,	47
Right of blood,	176
Robbery,	464

S.

Satisfaction,	47
Seamen,	281
Servant,	

INDEX.

Servant,	Page 271	Timber,	Page 93
Settlements,	261, 335, 338	Tithe,	67
		Tolls,	88
Sheriffs,	412, 417	Treason,	440
Slander,	64	—Petit,	447
Sodomy,	469	Trees,	93
South-Sea Stock,	345	Trespass,	76
Special Bail-piece,	23	Trials,	156
Statutes,	79, 140, 171, 367, 383, 387, 388	*Trover,*	59
Subpœna,	155		
Surrenders,	220, 222, 305	**W.**	
		Warrant,	109
		Writs,	10, 155
		Waste,	93
T.		Widow,	302
Tallage,	387	Wife,	332
Tenant,	6, 286	Will,	253, 259, 261, 308
—For Life,	292	Witnesses,	155
—In Tail,	287, 289	Women,	353, 356
—For Years,	294	Warranty,	45
—At Will,	296		

FINIS.

www.ingramcontent.com/pod-product-compliance
Lightning Source LLC
Chambersburg PA
CBHW031943290426
44108CB00011B/660